Potentia

Potentia

Hobbes and Spinoza on Power and Popular Politics

SANDRA LEONIE FIELD

OXFORD
UNIVERSITY PRESS

OXFORD
UNIVERSITY PRESS

Oxford University Press is a department of the University of Oxford. It furthers the University's objective of excellence in research, scholarship, and education by publishing worldwide. Oxford is a registered trade mark of Oxford University Press in the UK and certain other countries.

Published in the United States of America by Oxford University Press
198 Madison Avenue, New York, NY 10016, United States of America.

Library of Congress Cataloging-in-Publication Data
Names: Field, Sandra Leonie, author.
Title: Potentia : Hobbes and Spinoza on power and popular politics / Sandra Leonie Field.
Description: New York, NY : Oxford University Press, 2020. |
Includes bibliographical references and index.
Identifiers: LCCN 2020008321 (print) |
LCCN 2020008322 (ebook) | ISBN 9780197528242 (hardback) |
ISBN 9780197533864 (paperback) | ISBN 9780197528266 (epub) |
ISBN 9780197528259 (updf) | ISBN 9780197528273 (online)
Subjects: LCSH: Political science—Philosophy. |
Power (Philosophy) | Hobbes, Thomas, 1588–1679. |
Spinoza, Benedictus de, 1632–1677.
Classification: LCC JA71 .F4934 2020 (print) |
LCC JA71 (ebook) | DDC 320.01/1—dc23
LC record available at https://lccn.loc.gov/2020008321
LC ebook record available at https://lccn.loc.gov/2020008322

1 3 5 7 9 8 6 4 2
Paperback printed by Marquis, Canada
Hardback printed by Bridgeport National Bindery, Inc., United States of America

For Simon

Contents

Acknowledgements

Writing this book has been a long and uncertain journey, over many years and across several continents. My worries about the shape of human collective life, and philosophy's capacity to grasp it, were already were brewing as a student. I had my formative intellectual experiences in Australia with Moira Gatens and Paul Patton, against the backdrop of the University of Sydney's lively and fractious student politics; then I swam in the rich scholarly soup of the Princeton Department of Politics and the Princeton University Center for Human Values, under the guidance of Philip Pettit, Dan Garber, and Alan Patten. Over the eight years since I graduated, I have been working at Yale-NUS College, where the book's progress has been delayed but simultaneously immensely enriched. Coming to grips with postcolonial Singapore's ambivalent political legacy has forced me to get serious in my political thinking; the intense, student-focussed environment of the college has forced me to maintain broad intellectual horizons rather than settling into some comfortable narrow specialization.

Yale-NUS College has provided for me richly in financial and organizational support. Senior colleagues Rajeev Patke and Nomi Lazar were patient and encouraging during the long period of the book's gestation. Facing difficulty in bringing North American scholars to Singapore, instead a manuscript workshop for the book was held at the Princeton University Center for Human Values. The event was facilitated by Philip Pettit; Dan Garber graciously acted as host; and Steven Nadler, Arash Abizadeh, Michael Rosenthal, and Hasana Sharp served as my respondents. Funding for the event was provided by Yale-NUS College, through a Book Manuscript Workshop Grant (BMW18-002). Other Yale-NUS funding for the book includes Start-up Grant (R-607-263-181-121); Political Theory Research Cluster Grant (IG16-RCS004-CWG); Subvention Grant (C-607-261-042-001); and Internal Grant (IG17-SR101). Jade Koh Gek Hiang and Jessie Wong Fong Kee have been unfailingly helpful as I negotiated administrative matters. I also received assistance from student associates Theo Lai Wenming, Ng Sai Ying, Patrick Wu, and Vincent Lee Zheng Yang.

Chapters 2–4 rework material that was first published as Sandra Field, 'Hobbes and the Question of Power', *Journal of History of Philosophy* 52, no. 1 (2014): 61–86; with permission from Johns Hopkins University Press.

The full circle of those who helped in one way or another in the development of the manuscript includes too many to list. Here I indicate only those who very directly contributed, providing feedback on drafts at varying stages of completion: Sinja Graf, Kinch Hoekstra, Gordon Hull, Mike LeBuffe, Neil Mehta, Haig Patapan, Ben Schupmann, Ericka Tucker, and Robin Zheng. There are a few friends in political theory to whom I am especially thankful, not just for comments on my drafts, but for their special role in helping me keep up my stamina to complete the project: in the United States, Loubna El Amine and Geneviève Rousselière; and in Singapore, Koh Tsin Yen and Christina Tarnopolsky.

Finally, some more personal thanks. Always my biggest cheerleaders, my parents are reliable enthusiasts for whatever scholarly project I may be working on, and they have always done everything in their power to smooth the way for me. To their and my delight, alongside this scholarly work, I have become a parent myself, to three wonderful little people, Samuel, Oscar, and Eamon. Life is larger than scholarship, and the kids force me to keep the demands of scholarly work in perspective and within strict temporal limits. But none of this, neither the scholarship nor the family life beyond it, would be possible without my partner Simon: his labour, his ideas, his love. I dedicate this book to him.

Note on Sources

1. Note on Gendered Language

I generally reformulate Hobbes's and Spinoza's arguments in gender-neutral language, as I do not believe that the specific points on which I focus rely essentially on the gendered language in which they were originally framed. There is one point at which the gendering is more problematically imbricated in the analysis, as I will specifically discuss (Chapter 9, Section 9.2).

2. Editions for Primary Sources

Hobbes

Hobbes's complete works (excepting the *Short Tract* and the *Anti-White*) are available in English and Latin in the 1839 Molesworth edition, but in light of the inadequacies of that edition, I have used a number of later editions.

I primarily rely on chapter/paragraph referencing, because all of Hobbes's texts (apart from *Behemoth* and *Liberty and Necessity*) are divided into short paragraphs that are standardly numbered between English and Latin versions.

Short Tract (ST) (?1630)

Hobbes, Thomas. 'A Short Tract on First Principles'. In *The Elements of Law, Natural and Politic*, edited by Ferdinand Tönnies, 2nd ed. (London: Frank Cass, 1984), 193–210.

The Elements of Law (EL) (composed 1640, published 1650)

The Elements of Law, Natural and Politic, edited by Ferdinand Tönnies, 2nd ed. (London: Frank Cass, 1984).

De Cive (DC) (1642)

Latin: De Cive, edited by Howard Warrender (Oxford: Clarendon Press, 1983).
English: On the Citizen, edited and translated by Richard Tuck and Michael Silverthorne (Cambridge: Cambridge University Press, 2014).

Anti-White (AW) (1643)

Latin: Critique du De Mundo de Thomas White (Paris: Vrin, 1973).
English: Thomas White's De Mundo Examined, translated by Harold Whitmore Jones (London: Bradford University Press, 1976).

Leviathan (L)

English (1651) and *Latin* (1668): *Leviathan*, edited by Noel Malcolm (Oxford: Clarendon Press, 2014).

NB: I have used the Clarendon edition text and pagination, but I have additionally included the chapter/paragraph numbering from the Hackett edition, Thomas Hobbes, *Leviathan: With Selected Variants from the Latin Edition of 1668*, edited by Edwin Curley (Indianapolis: Hackett, 1994).

Liberty and Necessity (LN) (1652)

The English Works of Thomas Hobbes of Malmesbury, Vol. 4, edited by William Molesworth (London: John Bohn, 1839).

De Corpore (DCo) (1655)

Latin: Thomæ Hobbes Malmesburiensis Opera philosophica quæ latine scripsit omnia, Vol. 1, edited by William Molesworth (London: John Bohn, 1839).
English: The English Works of Thomas Hobbes of Malmesbury, Vol. 1, edited by William Molesworth (London: John Bohn, 1839).

De Homine (DH) (1658)

Latin: Thomæ Hobbes Malmesburiensis Opera philosophica quæ latine scripsit omnia, Vol. 2, edited by William Molesworth (London: John Bohn, 1839).

English: 'On Man'. In *Man and Citizen*, translated by Charles T. Wood, T. S. K. Scott-Craig, and Bernard Gert, edited by Bernard Gert (Indianapolis: Hackett, 1991), 33–86.

Behemoth (B) (completed 1668, published 1682)

Behemoth, or The Long Parliament, edited by Paul Seaward (Oxford: Clarendon Press, 2014).

Spinoza

Matters are simpler for Spinoza's works: there is a complete standard Latin edition and a complete standard English translation.

Latin: Spinoza Opera, edited by Carl Gebhardt (Heidelberg: Carl Winter, 1972).

English: The Collected Works of Spinoza, Vols. 1 and 2, translated by Edwin Curley (Princeton: Princeton University Press, 1985, 2016).

I make use of the following abbreviations:

Tractatus Theologico-Politicus (TTP) (1670)
The *Theological-Political Treatise*. I have used Curley's chapter/paragraph numbering, but I have additionally provided the Gebhardt volume number and pagination.

Ethica (E) (completed 1675, published 1677)
The *Ethics*. I have used the following system of abbreviations:

a: axiom
d: definition (if followed by a number); or demonstration (if not)

p: proposition
c: corollary
s: scholium
app: appendix

Tractatus Politicus (TP) (1677)
The *Political Treatise*. I have used the Gebhardt chapter/paragraph numbering.

Epistolae (Ep)
The correspondence. I have used the Gebhardt letter number, volume number, and pagination.

1
Introduction

1.1. Context

The idea of the power of the people regularly resurfaces in our political discourse and practice. Mass plebiscites and referenda are hailed as revealing a true will of the people, superior in its political authority to the deliberations of parliaments; governments must defer to them, if they are to be anything other than oligarchic regimes masquerading as democracies.[1] Mass protest movements understand themselves as asserting the moral and political primacy of the people, and celebrate their unstructured spontaneity as revealing a democratic authenticity; they hope to disrupt the ossified and elitist structures of institutionalized politics.[2] In both cases, the power of the people is distinguished from the institutional forms that constrain or thwart it: 'constituent power' is distinguished from 'constituted power'. In an age of growing disaffection with the standard operations of parliamentary democracy, the idea of a popular power distinct from the institutionalized forms of politics is a highly relevant one, and the hope to bring politics under its control is widespread.

Without denying the problems of institutionalized forms of politics, nonetheless a solution appealing to spontaneous popular power as the foundation of democracy invites some obvious critical questions. Are plebiscites and social movements themselves always so pure? In what sense are their decisions and actions more truly reflective of popular power, whatever that might mean, than the institutionalized forms of politics? Consider first plebiscites. Plebiscites are all-inclusive in the sense that they invite an entire political community to vote, but how meaningful are their results? Highly emotive advertising notoriously played some role in the Brexit decision. Joseph Schumpeter famously drew attention to what

[1] For example, the 2016 UK Brexit Referendum; the 2017 Australian Same Sex Marriage Postal Survey.
[2] For example, the antiglobalization protests of the late 1990s; the 2011 Occupy movement.

Potentia. Sandra Leonie Field, Oxford University Press (2020). © Oxford University Press.
DOI: 10.1093/oso/9780197533864.001.0001

he called 'human nature in politics'. The majority of people do not generally have clearly formed political opinions, and even when they do, they often fail to take serious cognizance of the implications of their positions, because the impact of their political action is so infinitesimal in national politics. Many people come to assent to political positions that are gratifying to them, regardless of their coherence. In result, the 'popular will' is the complex outcome of many causal factors in a political system, not least the efforts of opportunistic political entrepreneurs who, like advertisers, seed and cultivate political views in order to harness 'the people' to their own ends.[3] Schumpeter concludes that the popular will does not drive democratic political systems: 'The will of the people is the product and not the motive power of the political process.'[4]

Perhaps it can be objected that this troubling possibility of strategic capture of popular will does not apply so intensely to social movements, because they do not rely on a single punctual moment of voting, but instead extend over time and demand deeper involvement and commitment from their participants. But then a second Schumpeterian problem comes into play: value pluralism.[5] The democratic credentials of social movements might seem obvious when it comes to the case of an entire population opposing a narrow elite. But those credentials are less obvious when it comes to the more standard situation of a partial social movement that does not find universal support from the populace, and may even find itself in opposition to another partial movement.

What is the significance of these critical observations for democratic theory? Is it the case that there is a coherent concept of popular power, which regrettably often fails to be met in practice (as would be the view of many radical democrats)? Or is the problem deeper: is the very concept of popular power irredeemably confused, such that democratic politics would benefit from the concept being abandoned? Schumpeter himself presents his critical observations not in order to call for a better realization of popular power, but to excoriate the theoretical incoherence and practical danger of any concept of popular power. Schumpeter was a reactionary who assented to the gloomy status quo predicament of democratic politics as he characterized it. On his own proposed

[3] Joseph A. Schumpeter, *Capitalism, Socialism and Democracy*, 3rd ed. (New York: Harper Perennial, 2008), 256–264.

[4] Ibid., 263.

[5] Ibid., 251–256.

positive conception, democracy is nothing more than technical term for a system of government organized around a competition for political leadership: an 'institutional arrangement for arriving at political decisions in which individuals acquire the power to decide by means of a competitive struggle for the people's vote'.[6] The very ideas of popular power, popular will, or mass political agency are altogether abandoned as untenable and naive relics of eighteenth-century thought; he is entirely uninterested in establishing any new criterion to identify more or less genuine expressions of popular power. Beyond the minimal presumption of a free press, Schumpeter makes no discrimination between better or worse ways for this electoral competition to run; he accepts that the standard result is a system of inequality and manipulation.[7] For Schumpeter, there is just an incorrigible imperfection to human existence, and nothing is legitimately to be gained by promoting incoherent ideas of popular power. Indeed, such ideas are dangerous: the leaders who most ardently invoke the lofty name of the people are generally demagogues, using it as cover for their nefarious attempts to crush their political opponents.[8]

Schumpeter's concerns are often discounted.[9] Certainly, his positive proposal to abandon the very idea of popular power altogether may strike us as defeatist. But his critique of romantic tendencies in theories of democracy, and, in particular, his critique of the conceptual difficulties that beset appeals to popular power, cannot be so swiftly dismissed. In this book, I explore some current approaches to theorizing popular power, arguing that they rely on an uncritical conception of the populace, as well as a problematic analysis of power. But the central goal of this book is fundamentally anti-Schumpeterian. In the face of conceptual difficulties, rather than abandoning the very idea of popular power, I put forward a new and better conception. I offer a path beyond the analytical slipperiness and practical romanticism of prevalent conceptions of popular power, articulating and defending an analytically clear and practically robust theoretical account of popular power.

[6] Ibid., 269, also 269–283.
[7] Ibid., 271–272.
[8] Ibid., 268.
[9] Lynn M. Sanders, 'Against Deliberation', *Political Theory* 25, no. 3 (1997): 354–357; Bruce Ackerman, *We the People: Foundations* (Cambridge, MA: Belknap Press, 1991), 308–309.

I take my point of departure from recent efforts to understand popular power and radical democracy through the thought of seventeenth-century philosophers Thomas Hobbes and Benedict de Spinoza. In these recent interpretations, Hobbes and Spinoza have been invoked as providing the historical and conceptual foundations for the anti-institutionalist idea whereby popular power finds its exemplary expression in plebiscites or social movements. In this book, I heartily agree that the recourse to those philosophers is fruitful, but I argue that it is fruitful for reasons diametrically opposed to those normally offered. I use Hobbes's and Spinoza's analyses to demonstrate that the phenomena of plebiscites and social movements have only a weak claim to express popular power, both because they are insufficiently popular (they either fail to eliminate their own internal oligarchic structure, or they fail to encompass the whole populace) and because they are the wrong kind of political phenomenon to count as a power (they produce merely secondary effects that are often weak or evanescent, and in any case can only be properly understood in relation to the larger social and institutional ecology of society). Drawing on Hobbes and Spinoza, I articulate a precise concept of and standard for popular power: I propose that a political phenomenon should be said to express popular power when it is both popular (it eliminates oligarchy and encompasses the entire polity) and also powerful (it robustly determines political and social outcomes). The result is a chastening of expectations regarding the spontaneous expression of popular power. First, there is no such thing as a pure or authentic popular multitude. Human collective life is always already institutionally shaped, for better or for worse; and only some of the shapes that it might take deserve to be counted as genuinely popular. Second, the existence and strength of popular power cannot be established by momentary or transient phenomena; the measure of popular empowerment in a society will be the ongoing manifestation of the multitude's equal and inclusive popular form in political and social outcomes over time.

Once popular power is understood as I propose, it becomes clear that it is a mistake to pin all one's democratic hopes on mass movements or on plebiscites with an aspiration to transcend ordinary institutional politics. Rather, the slow meticulous work of organizational design and maintenance is the true centre of genuine popular power. Within this framework, mass movements and plebiscites surely may serve important roles, but not because they are themselves fundamental sources of popular legitimacy or the privileged site of mass agency. Or so I will argue.

1.2. Hobbesian and Spinozist Radical Democracy

I establish my new conception of popular power against the alternatives posed by two broad radical democratic traditions that celebrate popular power: the American public law tradition and the European post-Marxist tradition. In particular, I focus on two recent exemplary efforts to trace an early modern European philosophical lineage for contemporary radical democracy. First, standing as a representative of the American public law tradition, Richard Tuck recuperates Hobbes as a theorist of radical plebiscitary democracy; and second, standing as a representative of the European post-Marxist tradition, Antonio Negri invokes Spinoza as the paradigmatic theorist of the radical insurgent democracy and spontaneous social movements. In this section, I sketch Tuck's and Negri's views, along with their exegetical basis in Hobbes's and Spinoza's texts; I then also indicate their contemporary practical political context and implications.

Hobbes is the canonical theorist of absolutism. In his view, in any state there must be a single unitary holder of sovereignty who has the absolute authority to rule and to make ultimate decisions. The practical motivation of this absolutism is clear: Hobbes argues that any division of sovereignty opens the door to political breakdown and civil war. If any constraint is recognized on the sovereign's power, then when subjects make allegations of sovereign overreach, there is no higher authority to judge the case, and the disagreement can be settled only by fighting. Hobbes gives juridical expression to this fundamental political commitment through his famous device of a covenant establishing sovereignty. From an anarchic and hostile state of nature prior to politics, Hobbes argues that it is rational for individuals to establish a sovereign over them who will speak with one voice on their behalf; the sovereign's single voice is only possible if they hand over their rights fully and irrevocably.

Where does Hobbes stand with respect to democracy? Certainly, he is often characterized as authoritarian and anti-democratic. First, he endorses a political order with a monarchical sovereign holding the absolute right to make decisions, and within this order he allows no recourse for aggrieved subjects. Second, he identifies various practical disadvantages facing democracy compared to other regimes. Nonetheless, at the level of right, Hobbes insists that all proper forms of sovereignty—monarchy, aristocracy, and democracy—are equal; and when his absolutist commitment to unrestrained sovereignty is applied to a democratic sovereign, the result is an unflinching commitment to popular decision-making. Hobbes sharply opposes mixed constitutionalism, a form of political organization in which the people are conceived as just one partial element of society, whose interests need to be tempered and balanced against the interests of the nobles. In Hobbesian democratic sovereignty, there is no need to 'balance' the demands of the people with those of the elite. Indeed, generations of thinkers after Hobbes seized on this feature of Hobbes's theory to develop their own accounts of radical democratic absolute sovereignty. Rousseau and Kant were both close readers of Hobbes; they differ from him only in denying that a sovereign could be other than popular.

Tuck has laboured to uncover this Hobbesian genealogy of later democratic thought,[10] and the idea of radical democratic absolute sovereignty has taken an increasingly central place in Tuck's work. On Tuck's interpretation, even Hobbes himself does not see the practical objections to democracy as insurmountable; Tuck has argued that Hobbes was in fact strongly favourable to democracy.[11] The key to this interpretation is the distinction between sovereignty and government. In any state, the sovereign is the ultimate holder of right and authority; the government is the body that carries out the mundane affairs of ruling on a day-to-day basis. The government stands as the delegate and executor of the fundamental authority of the sovereign. Tuck promotes Hobbes's model of a 'sleeping sovereign', according to which the sovereign is mostly inactive, allowing the government to carry out its everyday business. But the real locus of political power remains with the holder of sovereignty: for from time to time the sovereign 'awakes' to check the operations of government, and when it does so, its rulings are authoritative.

Through the distinction between sovereignty and government, Tuck is able to account for Hobbes's apparent hostility to democracy. Hobbes is certainly hostile towards direct democratic government. Mass deliberative assemblies generate many problems that can be avoided in monarchical government. But this difficulty of democratic government has no bearing on the question of sovereignty. According to Hobbes's *De Cive*,[12] the populace must always first come together to become a democratic sovereign, even if it subsequently transfers sovereignty to a monarch or aristocratic assembly. In principle any kind of sovereign could be a sleeping sovereign (for instance, a king

[10] Richard Tuck, *The Sleeping Sovereign: The Invention of Modern Democracy* (Cambridge: Cambridge University Press, 2015), 121–142.

[11] Ibid., 86–107; Richard Tuck, 'Hobbes and Democracy', in *Rethinking the Foundations of Modern Political Thought*, edited by Annabel Brett, James Tully, and Holly Hamilton-Bleakley (Cambridge: Cambridge University Press, 2006), 171–172, 181–189.

[12] The second of Hobbes's three books laying out his systemic political philosophy.

designating a vizier). However, in Hobbes's own key examples, the sleeping sovereign is the entire populace, with their will defined by their mass non-deliberative vote. This is Tuck's favoured vision of radical democracy, and in his view it is the properly modern conception of genuine democracy: the voice of the people, via mass vote and without the distortions of deliberation, suspending and cutting through all normal operations of politics.[13]

The distinction between popular sovereignty and the form of government to which everyday rule is delegated is often expressed through the terminological distinction between constituent and constituted power. According to Sieyès, the popular sovereign is the constituent power, by whose authority the constituted powers of government are put in place.[14] But Tuck argues that the Hobbesian democratic sovereign offers a better and more radical model of popular power than Sieyès's classic account. Tuck points out that even as Sieyès identifies the constituent power as the source of legitimacy of government, he still insulates politics from the populace. For Sieyès the constituent power cannot act by itself; instead, it needs to be represented in a constituent assembly of delegates.[15] By contrast, for Hobbes, constituent power (in the form of the sleeping democratic sovereign) can directly act, by taking a mass plebiscitary vote on any issues it should choose.[16] In a curious inversion of the standard view, Tuck positions Hobbes as the true thinker of constituent power.[17]

Through his focus on Hobbes's sleeping sovereign, Tuck links Hobbes to the tradition of French and American constitutional plebiscites, and celebrates this as the most worthy conception of popular power for our contemporary world. His view stands in contrast both to more liberal views that are happy to limit popular power in the name of other values or constitutional commitments; and to more institutional democratic views that deny any voice to the people as such, apart from their ordinary political representation. Indeed, Tuck's view aligns neatly with an American

[13] Indeed, Tuck criticizes the constitutional order of the United Kingdom for lacking the properly modern separation between sovereignty and government (Tuck, *The Sleeping Sovereign*, 250–251).

[14] Emmanuel Joseph Sieyès, 'What Is the Third Estate?', in *Emmanuel Joseph Sieyès: The Essential Political Writings*, edited by Oliver W. Lembcke and Florian Weber (Leiden: Brill, 2014), 88–96. Lee has traced the origin of the conceptual pair constituent power / constituted power even earlier, to the sixteenth century. Daniel Lee, *Popular Sovereignty in Early Modern Constitutional Thought* (Oxford: Oxford University Press, 2016), 113.

[15] Sieyès, 'What Is the Third Estate?', 92; Tuck, *The Sleeping Sovereign*, 162–180.

[16] Tuck, *The Sleeping Sovereign*, 101–103.

[17] Ibid., 255–257. See also Murray Forsyth, 'Thomas Hobbes and the Constituent Power of the People', *Political Studies 29*, no. 2 (1981): 191–203.

valorization of 'the people' who express their power by rising up in occasional 'constitutional moments'. According to this understanding, the legitimacy of the US Constitution itself lies in popular support; hence it is possible for the populace to change the Constitution through a direct vote, not only through the procedures specified within the constitutional document itself.[18] Tuck draws broad contemporary lessons from his reading of Hobbes's sleeping sovereign: he is in favour of more frequent plebiscitary decisions (such as the Brexit vote) disrupting ordinary operations of modern democratic states, characterizing these plebiscites as a voice of the people and a solution to governmental unresponsiveness and elitism.[19]

I now turn to consider the legacy of Benedict de Spinoza, whose thought has been central to a quite different tradition of popular power: that of European Marxism.[20] The neo-Marxist appropriation of Spinoza is carried out against the backdrop of a less sympathetic reading of Hobbes. Whereas the American tradition aligns constituent power with popular sovereignty, for the Marxist tradition, by contrast, it is sovereignty that suppresses constituent power. The critical distinction is not between sovereignty and government, but between the politics of concrete power *potentia* and the politics of authorized power *potestas*. Sovereignty (*summa potestas*) is nothing but the highest form of authorized power. On this schema, Hobbes stands as the enemy, for he is the partisan of irresistible authority (*potestas*). Spinoza is the radical democratic saviour, for he is the champion of irrepressible popular multitude and its power as *potentia*, which finds its true expression in spontaneous popular movements. This conception of radical democracy has found most prominent popular expression in Hardt and Negri's immensely influential trilogy *Empire* (2000), *Multitude* (2004), and *Commonwealth* (2009). They repeatedly claim that the theoretical core of these works is Spinozist constituent power *potentia* against Hobbesian constituted power *potestas*,

[18] Akhil Reed Amar, 'Philadelphia Revisited: Amending the Constitution outside Article V', *University of Chicago Law Review* 55, no. 4 (1988): 1043–1104; Ackermann, *We The People*, 3–33; Joel Colon-Rios, 'The Legitimacy of the Juridical: Constituent Power and Democratic Reform', *Osgoode Hall Law Journal* 48, no. 2 (2010): 199–245.

[19] Tuck, *The Sleeping Sovereign*, 248–283; Tuck, 'Hobbes and Democracy', 185–190.

[20] Not all neo-Marxists subscribe to this interpretation of Spinoza. Indeed, Althusser's interest in Spinoza runs along quite different lines than Negri's: for Althusser, Spinoza offers a way to remove problematic Hegelian elements from Marx (the teleology; the conception of ideology as error; the primacy of the whole over parts) (Louis Althusser, *Essays in Self-Criticism*, translated by Grahame Lock [London: NLB, 1976], 135–142). In Chapters 6–9, I will characterize Matheron and Balibar as importantly opposed to core elements of Negri's view.

and advert to Negri's earlier scholarly monograph *The Savage Anomaly* to support this claim.[21]

In order to understand what is at stake in the contemporary radical democratic appropriation of Spinoza's idea of the multitude's *potentia*, it is first necessary to provide a standard sketch of the key theses of Spinoza's political philosophy, which is likely to be less familiar to an anglophone audience compared to that of Hobbes. Spinoza's *Theological-Political Treatise* initially provides a fairly straightforwardly Hobbesian analysis of politics in Chapter 16, only to challenge its very foundations in the following chapter. Hobbes's theory of sovereignty would be fine in theory, but Spinoza argues that it does not function in practice. In theory, subjects transfer all right and power *potentia* to establish a sovereign as *summa potestas* over them. But in practice, nobody can transfer all right and power without limit: regardless of any transfer of right or promise of obedience, each person's power *potentia* remains physically located in the person's body, and some sovereign commands simply will not be carried out. The result is devastating for Hobbes's project of overcoming war: indeed, historically Spinoza points out that sovereigns are more troubled by internal dissent than by external enemies, even when they are technically absolute in the Hobbesian sense. When the primary theoretical focus is shifted from questions of right and authority *potestas* to questions of concrete power *potentia*, it becomes clear that nothing is gained by insisting upon Hobbesian absoluteness, not even for a democratic sovereign. In result, liberal democracy emerges as a regime that best accommodates and channels subjects' individual *potentiae*.

Spinoza's second political work, the *Political Treatise*, follows through more deeply on the political ramifications of an analytical focus on *potentia*. The critical theoretical innovation is the concept of the multitude, *multitudo*. The multitude is the populace considered apart from any juridical structure; Spinoza argues that the multitude and its power *potentia multitudinis* are the foundation of any political order whatsoever. This gives rise to a new way of privileging democracy. Whereas the *Theological-Political Treatise* promotes liberal democracy, the *Political Treatise* now considers the inner power structure of any regime, regardless of the official designation of regime type

[21] Michael Hardt and Antonio Negri, *Empire* (Cambridge, MA: Harvard University Press, 2000); Michael Hardt and Antonio Negri, *Multitude: War and Democracy in the Age of Empire* (New York: Penguin Press, 2004); Michael Hardt and Antonio Negri, *Commonwealth* (Cambridge, MA: Belknap Press, 2009); Antonio Negri, *The Savage Anomaly: The Power of Spinoza's Metaphysics and Politics*, translated by Michael Hardt (Minneapolis: University of Minnesota Press, 1991).

according to the formal holder of sovereignty. In all cases, the central question is how the internal organization of the regime channels, develops, or thwarts the actual passions and desires of its subjects. The more democratic the internal structure (the more inclusive and participatory its decision-making structures, the more responsive it is to popular needs), the stronger the regime, even if it remains officially a monarchy or an aristocracy.

The radical democratic interpretation of Spinoza's political philosophy develops its conception of popular power by homing in on the idea of the multitude's power. Spinoza believes it is important to understand the concrete determinants of human action, even troubling disruptive action: centrally, it is important to understand that popular indignation can lead people to rise up against formally rightful regimes. The democratic Hobbes stands resolutely opposed to such spontaneous movements of the multitude. Hobbes insists that 'the people' can only speak through their sovereign representative; he denies there even is such a thing as popular power apart from its expression through the state. Outside of sovereignty, the multitude is an amorphous mob without any ability or authority to act. From the radical Spinozist point of view, to the contrary, moments of insurgency attest to the power of the multitude as such, and this power is an irrepressible real force in the world, fundamentally oriented towards equality. The multitude will rise up against even a democratic sovereign, because democratic sovereignty may not link well with *potentia* of people: for instance, majority tyranny may provoke indignation and sedition. For Spinozist radical democrats, when Spinoza embraces the power *potentia* of the popular multitude as the real foundation of all politics, he thereby shows the disruptive 'inner truth' of all regimes, and endorses the world-historical agency of the rising multitude as it resists unjust regimes. Popular power is the power of the multitude, and it finds its exemplary expression in social movements.

One might wonder why radical democrats in a Marxist tradition find it necessary to turn to Spinoza. After all, Spinoza himself was a member of the bourgeoisie, and his seventeenth-century viewpoint has no premonition of the future developments of capitalism.[22] But observe that Marx and Spinoza both deprioritize the formal juridical question of right: just as Spinoza takes seriously popular indignation even against formally rightful political orders, similarly Marx argues that a formally universalistic political order (such as

[22] Spinoza was the son of dried-fruit importer, and spent time running the business on his father's death. Steven Nadler, *Spinoza: A Life* (Cambridge: Cambridge University Press, 1999), 81–89.

bourgeois representative democracy) can be the ideological instrument of class rule; it is necessary for the class that has no class (the proletariat) to rise up and overthrow it.[23] Furthermore, the turn to Spinoza promises to answer some of the difficulties of twentieth-century Marxism.[24] First, Marxist social theory offers an unduly reductive conception of social struggle and progress, often privileging the struggles of the male industrial proletariat against capitalists, to the neglect of other sites of domination and resistance (women, the indigenous, the unemployed, and so on). By contrast, Spinoza's account does not prejudge the possible forms that human domination and resistance may take. Second, even at the same time as Marxist organizations fought the capture of state power by the ruling class, they themselves often took a hierarchical bureaucratized form, alienating power from the masses. By contrast, Spinoza's analysis of the power of the multitude promises to undermine the structures of domination in any organization whatsoever. Thus, the old Marxian idea of the universal class (the proletariat) as a mass agent which rises through history is given some democratic fine-tuning by being reconceived as a Spinozist multitude tending towards unalienated and inclusive horizontality.

Neither the radical Hobbes nor the radical Spinoza matches the mainstream view within the respective scholarly fields of study. It is more commonplace to read Hobbes as a thinker who is equally or more comfortable with absolute monarchy; it is more commonplace to read Spinoza as a liberal democrat who is leery of insurgency. But the radical Hobbes and the radical Spinoza pose challenging questions for politics, beyond the narrow exegetical context of their writings. Tuck points to various eighteenth-century French and American constitutional plebiscites that showed optimism and trust in the people:[25] his defence of Hobbesian democratic sovereignty leaves us with the question, how can we not favour more extensive use of democratic plebiscites? Negri points to social movements that have justice on their side and which, through history, have assumed an ever more open and inclusive

[23] Karl Marx, 'Contribution to the Critique of Hegel's *Philosophy of Right*: Introduction', in *The Marx-Engels Reader*, edited by Robert C. Tucker (New York: Norton, 1978), 62–65.

[24] In particular, the difficulties that troubled Italian autonomist Marxists. For a brief historical overview, see Sylvère Lotringer, 'Introduction', in *A Grammar of the Multitude: For an Analysis of Contemporary Forms of Life*, edited by Paolo Virno (Los Angeles: Semiotext(e), 2004), 7–20; Kathi Weeks, *The Problem with Work: Feminism, Marxism, Antiwork Politics, and Postwork Imaginaries* (Durham, NC: Duke University Press, 2011), 92–96. See also Enrique Dussel, *Twenty Theses on Politics*, translated by George Cicciarello-Maher (Durham, NC: Duke University Press, 2008), xvi; Mario Tronti, 'The Strategy of Refusal', *Autonomia: Post-political Politics* 3, no. 3 (1980): 28–35.

[25] Tuck, *The Sleeping Sovereign*, 146–161, 189–237.

structure:[26] his celebration of the power of the multitude leaves us with the question, how can we not support the spontaneous upswell of mass power against constituted authorities? In sum, together the two traditions of radical democracy demand an answer to the question, what could be more desirable than the unfettered grounding of politics in popular power? Certainly, the Schumpeterian worries already outlined may still niggle, but insofar as Schumpeter himself seeks to eliminate any appeal to the power of the people, his worries are often dismissed as signs of a reactionary lack of faith in the people: an elitist anti-democratic tendency, or a privileged conservatism.

Given that Tuck's and Negri's positions are admittedly not the dominant views in the specialist literatures on Hobbes and Spinoza, should we simply assess their claims about popular power and democratic politics on their own terms and drop the reference to Hobbes and Spinoza? Or is something to be learnt from the very texts that they appeal to? This book pursues the latter possibility. First, I argue that the radical democratic accounts of Hobbesian and Spinozist popular power gravely misrepresent the philosophers' own views. Second, I argue that the ways in which the radical democrats go wrong are illuminating. Using the question of popular power as a focus for interpreting Hobbes and Spinoza can also enrich and improve the mainstream scholarly understanding of their respective philosophies. Third, and putting aside the specialist Hobbes and Spinoza literatures, I argue that the results of my investigation have significance for contemporary democratic theory more generally. I offer a new approach to conceptualizing popular power that overcomes the impasse between radical enthusiasm and Schumpeterian scepticism.

1.3. *Potentia*: The Core Argument of the Book

It is often claimed that the critical point of differentiation between the political philosophies of Hobbes and Spinoza is the concept of *potentia*: Spinoza's concrete power *potentia* of the multitude is contrasted with Hobbes's authorized power *potestas* of the people. This Latin distinction, sometimes obscured by an indifferent English translation of both terms as 'power', is especially central to the radical democratic appropriation of Spinoza's work. But it is not often noted that Hobbes offers a very interesting conception of *potentia*

[26] Hardt and Negri, *Multitude*, 69–88.

of his own. In this book, the term *potentia* serves as the guiding thread for exploring popular power.

For both Hobbes and Spinoza, power *potentia* is a term not limited to human action, but is part of a broader natural philosophy. In their natural philosophies, any thing's *potentia* is relational and actual: analysing power involves analysing what occurs, not analysing some unexpressed substrate of what could potentially occur. I will argue that this has consequences for understanding human action. For the power of a collectivity cannot simply be conceived as the equal horizontal addition of individual powers. Insofar as actual human relations may be harmonious or conflictual, equal or hierarchical, helpful or exploitative, correspondingly the *potentia* of human collectivities reflects those characteristics: the power of a patron together with the patron's clients differs from the power of a band of friends. In consequence, for neither thinker is there anything necessarily good or authoritative in itself about the *potentia* of a human collectivity. Only under some circumstances does the *potentia* of a collectivity deserve to be called popular power; that is, popular power is a success term. Equally on a Hobbesian or a Spinozist account, I will argue that a popular power worthy of the name will be both popular (inclusive, equal, and not structured by oligarchic relations of dependency) and powerful (durably productive of effects). Such power is difficult to achieve, because forms of interpersonal dependency constantly emerge in social relations. For my purposes, the major disagreement between Hobbes and Spinoza lies in the disparate institutional-organizational models that each thinker believes optimally expresses popular power in this sense: I have dubbed Hobbes's model repressive egalitarianism; and Spinoza's, civic strengthening.

Despite Hobbes's and Spinoza's differences of substantial vision, more significant is their shared understanding of state institutions as at least partially constitutive of collective power. Against both the American neo-Hobbesian celebration of direct democratic voice and the Marxist neo-Spinozist romance of the multitude, Hobbes and Spinoza display no radical democratic suspicion of the state. Both camps of radical democrats worry about the oligarchic and elitist state, and valorize popular power as that which opposes the state. In so doing, they presume that non-state forces have an inherently horizontal structure and a meaningful direction, and that they can be genuinely powerful when they are not suppressed. But first, this presumption fails to recognize and address the private powers emergent within the multitude, which may be just as oligarchic and oppressive as the state. Second, this presumption rests on a feeble account of political causality. The juridical authority of plebiscites and the insurgent disruption of social movements both stand as superficial phenomena compared to quotidian relational processes that substantially determine political outcomes. Taking these two points on board, complex political institutions need to be conceived as fundamentally ambivalent with respect to popular power. On the one hand, it is surely possible for them to be alienating and oppressive and for them to be captured by special interests. But on the other hand, they are indispensable for addressing and containing informal oligarchy and for having real impact such that popular power becomes something more than a mere tragic gesture.

1.4. Conceptual Transformations and Political Models

Having provided a high-altitude overview of the book's argument, I now provide an outline of my engagement with Hobbes's and Spinoza's texts. The concept of power, *potentia*, serves as the book's guiding thread, but the concept proves exegetically and analytically slippery. The existing specialist literatures are of little assistance. On the side of Hobbes studies, the Latin distinction between *potentia* and *potestas* is generally obscured under the common English term 'power'; even when the distinction is noted, *potentia* is given little philosophical attention. On the side of Spinoza studies, the standard accounts of *potentia*, and in particular the *potentia* of the multitude, remain equivocal, sometimes glossed as merely the production of effects, but other times carrying ethical weight. To cut through the confusion, I start by contextualizing the concept within its overwhelmingly dominant frame of reference in the early modern period: scholasticism. Scholasticism, the Christianized Aristotelianism that dominated European intellectual life over the centuries leading up to Hobbes's and Spinoza's own time, placed a conception of *potentia* at the very foundation of philosophy, and indeed of all systematic thought from natural science to theology. On the scholastic view, a thing's *potentia* identifies its own proper nature, which (at least in natural entities where free will does not intervene) tends to be expressed for the most part. It offers an explanation of phenomena that is simultaneously descriptive and normative: the natural world is understood as a domain of proper entities endowed with natural and proper tendencies. In seventeenth-century Europe, the scholastic conception of *potentia* was the focus of a fight over the very nature of the scientific enterprise, and self-styled new scientists such as

Descartes committed themselves to purging 'occult powers' in the name of a more adequate mode of scientific mechanistic explanation. When Hobbes and Spinoza appeal to *potentia*, despite being fully aware of and engaged in the new science, we must be on our guard against uncritically attributing to them an account of power reflecting the old scholastic patterns of thought.

In the first half of the book, Chapters 2 through 5, I discuss Hobbes. I argue that Hobbes's understanding of *potentia* undergoes a striking development between his early and late works, with significant ramifications for his science of politics. Undeniably, the tumultuous political events of the period during which he was writing would have provided external impetus for shifts in his political analysis; but this book's contribution is to trace the conceptual transformations within which the shifting political analysis finds its voice. Early and late, Hobbes denies free will; thus, when he offers a model of human *potentia*, it is more or less continuous with a model of the *potentiae* of natural objects. But Hobbes's early view reflects his early education in scholastic natural science, whereas his later view reflects the new mechanistic natural science. On the early scholastic-influenced view, individual human power *potentia* is understood as human faculties, which are more or less equal in all adults. Individual humans can properly combine their powers together only as a formal union, because any informal association lacks a unifying principle. This neatly meshes with Hobbes's juridical theory of state authority *potestas*, which receives a *potentia* commensurate to its *potestas* in virtue of the covenantal combination of individual *potentiae*. But on the later view, reflecting the new mechanistic science that seeks to eliminate the explanatory appeal to inherent dispositional powers, individual human *potentia* is understood as whatever means a person may have to pursue their ends, including the assistance or deference of other people. As such, human *potentia* is relational and actual, and subject to great inequalities. Furthermore, individual human powers can accumulate into relatively stable informal allegiances and social groupings, endowed with their own power, even without any formal union. These private power blocs may sometimes be appealing, but more likely they will be oligarchic and objectionable. The new conception of *potentia* sits uncomfortably with the juridical theory of absolute state *potestas*, because in the face of competition from private informal powers in the political domain, the state may not have *potentia* commensurate to its *potestas*: call this mismatch 'the political problem'. The political problem can be solved only by looking beneath the juridical order of *potestas* to consider the concrete determinants of a stable collective power *potentia* of the populace.

In the light of Hobbes's changing understanding of *potentia*, it becomes easy to see why Tuck's preferred plebiscitary model of sleeping sovereignty only features in Hobbes's earlier text, *De Cive*, and is dropped in *Leviathan*. First, sovereignty separate from government is likely to have very little power *potentia*. The real seat of power *potentia* is the dense circuits of allegiance and deference that structure the quotidian functioning of the society. A sovereign standing separate from this structure but occasionally rising up to issue a ruling can make only a minor impact on the everyday production of effects in society, even if its ruling is respected; but even worse, such a sovereign gravely risks encountering the political problem, as it may find that much of the society has stronger allegiance to the government. A prudent sovereign might skirt this difficulty by accepting its lack of power and never issuing any controversial rulings, but the likelihood of such a strategy underscores the superficiality of focussing political analysis on the juridical holder of sovereignty. Second, the claim of plebiscitary voting to give radical expression to the popular voice is weak: for without addressing the private powers in society, a vote tends to relay those unequal background conditions.

What might solve the political problem? I characterize Hobbes's proposal as repressive egalitarianism: the common good is achieved by trying to improve the political and moral judgement of the sovereign, and at the same time protecting the sovereign from the distorting pressure of formal and informal power blocs within society. In the face of private power, the appropriate response is to crush it, to break collective formations within the populace in favour of a fragmented equality of all subjects. Hobbes argues that governance will better promote the common good when it takes a less participatory form; he worries that democracy may undermine common good and lead to division. But if there must be popular political participation, if there must be a democratic assembly as sovereign, then it is especially important to repress informal powers that might seek to capture the democratic process. I characterize Hobbes's democratic repressive egalitarianism as a certain minimal expression of popular power: it is a durable institutional form that strives to eliminate unequal influence.

In the second half of the book, Chapters 6 through 9, I turn to Spinoza. Spinoza's concept of power *potentia* is central to his philosophical system, yet it remains elusive and difficult to characterize. In his magnum opus, the *Ethics*, the power *potentia* of any thing is linked to its essence and virtue; in particular for humans, *potentia* is linked to ethics. At the same time, *potentia* appears to relate to a more ordinary meaning of power as efficacy or causality. This combination of normative and descriptive elements is apparently similar to that of scholastic natural science. But applied to human affairs, the combination yields implausible results. The power of the multitude is supposed both to tend towards virtue and also to be efficacious, but surely there are cases where efficacy does not align with virtue. What of the sorry history of human oppression and injustice? The scholastics can readily accommodate human deviancy from the good by appeal to the disordering interventions of sinful free will, but this avenue is not open to Spinoza because he denies free will. Interpreters—whether radical democrats, or equally the more mainstream interpreters whom I will label 'constitutionalists'—tend to square this circle by echoing Seneca's dictum that tyrants never last long. They presume that unappealing political regimes will be transient, and claim that democracy is the inner truth of every successful regime.

Rather than defending the alleged rapprochement of efficacy and ethics in Spinoza's conception of power, to the contrary I explore their divergence. In the face of the democratic complacency of standard interpretations of Spinoza, I press Spinoza's philosophy for a response to three Hobbesian worries: first, the problem of the multitude's inner oligarchy; second, the problem of nonideal endurance; and third, the problem of democracy's perverse effects. Determining Spinoza's response demands a systematic reconstruction of his concept of power. In fact, I argue that Spinoza has two clearly distinct senses of *potentia*. On the one hand, there is the power to produce effects (*potentia operandi*); on the other hand there is the power of acting (*potentia agendi*): the difference is between an individual producing effects in general, versus an individual producing effects that can be understood through the individual's own nature. Individuals can have a high degree of *potentia operandi* despite a low degree of *potentia agendi*: as, for example, a state under colonial rule, or an irascible individual whose partner calms the other's outbursts. I argue that it is only by appreciating the two senses of power and their interplay that a proper understanding of Spinoza's politics can be reached, but the plain textual distinction between the two senses has been obscured by the division of labour between Spinoza's texts. For in the *Ethics*, oriented towards individual self-cultivation, the primary focus is *potentia agendi*; whereas in the political texts, the foundational frame of right is linked to primarily to *potentia operandi*, and only secondarily to *potentia agendi*. Building on this distinction, I offer a systematic reconstruction of

Spinoza's politics that acknowledges its deep antinomianism. An individual's right and a state's right are coextensive with their *potentia operandi*, which is their power of producing effects of whatever sort, for better or for worse. Granted, only in those cases where they act from their own proper power (*potentia agendi*) alone are they in control of their own right (sui juris). This consideration of being sui juris (both the state itself being sui juris, and individuals within the state being sui juris) constitutes the ethical element of Spinoza's political philosophy, and it is undeniably important. But my analysis emphasizes that the ethical element is only one component of a larger analysis of political power.

This reconstruction of Spinoza's politics enables me to argue that Spinoza can and must accept my three Hobbesian problems. I argue that Spinoza accepts the first Hobbesian problem, the problem of the multitude's inner oligarchy. *Potentia operandi* is very similar to the late Hobbesian *potentia*; thus, the Spinozist multitude tends to feature Hobbesian oligarchic informal power blocs. I paint radical democratic Spinozists as neo-scholastics: for they understand the multitude's active power as a normatively appealing disposition that tends increasingly to express itself through history. But for Spinoza unlike the scholastics, all power is fully actualized, and a multitude has precisely the degree of power that it expresses at any given time. If a multitude is not horizontal and equal, then it lacks the power to be so. Nor even does the existence of egalitarian and inclusive social movements establish the underlying goodness of the multitude. I argue that an entity's action is determined by its own active power alone (it is sui juris) when it maintains itself homeostatically. Thus, a multitude's power sui juris cannot be established by appeal to behaviour shaped by its opposition to the state. A multitude sui juris must have established the forms of self-regulation to maintain itself over time, and this will mean establishing an institutional structure. The multitude sui juris amounts to a Hobbesian state that has solved the political problem: a state that has established a configuration of individual *potentiae* that can hold itself together over time.

Next, I argue that Spinoza accepts the second Hobbesian problem: the problem of nonideal endurance. Allegedly Spinoza shows that the only durable independent states (the only states that have solved the Hobbesian political problem) are those that have good institutions, fitting with the intuitive desiderata of a normatively appealing democracy. Radical and constitutionalist interpretations alike insist that, for Spinoza as for Seneca, tyrannies never last long: great political power presupposes a deep ethical structure to the political order. To the contrary, I argue that a state can be durable in non-democratic ways, whether due to the stabilizing pressure of external forces, or due to well-crafted internal structures of dependency: the challenge for politics is not only for a state to achieve durability and address the Hobbesian political problem, but to do so in a way that more robustly expresses popular power.

In Chapter 9, I draw together the various argumentative threads of the book to propose a neo-Spinozist criterion of popular power. First, as to power: I propose that a collectivity expresses its power to the degree it is sui juris, or in other words, to the degree it homeostatically maintains itself and produces characteristic effects. Effects that either are produced sporadically or erratically or are produced durably but only due to pressure from an external force (for instance, under the tutelage of a colonial power) attest less to the collective's own power. Next, as to popularity: I propose that a collectivity's power counts as popular if it effectively self-regulates itself in accord with a fundamental principle of equality and participation. A collectivity producing hierarchized dependency amongst its members counts to that extent as less popular. What regime might meet this two-part criterion of popular power? I argue that Spinoza takes very seriously the problem of democracy's perverse effects (the third Hobbesian problem); but whereas the Hobbesian solution is repressive egalitarianism, I characterize Spinoza's solution as civic strengthening. Hobbes views all collective organization as a force of oligarchy and therefore seeks to individualize the multitude and fragment its collectivities as much as possible. By contrast, Spinoza seeks to enhance the positive potentiality of human collective action, encouraging sociable and civic collective forms, and diminishing the passions that entrench problematic oligarchies. Once the use of egalitarian organizational mechanisms such as sortition breaks the perverse incentives for oligarchic consolidation, the possibility emerges for formal and informal counterpowers to be welcomed as a beneficial part of a political system's self-regulation.

1.5. Outcome

From a detailed study of the historical texts of Hobbes and Spinoza, this book renders contemporary lessons for a theory of popular power. First, a thesis on popularity: the multitude is not a locus of ontological purity or political authenticity. For neither Hobbes nor Spinoza is there any underlying disposition of human collectivities towards goodness, just waiting for the chance to express itself. To the contrary, the *potentia* of a human multitude is deeply normatively ambivalent. Hierarchy and domination are not merely external impositions of the state, but are emergent within the body politic; the challenge of politics is to bring these internal dynamics to heel. Second, a thesis on power: power is the production of effects, and power in human societies operates through a complex and continuously generated relational structure throughout the social body. The power governing a particular political community must be assessed at the level of this structure, within which particular expressions of popular feeling (in votes or social movements) are merely partial mechanisms.

Combining these theses, I have established a criterion of popular power: a political system expresses popular power to the extent that it manifests an institutional structure robustly generating equality and participation. Many formally democratic orders fall far short against this criterion. But the solution is not to fetishize the tragic and ephemeral popular upswell of plebiscitary votes or of social movements. The radical democratic celebration of plebiscites or social movements as the quintessential expression of popular power has the perverse consequence that a society that achieves substantive democratic equality through excellent institutional structure and well-conceived ongoing functions of representation will count as less expressive of popular power than one that is effectively an oligarchy but which occasionally hears the voice of people in plebiscites or mass uprisings of public outrage. Rather, the solution to the deficiency of popular power in formally democratic states should be to investigate and construct the organizational forms that better meet my Spinozist criterion.

This approach does not rule out popular plebiscites or unruly social movements. We need not follow the Hobbesian path of viewing any centre of collective power distinct from the holder of sovereignty as an oligarchic threat. But this approach does decentre those erstwhile paradigmatic forms of popular power. It is not the bare presence of social movements and plebiscites that establishes the state's popular credentials: the evidence of real popular power lies in how plebiscites or social movements may contribute positively to the popular state's durable maintenance of equality and participation amongst its citizens. I sketch a defence of the plausibility of Spinoza's model of popular power through 'civic strengthening': like Hobbes, constraining bad oligarchic collective power; but unlike Hobbes, taking on the project of cultivating collective power's good and helpful forms.

1.6. Note to Readers

In writing this book, I have tried to hold myself to standards of philological and philosophical rigour with respect to my interpretations of Hobbes and Spinoza's texts, and with respect to my analysis of the concept of *potentia*. However, in common with Tuck and Negri, I draw on historical texts out of a robust sense of their relevance to contemporary politics. Readers interested primarily in contemporary democratic theory (and less in the philological and genealogical background) might find they can still follow the overall argument of the book even if they skip the following sections: Chapter 2, Sections 2.2–3 and 2.5; Chapter 3, Sections 3.2–4; Chapter 7, Sections 7.2–3.

As for readers hoping for a more detailed account of the historical context—both material and intellectual—in which Hobbes and Spinoza were writing, I encourage them to consult the fairly comprehensive extant literature on that topic;[27] my own research does not pretend to contribute to those kind of investigations. My arguments do propose some periodization of Hobbes's and Spinoza's texts, and I do not deny that broader consideration of historical context would further illuminate the shifts in their views. Certainly, how could it not: both England and the Dutch Republic experienced immense political turmoil during the very time that Hobbes and

[27] For a general history of the period, see, for instance, Robert Buchholz and Newton Key, *Early Modern England, 1485–1714: A Narrative History*, 2nd ed. (Malden, MA: Wiley-Blackwell, 2009); J. L. Price, *The Dutch Republic in the Seventeenth Century* (New York: St. Martin's Press, 1998). For an intellectual history of the period, see, for instance, Perez Zagorin, *A History of Political Thought in the English Revolution* (London: Routledge & Kegan Paul, 1954); Johann P. Sommerville, *Thomas Hobbes: Political Ideas in Historical Context* (Houndmills: Macmillan, 1992); A. P. Martinich, *Hobbes: A Biography* (Cambridge: Cambridge University Press, 1999); Samuel I. Mintz, *The Hunting of Leviathan; Seventeenth-Century Reactions to the Materialism and Moral Philosophy of Thomas Hobbes* (Cambridge: University Press, 1962); Jonathan I. Israel, *Radical Enlightenment: Philosophy and the Making of Modernity, 1650–1750* (Oxford: Oxford University Press, 2001); Eco O. G. Haitsma Mulier, *The Myth of Venice and Dutch Republican Thought in the Seventeenth Century*, translated by Gerard T. Moran (Assen, The Netherlands: Van Gorcum, 1980); Susan James, *Spinoza on Philosophy, Religion and Politics: The 'Theologico-Political Treatise'* (Oxford: Oxford University Press, 2012); Lucien Mugnier-Pollet, *La philosophie politique de Spinoza* (Paris: Vrin, 1976), 13–80, 175–213; Nadler, *Spinoza*; Steven Nadler, *A Book Forged in Hell: Spinoza's Scandalous Treatise and the Birth of the Secular Age* (Princeton, NJ: Princeton University Press, 2013), 1–51, 215–240; Raia Prokhovnik, *Spinoza and Republicanism* (Houndmills: Palgrave Macmillan, 2004).

Spinoza were composing their texts. However, the relation between Hobbes and Spinoza's texts and their own historical experiences have been amply discussed by other authors.[28] My project is different: I seek to take advantage of variations of the underlying conceptualization of power manifested in the various stages of Hobbes's and Spinoza's writings as a testing ground for understanding the logic of popular power.

[28] For instance, Richard Tuck, *Hobbes* (Oxford: Oxford University Press, 1989), 1–39; Lewis Samuel Feuer, *Spinoza and the Rise of Liberalism* (Boston: Beacon Press, 1958); Étienne Balibar, *Spinoza and Politics*, translated by Peter Snowdon (New York: Verso, 1998); Perez Zagorin, *Rebels and Rulers, 1500–1660*, Vol. 2 (Cambridge: Cambridge University Press, 1982), 130–186.

PART I
HOBBES

2
Relational Power

2.1. Introduction

The fundamental question for this book is how to understand popular power in politics. Through the book, I will develop and defend a new conception of popular power, grounded in a new interpretation of the philosophies of Hobbes and Spinoza, according to which a political system expresses popular power to the extent that it manifests an institutional structure robustly generating equality and participation. The stakes of this new conception of popular power can be appreciated by contrast with the alternative conceptions put forward by radical democrats, which (I will argue) are unsustainable in the face of a proper consideration of the structure and dynamics of human collective life. In the first half of the book, I focus on Hobbes.

What even is Hobbes's understanding of popular power? Tuck locates a radical democratic proposal in Hobbes's second political tract, *De Cive*: popular power finds its exemplary expression in a political order with a democratic 'sleeping sovereign' that awakes to express its will through occasional mass plebiscites. Hobbes himself no longer mentions this proposal in his later tract *Leviathan*; for Tuck, this omission is of no significance, a mere matter of diplomatic prudence.[1] But to the contrary, I will argue that the omission reflects a foundational conceptual revision between Hobbes's early and late science of politics: a change to the conception of power. I will argue that viewing the sleeping democratic sovereign as a vehicle of popular power is possible only on the basis of Hobbes's early and entirely inadequate analysis of power. Hobbes's later relational and actual analysis of power is far superior to the early neo-scholastic view; compared to Hobbes's erstwhile breezy juridicism, this later view of power demands more subtle attention to organizational forms and interpersonal structures.

[1] Hobbes planned to present *Leviathan* to the King of Scots; Tuck speculates that Hobbes wished to avoid being needlessly inflammatory by making too obvious his advocacy for democracy. Tuck, *The Sleeping Sovereign*, 104–105.

Potentia. Sandra Leonie Field, Oxford University Press (2020). © Oxford University Press.
DOI: 10.1093/oso/9780197533864.001.0001

The changed analysis of power has not been noticed because interpretations of Hobbes's political philosophy nearly universally focus on his theories of authorized power (*potestas*) and right (*ius*); whereas the critical developments fall under the heading not of power as *potestas*, but of power as *potentia*. In the first half of this book, I focus on Hobbes's contribution to the conceptualization of *potentia*, its deep systematic importance for understanding Hobbes's political philosophy, and its broader political ramifications. In the second half of this book, I offer a parallel analysis of Spinoza's conception of *potentia*, arguing that it lies closer to the late Hobbesian view than is normally appreciated. For both thinkers, I will show that popular power worthy of the name is not an underlying force waiting to express itself, but rather it is an achievement, the outcome of patient and arduous institutional development.

My discussion of Hobbes spans four chapters, treating individual *potentia*, the early account of composition of *potentiae*, the late account of composition of *potentiae*, and the political implications of *potentia*, respectively. The present chapter, Chapter 2, establishes a distinction between Hobbes's early and late conceptions of individual *potentia*: a power initially understood as an internal faculty comes to be reconceived as irreducibly relational. Chapters 3 and 4 draw out the ramifications of these respective conceptions of individual power for modelling social and political dynamics: finding that the relational conception of power casts suspicion on any idea of spontaneous prepolitical human equality. To the contrary, it raises the problem of informal competitive oligarchy. Chapter 5 interprets Hobbes's hostility to popular political agency as a drive to crush oligarchic informal powers, and characterizes his preferred model of popular power as repressive egalitarianism. Through these investigations, I will show that a democratic sleeping sovereign cannot be the exemplar of popular power: for it is revealed as neither particularly powerful nor meaningfully popular.

In this present chapter, I argue that human *potentia* changes across Hobbes's oeuvre from an essential to a relational property. Early and late, Hobbes's theory of *potentia* is intended to explain actual human behaviour. In Hobbes's early texts, individual power is conceived as capacities or faculties possessed by and internal to the individual; any social ramifications of these capacities or faculties are conceived as secondary. In Hobbes's later texts, individual power is relational and inessential, emergent from the rich texture of human social interaction; as a corollary, it is not possible to analyse power in abstraction from the concrete net of human relations in which it is manifested. This amounts to a shift from understanding power as an inner, stable, more or less equal property with (admittedly minimal) moral character, to understanding power as neither inner, nor stable, nor equal, and (as will become clear in Chapter 4) as fundamentally lacking any moral character whatsoever. In this chapter and the next, I situate Hobbes's changing theory of human power alongside his broader negotiation with a scholastic conceptual inheritance. The changing conception has implications for politics: for whereas on the early science of *potentia*, actual human behaviour and power are expected to conform largely to the juridical demands of natural law,[2] on the later view conformity becomes elusive, as will become clear when human collective action is considered in Chapters 3 and 4.

In my argument, I periodize Hobbes's texts, counting *The Elements of Law* (1640), *De Cive* (1642), the *Anti-White* (1643), and the contested *Short Tract* (1630) as early; and *Leviathan* (English [1651] and Latin [1668] editions), *De Corpore* (1655), and *De Homine* (1658) as late. I draw on both the Latin and the English. Close correlations of the structure and content of large swathes of the texts make it possible to determine with confidence when an English discussion of power does indeed map onto *potentia* and not *potestas*. In particular, the explicit discussion of human power in *Leviathan*'s Chapter 10 is available both in English and in a direct Latin translation by Hobbes's own hand, and throughout the chapter power is systematically translated as *potentia*. Furthermore, this discussion is a clearly recognizable descendant of the early *Elements of Law*, Part I Chapter 8.[3] I rely primarily on the English-language discussion of power in *The Elements of Law* to reconstruct Hobbes's early view of individual human *potentia*,[4] because unfortunately there is no corresponding passage in the early Latin text *De Cive*.[5] *De Cive*'s contribution to the conceptualization of *potentia* will come to the fore in the context of political collectivities, as I will lay out in Chapter 3.

[2] Both in the state of nature and in the well-constituted commonwealth, but not in the poorly constituted commonwealth, as I will show in Chapter 3.

[3] The two passages stand in the same place in the text, after the discussion of the passions and before the establishment of the commonwealth; the internal sequences of the analyses of power are very similar (starting with natural power, then instrumental powers, then honour); many of the same examples are used.

[4] I also corroborate this interpretation with the briefer Latin discussion of human power in *Anti-White*.

[5] In the face of political strife, Hobbes put aside the first two sections of his *Elementa Philosophica* to work on the more directly political *De Cive*; the passage corresponding to the discussion of power/*potentia* in *The Elements of Law* I.8 and *Leviathan*, Chapter 10, eventually appeared in *De Homine*, but it was completed so late as to count as a late work by my periodization.

In my argument, I refer to an early and a late theory of human *potentia*, and the question has been raised, how strongly do I wish to assert a sharp distinction (rather than just a gradual evolution) between these theories. I am willing to grant that the chronological distinction between the theories may not be perfect: in particular, there are elements of both theories in *De Cive*.[6] However, granting some chronological messiness in Hobbes's transition from one view to the other in no way impugns the bright conceptual distinction between the views, as I will now endeavour to show.[7]

2.2. Human Power as Faculties in Hobbes's Early Writings

In this section, I argue that Hobbes's early political text *The Elements of Law* conceives individual human power (corresponding to the Latin *potentia*) as a collection of faculties possessed by the individual. I acknowledge that Hobbes discusses (what I will call) secondary powers, and (what I will call) the positionality of power, both of which apparently challenge the conception of power as faculties. But in both cases, I demonstrate that the core defining conception of power remains human faculties. This will stand in sharp contrast to the relational view of power/*potentia*, to be developed in subsequent sections.[8]

The discussion in *The Elements of Law* provides prima facie support for glossing individual human power as faculties. A human individual's power is 'the faculties of body and mind . . . that is to say, of the body, nutritive, generative, and motive; and of the mind, knowledge' (EL I.8.4). This connection is reiterated through the text, establishing an equivalence between human power, faculties, and human nature itself.

> Man's nature is the sum of his natural faculties and powers, as the faculties of nutrition, motion, generation, sense, reason, etc. For these powers we do unanimously call natural, and are contained in the definition of man, under these words, animal and rational. (EL I.1.4. See also EL I.14.1; DC 1.1)

[6] See footnotes 8 and 56.

[7] The bright conceptual distinction applies to the philosophical analysis of power, both individual and collective: the topic of this chapter and of Chapter 3, Section 3.2 and Chapter 4, Section 4.2. I accept that the change is gradual regarding more loosely political questions, for instance regarding the importance of the teaching of duties (Chapter 5, Section 5.2).

[8] While this general characterization holds true of *De Cive*'s discussion of power, there are some emergent hints of the later view, most notably in *De Cive*'s theology (DC 15.13).

Nonetheless, Hobbes also provides a suggestion for a more expansive conception of power, extending beyond faculties also to encompass what I will call secondary powers:

> such farther powers, as by them [the faculties of body and mind] are acquired (viz.) riches, place of authority, friendship or favour, and good fortune; which last is really nothing else but the favour of God Almighty. (EL I.8.4)

The more expansive conception of power includes all manner of other contextual and social considerations contributing to a person's capacity to achieve their ends. This revised conception has often been accepted as definitive; after all, it appears to align nicely with the view expressed in *Leviathan* (L 10.1–2).[9] I claim, to the contrary, that Hobbes's early analysis of power always privileges natural faculties, conceiving power as the causal potentiality proper and internal to an individual. Even if Hobbes recognizes secondary powers to be crucially important in human life, they are powers only in a derivative sense, as the conduits for or indicators of faculties. I demonstrate this claim by considering Hobbes's accounts of equality, honour, and glory.

First, consider equality. If secondary powers are part of an individual's power in the proper sense, then they must factor into the assessment of an individual's power. However, to the contrary, when arguing that people are more or less equal in power, Hobbes does not see it necessary to demonstrate that people's secondary powers, such as the assistance and favour they receive, are equal. Rather, the equality of power is established merely by considering equality in faculties: strength, wit, and knowledge. Correspondingly, the true measure of any inequality of power that does exist is determined not through comparison of secondary powers, but through the clash of bodily strength (EL I.14.1–5; DC 1.3–4, 1.6).

Second, consider honour. Honour is the internal conception of the superiority of another person's power.[10] The signs[11] by which power or its excess

[9] C. B. Macpherson, *The Political Theory of Possessive Individualism: Hobbes to Locke* (Oxford: Clarendon Press, 1962), 35–46; James H. Read, 'Thomas Hobbes: Power in the State of Nature, Power in Civil Society', *Polity 23*, no. 4 (1991): 505–506; Richard Tuck, 'Introduction', in *On the Citizen*, edited by Richard Tuck and Michael Silverthorne (Cambridge: Cambridge University Press, 2006), xxi; M. M. Goldsmith, *Hobbes's Science of Politics* (New York: Columbia University Press, 1966), 66–71.

[10] This superiority is initially characterized with respect to the power of the beholder, but Hobbes later generalizes it to mean superiority with respect to the relevant comparison class. For instance, a powerful individual can honour a subordinate by praising this person above other subordinates (EL I.8.6).

[11] A sign is a thing that a person has experienced as regularly occurring antecedent or consequent to something else, which the person conjectures will occur in this combination again in the future (EL I.4.9–10).

above that of others can be recognized are called honourable. They include not only the direct effects of a power, but also effects at several causal steps away from that power, by which its existence is indirectly inferred. For instance, 'general reputation amongst those of the other sex' is honourable as a sign directly consequent of 'power generative'; boldness is honourable via a more indirect signification: it is 'a sign consequent of opinion of our own strength: and that opinion a sign of the strength itself' (EL I.8.5). If secondary powers are powers in the proper sense, then their superiority should merit honour, even without reference to faculties. However, to the contrary, whenever Hobbes proposes superiority of secondary powers to be honourable, he takes care to trace the chain of signification back to an individual's possession of a faculty. Riches are honourable, not because they themselves are power, but 'as signs of the power that acquired them'; authority is honourable, not because it itself is a power, but 'because a sign of strength, wisdom, favour or riches by which it is attained' (EL I.8.5). Hobbes does not discuss friendship per se, but he does analyse some attributes thereof, again reducing them back to faculties: persuasiveness is honourable, as a sign of knowledge; 'general reputation amongst those of the other sex' is honourable, as a sign of bodily vigour (EL I.8.5).

Third, consider glory. If secondary powers are powers in the proper sense, then it is not false to glory in them. Glory,

> or internal gloriation or triumph of the mind, is that passion which proceedeth from the imagination or conception of our own power, above the power of him that contendeth with us. (EL I.9.1)

A person has reason to glory when their feeling of superiority of power is grounded in reality, whereas false or vain glory are the feelings without the real power. However, Hobbes directly denies that association with others gives rise to justifiable glory. '[N]or does association with others increase one's reason for glorying in oneself, since a man is worth as much as he can do without relying on anyone else' (DC 1.2).[12] Similarly, Hobbes insists that reliance on fame to achieve glory indicates a lack of power (EL I.9.20). In both cases, the secondary power (association, or the deference and assistance of those who recognize one's fame) is not by itself reason for glory; in other

[12] The *Anti-White* goes so far as to deny that friends even count as a secondary power, because real power (presumably, formidable faculties) inspires hate and fear, not love (AW 38.8).

words, it is not a power in the proper sense.[13] Rather, proper glory is tied to awareness of one's own superior faculties. In sum, while glory itself is intrinsically relational insofar as it is defined by comparison of powers, the power that it compares is clearly non-relational.

Thus, despite the initial presentation of secondary powers as powers in their own right, they are incorporated into the analysis only insofar as they are reduced back to natural faculties:[14] they are mere conduits for or indicators of the only things properly called powers, which are natural faculties.

I turn now to the question of positionality. The text provides some suggestion that power should not be conceived as faculty, but instead as a differential of faculties. Indeed, often Hobbes is interpreted as offering a 'zero-sum' conception of power.[15] In what I call the 'positionality claim', Hobbes asserts that power is intrinsically positional.

> And because the power of one man resisteth and hindereth the effects of the power of another: power simply is no more, but the excess of the power of one above that of another. For equal powers oppose, destroy one another; and such their opposition is called contention. (EL I.8.4)[16]

The analytical part of this positionality claim is reiterated and relied upon constantly throughout Hobbes's early texts. Capacities are only effective in their excess over one another; if you and I race to grab an apple, but I am faster, then I have the effective capacity to grab the apple. Your capacity, because comparatively inferior, is entirely ineffective. Hobbes elaborates this

[13] In the *Anti-White*, Hobbes insists we feel our power from our own deeds (AW 38.7) and from our own faculties: we feel glory in civil powers and honours because they are evidence of our superior mental powers, and we envy others who rise in wealth and honours because it is evidence of their superior mental power (AW 28.7). He makes only two very brief mentions of *potentiae* not reducible to our own faculties or deeds, or in other words, where the power of others itself constitutes one's own power rather than merely indicating one's own prior underlying power: kings and victors in battle (AW 38.8, 38.17). However, in Chapter 3, I will show that these kinds of cases fit neatly into Hobbes's early juridical conception of collective power.

[14] There are also other corroborations in the text. First, the definition of secondary powers—'such farther powers, as by them are acquired' (EL I.8.4)—already indicates that for something to be a secondary power, it must have a connection to faculties. Similarly, in the *Anti-White*, Hobbes claims honours and riches count as part of power *because* they are its consequents: '*partes esse potentiae, potentiam enim honores & divitiae sequuuntur*' (AW 38.8). Second, Hobbes says that power is known by the actions that it produces; he does not countenance that it might be known directly, as would be the case if secondary powers such as riches and friends were themselves truly powers in their own right (EL I.8.5).

[15] Macpherson, *Political Theory of Possessive Individualism*, 35; Thomas A. Spragens, *The Politics of Motion: The World of Thomas Hobbes* (Lexington: University Press of Kentucky, 1973), 190–191.

[16] See also AW 38.7.

point in an extended reflection on the analogy between human life and a race (EL I.9.21). Indeed, his definitions of glory, honour, and the honourable all involve comparison of power.

However, even if the positionality claim is indisputably analytically central, there still remains a terminological question. The positionality claim proposes a new use of the word 'power'. Power is no longer an individual's capacity (whether their faculties or also their secondary powers), but rather the excess of the person's capacity over the capacity of relevant others: for instance, it is the superiority of my strength that is a power, not the strength itself. The terminological question asks, in these early texts, is the term 'power' used equivocally for both these meanings, or is it reserved for one or the other? In fact, the use of the term 'power' to mean non-comparative capacity is clearly dominant in the text. To start, Hobbes frequently characterizes human power as faculties, not as the comparative excess of faculties (EL I.1.4, I.8.4, I.14.1). Furthermore, glory and honour are defined in terms of the comparative excess of power; if power already meant this comparative excess, Hobbes would need instead to define glory and honour directly in terms of power (EL I.8.5, I.9.1). Similarly, if power were already comparative, Hobbes should not speak of a situation of equal forces as a situation in which there is equal power, but rather as a situation in which there is no power at all (EL I.14.3).

In this section, I have established Hobbes's early conception of human powers: power is conceived as faculties, and as such it is internal and non-relational. I fully grant that relationality enters secondarily into the analysis of human affairs. Relationality is indispensable to understanding both the psychology of glory and the outcome of clashing powers. Nonetheless, relationality is not built into the concept of power itself.

2.3. Hobbes's Early Debt to Scholasticism

In his discussion of power, Hobbes was not taking an everyday term and giving it for the first time a technical meaning. To the contrary, the concept of power/*potentia* was a centrepiece of scholastic metaphysics. In this tradition, scientific understanding of each thing consists in discerning its *potentia*, which is at the same time its nature. Although *potentia* is now often translated as potentiality, in Hobbes's time it was translated as power. In his mature writings, Hobbes polemically opposed scholasticism. But Hobbes's Oxford education followed a standard scholastic curriculum, and secondary literature has meticulously documented the debt of his natural philosophy to this scholastic education.[17] This excellent secondary literature nonetheless has its limits. It is concerned with the history of philosophy of natural science; accordingly, its interest in human *potentia* extends only to narrow questions of optics and perception. In this section, I extend the scholastic framing of Hobbes's early philosophy beyond the science of natural objects to consider human action. I start by presenting a stylized sketch of the scholastic conception of *potentia*, in particular as it is found in Aquinas.[18] I then situate Hobbes's early conception of human power/*potentia* against this background, arguing that Hobbes's scholastic inheritance explains his peculiar insistence in *The Elements of Law* on conceiving of human power as inner faculties. However, due to Hobbes's denial of free will, I show that his conception of human power maps not onto the scholastic science of free human moral action, but onto the scholastic science of natural bodies: identifying a stable inner disposition that enables a simultaneously normative and descriptive understanding of the body in question. This frame will be important for understanding Hobbes's early conception of political power as *potestas*, as I will discuss in Chapter 3, Section 3.3.

The scholastic tradition of philosophy synthesizes Aristotle's physics and metaphysics together with Christian theology. It was the dominant tradition in Europe for several centuries following Aquinas's magisterial works.[19] But it was noisily superseded in the 'scientific revolution', displaced by the modern

[17] Cees Leijenhorst, *The Mechanisation of Aristotelianism: The Late Aristotelian Setting of Thomas Hobbes' Natural Philosophy* (Leiden: Brill, 2002), 1–16; Frithiof Brandt, *Thomas Hobbes's Mechanical Conception of Nature* (Copenhagen: Levin & Munksgaard, 1928), 9–85.

[18] My presentation largely follows Leijenhorst, *The Mechanisation of Aristotelianism,* who frames Hobbes's arguments with great specificity within his late scholastic intellectual context. In my own discussion, I do not pretend to provide an account of Hobbes's actual proximate philosophical influences, which include—in addition to scholasticism—also Averroism, humanism, and epicureanism. Readers interested in these topics can consult, in addition to Leijenhorst's book, his article 'Sense and Nonsense about Sense: Hobbes and the Aristotelians on Sense Perception and Imagination', in *The Cambridge Companion to Hobbes's 'Leviathan'*, edited by Patricia Springborg (Cambridge: Cambridge University Press, 2007), 82–108; as well as Gianni Paganini, 'Hobbes's Critique of the Doctrine of Essences and Its Sources', in Springborg, *Cambridge Companion to Hobbes's 'Leviathan'*, 337–357; J. Prins, 'Hobbes and the School of Padua: Two Incompatible Approaches of Science', *Archiv für Geschichte der Philosophie 72*, no. 1 (1990): 26–47; Gordon Hull, 'Hobbes's Radical Nominalism', *Epoché 11* (2006): 201–223; and Simon Friedle, 'Thomas Hobbes and the Reception of Early-Modern Epicureanism' (PhD dissertation, University of Cambridge, 2012).

[19] Centrally, St. Thomas Aquinas, *Summa Theologica: Complete English Edition in Five Volumes*, translated by Fathers of the English Dominican Province (Notre Dame, IN: Christian Classics, 1981).

science and mechanical philosophy of the likes of Galileo and Descartes.[20] Scholastic philosophy advances a hylomorphic metaphysics, so named for its focus on matter (Greek *hyle*) and form (Greek *morphē*). Undifferentiated inert matter is divided into natural bodies by substantial forms. This metaphysics characterizes the world in terms of a natural order. Des Chene provides a concise overview:

> The phenomena it [scholasticism] studies are in large part the regularities of everyday life: fire heats, water left alone cools, animals reproduce according to kind, excess is painful to the senses. There are phenomena that lie outside that sphere—miracles, monsters, the fortuitous. But the scientific study of change relies in the first instance on their regular effects. We know nature first of all not when it is frustrated, but when it succeeds.
>
> The task of natural philosophy is to understand that order, which Aristotelianism founded on the natural necessity of the progression from what is potentially so to what is actually so. That necessity was conceived not as the instantiation of natural law but as that of tendencies to ends. Natural things are divided into kinds according to those tendencies, or, to use an Aristotelian term, their active *potentiae*. Behind the set of *potentiae* belonging to each individual lies a substantial form, that at once individuates it, unites its powers, and determines its destiny.[21]

Forms are intrinsic principles of motion of natural bodies, including not only movement from one place to another, but also other kinds of natural change. In Aquinas's words, '[U]pon the form follows an inclination to the end, or to an action, or something of the sort; for everything, in so far as it is in act, acts and tends towards that which is in accordance with its form'.[22] For instance, the stone's substantial form explains why it falls to the ground, but equally the acorn's substantial form explains why it grows to be an oak tree. When natural change occurs, this is conceived as a potentiality being actualized, or a power being put in act. When the change is transitive, for instance, a fire burning wood, then two potentialities are involved: both the fire's

[20] For an overview, see Steven Nadler, 'Doctrines of Explanation in Late Scholasticism and in the Mechanical Philosophy', in *The Cambridge History of Seventeenth-Century Philosophy*, edited by Daniel Garber and Michael Ayers (Cambridge: Cambridge University Press, 1998), 513–522.

[21] Dennis Des Chene, *Physiologia: Natural Philosophy in Late Aristotelian and Cartesian Philosophy* (Ithaca, NY: Cornell University Press, 1996), 17. See also Leijenhorst, *The Mechanisation of Aristotelianism*, 138.

[22] Aquinas, *Summa Theologica*, I Q5A5.

active potentiality to burn and the wood's passive potentiality to be burned.[23] A thing's *potentia* characterizes its natural behaviour; consequently, a thing's *potentia* can be identified with its nature.

A substance operates, or is at work, insofar as its potentiality is being actualized. But identifying a potentiality is not sufficient to determine that something will in fact occur: for the natural motion of a natural body might be blocked or countered. In this case, the natural body undergoes unnatural, or 'violent', motion. A stone may naturally fall down, but it could also be thrown upwards; a seedling might be deformed by disease. Aquinas is emphatic that there is no formal cause for unnatural behaviour: 'Now it is manifest that a cause which hinders the action of a cause so ordered to its effect as to produce it in the majority of cases, clashes with this cause by accident: and the clashing of these two causes, inasmuch as it is accidental, has no cause'.[24] Correspondingly there is no separate science studying it; the aberrant behaviour is understood not in itself but in its deficiency compared to the natural tendency.[25]

In his study of the relation between Hobbes and Aristotle, Spragens characterizes Hobbes's philosophy as having wholly eliminated scholastic innate powers, including innate powers of human beings.[26] But he supports his claim by appeal only to Hobbes's later works; I will show that attention to Hobbes's early writings provides a rather different picture. For as I have argued, Hobbes's early works display a certain conception of human power as internal faculties; I now connect this conception of human power with Hobbes's scholastic intellectual context and training.

On the side of natural philosophy, by the early 1640s, Hobbes had moved a long way from scholasticism. To be sure, his much earlier *Short Tract* (1630) still bears the mark of his Oxford scholastic education.[27] It sketches out a metaphysics of agents with power to move, and patients with power to be moved (ST Ip3–4). Agents and patients are both substances, each with their respective powers 'inherent' in them. These inherent powers can then either be 'in act' or not, according to whether the agent is working or not (ST Ic1, Ic6–7). The authorship of the *Short Tract* remains controversial;[28] but even

[23] Ibid., I Q25A1. Later scholastics complicate this distinction (Des Chene, *Physiologia*, 46–51).
[24] Aquinas, *Summa Theologica*, I Q115A6.
[25] Ibid., I-II Q6A1, II-II Q95A5.
[26] Spragens, *The Politics of Motion*, 89–90, 102.
[27] Brandt, *Thomas Hobbes's Mechanical Conception*, 9–46, 55–73; Leijenhorst, *The Mechanisation of Aristotelianism*, 140–145, 172–179.
[28] Leijenhorst provides an overview, concluding that 'after more than a century of debate, Hobbes' authorship of the *Short Tract* is now beyond doubt' (*The Mechanisation of Aristotelianism*, 13).

if the text does provide insight into Hobbes's position in 1630, certainly over the subsequent years, the scholasticism of the conception of power of natural objects is substantially abandoned. During 1634 to 1636, and again from 1640 onwards, Hobbes was deeply immersed in the Parisian philosophical circle centred on Marin Mersenne. By the early 1640s, Hobbes's natural philosophy was already swept up in this circle's self-conscious intellectual shift away from scholastic hylomorphic metaphysics.[29]

I will discuss Hobbes's mature natural philosophy in more detail in Section 2.5, drawing attention in particular to its rejection of three features of a scholastic analysis of power: rejecting (i) any strong distinction between power and act; (ii) any conception of power as something internal to the body whose power it is; and (iii) any normative grain to a body's power. For now, the critical point is that these changes had not percolated through to Hobbes's treatment of humans and politics during the same period.[30] For in both his early political texts, the *Elements of Law* (1640) and *De Cive* (1642), Hobbes seeks to understand human nature through its powers (EL I.1.1, I.1.4; DC 1.1), and I claim his analysis retains these three critical features of the scholastic approach to power. As demonstrated in Section 2.2, the powers of an individual human are characterized as causal capacities originating in their nature conceived as a collection of faculties. To be sure, the powers are not taken as brute givens; rather, Hobbes attempts to provide an account of their genesis from motions of lesser bodies (EL 1–8).[31] But the key point is that the powers are conceived as distinguishing an internal, proper, and relatively stable human nature, which explains human acts; and that that nature is taken as the only proper object of science.[32] These inherent powers may well generate secondary powers, but secondary powers do not independently contribute to

[29] Brandt, *Thomas Hobbes's Mechanical Conception*, 143–165. Brandt dates the decisive break in Hobbes's natural science at 1641, which is just after the composition of *The Elements of Law* (ibid., 99); Tuck and Brandt both argue that the late *De Corpore* (1655), which clearly takes a step away from the scholastic frame, was already partly drafted in the early 1640s; indeed, its views have strong similarities to those expressed in the 1643 *Anti-White*. Brandt, *Thomas Hobbes's Mechanical Conception*, 171–175; Tuck, 'Introduction', xi–xii.

[30] The conceptual discontinuity in Hobbes's early works between power in natural objects and power in human beings is particularly stark in his *Anti-White*, which combines the new mechanical natural science with the early view of human power.

[31] This admittedly represents a certain departure from scholasticism, and may reflect Hobbes's encounter with neo-Epicureanism. I thank Stephen Nadler for this suggestion; for a fuller discussion of Hobbes's Epicurean influences, see Friedle, 'Thomas Hobbes'. By contrast, at the time of the very early *Short Tract*, he conceives of agents as qualitatively distinct substances (ST Ip15).

[32] To be sure, *De Cive* also characterizes humans in terms of their duties as citizens (DC Pref.10), as I will discuss in Chapter 3. For now, I focus on the characterization of human nature as such (DC 1.1).

the human individual's causality properly understood, especially not when they emerge without or out of proportion to their true power.

What of the third critical feature of the scholastic approach to power, regarding its normative grain? Here an ambiguity needs to be dispelled. Hobbes's analysis of human power seeks to explain actual human behaviour, not a lofty standard of behaviour from which humans regularly fall short; whereas the scholastic treatment human action is strongly moralized. But this does not eliminate the normative character of Hobbes's analysis: for I claim that Hobbes's descriptive treatment of human power corresponds to the scholastic science of natural bodies (not the scholastic practical science of human action). Scholastic natural science retains some residual normative grain, through the distinction between natural and (rare but still possible) degenerate motion.

My earlier sketch of Aquinas's hylomophism focussed on the metaphysics of natural bodies of the sort that interest natural scientists. But natural bodies exhibit just one of three possible ways that a thing's *potentia* can relate to its observable conduct.[33] First, heavenly bodies operate perfectly in accord with their nature. Heavenly bodies such as stars actualize their *potentiae* in circular motion, a form of motion with no contrary tendency; and they are incorruptible: so their motion is never violent.[34] Second, natural 'elemental' bodies such as animals, plants, and stones do have contrary tendencies, which can be brought about by an external 'violent cause': the stone's tendency down can find its contrary in upwards motion, or the seedling can rot instead of grow. But *potentia* still illuminates what in in fact occurs: for natural bodies operate in accord with their nature for the most part.[35] Third and finally, humans are distinct from the rest of nature insofar as they possess free will. This free will allows them to choose to behave in a manner that diverges widely and systematically from their true good nature, even without the intervention of violent external causes. Humans can and should use reason to direct themselves to morality,[36] but equally they can and frequently do choose to sin and to indulge in vicious habits instead.[37]

[33] Aquinas, *Summa Theologica*, II.II Q95A5. This sketch draws on the discussion in Alexandre Matheron, 'Spinoza et la décomposition de la politique thomiste: Machiavélisme et utopie', in *Études sur Spinoza et les philosophies de l'âge classique* (Paris: ENS Éditions, 2011), 82–87.

[34] Aquinas, *Summa Theologica*, I Q66A2.

[35] Ibid., I Q103A5, I Q115A6, I-II Q6A4.

[36] Ibid., I-II Q1A2–3.

[37] Ibid., I Q83A1, I-II Q6A4.

Science in relation to the first two cases explains what in fact occurs, either perfectly (in the case of heavenly phenomena) or for the most part (natural elemental phenomena). By contrast, the sciences of human beings do not even purport to do this. The science of human nature becomes a practical science of how humans *ought* to behave.[38] Natural law establishes moral ends of human action, and prescribes to humans all acts of virtue.[39] Actual human behaviour is scientifically considered only in relation to the moral norm that it may or may not meet.[40] There is no science of degeneracy per se; for evil and imperfection are a deprivation of being.[41]

In contrast to Aquinas's single unified normative science of human beings, when Hobbes poses a natural law in addition to his account of human power, he appears to offer a dual-track analysis. On the one hand, the science of human *potentia* laid out in Section 2.2 concerns actual tendencies of behaviour, like Aquinas's science of natural bodies; on the other hand, his natural law appears to offer a strongly normative science, corresponding to Aquinas's practical science of human action. For Hobbesian natural law delineates a standard of virtuous human behaviour. It is demanding, even though it is reduced to reason's dictates for pursuing self-preservation (EL I.15.1; DC 2.1). This is because effectively serving one's preservation requires significant constraint and foresight (EL I.15–16, I.17.14; DC 2–3). For instance, natural law requires that revenge consider future good and not past evil (EL I.6.10; DC 3.11); and that no one should insult another (EL I.16.11; DC 3.12). Either people may fail to reason correctly because they are too easily satisfied with platitudes, or because they make careless and imprecise use of words (EL I.5.11–13); or their reasoning may fail to be sufficiently motivating, overwhelmed by passions or pursuit of glory (EL I.15.1; DC 1.1) or their 'inordinate desire for an immediate good' (DC 3.27).

But this apparent analogy between Hobbes's natural law and Aquinas's practical science quickly vanishes: at every point in his early texts, Hobbes takes pains to qualify or discount the natural law so that normative standards on

[38] Aquinas divides knowledge into speculative knowledge, oriented towards truth, and practical knowledge, oriented towards action, or more precisely towards 'operation' (actualizing the *potentia* of a thing) (ibid., I Q14A16).

[39] Ibid., I-II Q94A2-A3.

[40] Ibid., I-II Q7A2.

[41] Ibid., I Q5A5. Spragens claims that the 'Aristotelian-Scholastic cosmos' is 'homogeneous in its basic pattern of action' across humans, plants, animals, stones; and identifies this as a structural similarity to Hobbes's system (*The Politics of Motion*, 167–168). But Spragens's textual focus on Aristotle leads him to miss the fundamental scholastic distinction between humans and the rest of nature.

action[42] only remain where they will be met for the most part. The applicability of natural law's more demanding precepts in the state of nature (and, as we will see in Chapter 3, in the well-ordered commonwealth) is constrained to be compatible with the actual ordinary tendencies of human power. In the state of nature, people generally do everything they can to preserve their lives according to their own judgement, at whatever cost to their fellow humans and regardless of its conflict with traditional morality and with many of Hobbes's own specific laws of nature. But *inter arma silent leges* (EL I.19.2; DC 5.2):[43] when there is no clear prospect of peace, reason itself directs self-defence, and rules that none of the other laws of nature apply (EL I.14.14). Correspondingly, Hobbes claims that in the state of nature, what people *in fact* generally do is simultaneously done *from right reason* (EL I.14.6–10; DC Ep.10, 1.15). Beyond merely permitting this antisocial conduct, reason's law of nature commands that, in the absence of security, people should be formidable and hostile to one another (EL I.17.15).

This collapse of Hobbes's practical science as a lofty moral standard is easily explicable. Aquinas's fundamental separation of humans from the rest of the natural world relies on their free will, either to put to work their moral *potentia* or not. By contrast, Hobbes resolutely denies free will. Already in the *Short Tract*, he argues that if a free agent is defined as 'that, which, all things requisite to worke, being putt, may worke, or not worke', then there is no such thing: the definition is contradictory (ST Ic11).[44] Human action is understood as the operation of *potentia* directed by a drive for self-preservation, without the mediation of free will (EL I.14.6; DC Ep.10, Pref.10, 1.7). To maintain a scholastic practical science demanding virtue, while at the same time posing a deterministic account of the causes of non-virtuous behaviour, would be to egregiously violate the principle of 'ought implies can'.[45] His apparently dual science

[42] This striking feature of Hobbes's theory only applies to action. I grant that there are also laws of nature applying to conscience, and in that domain perhaps there are likely to be divergences—see Hobbes's discussion of natural laws *in foro interno* (EL I.17.10; DC 3.17).

[43] 'Laws are silent among arms' (DC 5.2).

[44] The argument is repeated in LN 277–278. Leijenhorst provides an overview of the argument, including its continuities and ruptures with late scholastic thinkers. Leijenhorst, *The Mechanisation of Aristotelianism*, 173–186.

[45] I grant that in *Liberty and Necessity*, Hobbes asserts that practices such as blame and punishment of noxious actions are coherent even in the absence of any metaphysical free will. However, observe his primary argument in defence of his view: Hobbes defends practices of blame and punishment because they will be efficacious in reducing noxious actions in society (sometimes through reforming the malefactor, but more significantly by shaping the deliberations and conduct of others who witness the malefactor's suffering) (LN 248–255). This argument rests on a weak version of 'ought implies

collapses back into a single science of humans as natural bodies; his normative standards are flattened onto what actually tends to occur. Human *potentia* generates appropriate behaviour for the most part, just as with any other elemental body. Without the possibility of differentiating humans from the rest of nature in terms of their free will, Hobbes instead differentiates them in terms of their linguistic capacity (EL I.5.4).[46] But this is a much less profound distinction: it amounts to simply attributing a different collection of particular powers to humans than to animals, not to a metaphysical difference in how those powers operate.

The resultant Hobbesian human science has a structure similar to the scholastic science of natural bodies. Human power is simultaneously descriptive and normative. It is descriptive insofar as it explains human behaviour for the most part, even the conflictual behaviour of the state of nature. It is also normative, defining proper behaviour and distinguishing it from degenerate behaviour. But truly degenerate behaviour is a very marginal phenomenon. Far from accounting the hostile and antisocial behaviour that is observed in the state of nature as irrational and a perversion of human faculties, to the contrary, Hobbes is able to account it as the proper outcome of those faculties. Degeneracy is limited to antisocial conduct not even conceived as self-preserving, such as cruelty and drunkenness (EL I.19.2; DC 1.10, 3.25).[47] Human self-preserving behaviour is driven by 'a real necessity of nature as powerful as that by which a stone falls downwards' (DC 1.7). Just like Aquinas's stone falling to earth, which might occasionally be thrust upwards, ordinary human behaviour follows properly from its own nature, except for occasional bouts of drunkenness and cruelty.

can'. Certainly, in any particular case of wrongdoing, the malefactor did the noxious action, therefore they could not have avoided doing the noxious action. But they are held blameworthy because it is possible that society could avoid those noxious actions for the most part. Conversely, if certain actions cannot be avoided for the most part, regardless of practices of blame and punishment, then the coherence of those practices is in question. I thank Arash Abizadeh for pressing me on this point.

[46] An extended discussion is found in Philip Pettit, *Made with Words: Hobbes on Language, Mind, and Politics* (Princeton, NJ: Princeton University Press, 2008).

[47] A similar structure is evident in Hobbes's characterization of basic human motivation. Johnston demonstrates that Hobbes universally attributes to humans a fear of death as the greatest of evils; but at the same time, he recognizes that some humans do not feel this way. Johnston argues that the discrepancy does not show a failing of the science; rather, the science poses a standard to which reality ought to conform. David Johnston, *The Rhetoric of 'Leviathan': Thomas Hobbes and the Politics of Cultural Transformation* (Princeton, NJ: Princeton University Press, 1986), 50–54. My suggestion is that such an approach to a science of human behaviour parallels scholastic accounts of natural bodies.

2.4. Relational Human Power in Hobbes's Later Writings

In this section, I turn to Hobbes's later texts, and I argue that there is a striking change in how power/*potentia* is conceived. Rather than locating individual human power in the faculties internal to the individual, I argue, *Leviathan* offers a new analysis by which human power is externally constituted in relations with other humans. My argument rests primarily on *Leviathan*, Chapter 10 (both English and Latin editions), which is a recognizable descendent of the discussion of human power in *The Elements of Law* (EL I.8). The very close similarity of the two passages[48] makes the small changes I identify more significant.

I start by showing that in *Leviathan*, secondary powers are now included as genuine powers in their own right; their status as genuine powers is not understood through a connection with natural faculties. This outcome is not actively argued for in the literature on Hobbes's politics because it is generally taken for granted:[49] but against the sharply contrasting view that I have established for *The Elements of Law* and the *Anti-White*, it is useful to demonstrate it specifically.[50] Where *The Elements of Law* defined power as faculties (EL I.8.4), *Leviathan* opens with a definition of power that enshrines a privilege to effects:

> The POWER [*Potentia*] *of a Man* (to take it Universally,) is his present means, to obtain some future apparent Good. (L 132–133, 10.1)

Secondary powers also find a new definition, newly supplementing the backward relation to faculties from *The Elements of Law* (EL I.8.4) with a forward relation to effects. They are now called '*Instrumentall*' powers, and are

[48] As established in footnote 3. By the time of the very late *De Homine*, the structure of the text has shifted, leaving only a vestigial discussion of individual power. *De Homine*, Chapter 11, is clearly the relevant passage: its discussion of *pulchrum*/*pulchritudo* is a truncated version of the other texts' discussion of honour/*honorare*/honourability/*honorabilis*. *Pulchritudo* is the quality in an object that is an indication of future good (DH 11.5), but what is a means to a future good but power (L 132–133, 10.1). However, *De Homine*'s discussion does not provide any direct analysis of *potentia*. Its purpose is to characterize pleasure and displeasure; and it considers power incidentally only in relation to this purpose (DH 11.6, 11.13).

[49] See footnote 9; see also Christian Lazzeri, *Droit, pouvoir et liberté: Spinoza critique de Hobbes* (Paris: Presses universitaires de France, 1998), 66–77, 118–121; Gregory S. Kavka, *Hobbesian Moral and Political Theory* (Princeton, NJ: Princeton University Press, 1986), 93–94.

[50] Complementary accounts of the textual shift are provided by Ross Rudolph, 'Conflict, Egoism and Power in Hobbes', *History of Political Thought* 7, no. 1 (1986): 73–88; F. S. McNeilly, *The Anatomy of Leviathan* (London: Macmillan; New York: St. Martin's Press, 1968), 137–147; D. J. C. Carmichael, 'C. B. Macpherson's 'Hobbes': A Critique', in *Thomas Hobbes: Critical Assessments*, edited by Preston King, Vol. 1 (London: Routledge, 1993), 361, 368–369.

defined as those 'which acquired by these [natural powers], or by fortune, are *means and Instruments to acquire more*' (L 132–133, 10.2; emphasis added). Because the criterion for being counted as a power points forward to effects, not back to origins, any causal genesis for a power is acceptable: secondary powers are explicitly included in the general definition of power in equal standing with natural faculties (L 132–133, 10.1).

Macpherson draws liberally on examples from *The Elements of Law* to illustrate *Leviathan*'s conception of power,[51] but this is unsustainable: Hobbes's changed explanations of examples systematically reflect the new definitions' refusal to privilege faculties and the shift of focus to effects. Something is honourable if it is a sign of power. In early and late texts alike, nobility or good birth is certainly honourable, but in *The Elements of Law*, it is by reflection as a sign of power of ancestors (EL I.8.5), whereas in *Leviathan* it is a sign that one may easily obtain aid (L 140–141, 10.45). Riches were previously honourable 'as signs of the power that acquired them' (EL I.8.5);[52] now 'Riches joyned with liberality, is Power [*Potentia*]; because it procureth friends, and servants: Without liberality, not so; because in this case they defend not; but expose men to Envy, as a Prey' (L 132–133, 10.4).

It is not controversial that in *Leviathan*, power includes secondary powers in good standing. But I argue now that the new conception of power is not simply an enlargement of the scope of the previous conception to include additional discrete examples of power: rather, the addition of these examples displaces and transforms the (formerly) core cases. Specifically, first I demonstrate that the (previously degenerate) case of secondary powers that arise in the absence of grounding faculty powers (or out of proportion to the grounding faculty powers) becomes the exemplary case of human power. And second, I show that the resultant conception of power is deeply relational and resists abstraction from social context.[53]

51 Macpherson, *Political Theory of Possessive Individualism*, 39.

52 In the *Anti-White*, Hobbes counts others' hostility as a secondary power because it is a consequence of one's power (AW 38.8). This sharply illustrates the early understanding of secondary powers as signs of faculties: here, a consequence of faculty power counts as secondary power, even though it presumably may reduce efficacy.

53 Complementary characterizations of *Leviathan*'s conception of power can be found in Rudolph, 'Conflict, Egoism and Power', 80–88; Ross Rudolph, 'The Microfoundations of Hobbes's Political Theory', *Hobbes Studies* 4, no. 1 (1991): 50–51; and Samantha Frost, *Lessons from a Materialist Thinker: Hobbesian Reflections on Ethics and Politics* (Stanford, CA: Stanford University Press, 2008), 7–11, 144–145, 150–156. Kavka's rational choice reconstruction picks up on some of these themes. However, it is explicitly committed to (and attributes to Hobbes) a 'descriptive' account of human conduct as the conduct of an ideally rational individual, not as the conduct of actual individuals as per my reading of Hobbes's *potentia*. Kavka, *Hobbesian Moral and Political Theory*, xiii, 19–20.

Consider secondary powers arising without or out of proportion to underlying faculties. The new definition of power no longer renders such secondary powers degenerate; and I argue that Hobbes embraces this consequence. Early and late, Hobbes recognizes that secondary powers can outstrip faculties. Whereas this is an afterthought and an aberration to the core analysis in *The Elements of Law*, I argue that *Leviathan* systematically brings this phenomenon to the fore.

In *The Elements of Law*, secondary powers are 'acquired' through the natural faculties (EL I.8.4); but how exactly? It is easy to reconstruct the mechanism: honour bridges from faculties to secondary powers through the mediation of people's subjective conceptions. Honour is the internal conception of the superiority of another person's power, and it gives rise to certain characteristic external actions (EL I.8.6). If I think someone else is more powerful than I, I will tend to defer to, obey, and be polite to that person. For this reason, deference, obedience, and politeness are all signs of honour. But these signs of honour from others simultaneously contribute to the honoured individual's capacity to achieve her ends. They constitute secondary power (favour and perhaps friendship) for the honoured individual.

In the initial presentation, the mechanism appears straightforwardly reliable. It is not difficult to know someone's power and therefore to honour it correctly: we simply need to attend to 'such actions, gesture, countenance and speech, as usually such powers produce' (EL I.8.5). But in his discussion of false glory in the following chapter, Hobbes indirectly addresses the possibility of the mechanism malfunctioning, of people misidentifying power and misdirecting their honour. It is possible to feel glory 'not from the conscience of our own actions, but from fame and trust of others, whereby one may think well of himself, and yet be deceived' (EL I.9.1).[54] Insofar as people revere and trust an individual, they honour them. Their deference is no less real even in cases where it has faulty grounds. Nonetheless, Hobbes treats this malfunction as an aberration that has no implications for the analysis of power. He counts glory from misplaced deference as false glory, or in other words, as not indicative of real power. Such deference grounded in misdirected honour and not linked to faculties can be counted as secondary power only in a degenerate sense, and falls outside the scope of scientific analysis of the individual's power. In any case, Hobbes suggests that this degenerate power

[54] See also AW 38.7.

will be unreliable: aspiration grounded in false glory 'procureth ill-success' (EL I.9.1).[55]

In *Leviathan*, near the start of the discussion of power, there is a new topic without parallel in *The Elements of Law*: reputation, or in other words, others' conception of one's power, considered without regard to its accuracy. Reputation is power 'because it draweth with it the adhaerence of those that need protection' (L 132–133, 10.5).[56] Hobbes's explicit treatment of reputation makes clear the role of subjective conception as such in generating secondary power. Hobbes doubly insists that secondary power disconnected from faculties is genuine power:

> [*W*]*hat quality soever* maketh a man beloved, or feared of many; *or the reputation of such quality*, is Power [*Potentia*]. (L 134–135, 10.7; emphasis added)[57]

First, the 'what quality soever' underscores the point that the content of the reputation generating secondary power need not even be a reputation of superior natural faculties. Second, the contrast between the 'quality' of the first phrase and the 'reputation of a quality' in the second underscores the point that reputation remains a power even when it is contrasted with fact.

These two dimensions of disconnection are reinforced in the discussion of honour and honourability. Honour is still the dominant mechanism for generating secondary power: secondary powers of friendship, obedience, allegiance, and assistance are all also analysed as forms of honour (L 136–139, 10.17–36). But first, a new definition of honour eliminates the priority for natural faculties in generating secondary power. Honour is redefined as the manifestation of the value that we set on one another's power, where value is 'not absolute; but a thing dependant on the need and judgment of another' (L 134–137, 10.16–17). Indeed, the examples of honour all emphasize the honouring individuals' belief in the honoured individual's capacity to help or harm them, without reference to faculties (L 134–137, 10.16, 19, 20, 21, 22, 24, 26). Second, Hobbes indicates that the honour can be merited even when

[55] Similarly, in the *Anti-White* Hobbes grants that honour can mismatch with faculty power, but there is no hint that such misplaced honour itself could constitute power (AW 38.18).

[56] This is also foreshadowed in *De Cive*'s theology (DC 15.13), although not in its discussion of human power.

[57] See also L 132–135, 10.5–6, 8, 10.

there is no prior underlying capacity or property of any sort that that honour recognizes, through a circle of compounding perceptions:

> Honourable is whatsoever possession, action, or quality, is an argument and signe of Power [*Potentiae*].
>
> And therefore To be Honoured, loved, or feared of many, is Honourable; as arguments of Power [*Potentiae*]. (L 140–141, 10.37–38)

Being honoured by many people is itself honourable, without regard to the basis for that honour; and being honoured constitutes power.[58]

Hobbes thus removes the distinction between proper and degenerate honour, and between proper and degenerate secondary power. Even if the honourer values something other than faculties, and even if they are mistaken to think that the thing they value is truly present, their behaviour is still honour and still constitutes power. Thus, on the late view, power arises from a reverberation of appearances and reputations in a network of social relations: insofar as the power so generated has effects, it has full status as power. In Chapters 4 and 5, I will delve into the implications of this analysis of power for politics, but for now, a simplified model of the commonwealth provides an image of the generation of power through a complex interplay of perceptions without a grounding in natural faculties. As Hobbes remarks in *Behemoth*, '[T]he Power of the mighty has no foundation but in the opinion and beleefe of the people' (B 128). In what sense does a sovereign ruler installed by the agreement of the people (a sovereign by institution) have the effective ability or power (*potentia*) to enforce covenants (L 262–263, 17.15)? The sovereign by institution does not possess overwhelmingly superior force as a natural person. However, when soldiers, guards, judges, executioners, and subjects in general play their commanded roles in wielding the metaphorical sword of justice and do not thwart its operation, anyone seeking to disobey will be punished. But why do the soldiers, guards, judges, and executioners do their part even though the sovereign does not personally have a sword sufficiently mighty to compel them? They do so because each of them believes that every other subject will uphold the command of the sovereign, including wielding

[58] Strauss also recognizes that honour shifts from being independently grounded in *The Elements of Law* to being subordinated to its power effects in *Leviathan*. But he interprets this as Hobbes's attempt to hide the humanistic moral basis of his thought. Leo Strauss, *The Political Philosophy of Hobbes: Its Basis and Its Genesis*, translated by Elsa M. Sinclair (Chicago: University of Chicago Press, 1963), 115 n. 2, 169. On my reading, there is no such subterfuge, but rather a substantive change of analysis.

its sword as commanded. This network of belief and compliance is a real power for the sovereign, no less than the direct superior force of a conqueror (L 260–263, 17.13).[59]

In light of this analysis, I propose characterizing Hobbes's later conception of power as relational. For power is conceived through its effects, and the central generator of human effectiveness turns out to be secondary powers, and in particular, formations of human deference, assistance, obedience, and allegiance: or in other words, social relations with other human beings. I now elaborate just how significant a change this is: on the new conception, any attempt to talk of individual power non-relationally, apart from the concrete net of human relations, is an abstraction, often a pernicious one.

Already *The Elements of Law* recognizes some kind of relationality of power insofar as it stresses what I called the 'positionality' of power. In that text, a person's power itself is not relational because this power properly speaking is the person's natural faculties. Nonetheless, there is a sense of positionality involved in power analysis insofar as their causal effectiveness lies in the superiority of their faculties in relation to others. Two competitors race for an apple; if I am the slower runner, then I do not get the apple (EL I.8.4, I.9.21). Power's effectiveness is relational insofar as it is generated by the differential objective quality of competitor's faculties. Is *Leviathan*'s power relational just insofar as it extends the analysis of positionality, already used in the earlier text for faculties, to include secondary powers? To the contrary, I argue that the inclusion of secondary powers transforms the relationality at stake, as becomes clear in the discussion of eminence.

It is common to equate *Leviathan*'s concept of eminence to the early 'positionality' of power.[60] After all, to say that natural faculties are power only insofar as they are *eminent* (L 132–133, 10.2) is to say that they are superior in relation to others. But this misses a crucial change: eminence pinpoints the relative superiority of one person's power over that of others, not (as with positionality) in terms of objective difference of faculties, but in terms of its prominence or conspicuousness in the eyes of others. This

[59] Kavka, *Hobbesian Moral and Political Theory*, 254–264.

[60] Macpherson, *Political Theory of Possessive Individualism*, 35–36; Spragens, *The Politics of Motion*, 191, 200–201; C. B. Macpherson, 'Introduction', in *Leviathan*, edited by C. B. Macpherson (London: Penguin, 1985), 34–35; Barry Hindess, *Discourses of Power: From Hobbes to Foucault* (Oxford: Blackwell Publishers, 1996), 26; Lazzeri, *Droit, pouvoir et liberté*, 74 n. 1.

eminence has two dimensions. First, the faculty needs to be perceived as superior. For example, Hobbes considers science to be a small power, because even though taken by itself it enormously improves a person's capacity to manipulate the world around her to her ends, it is not *recognized* as a power: 'The Sciences, are small Power [*Potentia est; sed parva*], because not eminent; and therefore, not acknowledged in any man' (L 134–135, 10.14). It is little use to the scientist to have a capacity to manipulate nature if the people among whom the scientist lives and works thwarts their activities.[61] Second, that superiority needs to be considered significant in the given situation. 'A learned and uncorrupt Judge', superior in wisdom, is valuable in peace but not in war (L 134–135, 10.16). Examples could be multiplied: for instance, a slave may have recognized superiority of bodily strength, but this particular superiority does not constitute a power in stable slaveholding society because of the other aspects of the social domain. If we return to my earlier example of a race through the lens of *Leviathan*'s analysis, we see that the example has background assumptions. Speed alone will be the criterion of success only when the race is a well-regulated competition in which the rules are respected. Outside of this special case, my slowness may not prevent me from gaining the apple, for perhaps I have a greater band of friends or supporters willing to help me and obstruct my competitor; or perhaps I have sufficient riches to buy the apple.

The requirement for eminence forces the analysis of power to be deeply and inextricably bound to the human social context in which the power occurs.[62] In *The Elements of Law*, natural faculties are powers intrinsically and non-relationally, regardless of how they may subsequently be put into relation. But in *Leviathan*, these faculties or capacities become power only through the mediation of relational secondary powers; and this mediation is non-trivial. Macpherson

[61] Is this a pointed criticism of Bacon's view of scientific knowledge as power? Knowledge may be power, but it is insignificant in the context of human existence in society.

[62] Hindess, attributing to *Leviathan* an analysis of power as a zero-sum conflict between fixed capacities (similar to the view I outlined in Sections 2.2 and 2.3 for *The Elements of Law*), complains that such an analysis fails to take into account the role of context in determining outcomes, and the corresponding indeterminacy of human conflict (Hindess, *Discourses of Power*, 26–32). But on my reading, Hobbes's appreciation of context and indeterminacy is the signal contribution of *Leviathan*'s discussion. Baumgold's thesis, that Hobbes is not an abstract individualist but rather is concerned with roles within a political structure, differs from my claim but does not conflict with it. For Baumgold primarily offers a juridical consideration of roles (for instance, the right to refuse military service). Deborah Baumgold, *Hobbes's Political Theory* (Cambridge: Cambridge University Press, 1988), 10–15, 31–35.

complains that Hobbes 'neglects human power to transform nature.[63] But this is no accidental neglect: it is a challenging positive feature of Hobbes's analysis of power. Hobbes places front and centre the observation that exercising any capacity in a world populated by other people relies on their conduct, perhaps their aid but at minimum their non-interference. Relationality in *Leviathan* is a question of human relations: how humans are disposed to one another and behave towards one another, which frequently is unmoored from objective comparison of the faculties of the parties to the relationship. The depth of the relationality of power is also corroborated in *Leviathan*'s analysis of secondary powers. To return to *Leviathan*'s account of riches, riches do not count as powers simply because they can be exchanged for specific goods: for Hobbes states that riches are only a power when combined with liberality (L 132–133, 10.4). Liberality makes no difference to the capacity to carry out direct exchanges, but it does make a difference for allegiance. People desiring to advance or protect their own general power will give the possessor of riches their allegiance insofar as they hope to receive whatever unspecified assistance they may require from those riches in the future. Liberality gives rise to this hope; illiberality quashes it (L 132–133, 10.4).

In result, the behaviour and causal efficacy to be explained have changed. It is always possible to restrict one's analysis to consider faculties, capacities, or even secondary powers themselves in artificial isolation and to abstract away from this looser social terrain that shapes their effects: one can always consider the scientist apart from the mob, the race competitors apart from their supporters, the money apart from the hopeful clients. This was the procedure of *The Elements of Law*. In that text's analysis of power, it was meaningful to ask about human power with respect to specific narrow targets in abstraction from a larger social context. But if the phenomenon to be explained under the rubric of power is human effectiveness, and if, as *Leviathan*'s account proposes, allegiance is the central determinant of this effectiveness, then such abstraction vitiates the analysis of power. On this new account, power is neither natural faculties nor any other attribute that could be neatly accommodated as a possession of the individual: human power lies fundamentally in relations, and the focus of the analysis of power is generalized efficacy understood through an individual's position in a complex social field. In contrast to *The Elements of Law*, *Leviathan* finds an individual's human nature and power to lie outside of her or him, both physically and conceptually, in her or his potentially shifting and relational social context.

[63] Macpherson, *Political Theory of Possessive Individualism*, 37.

2.5. Hobbes's Departure from Scholasticism

I have argued that Hobbes changed his conceptualization of individual human power *potentia* between his early and later political works. In this section I situate Hobbes's later conception of individual human power within his broader move away from scholastic science. Frost argues that Hobbes's interrelational and interdependent conception of human power is generated by his insistence on treating humans as natural bodies, rather than as something possessing free will and thereby liberated from nature.[64] But this connection between a naturalistic view of humans and a relational view of power does not necessarily hold: it all depends on how the natural bodies are conceived. In Hobbes's early view, humans are very much natural bodies lacking free will, but their power is not relational. The relational conception of power presupposes the evacuation of the remnant scholastic metaphysics of innate powers. In order to understand human power and its socially embedded character, the key contrast is not to Cartesianism (as Frost would have it), but to scholasticism.

While the very early (and contested) *Short Tract* offers a metaphysics retaining certain scholastic elements, from the 1640s onwards, Hobbes's natural science is systematically mechanized.[65] During the years 1640–1651, Hobbes lived in France, and associated with the Mersenne circle. Descartes and others in the circle aspired to a mechanical understanding of nature, striving to reduce the study of nature to mechanical interactions and efficient causes, without scholastic formal or final causes.[66] Hobbes enthusiastically involved himself in this project,[67] praising their efforts (DCo Ep)[68] and expressing an increasingly polemical hostility towards scholasticism. He describes 'school divinity' (*scholastica*, scholasticism) as having one healthy foot (scripture) but the other foot rotten: the 'many foolish and false [ideas] out of the physics and metaphysics of Aristotle' (DCo Ep).[69]

64 Frost, *Lessons from a Materialist Thinker*, 1–13.

65 My subsequent presentation focusses on the late *De Corpore*, but a very similar conceptual scheme for natural science is evident in the early *Anti-White*, albeit with slight differences of terminology.

66 Des Chene, *Physiologia*, 17, 53.

67 Brandt, *Thomas Hobbes's Mechanical Conception*, 129–166.

68 Thomas Hobbes, *The English Works of Thomas Hobbes of Malmesbury*, edited by William Molesworth, Vol. 1 (London: John Bohn, 1839), ix. The Epistle to *De Corpore* is not subdivided into sections, nor is it even paginated in the Latin.

69 Ibid., x. Hobbes closes the book with a polemical spray against scholastic philosophy: 'For as those that say anything may be moved or produced by *itself*, by *species*, by *its own power* [*potentia*], by *substantial forms*, by *incorporeal substances*, by *instinct*, by *anti-peristasis*, by *antipathy*, *sympathy*, *occult quality*, and other empty words of schoolmen, their saying so is to no purpose' (DCo 30.15).

Recent scholarship has established that Descartes's and Hobbes's revolutionary self-conception rests on a caricature of scholasticism: scholasticism was an internally diverse tradition, and in particular, late scholastic thinkers were already strengthening their conception of matter and reducing their reliance on form. The new philosophy and science can be understood as an extension of existing trends rather than a new start ex nihilo.[70] Nonetheless, for the purposes of my argument, it is not important whether Hobbes was truly revolutionary compared to his contemporaries or not. Rather, my focus is, first, to establish the specific manner in which Hobbes's mature natural science repudiates the traditional scholastic conception of power, resulting in a new notion of power as not inherent and internal but relational and contextual, and as lacking in any normative grain; and, second, to establish the parallels between this anti-hylomorphic natural science and Hobbes's late conceptualization of human power.

If this argument is persuasive, it raises the question of why the mature mechanistic rethinking of the power of natural bodies—already developed in the early 1640s and therefore contemporaneous with Hobbes's early political writings, according to my periodization—was not immediately also applied to human power, but instead only with delay in the late political writings (1650s onwards). I can only speculate that the profound traditional division between the practical and speculative sciences constituted a barrier; despite their radical innovations in natural science, other proponents of the new science certainly were careful to maintain a sharp break between natural objects and human beings.[71] But Hobbes's greater interest in politics may have forced him to transgress this line. In Chapters 3 and 4, discussing human collective formations, I will argue that Hobbes's early neo-scholastic account of human power is poorly equipped to grasp certain social phenomena; surely it was the turbulent political events of the 1640s that provided impetus to try out new forms of thought.

Let me sketch the key antischolastic elements of Hobbes's mature natural science, focussing on the conceptions of form and power. While Hobbes retains residually the concept of form, he radically changes its meaning. Far from generating or explaining a body's motion, form is now explained by that motion, via new conceptions of *body*, *accident*, and *name*. He denies that there is such thing as entirely undifferentiated matter. Rather, there are

[70] Des Chene, *Physiologia*, 5, 81–83; Leijenhorst, *The Mechanisation of Aristotelianism*, 1–16, 139.
[71] Most famously, Descartes: see discussion at Chapter 7, Section 7.2.

bodies in motion (DCo 8.24). Each body has *accidents*, which are its motion insofar as it works on our sense organs to generate our conception of it (DCo 8.2). We attribute *names* to bodies in accord with their effects on us, to mark their similarities and to use for remembrance (DCo 2.4). The form or essence is just those accidents for which we give a body its name (DCo 8.23). So for instance, to say that human essence or form is rational is not to identify an inner rational principle that explains and generates human behaviour. To the contrary, it is to say that humans strike us as similar insofar as they are rational, and in light of this rationality we have classed them together under the name 'human'. This redefinition deflates the concept of form. The form is no longer the cause of a thing, but a cause of our knowledge of the thing: when I know a thing is rational, I know I am dealing with a human (DCo 10.7).[72] Form no longer explains phenomena, but rather it needs itself to be explained—what generates the rationality that these humans observably share?—and a focus of Hobbes's science is to understand the generation of these forms (DCo 1.2).[73]

Turning now to power: again, the scholastic vocabulary is retained with a radically new meaning.[74] Far from identifying an internal property metaphysically distinct from the motions that it produces, power becomes just a set of motions in the agent. Hobbes lays out the new conception in parallel with an account of causation. The 'entire cause' of an effect is the sum total of accidents in the bodies of an agent (or agents) and a patient that bring the effect about. The scholastic efficient cause is redefined to become the accidents in the agent, and material cause becomes the accidents in the patient (DCo 9.3–5). But all these accidents themselves are nothing but motion (DCo 8.2). Power is then just another name for this same thing, with the only difference that we tend to use causation to refer to the past and power to refer to the future. Entire cause corresponds to 'plenary power' (*potentia integra vel plena*); act corresponds to effect; the agent's power corresponds to the efficient cause; and the patient's power corresponds to the material cause (DCo 10.1).

In the scholastic frame, motion is the result of power, or in other words, it is an act; it is not itself power. Hobbes emphatically rejects this distinction. Power and act are distinguished only by the frame of analysis.

72 See also AW 27.1–2, 28.5.
73 Leijenhorst, *The Mechanisation of Aristotelianism*, 164.
74 Ibid., 203–217; Spragens, *The Politics of Motion*, 53–74. A parallel account is found at AW 27.3–4.

> [P]ower is not a certain accident, which differs from all acts, but is, indeed, an act, namely, motion, which is therefore called power, because another act shall be produced by it afterwards. For example, if of three bodies the first put forward the second, and this the third, the motion of the second, in respect of the first which produceth it, is the act of the second body; but in respect of the third, it is the active power of the same second body. (DCo 10.6)[75]

Power is not separate from the act, but is just the prior temporal moment in a necessary chain of events. Any power can itself be conceived as act in relation to an earlier power. To conceive something as a power is simply to focus one's attention on its forward role in causation, rather than its status as the outcome of previous causation. For instance, a white billiard ball has power with respect to the act of hitting the red ball, even if that power itself is merely the act with respect to the prior power of the cue stick.

What of the active power of an agent? Surely any conception of power needs to identify a dispositional property of an agent, something (positively) that can be said of it outside the moment of acting, and (negatively) which distinguishes its proper actions from its motions merely driven by the power of others?

On the positive point, Hobbes allows attributing power to an agent outside the moment of acting, but with sharp caveats that prohibit giving an abstract, decontextualized account of the power. Power is not properly predicated of a body in isolation, but of the total combination of bodies whose accidents combine to bring a particular act about: in other words, the plenary power. Hobbes is quite explicit that strictly speaking, there is no such thing as an agent's power, except in the context of plenary power.

> [P]ower, active and passive, are parts only of plenary and entire power; nor, except they be joined, can any act proceed from them; and therefore these powers . . . are but conditional, namely, *the agent has power, if it be applied to a patient; and the patient has power, if it be applied to an agent*; otherwise neither of them have power, nor can the accidents, which are in them severally be properly called powers. (DCo 10.3)[76]

[75] See also AW 34.3.

[76] See also AW 35.2–5, 34.7. Correspondingly, Hobbes's mature science centres not on bodies' powers, but on the causes or generations of bodies (DCo 6.10, 6.13).

When there is plenary power for an act, the agent clearly has active power. Outside of the moment of an act, we can still attribute active power to the agent if the act is *possible* (DCo 10.4). But Hobbes's notion of possibility still ties power closely to what actually occurs. Nothing is truly contingent: everything is the result of necessary causes. Possibility does not mean contingency, but, rather, it means that the act is not impossible: at some point of time there will be plenary power to produce it (AW 37.5). In our ignorance of the future, we loosely attribute active power to an agent for an act when there may (for all we know) be plenary power for the act in the future; and this is harmless enough (DCo 10.5; AW 35.6–10). However, if plenary power is in doubt—for instance, if there is reason to think that the act would require coordination with multiple other agents, and if there is reason to think that that coordination of multiple agents is unlikely itself to be produced—then active power cannot be attributed to the agent.[77]

But on the negative point, Hobbes is less compromising. Hobbes explicitly rejects the scholastic distinction between natural and violent motion: he remarks sharply that philosophers tend to classify some motions as natural, others as violent, simply in proportion to how clearly or unclearly they perceive their causes. On Hobbes's view, by contrast, every movement of a body is natural to that body, and flows from its own power (AW 6.6).

This new conception of powers in natural science corresponds point by point to the deeply relational reconceptualization of human power that I have laboured to establish in Section 2.4.[78] First, just as power in Hobbes's natural science is not metaphysically distinct from acts, so too in *Leviathan* there is no fundamental distinction between human power and what it produces. Honour is produced by power, but that honour sometimes itself serves as a power. Second, just as the agent's active power in natural science cannot properly be abstracted from the plenary power to a specific act of which it is a component, so too in *Leviathan*, to consider an individual's power apart from the social context is a misleading abstraction.[79] In other words,

[77] As he explains in the course of criticizing his opponent's view: 'We may say . . . that an axe can cut because there is nothing in the axe that stops it from cutting. Yet there may well be, in the nature of things, causes that make it impossible for the axe—or anything else—ever to be picked up, and as a result the axe cannot cut' (AW 37.11).

[78] See also Frost, *Lessons from a Materialist Thinker*, 135–140, 143.

[79] Other aspects of Hobbes's science of man display similar conceptual shifts: for instance, moving from understanding passions as drives to understanding them as contextually determined (Rudolph, 'Conflict, Egoism and Power', 34–52); for instance, moving from taking reason to be an innate capacity clouded by sophistry to seeing reason as an achievement that counters naturally emergent superstition (Johnston, *The Rhetoric of Leviathan*, 106–113).

an individual's power is not purely an internal property of that individual. Accounting for the plenary power necessary for the success of an individual's projects requires ensuring that people in a society cooperate with and do not obstruct the individual's efforts, and ensuring this cooperation is a non-trivial task. Third, any residual normativity is evacuated from the analysis of power. Whenever effects are produced, there is power, with no distinction between proper and degenerate cases. As will become clear in Chapters 3 and 4, on this late analysis (and contrary to his earlier analysis), power will diverge from natural law, even within a well-constituted commonwealth.

Hindess complains that, when *Leviathan* characterizes power as deeply heterogeneous in its causes and its effects, it precludes anything meaningful being said about power in general. To the extent that Hobbes goes on to combine and compare powers, Hindess argues that Hobbes must implicitly be relying upon a prior notion of power unifying those heterogeneous causes, as 'underlying capacity or essence of effectiveness'.[80] But this is precisely the attitude that Hobbes's later mechanistic philosophy seeks to displace. His new account of power resolutely refuses inner causal principles: a particular thing or person displays de facto regularities in causes and effects, and this is that thing's or that person's power, without appeal to any underlying substrate. On this new account, individual power is not essential, stable, and equal, but rather is relational, shifting, and unequal; the change unsettles the juridical simplicity of Hobbes's early civil science, as I will now show.

[80] Hindess, *Discourses of Power*, 25.

3

Juridical Politics

3.1. Introduction

It is not for its own sake that I have focussed on the minutiae of the evolution of Hobbes's treatment of human power/*potentia*, but in service of the book's larger goal: namely, developing a coherent account of popular power. In Chapter 2, I laid out Hobbes's account of individual human power *potentia*; now I turn to consider what power human collectivities might hold. The most obvious answer lies in Hobbes's account of the sovereign state (or, in more Hobbesian language, of the commonwealth *civitas*), which possesses power as authority *potestas*. The vexed and contentious question will be whether popular power must be understood as state *potestas*: or to the contrary, is there such a thing as the people apart from the commonwealth, and if so, how to characterize this collectivity, what might its properties and capacities be? If a political ontology is an account of the kinds of entities that exist in the political domain, then this question boils down to a question of political ontology. Together, Chapters 3 and 4 provide Hobbes's answer, through an investigation of collective *potentia*.

Many readers of Hobbes (whether his orthodox interpreters, or his Spinozist critics) have claimed that Hobbes is unable to conceive collective human power apart from its mediation by sovereignty.[1] The political valence attached to this observation about Hobbes's political ontology is variable. On the side of the American public law tradition, the valence is positive: because the power of the people can be fully expressed by the decisions of a certain authorized body, radical plebiscitary democracy is possible (where the body holding authority is the citizenry taken as a whole, making decisions via

[1] Macpherson, *Political Theory of Possessive Individualism*, 93; Macpherson, 'Introduction', 55–56; Michael Oakeshott, 'Introduction to *Leviathan*', in *Rationalism in Politics and Other Essays* (Indianapolis: Liberty Press, 1991), 280–283; Read, 'Thomas Hobbes', 514; Warren Montag, *Bodies, Masses, Power: Spinoza and His Contemporaries* (New York: Verso, 1999), 90–103; Baumgold, *Hobbes's Political Theory*, 14, 36–55; Annabel Brett, '"The Matter, Forme, and Power of a Commonwealth": Thomas Hobbes and Late Renaissance Commentary on Aristotle's Politics', *Hobbes Studies 23* (2010): 99; Lee, *Popular Sovereignty*, 309–319.

Potentia. Sandra Leonie Field, Oxford University Press (2020). © Oxford University Press.
DOI: 10.1093/oso/9780197533864.001.0001

plebiscitary votes). This appealing possibility finds its canonical presentation in the Hobbesian idea of a 'sleeping sovereign' as holder of ultimate authority and power *potestas*. But on the side of the European post-Marxist tradition, the valence is negative: this very same absence of any conception of collective power distinct from the sovereign state is taken to be a fundamental deficiency of Hobbes's view. Relying heavily on Macpherson's interpretation of Hobbes as an individualistic thinker, many Spinozists dismiss Hobbes's philosophy as fundamentally unable to understand emergent collective action and, correspondingly, unable to provide insight into popular power.

It is certainly true that throughout his writings, Hobbes expresses a persistent and polemical hostility towards the people separate from the commonwealth, what he often calls the multitude (*multitudo*). Nonetheless, beneath the superficial continuity of his polemic, this chapter and the next argue, he presents two quite distinct political ontologies. Chapter 3 establishes Hobbes's early view, whereby (in line with the common interpretive view) popular power must indeed be understood as juridically constituted *potestas*. In particular, I show that the early texts have difficulty even conceiving the possibility of collective power apart from the commonwealth. By contrast, in Chapter 4, I show that the later texts can conceive collective power apart from the state, but they cast it in a deeply unflattering light. I do so by establishing and developing a little-noticed new element in Hobbes's later writings: his new theory of informal oligarchic power blocs. To sum up the shift in Hobbes's view, an ontology of fragmented equality is discarded in favour of an ontology of spontaneously emerging oligarchic groups. Just as in Chapter 2, I will insist that there is a perfectly sharp conceptual distinction between the early and late views, even if the textual transition between the two conceptual schemes is less clear. My analytical focus on *potentia* will reveal the limits to the exegesis of both democratic proponents and democratic detractors of Hobbes. On the one hand, it reveals one fundamental reason why, in Hobbes's later texts, Tuck's sleeping sovereign no longer features as a possible mode of expression of popular power: such a sovereign simply is not powerful in the relevant sense. But on the other hand, it poses a sharp challenge to anti-Hobbesian champions of the multitude. For in his later texts, Hobbes proves to be perfectly capable of analysing non-state collective power, but he shows that such power hardly necessarily merits being called popular.

In this chapter I lay out the structure of Hobbes's early political ontology in terms of a distinction between informal and formal human collectivities, or in other words, between associations and unions, the key example of the latter being the commonwealth; and I connect this ontology to Hobbes's residual scholasticism. On the early political ontology, individual human power *potentia* is conceived as an essential property, and more or less equal. These human individuals may certainly combine into informal collectivities based on horizontal agreement to direct their individual powers to a common end. But conceptually, informal political associations lack power of any sort, having neither *potentia* nor *potestas*; and practically, they are fragile. By contrast, if the human individuals combine instead into a formal union, then conceptually they have power as both *potentia* and *potestas*, where *potentia* becomes just another name for collective *potestas*; and practically, they are robust.

In this chapter, I also lay out what I call the political problem: that the allegiance to which a state is entitled by right might not in practice be forthcoming. The political problem might arise if insubordinate groups within the commonwealth dilute or fragment the sovereign's supreme command of subjects' allegiance. I argue that the problem is marginal in Hobbes's early texts and readily solved, due to Hobbes's early confidence in the fragility of associations. The result is a neat picture of juridical politics: so long as the political order has the correct juridical structure of *potestas*, Hobbes's early science of politics envisions the possibility of a democratic sleeping sovereign retaining full power. Unfortunately, as I will argue in Chapters 4 and 5, Hobbes's revisions to his conception and analysis of collective power reveal that a democratic sleeping sovereign is likely to be neither popular nor powerful; but the emergent new conception of non-state collective power hardly offers a more appealing alternative.

3.2. Formal and Informal Political Collectivities in Hobbes's Early Writings

Hobbes's political ontology, early and late, is framed by a distinction between two possible modes of combination of individual human powers, a distinction between (what I will call) informal and formal collectivities. In this section, I argue that informal associations are both conceptually and practically marginal in Hobbes's early politics; and correspondingly, I characterize Hobbes's early political ontology as an ontology of fragmented equality.

In Hobbes's early political works, he characterizes the distinction between informal and formal collectivities as follows. On the one hand, informal collectivities: if a number of individuals, each retaining their own distinct will, nonetheless coordinate to act toward a shared end, then this concourse of their wills is called concord, consent, or *consensio*, forming an association, or *societas*. Their wills are temporarily aligned but remain distinct (EL I.12.7, I.19.4; DC 5.3–5). On the other hand, formal collectivities: if a number of individuals combine their separate wills to form a single collective will, then this is called a union, *unio* (EL I.12.8, I.19.6; DC 5.6–7).

Consider first associations, or informal collectivities. I will show that in Hobbes's early view, humans forming concrete relations and coordinating behaviour together does not constitute collective power. For informal collectivities are not true entities endowed with a proper power in their own right—in Latin, they have neither *potestas* nor *potentia*—and consequently they fall outside of the purview of scientifically studiable phenomena. Hobbes uses the word multitude/*multitudo* (crowd) to refer to a number of people, lacking (or considered without regard to) the structure of a formal union; a 'heap' of people (EL II.2.11; DC 6.1). Sometimes a multitude forms an association, when it is coordinated towards a single end. But Hobbes is quite explicit that there is a problem with conceiving such an informal collectivity as a proper entity: for such a collectivity is a mere aggregation, and not really a single thing at all. A multitude can only be said to perform a single act under very specific conditions:

> [N]or can any action done in a multitude of people met together, be attributed to the multitude, or truly called the action of the multitude, unless every man's hand, and every man's will . . . have concurred thereto. (EL II.1.2)

And even in the moment of performing an act, the multitude still has no single will (EL I.12.7). In *De Cive*, Hobbes is even more ontologically uncompromising: even when all persons in the multitude concur in action, 'one must not attribute to it [the multitude] a single action of any kind', but rather, so many actions as there are separate wills (DC 6.1). Human beings cannot have group agency insofar as their collectivities remain informal, and it is never appropriate to attribute power (whether *potentia* or *potestas*) to an association as such. A fortiori, unified agency certainly cannot be attributed to a multitude when there are divergent wills within it. Nothing licences attributing the view of a majority of members of the multitude to the entire group: the view can only be attributed to the persons who actually hold it (EL II.1.2; DC 6.1). If the members of the multitude do agree to be bound by the majority decision, then they cease to be an association and they constitute themselves as a formal union. If they do not so agree, then each member retains their own individual right; they remain in a condition of war against all the others, regardless of ad hoc cooperation (DC 7.4).

The conceptual difficulty concerning informal groups is matched by a denial of their practical political significance: any informal collectivity is transient and unstable. To be sure, associations play an important theoretical role in the genesis of the commonwealth. Although the state of nature is at first characterized as a domain of isolated individuals, very quickly Hobbes imagines the formation of protective associations, as indeed is recommended by reason (EL I.14.14, I.19.3–4; DC 1.13, 1.15, 5.1–4). But these protective associations are important only to be superseded: informal human associations are not sufficiently durable and robust to break the isolated equality of the state of nature. Animal multitudes endure and flourish because animals' faculties are different from those of humans. It is 'the work of God by the way of nature' that animals find themselves in concord, with cooperative rather than dissociative passions (EL I.19.5; DC 5.5). By contrast, for humans, endowed with reason, speech, conceptions of right and wrong, and the corresponding capacity to be inflamed by comparisons and contentious words, their associations tend to dissolve after brief periods of cooperation. Although an association may be prompted by 'the fear of a present invader, or by the hope of a present conquest, or booty', Hobbes claims that it only 'endureth as long as that action endureth' (EL I.19.4; see also DC 5.4). Human associations organized around shared ends are destabilized by the other ends of their particular individual members: by passions of resentment and envy, by competition for scarce goods. Even focussing on ends that are shared, individuals disagree on the most prudent way to proceed (EL I.19.4–5; DC 5.4–5). Correspondingly, despite protective associations, I characterize Hobbes's early political ontology as an ontology of fragmented equality: associations are profoundly fragile, and when associations fall apart, individuals are returned to isolated equality and general diffidence of one another (EL I.14.3).

In Hobbes's early writings, a picture of associations as horizontal, deliberate coordination on shared ends is regularly and prominently reiterated. Individuals come together for mutual aid with respect to a shared purpose (EL I.14.14, I.19.3; DC 1.13–14, 2.2, 5.3–4). Hobbes's account of the extreme fragility of associations rests on this picture. But one might wonder, surely there are other durable forms of association, notably hierarchical forms. Hobbes himself recognizes that the picture of equality in the state of nature is hopelessly stylized, posing the idea of humans popping up 'like mushrooms' (DC 8.1). In reality, there are always human groupings: it is more realistic to imagine a state of nature inhabited by families with children and masters with slaves (EL II.3–4; DC 8–9). But on Hobbes's analysis, in all these cases, there is sufficient inequality that they no longer count as mere associations, but dominions, which are a species of juridical union. By natural law, when greatly unequal powers face one another, the weaker power can be taken to have submitted its will to the stronger: in the biblical phrasing, do not kick against the pricks (DC 15.7). The overwhelming superiority of force of the parent over the child in a family grouping generates an implicit covenant of submission from the child. A person becomes a slave because they find themselves threatened with death by an assailant, and they choose submission to avoid death (EL I.14.13, II.3.2, II.4.3, II.4.10; DC 1.14, 9.3–4). If the domestic unit of father (or mother) with children and slaves grows larger, then it becomes indistinguishable in its power from a monarchical polity, despite its different historical origin (EL II.4.10; DC 9.9–10).[2] In the absence of formal union, we are left with a binary choice between two possible modes of interaction between individual wills: either horizontal concurrence on a specific shared goal; or conflict (EL I.12.7).[3]

[2] Christov provides an extended discussion of both vertical dominions and horizontal associations within Hobbes's state of nature. Theodore Christov, *Before Anarchy: Hobbes and His Critics in Modern International Thought* (New York: Cambridge University Press, 2015), 36–102.

[3] Could there be anything else? There is a curious suggestion at the opening of *De Cive*: individuals may seek out the company and patronage of prestigious figures (DC 1.2). Surely the collectivity consisting of a prominent individual with allies constitutes a different non-horizontal form of combination of wills: clients cooperate not because of sharing a goal with their patron, but in deference to the patron's goal, for hope of advancing their own particular purposes. But the suggestion is not developed. Perhaps this is because, on Hobbes's early analysis, such an association will not be any more robust than horizontal association, and may well be less. The example is an instance of the secondary power of allegiance. As discussed in Chapter 2, Section 2.2, secondary powers flow from core faculties, and Hobbes is at pains to insist that there are not significant differences between individuals' faculties: '[C]onsider how little odds there is of strength or knowledge between men of mature age' (EL I.14.1; see also DC 1.3). Correspondingly, no one person merits more allegiance than another, so there is no natural division of society into allegiance groups. And any other division into allegiance groups would rely on the secondary power accruing degenerately, out of proportion to the underlying faculty. This is expected to be unstable: receiving adulation and trust of others out of proportion to what is merited by one's underlying faculties generates 'false glory' (a false feeling of power), and trying to act on the basis of such allegiance 'procureth ill-success' (EL I.9.1). Thus, the overwhelmingly dominant modelling of informal collectivities remains horizontal association on explicit shared ends.

Now I turn to consider formal collectivities, or unions, of which the exemplary case is the body politic or *civitas* (commonwealth). I will show that in Hobbes's early work, formal political collectivities (unions) do have their own proper power, the sovereign's power *potestas*, constituted through transfer of the *potentiae* of subjects. Furthermore, I argue that the transfer is understood juridically (in a sense that I will make precise subsequently). A union's *potentia* is simply defined as the juridically constructed *potestas*; the distinction between *potestas* and *potentia* makes no difference, because they are equivalent by construction. At a practical level, Hobbes anticipates unions will be robust.

Unlike associations, unions can be studied scientifically, because they are genuinely unified entities and not aggregates. A union is a single entity because by definition it has a single will. But what does it mean for a collectivity to have a single will, given that its human constituents remain physically distinct, with separate operation of their natural wills? The single will is founded on agreement. In the case of domestic dominion, the slave or child agrees to submit (or is taken to agree to submit) to the master or parent. This can equally occur on a political scale. In a commonwealth by conquest, or by what Hobbes calls natural power, an already mighty individual demands that a multitude submit. But Hobbes's own more canonical political case is a commonwealth by design or institution, where there is a lateral agreement among individuals of a multitude to establish a sovereign over them and submit to it[4] Either way, in a commonwealth subjects submit their multiple wills to the will of a single entity designated as sovereign, who may be an individual human or a council. In *The Elements of Law*, submitting one's will to another is directly glossed as a promise to obey; in *De Cive*, it is a promise not to resist, which indirectly generates an obligation to obey (EL I.19.6–8; DC 5.6–12, 6.13). Hobbes's account of formal union has the counterintuitive corollary that all regimes are always already popular:

> In every commonwealth the *People* [*Populus*] Reigns; for even in *Monarchies* the *People* exercises power [*imperat*]; for the *people* wills through the will of *one man*. But the citizens, i.e. the subjects, are a *crowd* [*multitudo*]. (DC 12.8; see also EL II.2.11, II.8.9; DC 6.1)

[4] In both cases, agreement is motivated by individuals' desire for enduring security, and their fear of its disruption, and in both cases it generates the same obligation to submit; but in the former they fear a conqueror's sword, whereas in the latter, they feel threatened by each other (EL I.19.11; DC 5.12).

For the will of each citizen is 'comprehended in' the will of the sovereign, and the will of the sovereign is 'taken for' the will of the whole commonwealth (DC 6.1, 6.14). A single will for a union is only constituted at all through covenantal obligation: insofar as the word 'people'/*populus* refers to a coherent entity with a single will, it must refer to the sovereign.[5]

The body politic or commonwealth possesses unity via the single will of the sovereign; it can be characterized in terms of its own proper power, which is the power of the sovereign. A number of equivalent terms are used to refer to this power:

> SOVEREIGN AUTHORITY (*SUMMAM POTESTATEM*) or
> SOVEREIGN POWER (*SUMMUM IMPERIUM*) or
> DOMINION (*DOMINIUM*). (DC 5.1)

I will primarily focus on *potestas*, which Hobbes himself renders not as 'authority', but as 'power' (EL I.19.10).[6] The sovereign's power is nothing other than the power/*potentia* of its subjects: '[I]t consisteth in the power and the strength that every of the members have transferred to him from themselves' (EL I.19.10).[7] There is an ambiguity in this formulation. Is its power constituted from its *entitlement* to the powers of its subjects (in which case, call it a juridical power); or is it constituted from the powers of its subjects, which it *in fact* succeeds in harnessing to its purposes (in which case, call it a concrete power)? To put it another way, does obedience constitute the sovereign's power (making the sovereign's power concrete); or is obedience owed to the sovereign in virtue of that power (making the sovereign's power juridical)? I argue that *potestas* is juridical and not concrete: sovereign *potestas* is the

[5] Tuck has argued that in *De Cive*, the first formation of the people is always democratic, in which the will is defined as the will of the popular majority; only after this can sovereignty be transferred to a monarch (Tuck, *The Sleeping Sovereign*, 97–99; see also Lee, *Popular Sovereignty*, 309–319). But Tuck's conclusion is immediately called into question by the equivalence between unions by institution and unions by acquisition or natural dominion: for there is no necessary democratic step in setting up dominion. Furthermore, even considering institution, there are textual suggestions that direct appointment of a monarchical sovereign would be possible (DC 6.1).

[6] For corroboration, see also L 262–263, 17.4. Some terminological connections and distinctions are obscured in the Cambridge translation of *De Cive*: first, translating *potestas* as authority rather than power; second, translating *imperium* inconsistently, sometimes as power, sometimes as government (Tuck, 'Introduction', xlii). Tuck himself comes to acknowledge the inadequacy of the edition's rendering of *imperium* (Tuck, *The Sleeping Sovereign*, 92 n. 26). However, given Hobbes's equivalence between *imperium* and *potestas*, instances of *imperium* in the text are also relevant to understanding power/*potestas*.

[7] It 'consists in the fact that each of the citizens has transferred all of his own force [*vim*] and power [*potentiam*] to that *man* or *Assembly*' (DC 5.11).

power that a sovereign is entitled to from subjects, regardless whether it is actually able to harness it or not. Returning to the crucial passages explaining the generation of the commonwealth, the covenantal ground of *potestas* is constantly reinforced. From the subjects' side, *potestas* is constituted by the transfer or laying down of subjects' rights and the corresponding generation of obligations, and not by the fulfilment of those obligations; from the sovereign's side, *potestas* is a right of giving commands, and not the successful implementation of commands (EL II.1.7; DC 5.8, 5.11, 6.13). Extending the quotation provided in truncated form previously, sovereign power

> consisteth in the power and the strength that every of the members have transferred to him from themselves, *by covenant.* And because it is impossible for any man really to transfer his own strength to another, or for that other to receive it; it is to be understood: that to transfer a man's power and strength, is no more but to *lay by or relinquish his own right* of resisting him to whom he so transferreth it. (EL I.19.10; emphasis added)

If subjects fail to obey, they violate their obligations and do a wrong; if the sovereign is ineffective, that is regrettable. But the subjects' wrong does not in any way invalidate the obligation; and the sovereign's ineffectiveness does not change the nature or extent of its power.[8]

Even though power itself is juridically defined, Hobbes expects that in a well-constituted commonwealth, juridical power leads subjects to actual compliance.[9] His own explanation is rather telegraphic:

> [H]e that is to command may by use of all their means and strength, *be able by terror thereof, to frame the will of them all to unity* and concord amongst themselves. (EL I.19.7; emphasis added)[10]

But it is possible to expand the explanation to make it clearer. If at any point (most of) a population complies with the sovereign's command, they comply

[8] Indeed, *De Cive* is even more strongly juridical than *The Elements of Law*. *The Elements of Law* analyses the nature of the body politic, which so happens to be constituted by right and obligation (EL II.1.1); by contrast *De Cive* takes the rights of the commonwealth and the duties of citizens as the direct primary focus of analysis (DC Pref.9).

[9] A well-constituted, or 'complete', commonwealth is one that does properly asserts its rights (such as the rights of making law, supreme judicature, nominating ministers), rather than mistakenly dividing up and handing over some of these rights. EL II.1.13; DC 6.12.

[10] See also EL II.1.6; DC 5.8, 6.4.

with any commands of the sovereign to serve as police, guards, executioners, and thereby they give force to the sovereign's punitive capacity. This momentary compliance becomes self-sustaining: the punitive threat brings about the submission of wills of would-be resisters to the sovereign, and it strengthens the submission of those already compliant. Moving forwards, the sovereign stably receives obedience in proportion to entitlement. Some foolhardy souls will still disobey even in the face of overwhelming punitive disincentive, and need to be punished (EL II.1.10; DC 6.7). Nonetheless, for the most part actual disobedience is presumed not to be too disruptive; it will be a marginal occurrence, not threatening the civil order.[11]

In *The Elements of Law*, the power of the sovereign is always juridical; and in *De Cive*, the juridical character of *potestas/imperium* is indisputable. But it might be objected, surely in *De Cive* the Latin term *potentia* must be reserved for the sovereign's concrete power? Indeed, Silverthorne considers the *potentia* of the sovereign in these texts as its actual effectiveness towards its ends, in contrast to juridical *potestas*.[12] Suppose that this is correct. Then we should expect the sovereign's *potentia* to be variable: for as established, subjects' actual obedience is imperfect. When a subject disobeys the sovereign, this should correspondingly diminish the sovereign's power. But in the text, following on from a discussion of the possible shortcomings of subjects' compliance, Hobbes insists that the sovereign's power is nonetheless constant.[13]

> [G]overnment [*imperium*] is a capacity [*potentia*], administration of government [*administratio gubernandi*] is an *act* [*actus*]. *Power* [*potentia*] is equal in every kind of commonwealth; what differs are the acts, i.e. the *motions* and *actions* of the commonwealth. (DC 10.16)

Sovereign *potentia* is constant, and, moreover, it is directly identified with sovereign power *imperium* (which already by definition is equal to *potestas*) (DC 10.16).[14]

[11] This reconstruction relies on a large number of persons forming a union. Despite the same juridical structure, smaller unions are likely to be less robust. For instance, a master may gain right over a single slave through skilful manoeuvres in battle; but outside of the particular circumstances of that battle, even if the slave by right should submit, there is little to compel the slave to do so (DC 8.3).

[12] Michael Silverthorne, 'Political Terms in the Latin of Thomas Hobbes', *International Journal of the Classical Tradition* 2, no. 4 (1996): 506–507.

[13] Except in extremis, when disobedience becomes so prevalent as to jeopardize the basic provision of security and thereby dissolve sovereignty (i.e., civil war) (EL II.8.1; DC 12.1).

[14] There are further textual corroborations. First, *potentia* is linked to the juridical question of right: 'To rule men as they are, there must be power [*Potentia*] (which comprises both right [*ius*] and

In sum, Hobbes's early science of politics remains thoroughly juridical, in the sense that it analyses sovereign power (*potentia* or *potestas*, without distinction) as an entitlement to certain capacities. It does not have any explicit rubric under which to perform a separate analysis of actual effective capacity: not for the commonwealth, and certainly not for any informal collectivity. It lacks the tools or motivation to analyse informal collectivities as such.

3.3. The Scholastic Context of Hobbes's Early Science of Politics

The persistent focus of Hobbes's early writings on juridical power might be puzzling to some contemporary eyes. For first, supposing that (against Hobbes's own expectation) an association should prove to be durable, wouldn't it be useful to characterize its de facto power? Second, surely the non-juridical concrete power of the sovereign (the actual variable harnessing of subjects' power) should be of at least equal concern to any analyst of politics as the juridical power, if for no other reason than to ensure the correspondence between the two? I make Hobbes's approach comprehensible by contextualizing his methodology in relation to his scholastic intellectual background, building on the analysis of Chapter 2, Section 2.3.[15] Even if Hobbes's natural science already was taking its mature mechanistic form in this period, I claim his science of politics remains heavily under the shadow of a scholastic inheritance. Certainly, Hobbes does not endorse the scholastic moralized natural teleology according to which humans are by nature political animals. But I will argue that Hobbes's conception of human power maintains a modified natural teleology centred on self-preservation in the case of individuals, and centred on juridical structure and obligations of obedience in the case of collectivities. In this light, it becomes clear how, despite its juridical focus, Hobbes's science of politics is understood to provide a guide to actual political functioning. Just like scholastic natural science, on the one hand Hobbes's science of politics is normative, establishing proper

strength [*vires*]) to compel' (DC 16.15). Second, the sovereign's *summum imperium* (sovereign authority) is equivalent to its *potentia absoluta* (absolute power, DC 6.17).

[15] A complementary explanation is Hobbes's engagement with the Roman private law, as explored at length in Lee, *Popular Sovereignty*.

inner powers for humans and polities; but on the other hand, it simultaneously ensures that the normative standard is for the most part met.

First, I argue that Hobbes's focus on juridical power corresponds to the scholastic preoccupation with identifying the proper powers of entities. As sketched in Chapter 2, scholastic philosophers conceive the world in terms of natural order. Science discerns the natural *potentiae* by which each thing is inclined towards its own proper end; there is no science of the causes of degeneracy as such. Even entities that are not natural bodies like a rock or an animal, but which are composed or constructed, have an analogous structure. For instance, houses are not natural objects but constructed by humans. Nonetheless, a house is properly understood in relation to its 'universal formal principles'.[16] For another instance, while a political society does not have its own *potentia*, its *potestas* will play an analogous explanatory role as the proper end for politics.

The structure of *potestas* is specified in the course of Aquinas's discussion of natural laws. God ordains order for the world through his natural laws.[17] The natural law for humans prescribes virtue in relation to their ends as entities (self-preservation); as animals (reproduction); and most importantly as rational beings (virtue properly speaking: knowledge of God and living in society).[18] Both the animal and rational ends of humans require society: for satisfying animal needs for food and shelter requires common industry, and learning the habits of virtue requires training from others who are already virtuous. If it were not for human depravity, perhaps these desiderata could be achieved through spontaneous association; but given human depravity, there must be political society, in which laws are coercively enforced:

> But since some are found to be depraved, and prone to vice, and not easily amenable to words, it was necessary for such to be restrained from evil by force and fear, in order that, at least, they might desist from evil-doing, and leave others in peace, and that they themselves, by being habituated in this way, might be brought to do willingly what hitherto they did from fear, and thus become virtuous.[19]

[16] Aquinas, *Summa Theologica*, I-I Q14A16.
[17] Ibid., I-II Q94-Q95.
[18] Ibid.,.I-II Q94A2-A3.
[19] Ibid., I-II Q95A1.

Coercive law is enacted and enforced by the power *potestas* of the prince. But the *potestas* of the prince is not an indiscriminate power for the prince to rule however he pleases. Rather, it is tightly bound to the natural law, which orders humans towards virtue in society with others.[20] A prince must frame his laws towards the common good, not private benefit; and the laws must provide the outer form of virtue within which subjects' inner disposition towards virtue can grow.[21] Law is only truly law insofar as it takes this form, and the prince's *potestas* only extends as far as true law. Pseudo-laws that deviate from this moral standard 'are acts of violence rather than laws': tyranny cannot be understood in terms of its own positive causes, but in terms of its corruption from genuine *potestas*. Nor does the corrupted *potestas* need to be obeyed: its corruption vitiates its function.[22] Thus just as *potentia* in the science of natural bodies prescribes a norm of naturalness against which degeneracy can be measured, the power *potestas* of the prince is a power in a normatively laden sense.

As I established in Chapter 2, the method of Hobbes's early analysis of individual human action is to identify characteristic inherent powers, distinct from and prior to the acts that they generate: to that extent, it echoes the scholastic focus on *potentiae*. Understanding Hobbes's early science as committed to identifying proper internal characteristics of a thing also makes sense of the strongly juridical focus of his analysis of human collectivities. First, there can be no science of mere ad hoc aggregates, to which there is no inherent principle; there can only be a science of proper things, either natural things or constructed things. This requirement excludes associations but includes unions, because they are unified by the principle of their construction. Furthermore, having identified the object of study, inquiry focusses on the entity's inner causal principle and order of its operation, and not on its accidental divergences from this order. Thus, when it comes to attributing *potestas* or *potentia* to a political union, Hobbes characterizes it according to the principle of its construction: according to its entitlement to subjects' obedience. For to characterize it instead in terms of its mere de facto capacity to garner obedience would be to fail to grasp the inner principle of union as such.

[20] Ibid., I-II Q95A2.
[21] Ibid., I-II Q96A1, Q96A3.
[22] Ibid., I-II Q95A4, Q96A4.

The preoccupation with, first, identifying proper entities for science and, second, identifying their proper characteristics is reflected in Hobbes's sketch of the domain of his science of politics. Hobbes constantly analogizes between the natural human individual and the state. *The Elements of Law* is divided into two parts: the study of persons natural; and the study of persons civil, or in other words of bodies politic (EL II.1.1; DC 5.9). Commentators have puzzled over the relation between the two parts of Hobbes's science: how can a descriptive science ground an account of rights and duties?[23] But there is an easy answer when we restrict the question to Hobbes's early writings: for in fact, both parts of the science display the mingling of descriptive and normative concerns that is characteristic of a science of proper powers of bodies. Just as a natural person (a human individual) has proper powers conceived as faculties, Hobbes attributes faculties to the sovereign. These faculties are the faculties of the sovereign conceived in its fictional unity: 'For the body politic, as it is a fictitious body, so are the faculties and will thereof fictitious also' (EL II.2.4). This fictional unity in turn is constituted by a covenant obliging subjects to fully transfer their powers (their faculties), whether they in fact deliver on their obligation or not.[24]

Thus, Hobbes's early methodology and conceptual frame militates strongly in favour of his political philosophy focussing on formally constituted entities, and on studying their juridical entitled power. But there is a difference between Hobbes and the scholastics in how they conceive this proper power of the commonwealth: Hobbes is confident that (in a well-constituted commonwealth) the juridical account of politics corresponds to what in fact occurs for the most part, without appeal to free moral choice. I argue that Hobbes's confidence regarding sovereign *potestas* is analogous to scholastic natural philosophy's confidence that (for entities lacking free will) the proper power of an entity should generate behaviour for the most part.

Recall from Chapter 2, Aquinas draws a significant distinction between humans and all other natural elemental bodies, due to human free will.

[23] John W. N. Watkins, *Hobbes's System of Ideas: A Study in the Political Significance of Philosophical Theories* (London: Hutchinson, 1965); M. M. Goldsmith, *Hobbes's Science of Politics* (New York: Columbia University Press, 1966), 228–242; Tom Sorell, *Hobbes* (London: Routledge & Kegan Paul, 1986), 7–21; Noel Malcolm, 'Hobbes's Science of Politics and His Theory of Science', in *Aspects of Hobbes* (Oxford: Clarendon Press, 2002), 146–155.

[24] Sorell argues that in *De Cive*, the science of the commonwealth is a science of duties (*Hobbes*, 7–31, especially 19); but Malcolm shows that equally often it is characterized as a science of the commonwealth as a body (Malcolm, 'Hobbes's Science of Politics', 149). The scholastic frame shows how these can be conceived as equivalent. See Brett for the scholastic genealogy of this feature of Hobbes's politics (Brett, 'Matter, Forme, and Power', 72–102.)

Humans' degeneracy with respect to their proper end is both more prevalent and differently explained than is the degeneracy of natural bodies. First, natural bodies are infrequently degenerate. The correctly identified *potentia* of a natural body must illuminate and explain its conduct for the most part, setting aside some marginal cases such as disease or other disruption. By contrast, human nature constitutes a moral standard that humans frequently violate, through their voluntary turning away from goodness. Second, the degeneracy of the malformed plant or diseased animal arises innocently from the intervention of a violent external cause. But failings in human conduct cannot be blamed on external causes: they are morally culpable failings through the misuse of free will.

This moralized view of human order and degeneracy is reflected in Aquinas's politics. Politics is a human activity, for which natural laws set a moral standard, as outlined earlier. But there is no claim that this standard is generally met; and imperfections against this standard are understood not as sicknesses of the political body inflicted by an external cause, but as human vice, both of rulers and ruled. '[T]he good of the state cannot flourish, unless the citizens be virtuous, at least those whose business it is to govern'.[25] In particular, the prince's *potestas* may degenerate to illegitimate pseudo-*potestas* if he is not virtuous. One might object that it is untenable to explain political malfunctions entirely in terms of freely chosen individual vice, without any role for structural factors. Indeed, when Aquinas considers the extreme case of a vicious tyrant who directly privileges himself over the community, he proposes some institutional measures to lessen the impact of a tyrant's vice on the population: he endorses a mixed form of government, in which *potestas* is not solely held by the king but shared with an aristocratic tier of judges and governors and tempered by some element of popular input.[26] Nonetheless, to the extent a political society falls short of realizing the proper moral end of politics, the failure is not explained by insufficient institutional creativity. Regardless of the institutional mediation, failings ultimately boil down to vice: the goodness even of the mixed polity relies on virtue from each tier of its structure, which itself relies on free moral choice.[27] There is no particular remedy to political degeneracy except to recommend more virtue.

[25] Aquinas, *Summa Theologica*, I-II Q92A1.
[26] Ibid., I-II Q105A1.
[27] Ibid.

In sum, for Aquinas, reason and moral law inscribe lofty standards within the *potestas* of the prince and the *potentia* of subjects, standards that could be met if they would all spontaneously deploy their free will to choose virtue, but which in practice are often not met. I argued in Chapter 2 that in his early texts, Hobbes understands humans as natural bodies lacking free will, offering a reductive model of human nature and power as faculties guided by self-preservation. Within this model, natural law, as reason's dictates for how to pursue self-preservation, in principle ranges widely from the tendencies of human behaviour because of imperfections of human reason. But such variance is quickly eliminated by qualifying and modifying natural law's applicability. Hobbes consistently seeks to show that in fact human behaviour conforms for the most part to its proper normative standard. It is possible to violate this normative standard, but such violation should be a marginal occurrence.[28] Now let me extend Chapter 2's analysis to human behaviour within the commonwealth. I claim that for Hobbes's early texts, the analysis of power, whether *potentia* or *potestas*, provides a simultaneously normative and descriptive account of human behaviour, at least in a well-constituted commonwealth.

In Chapter 2, I showed that in the state of nature, the divergence of the acts of human *potentia* from the demands of natural law is nullified because of the reduced applicability of the laws of nature. In the absence of personal security and of an agreed authority, the law of nature only prohibits marginal and obviously pointless behaviour such as drunkenness and cruelty.

In the commonwealth, there is security, so in principle all the specific and demanding laws of nature should apply. Nonetheless, if the commonwealth is well constituted, divergence between these laws and actual behaviour is again mostly eliminated. Consider first subjects within the commonwealth. Hobbes argues that once in the commonwealth, each person tends to follow the civil laws because of the sovereign's punitive incentive: the 'terror' of the sovereign will 'frame the will of them all' to submit to the sovereign's will (EL I.19.7; DC 5.8).[29] This amounts to following natural law, because natural law supports displacing its own more specific dictates by the civil law.[30] The

[28] This claim only concerns external conduct; I grant that natural law also prescribes internal attitudes (EL I.17.10; DC 3.17). There remains a possibility of wide divergence from the natural law *in foro interno*.

[29] In *The Elements of Law*, Hobbes presumes that humans fear violent death more than punishment in the afterlife; the possibility of motivation by otherworldly fear starts to emerge in *De Cive*. Compare EL II.8.5 with DC 12.2.

[30] See detailed discussion in Howard Warrender, *The Political Philosophy of Hobbes, His Theory of Obligation* (Oxford: Clarendon Press, 1957), 146–176.

first law of nature is to seek peace (EL I.15.1; DC 2.2), and only by deferring to an authorized interpreter of the natural law (the sovereign) can peace be achieved (EL II.1.10, II.7.11; DC 6.8–9, 6.16). Furthermore, a valid contract establishes sovereign power, and 'natural law commands that all civil laws be observed in virtue of the natural law which forbids the violation of agreements' (DC 14.10). Despite imperfections of individual rationality, the threat of punishment brings rationally recommended behaviour and likely behaviour into alignment, both with respect to the natural law to defer to the sovereign, and also with respect to other more specific natural laws, whenever the sovereign has enacted them into civil legislation.

In principle there can be conduct that is regulated only by natural law, and not by civil law, for instance, giving alms (EL II.10.5). But Hobbes's general strategy is to minimize the scope of natural laws outside of civil authority. Because of humans' self-serving inability to reason fairly about blameworthiness and desert, Hobbes endorses the civil laws encoding and thereby superseding the natural law in matters of external conduct, and he does not display any concern about sovereign overreach (EL II.10.8; DC 14.17). Even when civil law commands an action prima facie against natural law (for instance, civil laws stipulating that pilfering does not count as theft under certain circumstances), Hobbes argues that natural law upholds civil law's ruling (DC 16.10). Only inner conscience remains entirely beyond civil regulation (DC 14.17).

Finally, Hobbes grants that for certain kinds of commands, there cannot be any punitive incentive sufficient to enforce them. People are unlikely to comply with commands that offend against profound values, for instance, a command to kill their own parents. But in dealing with these cases, Hobbes again seeks to minimize the extent to which natural law and the actually expected behaviour of subjects diverge: he argues that natural law simultaneously supports the sovereign's right to command and the subject's refusal to comply (DC 6.13).[31]

Consider now the sovereign itself: the person (or assembly) holding sovereignty in a commonwealth. Aquinas's prince's *potestas* was tightly tied to virtuous rule for the common good; to the extent the prince governed despotically for their own self-interest, they lacked *potestas*. By contrast, for Hobbes *potestas* is fully held for the most part, so long as the commonwealth

[31] See extended discussion in Susanne Sreedhar, *Hobbes on Self-Defence: Defying the Leviathan* (Cambridge: Cambridge University Press, 2010).

is properly constituted. In a properly constituted commonwealth, the sovereign holds various essential rights, including rights of punishment, and the right of defining laws (EL II.1, DC 6). I already established that subjects obey the sovereign for the most part due to the sovereign's punitive threat. In result, the sovereign's *potestas* has full efficacy. It also has full status as *potestas*; for Hobbes eliminates the category of despotic rule, by refusing the distinction between the common good and the ruler's interest (EL II.5.1–2; DC 7.2). Rulers for their part seek to preserve and enrich themselves, and the best way to do this is by tending to the safety of the people (EL II.5.1, II.9.1; DC 13.2, 13.4). Furthermore, Hobbes argues that the duty placed by natural law on the sovereign is nothing other than ruling for the safety of the people (EL II.9.1; DC 13.2).

Without any distinction between virtuous and despotic rule on the basis of which to deny *potestas*, Hobbes insists that the sovereign holds full *potestas* regardless of the way it rules, so long as it is not conquered or usurped (EL II.2.15; DC 7.3). But one might worry, even if the sovereign's duty is in line with its self-interest, this still does not show that the dutiful behaviour occurs for the most part. Hobbes gives detailed policy prescriptions for ruling for the safety of the people (EL II.9.3–9; DC 6.6–17), which are hardly likely to be met by most sovereigns. For a sovereign (who has no greater likelihood of perfect long-term rationality than subjects) faces no immediate external constraint (punitive or otherwise) shaping its will. Nonetheless, Hobbes also suggests a weaker standard of conduct for a sovereign: basic rule for the people's security, which may neglect to fully implement best rational practice, but which is not wicked (DC 6.13). He is at pains to insist that achieving this weaker standard will occur for the most part. Regarding the possibility of wicked rule that preys directly on the people rather than protecting them, Hobbes asserts that 'there is no reason why [the sovereign] would want to spoil his citizens, since that is not to his advantage' (DC 6.13). That is, direct wickedness is so contrary even to immediate self-interest that it will be a marginal occurrence.

In sum, Hobbes's focus on juridically constituted unions, and on their juridically entitled powers, can be understood as a natural consequence of his methodological approach, whereby he seeks to identify proper (definitional and normative) powers that are nonetheless efficacious. Specifically, even though the power/*potestas* of the body politic identifies a juridical entitlement to subjects' obedience that could in principle fail to be fulfilled, fulfilment should be successful for the most part, without requiring moral effort of subjects. And for the most part, the sovereign performs its role adequately. Although the conceptual frame of Hobbes's early science of politics is juridical, it is intended simultaneously to supply a model of actual political functioning.

3.4. Sovereign Robustness in Hobbes's Early Writings

The sovereign possesses the authority to speak the people's will, and no one else does. Hobbes's insistence on the priority of formal collectivities allows him to deny any popular political agency apart from the agency mediated and expressed by the sovereign; a fortiori, he is able to deny the legitimacy of any popular critique or censure of sovereign power.

> [T]hey say the people rebelleth, or the people demandeth, when it is no more than a dissolved multitude, of which though any one man may be said to demand or have right to something, yet the heap, or multitude, cannot be said to demand or have right to any thing. (EL II.2.11; see also DC 6.1)

When a multitude speaks, it lacks the juridical structure to even possess a single will: it is just an aggregate of many people with separate wills.

This sketch of Hobbes's view of popular agency remains juridical. But it is unsatisfying. For one might wonder, under some conditions couldn't there be a de facto voice of the people? If there were a robust collectivity of subjects distinct from the formal union headed by the sovereign, couldn't it meaningfully be understood to speak the people's will? Nor is this question illegitimate, notwithstanding Hobbes's uncompromising rhetoric. Hobbes relies on the juridical *potestas* of the sovereign having real consequences, most pointedly, a capacity to deliver peace and security, through its effective mastery of its subjects, as established in Section 3.3. And these real consequences rely on there being no robust insubordinate collectivities below the sovereign: for a de facto mass popular political subject, emboldened to insubordination by its collective strength, can threaten the neat convergence between the sovereign's *potestas* and the actual obedience that it is able to garner. Call the gap between the sovereign's entitled obedience and actual obedience 'the political problem': if there is such a thing as usurpatory popular agency, then this problem is pressing.

In this section, I reconstruct the early Hobbesian response, showing that there is no such de facto mass popular political subject in a well-constituted commonwealth. The corollary of Hobbes's early social ontology of fragmented equality is the robustness of sovereign power.

As argued in the previous sections, the well-constituted sovereign's power is generally robust, due to its punitive incentive effectively conforming the wills of subjects. Nonetheless, sometimes it degenerates. Degeneracy is not understood through failure of the sovereign's or subjects' virtue, but rather through the political analogue of ill health. The body politic is naturally healthy, but it can face demise either through violent death (foreign invasion) or 'sickness and distemper' (sedition) (EL II.8.1). The critical factor in an outbreak of the disease of sedition is insubordinate groups. Hobbes assesses seditious disruption as a marginal possibility rather than a dominant reality for a properly constituted commonwealth, and I will show that this assessment rests on his ontology of fragmented equality.

There are three things required to dispose subjects to sedition: discontent, pretence of right, and hope of success. If any one of these three is lacking, rebellion will not occur (EL II.8.1; DC 12.1).[32] I will focus on the third, which *De Cive* foregrounds as the Achilles heel of rebellion:

> For men can be as steeped as may be in opinions inimical to peace and civil government; they can be hurt and exasperated by injuries and insults from those in authority; but if they have little or no *hope of winning*, no sedition will follow; individuals will hide their feelings and put up with a bad situation rather than risk a worse. (DC 12.11)

Hobbes clearly identifies collective strength as the fundamental ground of hope of success: for an individual taken alone could never hope to prevail against the sovereign. Within the body politic, there are four possible kinds of collectivities that might provide that strength: subordinate groups (associations or unions); and insubordinate groups (associations or illicit unions). Neither kind of subordinate group is any use, because by definition they respect the authority of the sovereign and are tolerated by it (EL I.19.9; DC 5.10). Sedition requires insubordinate groups: whether informal associations or illicit unions. Let me consider these in turn.

[32] Elsewhere, Hobbes asserts that bad doctrine or discontent at oppressive rule causes sedition (EL II.8.4–10, II.9.5–8, II.12.1, II.13.9–10; DC Pref.5–8). However, these must be read as contributing rather than sufficient causes.

First, informal association. Hobbes relies on his fragmented political ontology to rule out the relevance of informal association. A discontented multitude can have seditious discontent and a pretence of right

> when the commands seem hurtful to the people; and they think, every one of them, that the opinion and the sense of the people is the same with the opinion of himself, and those that consent with him; calling by the name of the people, any multitude of his own faction. (EL II.8.4)

But for Hobbes, it lacks hope of success. As I argued earlier, association is conceived as a deliberate, horizontal form of cooperation for shared ends. But Hobbes shows that in the state of nature, the diversity of individual human ends, combined with various antisocial passions, means such associations are prone to uncoordination, infighting, and dissolution. There is nothing to protect insubordinate associations within a commonwealth from these same sources of ineffectiveness and fragility.

Hope of success requires an illicit union:[33] rebels need to unify in order to be directed to a single action. Furthermore, Hobbes asserts that any union would need to be established deliberately by a seditious multitude mutually agreeing upon a leader to submit to and unify under (EL II.8.12; DC 12.11). In principle, unions could form either by lateral consent or by natural inequality, but within civil society no unions are naturally generated by inequality: for adult men are all more or less equal (EL I.14.2; DC 1.3). Nor is consent easy to achieve. In the state of nature, one of the main pressures to form a union by lateral consent is fear of one another: but in the commonwealth this fear is already under control. Hobbes suggests that seditious unions arise only under the spell of the extraordinary oratory of ambitious men. He emphasizes the specific premeditated directed effort that such men would have to make in order to carry off their plans.

> But those who want to turn that [seditious] disposition into action devote the whole thrust of their effort first to uniting the disaffected as a faction and a conspiracy; and then to getting the leading role in the faction themselves. (DC 13.13)

[33] Illicit unions merit being called unions insofar as they are collectivities in which members submit to a single will. But they differ from licit unions insofar as there is no genuine obligation with this submission (DC 13.13); genuine obligation is lacking because they are inconsistent with subjects' prior obligation to submit to the sovereign (DC 2.17, 6.20, 12.11).

This makes seditious unions easy for the sovereign to contain. To prevent sedition it is sufficient simply to undercut the formation of unions by targeting their would-be leaders: without them, the unions cannot form and the action cannot proceed. Hobbes belittles these leaders' claim to good judgment, points out their low odds of success (EL II.8.12–15; DC 12.10–13), and recommends to the sovereign that it should deploy harsh punitive measures specifically for the ambitious (EL II.9.7; DC 13.12).

The polemical force of this analysis is clear. I mentioned at this section's outset that the multitude is not a single thing, not a person, and can exercise no legitimate constraint on the sovereign: speaking in the name of 'the people' to criticize the sovereign is always an illicit rhetorical claim. But more importantly, Hobbes's analysis shows that there is also no practical constraint because associations are inherently weak. They can only become powerful if they cease being a multitude and structure themselves as a union, consciously deciding to join together and act by a single will under a leader (EL II.8.1, II.8.11; DC 12.11, 13.13). The multitude is only politically salient insofar as it ceases to be a multitude; and because such a transformation requires brazen deliberation and coordination, it can readily be prevented.

Sedition and rebellion are primarily analysed as strategic behaviours undertaken with the ultimate purpose of prevailing over the opposing party, causing war and conflict along the way. But Hobbes does consider a different, less strategic, source of war: doctrinal disagreement (on religion, science, or policy). In *De Cive*, Hobbes portrays prickly human beings who fight to defend their pride, without specific reference to hope of success (DC 1.5, 6.11). Nonetheless, Hobbes views this source of war as also readily containable.

> One cannot prevent such disagreements from occurring. However, by the use of sovereign power they can be kept from interfering with the public peace. (DC 6.11)

In a well-ordered commonwealth, the sovereign retains the right to determine doctrine. Most quarrelling can be tolerated, so long as the sovereign prohibits doctrine with seditious content.

One might wonder, is this resolution satisfactory? Or does the case of doctrinal quarrelling point to a larger problem for Hobbes's analysis: the possibility that subordinate unions might become insubordinate? An entity such as a church is structured as a subordinate union. As such, it does not face the organizational hurdle normally facing seditious union. It is ready to spring into action: all that is required is that its previously submissive leadership be inspired with seditious passions. And such inspiration may arise in response to the sovereign prohibiting its earnestly believed doctrine. Hobbes's lengthy theological discussions can be understood as an effort to head off this kind of problem with churches (EL I.18, II.6–7; DC Chs 4, 11, 15–18). But beyond religion, Hobbes's early works display a general optimism that the proper juridical specification of sovereignty concretely guarantees peace. In later work, as we will see, the robustness of the sovereign's peace is threatened not only by insubordinate churches, but also, more pervasively, by the emergent power dynamics of the multitude itself.

4

The Political Problem

4.1. Introduction

What is the power of the people for Hobbes? In Chapter 3, I sketched his view in the early texts. I argued that Hobbes offers a political ontology of fragmented equality. There is no such thing as human collective power outside of formal juridical union; and in particular, there is no power of the people apart from the commonwealth. Popular power is conceived as an authority *potestas*, and is exclusively expressed by the sovereign state. Outside the state, there are only the powers of individuals. This broadly accords with the standard interpretation of Hobbes.[1] However, this is far from the most interesting contribution that Hobbes offers to the conceptualization of popular power. Now in the present chapter, I argue that Hobbes's later writings develop a new account of non-juridical collective power as *potentia*. The emergence of a theory non-juridical collective power grounds a new approach to the question of popular power; in particular, it raises the troubling possibility that the phenomena commonly taken to be manifestations of popular power may in fact be neither deeply powerful nor meaningfully popular.

It is certainly true that throughout his writings, Hobbes expresses a persistent and polemical hostility towards the people separate from the commonwealth, what he often calls the multitude (*multitudo*). Nonetheless, I argue that the grounds of this hostility differs between his early and late works. In Chapter 3, I established that the early texts have difficulty even conceiving the possibility of collective power apart from the commonwealth, due to their political ontology of fragmented equality; and they have no framework to analyse any divergence of the efficacy of a commonwealth from its juridical entitlement. By contrast, now I show that the later texts can conceive collective power apart from the state, through a natural extension of the new relational conception of individual human *potentia* established in Chapter 2. To characterize the shift between the early and late texts, an ontology of

[1] See Chapter 3, footnote 1.

Potentia. Sandra Leonie Field, Oxford University Press (2020). © Oxford University Press.
DOI: 10.1093/oso/9780197533864.001.0001

fragmented equality is discarded in favour of an ontology of spontaneously emerging oligarchic groups. In result, Hobbes's later texts can conceive a divergence between the commonwealth's juridical authority and its concrete efficacy; the theory reveals Tuck's 'sleeping sovereign' to be strikingly lacking in power in the politically relevant sense, thereby explaining why it no longer features as a possible mode of expression of popular power in the later texts.

The later political ontology builds on the relational conception of power laid out in Chapter 2. If individual human power *potentia* is always already relational and unequal, then practically, there is a possibility of more robust informal collectivities, because groups need not be founded on explicit horizontal agreement on shared ends, but may be hierarchical entities emergent from the interaction of individual purposes that are diverse and crosscutting, as I will show. Conceptually, the de-essentialized conception of individual power opens the possibility to attribute *potentia* to any group, whether formal union or informal association; and the *potentia* of a collectivity is no longer equivalent to its *potestas*. I connect this change of political ontology to Hobbes's gradual shift away from scholasticism, building on the analysis from Chapter 2.

Hobbes hopes his juridical civil science might reliably generate actual political outcomes. But recall the political problem: that the allegiance to which a state is entitled by right might not in practice be forthcoming. The political problem might arise if insubordinate groups within the commonwealth dilute or fragment the sovereign's supreme command of subjects' allegiance. In Chapter 3, I argued that the problem is marginal in Hobbes's early texts and readily solved, due to Hobbes's early confidence in the fragility of associations. However, because of the changed political ontology, the political problem becomes significant in the later texts. On the later political ontology, associations within the commonwealth beneath the sovereign may have their own power *potentia*, and may de facto express the agency of some part of the population, generating a gap between the concrete power *potentia* and the juridical entitlement *potestas* of the sovereign. Indeed, such associations constantly tend to arise: as a result, sovereign security faces a persistent insurgent threat. But lest present-day readers celebrate the emergence of an autonomous popular political agent capable of exerting a normatively reassuring restraint on absolute state power, Hobbes's analysis casts suspicion on any idea of prepolitical human equality. Non-state collective power comes without any guarantee of an egalitarian internal structure, and it may well be unappealingly oligarchic. In result, Hobbes faces a pressing political problem, which non-state mass political agency inflames rather than resolves. In Chapter 5, I will lay out Hobbes's response to the problem.

4.2. Formal and Informal Political Collectivities in Hobbes's Later Writings

In this section I consider Hobbes's later texts, and I argue that there is a striking change in his political ontology, compared to his earlier political writings. The distinction between association and union (in my terms, informal and formal collectivities) as two possible modes of combination of human powers persists (L 132–133, 10.3). But now informal collectivities have a significant practical presence. I claim that *Leviathan* lays out a new model of association that lies between a momentary association motivated by specific goals and a formal union for the sake of permanent security. These associations are oriented toward mid-range goals and they come about in a new and less intentional fashion, which correspondingly endows them with the possibility of durability and political salience, even if not the supreme security of a permanent union.[2] In result, the fragmented human equality of the early texts' analysis is displaced by a new ontology of spontaneously emerging oligarchic groups. Furthermore, these informal collectivities can be attributed a power *potentia* of their own. I argue that their *potentia* is understood non-juridically, and that the possibility of a non-juridical conception of collective power corresponds to the late texts' de-essentialized, relational grasp of individual human power, established in Chapter 2. The new conception of *potentia* also has implications for unions. Unions are still conceived first of all in terms of juridically constructed *potestas*, but it is simultaneously possible to attribute to them a non-juridical *potentia* that may or may not correspond to their entitled *potestas*.[3]

To understand the formation of associations, it is first necessary to understand the motivations driving human action. In Hobbes's early view, individuals have no desire for power *potentia* as such. The lack of desire for power

[2] Similar themes are pursued in Charles D. Tarlton, 'The Creation and Maintenance of Government: A Neglected Dimension of Hobbes's *Leviathan*', *Political Studies 26*, no. 3 (1978): 307–327; Carmichael, 'C. B. Macpherson's "Hobbes"', 359–379; Frost, *Lessons from a Materialist Thinker*, 131–172. Tarlton and Frost draw only on *Leviathan*, whereas Carmichael also shows these themes to be new in *Leviathan* compared to earlier texts.

[3] In this light, Silverthorne errs in using *De Cive* to understand *Leviathan*'s Latin. Silverthorne, 'Political Terms', 499–509.

can be understood in light of the conception of individual human power as faculties, established in Chapter 2, Section 2.2. Each person's own faculties are more or less fixed, beyond a limited possibility of self-cultivation. In the early texts, humans are instead driven by desire for glory[4] (mental pleasure: the feeling of power, primarily from receiving honour) or advantages (sensual pleasure: including satisfying bodily needs) (EL I.7.9; DC 1.2).[5] At the outset of *De Cive*, Hobbes charts four ways in which these motivations can generate collectivities, finding three paths unstable or fruitless, before leading into an argument in favour of the fourth, the juridical formation of the commonwealth (DC 1.2). First is the pursuit of glory. Glory is an antisocial passion and offers only an unstable basis for association, because 'glorying, like honour, is nothing if everybody has it' (DC 1.2; see also EL I.14.3–4, 1.4). One way to achieve the feeling of glory is to receive the honour and deference of others; but this feeling of glory is rightful only if one's underlying power *potentia* is exceptional compared to everyone else. For most people, glory is actually vainglory or false glory, and associations built around a leader lacking genuinely exceptional faculties are anticipated to be degenerate and unstable (EL I.9.1). Second is the pursuit of advantages by means of domination.[6] Dominating others for the sake of advantages is effective in theory but is fruitless in practice. Given the approximate equality of power *potentia*, the pursuit of domination leads back into war amongst humans who will not defer to one another (DC 1.2).[7] Third is the pursuit of advantages by forming a cooperative association. As argued in Chapter 3, the model case of an association in the early texts is an aggregation of individual humans, who combine together in an accord (*consensio*) with specific shared ends in mind, for however long those ends continue to motivate each member. Such an aggregation is horizontal in the sense that all members' wills are on an equal plane: all have the same goal, in virtue of which they come together, and none

[4] Indeed, Hobbes's discussion of power is explicitly in service of explaining glory (EL I.8.3, I.9.1).

[5] The desire for a secondary power such as riches straddles this divide: for riches provide both mental pleasure (glory) and sensual pleasure (direct means to acquire advantages). In passing, Hobbes does acknowledge the desire for riches (EL I.7.7). But he does not see it offering any basis for association, perhaps because (as argued in Chapter 2) secondary powers out of proportion to faculty powers are regarded as degenerate and unstable; and in any case, the desire for riches does not effectively secure advantages, because riches vanish if the other causes of conflict are not addressed (EL I.14.12). The distinctive new move in *Leviathan* will be to give central place to the desire for secondary powers such as riches, as I will show.

[6] *Dominium* is a form of *imperium*, which is in turn equivalent to *potestas* (DC 5.11, 9.1–2). I emphasize that desire for dominion or domination is not a desire for power *potentia*: achieving dominion makes no difference for a person's *potentia*, which is an inner capacity.

[7] The same problem applies to domination motivated by desire of glory (EL I.14.3).

defers to any other (EL I.12.7, I.19.4; DC 1.14, 5.4). Individual wills exist in fragmentary independence of one another, and this independence is wholly undiminished by association. Whether because the shared ends that ground the association are superseded or because of other differences or passions, associations are fragile and tend to collapse.

In the face of the failures of the other three strategies, in his early texts Hobbes concludes that the pursuit of pleasures, whether glory or advantage, does not spontaneously produce durable human collectivities. Thus, the fourth and final strategy: individuals seeking advantage limit the spontaneity of their wills, submitting to the domination of a sovereign to form a union. In the commonwealth, the relation between wills is vertical: all particular wills are fully subordinated to the will of the sovereign, not for the sake of any specific short-term end, but for the permanent end of security. Unions are anticipated to be robust, because the juridical union of wills is made effective by the sovereign's punitive incentive (EL I.19.6–7; DC 5.6–8).

In *Leviathan*, by contrast, Hobbes directly asserts what has no parallel in the earlier texts: a desire for power *potentia* itself.

> [I]n the first place, I put for a generall inclination of all mankind, a perpetuall and restlesse desire of Power after power [*Potentiam unam post aliam*], that ceaseth onely in Death. (L 150–151, 11.2)[8]

This desire to increase power itself is possible because, as established in Chapter 2, Section 2.4, power *potentia* in *Leviathan* is not limited to faculties, but is relational: it is pre-eminently constituted from social allegiance and support, which (in sharp contrast to faculties) can certainly be increased. Furthermore, this desire is dominant. To be sure, specific pleasures and goods are also desired, but Hobbes is very clear that these specific desires will generally be submerged by the more general and abstract desire for power itself. Each individual has a restless desire of power after power because 'he cannot assure the power [*Potentia*] and means to live well, which he hath present, without the acquisition of more' (L 150–151, 11.2). As a corollary, the model of human motivation focuses on the desire for power and not for specific advantages.

I now show how for Hobbes, the individual pursuit of relational power generates associations of a different structure and greater durability than

[8] The discussion of power is no longer instrumental to the analysis of glory; contrast footnote 4.

in the early texts' associations for specific advantages; I show how this later analysis generates a new social ontology with a prominent place for non-juridical collective formations. In establishing the existence of a new associational social ontology in Hobbes's later writings, I push against the opposing view, that Hobbes envisages a fragmented social ontology in *Leviathan* just as in the earlier texts, a view that is directly expressed in the secondary literature and apparently supported by key textual passages. In the history of Hobbes scholarship, Macpherson famously characterizes Hobbes as a possessive individualist; he accuses Hobbes of holding an untenably fragmentary vision of society, and of focussing on centrifugal forces at the expense of centripetal ones.[9] For Macpherson, this vision is generated by the very same features that I claim lead to associational forms: the modelling of individuals as power seekers pursuing relational power. And indeed, textually, *Leviathan*'s direct characterization of the state of nature in Chapter 13 maintains the earlier texts' picture of fragmentation. There are equal individuals, forming only momentary and fragile associations in relation to specific and transitory shared goals; often they attempt (futilely) to dominate one another, resulting in a fragmenting diffidence between them (L 190–191, 13.3–4). This leads to Hobbes's infamous claim that life in the state of nature lacks society (*societas*)[10] and is '*solitary*, poore, nasty, brutish, and short' (L 192–193, 13.9; emphasis added).

However, I will argue that attention to *Leviathan*'s Chapter 10 reveals a different social ontology, in light of which the image of the state of nature appears in *Leviathan* as a vestigial remnant from an earlier theoretical frame.[11] It is critical to see that the relationality involved in *Leviathan*'s power

[9] Macpherson, *Political Theory of Possessive Individualism*, 93; Macpherson, 'Introduction', 55–56. It is commonplace to attribute to Hobbes a fragmented social ontology: see references at Chapter 3, footnote 1.

[10] In both early and late texts, Hobbes rhetorically denies the existence of any associations at all in the state of nature; yet then in his discussion of the emergence of the commonwealth out of the state of nature, there is an important role for cooperative associations for defence (EL I.19.3–4; DC 5.4; L 256–257, 17.3–4). A more precise claim would be that the state of nature features no lasting or durable association.

[11] Whereas other commentators may come to a misunderstanding of *Leviathan*'s new social ontology by their excessive focus on the description of the state of nature and insufficient attention to Chapter 10, Macpherson pays great attention to this chapter. In Macpherson's case, the error arises from modelling power relations as purely vertical, all on the model of domination: when each individual is seeking power, that just means that they are seeking full control over others. If this were the case, certainly, the result would be individualizing conflict and fragmentation. But as I now seek to show, the lesson of Chapter 10 is that power relations are not (in general) total vertical relations of domination. Christov attempts a criticism of Macpherson's view of fragmentation by drawing attention to the sheer proliferation of human groupings in the Hobbesian state of nature, and he insists on the persistent threat of degeneration of the commonwealth into war because of these groups. In general terms, this is congruent to my analysis. But Christov's account focusses almost exclusively on

is not (contra Macpherson) the essentially conflictual relationality of the early texts' zero-sum analysis, but rather the emergent relationality of layered dependencies generated by many individuals' simultaneous efforts to negotiate a complex social web of assistance and hindrance.

To see how the new conception of power *potentia* and, correspondingly, the desire for power *potentia* itself as a new fundamental motivation of human action generate a different social ontology, recall what it means to pursue this new power. As outlined in Chapter 2, Section 2.4, to say that each individual human seeks power amounts to saying that each seeks to placate and propitiate those whom they speculate could harm or assist their own ends. Individuals seek to ally themselves in such a way as to advance and protect their ability to live securely and pursue their more specific ends. Their own power is constituted in part by their success in this endeavour, but also in part by other actors in turn seeking to placate and propitiate them. However, this behaviour has an effect that is not directly intended either by those honouring or those honoured: it constitutes patronage networks, security blocs, gangs of followers, and allegiance groups. In other words, the desire for power leads to the spontaneous formation of associations, superseding the rough equality of individuals with the inequality of more or less mighty groupings (L 132–141, 10.5–9, 10.20, 10.38, 10.45). For instance, recall that riches are a power insofar as they garner allegiance (L 132–133, 10.4). When multiple individuals offer their allegiance to the possessor of riches, an association is constituted. These associations are emergent social formations that are unintentional and spontaneous in the sense that they are the result of individuals each pursuing their own status and relationship within a social domain; they are not the result of a shared equal intention to combine forces to secure a particular advantage collectively, nor do they rely on a mutual agreement or shared goal of the members. The rich person may garner clients whether or not they cultivate them; the poor person may become a client without sharing substantive goals with the patron.

As I argued in Chapter 2, Sections 2.4 and 2.5, Hobbes's later conception of power refuses abstraction from social context. To say that an individual has power to do something is to say they will be able to achieve the desired

covenantal groups (as is to be expected, given his primary focus on *De Cive*): either vertical relations of domination between unequals (parents over children, victors over the vanquished) or horizontal voluntary associations (Christov, *Before Anarchy*, 15–16, 35, 58–63, 71–102). I argued in Chapter 3 that such groups are not sufficient to threaten the sovereign's power; the real threat arises with the new form of association introduced in *Leviathan*, which is spontaneous rather than covenantal, and neither perfectly horizontal nor perfectly vertical, as I will now show.

outcome given the actual social context in which they find themselves. In result, the desire for power binds individuals to particular social contexts, and is potentially capable of motivating a commitment to maintaining an association over an extended period of time. Consider the factors that destabilize association that is founded on explicit agreement on specific goals: notably envy and disagreement. These do not arise so acutely in spontaneous associations of allegiance and patronage. If I envy my partner in a cooperative enterprise and covet their goods, it may be impossible to continue cooperating; by contrast if I envy the wealth and covet the goods of my patron, I am likely nonetheless to continue to be their client in hope of receiving some benefit (L 136–137, 10.19, 10.23). If I disagree with my patron's decisions but still hope to be favoured by my patron, then I have a strong reason to put my disagreement aside (L 136–139, 10.28, 10.30).

Beyond merely being stable, the spontaneously compounding of powers in associations builds upon itself.

> For the nature of Power [*Potentiae*], is in this point, like to Fame, increasing as it proceeds; or like the motion of heavy bodies, which the further they go, make still the more hast. (L 132–133, 10.2)

As discussed in Chapter 2, Section 2.4, power compounds itself through honour. Allegiance is not only a power in itself, but is also a sign of power. As a sign of power, it attracts honour, very likely in the form of more allegiance. X has a lot of friends, so I want to be her friend; Y has henchmen, so I do not want to annoy her; I heard that people plan to back Z, so I back Z too: in all cases the reputation of holding many people's allegiance leads to ever more people placating and propitiating, or, in other words, to a bigger and more solid social grouping (L 140–141, 10.38).

The resultant relation between wills in these associations is neither perfectly horizontal nor perfectly vertical, instead displaying multiple layered dependencies of will that fall short of total submission.[12] It is not horizontal: each individual displays variable degrees of de facto deference to various others. Associations are often stabilized by oligarchic relations of dependence: the result is a deeply uneven texture of social life.[13] At the same

[12] Insofar as this associational power is the exemplary form of human power, it undermines the commonly made distinction between power-to and power-over.

[13] May has attempted a Hobbesian analysis of emergent collectivities. However, taking his starting point in the juridical theory of authorization, he models a horizontal association of equals with a small number of leaders; he does not recognize the asymmetrical and hierarchical

time, it is not strict vertical subordination. For the wills remain formally independent, and whatever de facto submission is in play may well be partial and context-sensitive. Thus even in clearly hierarchical relationships, the stronger party is still dependent on subordinates. For instance, a patron needs to take care not to be too miserly to retain the loyalty of clients against competing patrons (L 132–137, 10.4, 10.21).

In sum, Hobbes envisages an active social domain from which groupings constantly emerge and persist apart from any process of covenant, and in which inequalities are constantly generated. The earlier political ontology of fragmented equality is replaced with a new political ontology of emergent power blocs. This is reflected in a critical revision that *Leviathan* makes to the argument of the earlier texts.[14] Right at the start of the discussion of power in *The Elements of Law*, Hobbes stresses the tendency of humans to isolation and fragmentation. What I called the positionality claim pits individual against individual, and the only salient possibility of human coalition is a formal union via covenant, a topic deferred to later in the book (EL I.8.4). In the corresponding point in the sequence of *Leviathan*'s argument,[15] Hobbes wholly excises the discussion of fragmentation and replaces it with a discussion of aggregation that is without parallel in the earlier text. He asserts that the greatest human power is 'strengths united', and makes explicit that this is achieved not only by a formal union bound by a permanent covenant into a single will, but also by compounds of powers 'depending on the will of each particular': in other words, associations (L 132–133, 10.3).[16]

texture of these collectivities. Larry May, *Limiting Leviathan: Hobbes on Law and International Affairs* (Oxford: Oxford University Press, 2013), 167–173.

[14] Indeed, even though I have generally characterized the state-of-nature discussion in *Leviathan* as a vestige of the earlier theory of power, there is an interesting change in the detail, reflecting the shift from a social ontology of fragmented equality to a social ontology of inequality. In *The Elements of Law* and *De Cive*, humans are equal because their faculties are more or less equal and therefore any can be killed by another, even the weakest. In *Leviathan*, humans are equal because any can be killed, but the claim that the weakest individual is really able to kill the strongest is dropped, to be replaced by the claim that the weakest may be able to kill the strongest through confederacy (EL I.19.1–2; DC 1.3; L 188–189, 13.1). I interpret this change as a reflection of Hobbes's new conception of power: equal faculties tell nothing about power. In the early texts, the problem generating war is that human faculties, or equivalently, human powers, are equal, leading to universal diffidence. But in *Leviathan*, power is relational, not faculty based, so there is no initial equality of power; and as I will argue in Chapter 5, it is only through active equalization of human power that war is overcome.

[15] Immediately after defining power and listing primary and secondary powers.

[16] To be sure, in the Latin edition there is a hierarchy: the greatest (*maxima*) power is the formal union of wills; a federation where wills remain separate is said to be second in power (*proxima*). Nonetheless, the point of the English edition still holds: an informal collectivity is a considerable power.

I am not claiming that these associations are perfectly durable. The very nature of their constitution carries a deep risk of instability: if my reason for offering allegiance to a powerful individual or organization is my perception their power and of the likelihood of benefiting from it, then should that perception change, I will withdraw my allegiance. Worse, given that my estimation of that power may be largely based on the evidence I see of others' opinions of that power, if ever I suspect that others are shifting their allegiance, I will be quick to do the same. For Hobbes, rationally speaking, humans should desire security to 'last all the time of their life', and this still requires a formal commonwealth (L 258–259, 17.5). But the fact that these associations may sometimes be unstable does not prevent them from proving quite durable under many circumstances.

I have established the mid-range durability of associations in Hobbes's later texts, durability that had been denied in the early texts. But the larger problem with associations in the early texts was that they were conceptually elusive, due to their status as mere aggregations without formal unification. They possessed no power themselves, neither *potentia* nor *potestas*. Now I argue that Hobbes's later texts are able to attribute power *potentia* to associations as such, and that this is a non-juridical conception of power.[17]

Recall that in Hobbes's late natural philosophy, the concept of power is reconceived to evacuate any appeal to internal motive properties (Chapter 2, Section 2.5). Power is plenary power: the sum total of all accidents in all agents and patients that combine to produce a specific act. Any attempt to characterize the power 'of' an agent is parasitic on this primary definition. First, strictly speaking the agent's accidents only count as power insofar as they combine with the accidents of other bodies to constitute a plenary power that produces an act. And second, if we wish to speak more loosely of the agent's power with respect to a class of possible acts, the power can only be attributed to the agent if it is likely (for all we know) that all the other elements of the plenary power will be forthcoming for the relevant acts. This conceptual frame makes it very easy to attribute power to an association as such. Power can only be attributed to an individual human when the full social context necessary to the success of the person's action is in place or ready to hand. And within this full social context, the individuation of the agent

[17] In her discussion of Hobbes's engagement with scholasticism, Brett argues that for Hobbes, a human collectivity without a sovereign has no form at all (Brett, 'Matter, Forme, and Power', 99). But contra Brett, informal collectivities persist in Hobbes's late civil science, because they do have *potentia*.

holding power is flexible and not tied to the boundaries of natural bodies: in Hobbes's own discussion of individual human power, accidents in other people count towards an individual's power (for instance, another person's helpfulness). Insofar as individual human power is defined to include the social allegiance that supports the individual's action, it is easy to slightly shift terminology and attribute power to the structure of social allegiance itself; or in other words, to association. Attributing power to an association does not require the association to have some inner essence or proper nature, whether inherently or by construction: rather, the power of a group of people is just what they actually tend to be able to do together. Indeed, this speculative consequence of the new doctrine of individual power finds direct textual support. A single *potentia* is attributed to associations, despite their lack of formal unity, even in the very moment that they are being contrasted with unions (L 132–133, 10.4).

I turn now to consider unions. Some commentators attentive to questions of concrete power have puzzled over Hobbes's characterization of sovereign power. Frost contrasts two images of sovereign power that can be seen in *Leviathan*: the 'fable' of power as domination linked to covenant, against a 'materialist' power grounded in human relations.[18] Hindess for his part complains that Hobbes's argument 'involves a confusion between the idea of power as a capacity and the idea of power as a right: a confusion that is endemic to modern political theory'.[19] But the duality in Hobbes's account of sovereign power does not reflect any confusion: rather, he offers a two-track account of formal collectivities. Unions have both a juridical power *potestas* generated by covenantal transfer of rights; and an analytically distinct concrete power, under the heading of *potentia*.[20] In *Leviathan*, Hobbes retains the image of the commonwealth as a deliberately created body with covenantally established *potestas* as its defining characteristic:

[18] Frost, *Lessons from a Materialist Thinker*, 133–135, 163.

[19] Hindess, *Discourses of Power*, 15. Hindess's capacity power corresponds to Frost's materialist power and my concrete power (*potentia*).

[20] See also Read, 'Thomas Hobbes', 505–525. Both Frost's and Hindess's analyses are perhaps hampered by presuming a single unified use of the English term 'power', and not observing the systematic Latin distinction *potentia*/*potestas*. Kavka distinguishes between Hobbes's 'descriptive' and 'normative' analyses, but this does not match my distinction exactly, because Kavka's 'descriptive' analysis models ideally rational behaviour, not actual behaviour (Kavka, *Hobbesian Moral and Political Theory*, xiii, 19–20). Kavka actually complains that Hobbes fails to model human irrationality (438). But on my reading this is exactly what Hobbes's *potentia* offers; Kavka's complaint is an artefact of his own methodological strictures.

> For by Art is created that great LEVIATHAN called a COMMON-WEALTH, or STATE (in latine CIVITAS) which is but an Artificiall Man . . . in which, the *Soveraignty* [*Is qui summam habet Potestatem*] is the Artificall Soul, as giving life and motion to the whole body. . . . the *Pacts* and *Covenants*, by which the parts of this Body Politique were at first made, set together and united, resemble that *Fiat*, or the *Let us make man*, pronounced by God in the Creation. (L 16–17, Intro.1)

There is a change of theoretical apparatus, but the fundamental character of sovereign *potestas* is consistent with earlier texts. Hobbes offers a new theoretical account of the formation of a single will for the commonwealth, introducing the new technical terms 'personation' and 'authorization' (L 16).[21] Rather than subjects simply covenanting to obey commands (EL I.19.7) or not to resist commands (DC 5.7), now they make a more demanding covenant: to acknowledge the actions of the sovereign as their own. They

> appoint one Man, or Assembly of men, to beare their Person; and every one to owne, and acknowledge himselfe to be the Author of whatsoever he that so beareth their Person, shall Act, or cause to be Acted, in those things which concerne the Common Peace and Safetie; and therein to submit their Wills, every one to his Will, and their Judgements, to his Judgment. (L 260–261, 17.13)

This constitutes sovereign power *potestas*:

> And he that carryeth this Person is called SOVERAIGNE, and said to have Soveraigne Power [*Summam Potestatem*].[22] (L 262–263, 17.14)

Despite its new mediation by 'personation' and 'authorization', *potestas* still boils down to a juridical power.[23] Frost attempts to reduce sovereign power to a special kind of concrete power, claiming that 'the authorization of the

[21] Omar Astorga, 'Hobbes's Concept of Multitude', *Hobbes Studies 24* (2011): 5–14.

[22] In Hobbes's Latin, *summa potestas* refers to both the person of the sovereign and the power that the sovereign holds. Curiously, the equivalent term *summum imperium*, strongly preferred in *De Cive* (see, for instance, throughout DC 6) is almost entirely absent from *Leviathan*. I speculate that this is merely a rhetorical choice, as *imperium* perhaps has harsher overtones than *potestas*.

[23] Skinner argues that the change is merely a polemical ploy to co-opt the rhetoric of Hobbes's radical political opponents. Quentin Skinner, 'Hobbes on Persons, Authors and Representatives', in Springborg, *Cambridge Companion to Hobbes's 'Leviathan'*, 161. For the origin of this conception of authority in Roman private law, see Lee, *Popular Sovereignty*, 128–129.

sovereign consists in obedience'.[24] But to the contrary, obedience is owed in virtue of the authorization; authorization means the sovereign is entitled to subjects' compliance. The sovereign is so entitled, not only because compliance has been promised to it through covenant, but also more importantly because natural law stipulates that such a covenant is needed for peace (L 198–201, 14.4–5). It is still very important to get the sovereign's juridical power correct: Hobbes places first in his list of causes of the dissolution of the commonwealth the sovereign resting '*content with lesse Power* [*potestas*] *than to the Peace and defence of the Common-wealth is necessarily required*' (L 498–499, 29.3).

Nonetheless, this is no longer the only way to analyse the commonwealth. In the early texts, there is explicitly only a juridical conception of a union's power, indicated indifferently by both *potentia* and *potestas*; there is no explicit rubric under which to analyse concrete power. In *Leviathan*, the new conception of *potentia* now affords just such a rubric.[25] Insofar as one individual obeys another's command, she gives power *potentia* to the one she obeys (L 136–137, 10.20). This analysis can be applied to the person holding sovereignty: they have *potentia* precisely insofar as they garner actual obedience. And again, the analysis of individual relational power can readily be extended to characterize the power of the collectivity as a whole. Just as associations had their own *potentia*, according to their actual concrete tendency to garner and deploy allegiance, so too the commonwealth's *potentia* can be characterized, independently of its *potestas*. Where *De Cive* asserts that all commonwealths alike possess a stable *potentia* that is equated with their *imperium/potestas*, now the corresponding passage in *Leviathan* raises the concern that despite its stable *potestas*, a commonwealth might suffer a diminished *potentia* (DC 10.16; L 288–289, 19.4).

The two registers of analysis of political power are certainly interrelated. Hoekstra has shown that sufficient concrete power generates sovereign authority (*summa potestas*); and that insufficient concrete power removes it.[26] In other words, actual obedience can generate an entitlement to obedience,

[24] Correspondingly, Frost reduces the rights of sovereign power to strategic practices to secure sufficient concrete compliance (Frost, *Lessons from a Materialist Thinker*, 156–159, 165–169). As will become clear in Chapters 6 and 7, such a strategic view of political rights might be fairly attributed to Spinoza, but I cannot grant it to Hobbes, who consistently gives his science of political rights and duties pride of place in his writings, way ahead of his theory of concrete power, and who proudly names this science as his most profound philosophical contribution.

[25] See also Frost, *Lessons from a Materialist Thinker*, 156–159.

[26] Kinch Hoekstra, 'The *n* Turn in Hobbes's Political Philosophy', in *Leviathan after 350 years*, edited by Tom Sorell and Luc Foisneau (Oxford: Clarendon Press, 2004), 33–73.

and actual disobedience can destroy the entitlement, even without contract.[27] But the two registers of analysis nonetheless remain analytically distinct. Even while the power *potestas* of the sovereign remains constant, there can be fluctuations in concrete power *potentia*; *Leviathan* offers an account of the dynamics of concrete power on their own terms. Concrete power is no longer presumed to be a stable possession but is reconceived as a variable and relationally constituted effective capacity. This transformed conception of power illuminates the domain of lived politics below the neat categories of the juridical sphere.

4.3. Hobbes's Imperfect Departure from Scholasticism

Having established in Section 4.2 that Hobbes develops a new, non-juridical science of human collectivities, now in this section I briefly explain why he does so, and also I account for why this theme has not generally been emphasized or even recognized.[28] Indeed, the reader might view my claims with scepticism, given that several eminent interpreters have directly denied that there is such a science of concrete power.[29] I ultimately find these interpretations to be mistaken, but they are understandable. For the new view is not laid out with deliberate clarity in Hobbes's texts: I have had to reconstruct it from textual fragments. In this section, I account for the new view's merely interstitial presence in *Leviathan* in terms of Hobbes's ongoing negotiation with his scholastic intellectual inheritance. I then characterize Tuck's favoured model of sleeping sovereignty as a vestige of a scholastic understanding of power that cannot be maintained in the face of the new non-juridical analysis.

I identify two causes of Hobbes's doctrinal shifts on human collective power. First is the new science. As discussed in Chapter 2, Section 2.5, Hobbes's dissatisfaction with the adequacy of scholastic natural science was cultivated and developed in the company of other new philosophers in the

[27] This relation already held in the earlier texts, even though an explicit rubric to discuss concrete collective power was lacking: see the discussion of union by natural inequality of power in Chapter 3, Section 3.2.

[28] Many commentators simply neglect the theme, attributing to Hobbes only a juridical science of *potestas* and rights, for instance, Pettit, *Made with Words*, 115–140; Spragens, *The Politics of Motion*, 151–158; Tuck, *Hobbes*, 64–76, 109; Skinner, 'Hobbes on Persons', 157–180; Oakeshott, 'Introduction to *Leviathan*', 260–267; Brett, 'Matter, Forme, and Power', 99; Lee, *Popular Sovereignty*, 309–319.

[29] Goldsmith, *Hobbes's Science of Politics*, 176; Hindess, *Discourses of Power*, 35–39; Montag, *Bodies, Masses, Power*, 90–103; Sorell, *Hobbes*, 7–21, especially 17.

Mersenne circle. By the 1640s, Hobbes had largely rejected the scholastic approach to natural philosophy, replacing it with a mechanistic treatment of bodies in terms of their actual motions, without reference to any inner causal principle or a proper power and form. In Chapter 2, I drew implications of this shift in natural philosophy's foundations for Hobbes's study of individual human power, identifying a change from an essential to a relational understanding. In Chapter 3 and the present chapter, I drew implications for human collectivities. In Chapter 3, I argued that certain features of Hobbes's early philosophy of human action are inherited from scholasticism, preventing him from readily conceiving the power of associations as such, or the concrete power of unions. This conceptual blind spot is met with practical confidence that associations for the most part will be weak and unstable; and that unions will have concrete capacities in line with their juridical entitlement. Then in this chapter's Section 4.2, I showed that a ramification of the new relational conception of individual power is the possibility of conceiving the power of associations as such.

But in no way do I wish to suggest this constitutes a complete explanation: in particular, it does not explain why Hobbes did not immediately carry across the implications of his antischolastic natural science to the study of human action and politics. Rather, the causal role of the new natural science in changing his civil science must be contextualized within a larger and more directly political explanation. Between Hobbes's early and late political writings, England was shaken by tumultuous political events. Other commentators have charted the impact of the shifting political context of Hobbes's various writings;[30] my purpose in focussing on natural science is not in any way to detract from such accounts, but to complement them by articulating the precise conceptual shape that Hobbes's changing politics takes. Specifically, through the period of the English Civil War, long-standing political structures crumbled away, forcing into the open the weaknesses of theorization of informal power and the unjustified confidence in the theorization of formal power. Robust rebel groups emerged to challenge legitimate sovereignty. Hobbes's early model of individual faculty power combined into juridical union has difficulty accounting for the durability of informal collective powers, and it cannot directly analyse the variable practical efficacy of formal collective powers. Historical events forced sharper attention to these phenomena, and the core achievement of Hobbes's later model of relational

[30] See Chapter 1, footnotes 27 and 28.

power and its ramification for analysing collectivities is a superior account of these phenomena.

I have striven to demonstrate the textual presence of the concrete non-juridical conception of the power of collectivities in Section 4.2, and further corroboration will be provided in the discussion of seditious associations in Section 4.4.[31] Nonetheless, I have to concede that it remains fragmentary in the texts. The analysis of concrete power of collectivities always remains subordinated to the primary analysis of sovereign juridical power *potestas*. (By contrast, the analysis of individual relational power is perfectly explicit and prominent [L Ch 10].) I account for the merely interstitial presence of this theme as a result of the prior frame of Hobbes's philosophical system being retained, even as it is populated by a fundamentally changed natural science.

In the *Elements of Law*, the primary division of Hobbes's philosophical system is between bodies natural and bodies political. In *De Corpore* Hobbes restates the division as follows:

> For two chief kinds of Bodies, and very different from one another, offer themselves to those who search after their Generation & Properties; One whereof being the work of Nature, is called a *Naturall Body*; the other is called a *Commonwealth*, and is made by the wills and agreements of men. And from these spring the two parts of Philosophy called *Naturall* and *Civill*. (DCo 1.9)

Similarly, *Leviathan* makes a contrast between human bodies made by God and civil bodies made by humans (L 16–17, Intro.1). Commentators have puzzled over the relation between these two parts.[32] I have argued that in the early texts, the relation is actually easy, because both parts are sciences of bodies conceived as endowed with proper power (Chapter 3, Section 3.3). But there appears to be a problematic gap in the later writings between a mechanistic (and purely descriptive) understanding of natural bodies and a juridical (and therefore normative) understanding of civil bodies.[33]

[31] It is matched by a wider move away from an exclusively juridical treatment of human relations: for instance, Curley observes that there is a shift between early and late texts in the characterization of the state of nature. Whereas before rights were the cause of the state of war, in *Leviathan* they become the result of that state of war. Thomas Hobbes, *Leviathan: With Selected Variants from the Latin edition of 1668*, edited by Edwin Curley (Indianapolis: Hackett, 1994), 78 n. 9.

[32] See Chapter 3, footnote 23.

[33] Watkins's solution, to demonstrate that civil science is prudential rather than properly moral (*Hobbes's System of Ideas*, 51–53, 120), fails to address the larger question of why there shouldn't be a descriptive science of politics.

The gap arises because of the difference between the method of explaining divine and human creation. Natural bodies are understood as God's creations, and the science of natural bodies needs to grasp principles 'placed in the things themselves by the Authour of nature' (DCo 25.1). But what does this entail methodologically? Despite the reference to divine authorship, natural bodies are conceived without reference to God's intentions or purposes. As shown in Chapter 2, Section 2.5, *De Corpore* radically redefines the form or essence or principle of natural bodies, such that it is no longer an inner generative force with normative direction: instead, it is a similarity in how the body's behaviour strikes us. By contrast, the artificial body of the commonwealth is a union conceived precisely in terms of intentions: in terms of the purpose for which it is humanly instituted. It is a power for the sake of 'Peace and Common Defence' (L 262–263, 17.13) and is understood in terms of normative rights and obligations generated by that goal.[34] From Hobbes's point of view, the latter science is more robust. Just as in geometry, in civil science the objects of study are human made so we can know their principles directly (DC Ep.5–6; L Intro.16–21; DCo 1.5).[35]

Despite this deep difference, Hobbes presents the two kinds of science as a seamless whole. Malcolm argues that Hobbes's eagerness and confidence to propound a unified system of science prevented him from recognizing the fundamental discontinuity between the two kinds of science.[36] To this argument, I would add two observations. First, perhaps Hobbes's eagerness and confidence for a unified science was carried over from his earlier and more scholastic sketch of a system of philosophy, in which (as I have argued in Chapter 3) it made a certain amount of sense.[37] Second, the striking side effect of this division of sciences is that the possibility of a science of human collectivities as natural bodies is obscured. Indeed, the place in Hobbes's various tables of science for considering political bodies is always characterized in a normative way, in terms of rights and duties (L 130–131, Ch 9; DCo 1.9).

Nonetheless, there is a nagging sense that the juridical account of human collectivities is inadequate. On the new natural science, any body at all should

[34] Malcolm, 'Hobbes's Science of Politics', 149–152.

[35] Steven Shapin and Simon Schaffer, *Leviathan and the Air-Pump: Hobbes, Boyle, and the Experimental Life* (Princeton, NJ: Princeton University Press, 2011), 149–152.

[36] Malcolm, 'Hobbes's Science of Politics', 155. In a similar vein, Sorell advances an 'autonomy thesis' regarding the status of civil science (*Hobbes*, 7–28).

[37] Relatedly, Strauss argues that the core of Hobbes's philosophy predates his turn to 'naturalism' (Cartesian mechanistic natural science), insofar as it retains a priority for right. Strauss, *Political Philosophy of Hobbes*, ix–x, 169–170.

be analysable mechanistically, regardless of whether it is a divine or human creation, because the mechanistic science doesn't depend on specifying the inner purpose of the creator. Indeed, even though the commonwealth is made by human intentions, its behaviour may or may not conform to that intention. Even when a formal account of *potestas* is secured, the question of the concrete conduct of human collectivities constantly presses, and Hobbes casts about to find a conceptual frame within which to address it. Sometimes he falls into a distinction between the sovereign qua sovereign versus sovereign as a natural individual. He differentiates amongst regimes that are equal in *potestas* according to differences in the interests and motivations of the natural person holding sovereignty. For instance, he accounts for the greater failure rate of democracies compared to monarchies by arguing that the monarchs' personal interests align better with common prosperity than the personal interests of members of an assembly (L 288–289, 19.4). Similarly, he analyses the sovereign's behaviour in appeasing powerful subjects as its behaviour qua natural individual; this is contrasted with its power as the person of the commonwealth, by which it is entitled to obedience (L 496–497, 28.25; see also L 524–525, 30.6). This frame is complementary to the analysis I have advanced, but I preferred to reconstruct and draw together textual fragments to construct an account of the power of associations as such, as it provides a single framework in which to understand both informal collectivities and the concrete power of formal collectivities. My account proves powerful help in understanding the dynamics of sedition and political disorder, as I will show in Section 4.4.

My account of Hobbes's changing understanding of power illuminates why the idea of the 'sleeping sovereign', recently promoted by Tuck, is prominent in *De Cive* but largely absent in *Leviathan*. Tuck emphasizes Hobbes's distinction between sovereignty and government.[38] This distinction allows the possibility of a sleeping democratic sovereign: the people are not involved in the day-to-day business of government, but they retain sovereignty nonetheless, which they exercise through occasional plebiscitary expressions of their will. Tuck may be correct that the distinction is a defining characteristic of modern conceptions of democracy (or at least of modern French and American conceptions of democracy),[39] but on my analysis, it

[38] Tuck, *The Sleeping Sovereign*, ix–x, 86–106, drawing on DC 7.5–17. See also Lee, *Popular Sovereignty*, 309–319.

[39] Tuck, *The Sleeping Sovereign*, 249–250; similarly, Lee, *Popular Sovereignty*, 309–319.

simultaneously appears as a vestige of an earlier scholastic conceptual universe, whereby power can be thought as inner inherent potential.

Tuck draws almost exclusively on Hobbes's early texts to establish the distinction between sovereignty and government; he notes that it is not so evident in Hobbes's later writings, and he speculates that strategic or polemical reasons are responsible for that omission.[40] But there is a more conceptual explanation: the distinction between sovereignty and government is bound up with a particular conception of the sovereign's *potentia.* As I have argued, in *De Cive* it is not possible for sovereign *potentia* to vary independently from sovereign *potestas*, because by construction, the *potestas/imperium* and *potentia* of the sovereign are equivalent. *Potestas/imperium* are dominant by far in *De Cive*; but it is striking that when *potentia* is discussed, it is part of a distinction between power and act, *potentia* and *actus* (DC 7.16–17). Consider the crucial *De Cive* passage discussing the 'sleeping sovereign', where the people remain sovereign even though they delegate governance:

> [T]he intervals between meetings of citizens may be compared to the times when a *Monarch* is asleep; for the power is retained though there are no acts of commanding [*vtrobique enim actus imperandi cessant, potentia retinetur*]. (DC 7.16)[41]

In the scholastic frame, there can be a strong distinction between power and act: power can be the inherent principle of a thing even if it is not put to work. And it is this way of thinking about power that allows the distinction between sovereign and government. The *potentia* of the sovereign is defined by its juridical structure, and so even if a sovereign should delegate the day-to-day running of its commonwealth to a government, and even if the government should thereby consolidate immense concrete capacity to ignore the rightful sovereign, the sovereign still holds full *potentia* in light of its rightful authority.[42]

[40] Tuck, *The Sleeping Sovereign*, 104–105.

[41] Relatedly, earlier in the same passage, Hobbes argues that the sovereign people hold a 'direct and immediate power of action [*in potentiâ proximâ & immediatâ est ad agendum*]' and are able actually to give commands [*possit actu imperare*] even when they delegate governance (DC 7.16).

[42] But cf. Hoekstra, who argues that already in the early texts, Hobbes displays a tendency to privilege the de facto rather than the formal holder of sovereignty. Kinch Hoekstra, 'A Lion in the House: Hobbes and Democracy', in Brett, Tully, and Hamilton-Bleakley, *Rethinking the Foundations*, 200–201.

But on the later analysis, the distinction breaks down. As I showed in Chapter 2, Section 2.5, in Hobbes's later natural science, power is not separate from the act, but is just a prior temporal moment in a necessary chain of effects; if the act does not follow, there cannot be said to be a power. Applied to the commonwealth, I have argued that on Hobbes's later conception, *potentia* is not some inner property inherent in the juridical construction of the commonwealth and equivalent to *potestas*, nor is it a mere 'possibility';[43] rather, it is a concrete capacity linked to actual occurrences. A sovereign's *potentia* consists in its concrete harnessing of popular obedience, and faces competition from the *potentia* of other entities vying for that obedience. This concrete analysis of *potentia* is distinct from but has implications for the juridical analysis of *potestas*. A sovereign is sovereign not only by having *potestas* to rule, but also by having sufficient *potentia* to match that *potestas*; should *potentia* fall below a certain level, then it undermines the sovereign's *potestas*. The sovereign's *potentia* is not separate from exercise, as it was in the early texts; power *potentia* is defined by its exercise, in actual events.

Let me now unpack the implications of this conceptual scheme for the practice of delegated governance. Certainly, in principle a sovereign can retain full *potentia* even as it delegates functions of governance. But on Hobbes's later view, this is not due to the inherent juridical structure of sovereign power. Rather, *potentia* is retained only insofar as concrete allegiance is maintained. Consider first the case of a captive sovereign, which Tuck takes to have a structure similar to the sleeping sovereign (L 346–347, 21.25).[44] One can imagine the people still feeling allegiance to a captive sovereign, and expressing this through continued obedience to the sovereign's magistrates, even as the sovereign is in prison and unable to rule directly. However, after a time, there is a risk that the allegiance de facto transfers to the magistrates, and if at a much later date the sovereign ruler is freed and wishes to exert their will against those magistrates, then the people might no longer be willing to comply. Turning to the core case of the sleeping sovereign, on the new analysis, there is only popular sovereignty if the decision of the popular assembly concretely garners obedience. And Hobbes expresses grave concerns that any sovereign assembly delegating the exercise of its sovereign power *potestas* will tend to provoke rebellion when it attempts to reclaim that power (L 498–501, 29.3): in other words, it will find that it has lost

[43] Tuck, *The Sleeping Sovereign*, 94.
[44] Ibid., 93–94.

its concrete *potentia*. Hobbes's later analysis of power would view 'sleeping sovereignty' as a risky distraction from the real locus of political control.

For Hobbes's later analysis, the sleeping sovereign is not in principle impossible, but it is highly risky, and its conditions of possibility vitiate the robust popular control that Tuck desires. In order to avoid provoking resistance and rebellion by pursuing more substantial and contentious goals, a democratic sleeping sovereign that wishes to keep its *potentia* never aspires to do anything beyond uncontroversial constitutional plebiscites every few decades.[45] But this is a pyrrhic victory: what use is a conception of a sovereign that retains sufficient popular *potentia* to render its *potestas* effective only insofar as it respects extreme limitations on its scope of action? In this light, it is easy to understand why Hobbes drops the sleeping sovereign when writing *Leviathan*.[46]

4.4. The Political Problem in Hobbes's Later Writings

The political problem, first introduced in Chapter 3, is that there may be a gap between the obedience to which the sovereign is juridically entitled and what it actually receives. Hindess observes that 'sovereign power is a *right* to make use of the powers of its subjects, but it does not follow from this, as Hobbes would sometimes have us believe, that the sovereign will therefore have an effective *capacity* to make use of those powers'.[47] In light of Hobbes's later texts' changed theoretical analysis of collective *potentia* and its separation from *potestas*, it becomes possible to reformulate: the political problem is the problem of a divergence between sovereign *potestas* and sovereign *potentia*. In his early texts, Hobbes presumes that the sovereign's punitive incentive

[45] The recent case of Brexit illustrates the problem with more controversial exercise of plebiscitary democratic sovereignty. The authority of the popular vote for the UK to leave the European Union was widely contested, with parliamentarians and members of the public seriously (although ultimately unsuccessfully) arguing that the decision to leave should not be implemented. Even if a sleeping sovereign is possible, it risks insurrection as soon as it attempts any controversial decision. And this insurrection is not necessarily merely the forces of reaction, the vested interests of the ruling government contrary to the interests of the sovereign. Rather, insurrection can be motivated by the suspicion that the very will of the popular plebiscitary sovereign itself has been insidiously shaped and formed by a different set of vested interests. See further discussion of the power distortions within democratic fora in Section 4.4, but also in more detail in Chapter 5, Sections 5.3–4.

[46] Beyond his principled defence of plebiscitary democracy, Tuck also defends the quality of such a democracy's decisions, remarking that on this point the historical record is not too bad (Tuck, *The Sleeping Sovereign*, 257 n. 8). But on my analysis, this is just a reflection of the powerlessness of the plebiscitary sovereign.

[47] Hindess, *Discourses of Power*, 15; see also 35–39.

will be sufficient to render subjects obedient, and to bring its effective power to meet the power to which it is entitled. In this section, I argue this picture comes under pressure in his later civil science: the political problem becomes pressing.[48] I already argued that a sleeping democratic sovereign faces very nigh insuperable difficulty in this respect, hence it is dropped from Hobbes's later texts. But now I show that even an ordinary active and governing sovereign faces a grave version of the political problem. The changed political ontology envisages a social sphere much less amenable to decisive unification, and consequently forces a potentially much greater gulf between the sovereign's entitled *potestas* and its concrete capacity.

To clear the ground, I wish to distinguish the political problem from a related issue in the contemporary literature: the threat to sovereignty from rightful rebel associations. For Hobbes, no one is obliged to cooperate in their own execution; thus, any subject who faces such penalty can rightly rebel. If there are many such subjects, this amounts to a collective right to rebel against the sovereign. Specifically, Hobbes argues that initially illegitimate seditious rebel associations have a right to continue their insurrection because, with a bounty on their heads, their ongoing action simply amounts to defending their own lives:

> [I]n case a great many men together, have already resisted the Sovereign Power unjustly, or committed some Capitall crime, for which every one of them expecteth death, whether they have not the Liberty then to joyn together, and assist, and defend one another? Certainly they have: For they but defend their lives, which the Guilty man may as well do, as the Innocent. There was indeed injustice in the first breach of their duty; Their bearing of Arms subsequent to it, though it be to maintain what they have done, is no new unjust act. (L 340–341, 21.17)

There has been considerable discussion of whether allowing such a right of rebellion is consistent with Hobbes's larger system of absolute sovereign right.[49] However, this juridical discussion of right is tangential to my investigation of the play of forces between sovereign and multitude: I focus on the

48 Johnston and Astorga both note an increase in the sovereign's vulnerability to a seditious multitude. Johnston, *The Rhetoric of 'Leviathan'*, 78–80; Astorga, 'Hobbes's Concept of Multitude', 5–14.

49 Kavka, *Hobbesian Moral and Political Theory*, 433–436; Sreedhar, *Hobbes on Self-Defence*, 132–175; Jean Hampton, *Hobbes and the Social Contract Tradition* (Cambridge: Cambridge University Press, 1986), 197–207.

non-juridical question, can the sovereign in a Hobbesian polity be expected to have sufficient concrete power to function as it is entitled to do? Whether a rebel association is rightful or not makes little difference to this question. The rebels' rightful status is readily within the sovereign's control: Hobbes argues that the right of continued rebellion disappears if the sovereign offers a pardon (L 340–341, 21.17). But the concrete threat that the rebels pose may continue unchanged even when their right is taken away. The political problem asks, quite apart from questions of right, will there in fact be rebellions in Hobbes's commonwealth, will moments of rebellion gain momentum or dissipate, and how successful can we expect a sovereign to be in containing them? Will Hobbes's commonwealth concretely deliver the peace that it promises?

In the early texts, there is no explicit rubric for the concrete power of the sovereign, but nonetheless Hobbes is confident that it will be sufficient, as I argued in Chapter 3. The multitude, or in other words the population beneath the sovereign, is constituted of flat, fragmented equality of power among subjects: it certainly lacks collective agency as such, and no individual within it has sufficient power to challenge the sovereign. The only way in which the sovereign order is threatened is when out of a multitude a formal faction is established for the express purpose of overthrowing the sovereign; associations are so ineffective that they pose no threat. Correspondingly, the commonwealth is secure so long as it can prevent the formation of seditious unions.[50]

In *Leviathan*, the multitude is populated by moderately durable associations. This is just the structure of social life: the associations simply emerge according to the spontaneous dynamics of the pursuit of power, as described in Section 4.2, and they are not formed with seditious intent. But Hobbes shows a new and persistent concern with these informal associations: worrying about eminent individuals, masters with too many servants, the immoderate greatness of towns, and the accumulation of treasure by monopolies or farms (L 372–373, 460–461, 516–517, 22.31, 27.15, 29.19, 29.21). He

[50] Abizadeh's argument identifying the cause of commonwealth breakdown fits better with this early view than with the later one. He argues that for Hobbes, disagreement is the primary cause of conflict, because disagreement constitutes dishonour, which diminishes the dishonoured person's feeling of power (i.e., their glory. Arash Abizadeh, 'Hobbes on the Causes of War: A Disagreement Theory', *American Political Science Review 105*, no. 2 (2011): 308–310. Abizadeh identifies this as a problem primarily afflicting the ambitious and idle (ibid., 311–313). However, as I will argue, on the later texts, conflict is not just a question of the hurt feelings of idle aristocrats, but a result of a concrete social power structure, in which the masses seek protection and avoid harm from whichever patron appears most promising to them.

also inserts a new anthropology of religion, tracing the constant tendency for the emergence of religious groupings from pervasive human passions of curiosity and anxiety, and worrying that new religions can resurge at any time (L 164–171, 176–179, 180–181, 12.1–11, 12.20, 12.23).[51] Any de facto social groupings are of concern: whether familial, socio-economic, or religious (L 372–373, 22.32).[52]

I now piece together Hobbes's scattered remarks to reconstruct exactly why he finds these associations so troublesome, even though they are not formed for the sake of sedition. I argue that once the multitude features an associational structure of powers, the punitive threat of the sovereign is no longer so effective in motivating subjects' conduct; but eliminating this structure is far from straightforward.[53]

First, the associations provide means for sedition, if the intent does arise. In the early texts, the means of sedition are secured only after an active decision to form a faction for the purpose of sedition, because the only effective faction is one structured as a formal collective. In *Leviathan*, the means (power blocs not dependent on the sovereign's pleasure) are always being generated, even without any seditious intent. Thus, should an ambitious individual develop seditious plans, they may already have at their disposal the means to put these plans into action; it will be that much more difficult for the sovereign to arrest these plans.[54]

> [P]opularity of a potent subject (unless the commonwealth has very good caution of his fidelity) is a dangerous disease, because the people (which should receive their motion from the authority of the sovereign), by the flattery and by the reputation of an ambitious man, are drawn away from their obedience to the laws, to follow a man of whose virtues and designs they have no knowledge. (L 516–517, 29.20)

[51] Religion poses two distinct threats: (i) it constitutes a this-worldly power bloc; (ii) it inspires subjects with a fear of otherworldly punishment (L Ch 38). In my argument, I focus on (i), but I do not deny (ii). Indeed, this is also a newly prominent theme in *Leviathan* (L 226–227, 15.8).

[52] Scientific and intellectual groups were also problematic. Shapin and Schaffer, *Leviathan and the Air-Pump*, 320–331. See Zagorin for a historical overview of the forms of social resistance in this period. Zagorin, *Rebels and Rulers*, 1–50.

[53] Montag also argues that Hobbes is acutely aware of associations as a threat to sovereignty, drawing most especially on *Behemoth*. Montag argues that Hobbes has no theoretical resources to grasp these associations (*Bodies, Masses, Powers*, 90–103). But this is exactly what the theory of collective *potentia* offers. (See also Kavka, *Hobbesian Moral and Political Theory*, 264–272.)

[54] In this light, Baumgold's characterization of the problem of *Leviathan* as elite conflict is correct but incomplete: the reason elite conflict is so troublesome is that elite power is deeply rooted in the everyday fabric of social relations. Baumgold, *Hobbes's Political Theory*, 2–3, 121–122.

This concern is further developed in *Behemoth*, in which the wealth, influence, and popular support of religious groupings and great towns are identified as the matrix of England's descent into civil war (B 108–111).

The second reason why these groups are dangerous to the sovereign is even more serious. The very existence of other powers within the social order in itself means the sovereign itself has less concrete power *potentia*. Powerful subjects tend to engage in the commonplace pursuit of advantage; they do not in general have the intent to seize power or to destroy the civil order, but they do want to have things their way. In particular, they think they ought not be punished, and hope to escape punishment.

> And that such as have multitude of potent kindred, and popular men, that have gained reputation amongst the multitude, take courage to violate the laws from a hope of oppressing the power to whom it belongeth to put them in execution. (L 460–461, 27.15)

The sovereign knows that when it wants to issue or enforce some command that is inconvenient to the powerful subject, it cannot presume it will secure obedience from that subject, and perhaps not from the subject's supporters either. For the powerful subject and their followers have the power simply not to comply. They may comply in some cases, they may limit their reaction to noncompliance, or they may be provoked into hostile retaliation to teach the sovereign not to trespass on their concerns. This is vividly illustrated by King Charles I's abortive attempts to impose the Book of Common Prayer on Scotland and to demand ship money (B 142–146, 155–157). In all cases, the sovereign's power is weakened. It cannot simply ignore the fact of powerful subjects in society and make no concessions to them, because any successful display of disobedience publicizes the subjects' power and gains them even more allegiance. For this reason, crime from presumption of strength giving impunity is much more politically pernicious than the everyday crime from hope of not being discovered (L 470–471, 27.30).

However, no alternative direct response from the sovereign is clearly better. For if the sovereign acknowledges the limits on its own concrete effective power, it is drawn into a game of appeasement, which can only end badly. The sovereign may bestow benefits on a subject (whether exempting from punishment or making policy to please) 'for fear of some power and ability he hath to do hurt to the Common-wealth' (L 496–497, 28.25). Such benefits are 'extorted by fear' and are in this sense sacrifices that the sovereign 'makes for the appeasing the discontent of him he thinks more potent than himselfe' (L 496–497, 28.25). However, this strategy does not encourage obedience; quite the opposite, it encourages increased extortion, as Charles I found after his attempts to appease the Scots and Parliament backfired[55] (B 204–205, 234–242, 260). For achieving the deference of the sovereign makes visible the subject's power, garnering more allegiance. Seeing the sovereign's weakness emboldens others to press for concessions too. This may defer civil war, '[Y]et the danger grows still the greater, and the public ruin is more assured' (L 544–545, 30.24).

The lesson from this analysis is a dispiriting one. Power groups spontaneously generate and, once established, cannot readily be eviscerated without negative consequences. Instead, powerful subjects need to be cut down before their influence grows (L 544–545, 30.24). There are measures that can, and indeed must, be taken to prevent power blocs from reaching politically disruptive dimensions. For instance, a sovereign should prohibit subjects from holding more servants than necessary (L 372–373, 33.31); and any assembly that cannot give an account of its reasons for existing should be disbanded and punished as seditious (L 374–375, 22.34). But these kinds of measures are difficult to implement, and will need to be undertaken with utmost skill and delicacy if they are not to backfire. For example, Hobbes says subjects should be prevented from honouring fellow subjects, for this would constitute unequal powers not subject to the control of the sovereign (L 526–527, 30.8). But almost all social conduct has a valence as honour or dishonour, and so it will be impossible to eliminate honour entirely (L 136–139, 10.19–36). Furthermore, functionally, not all power differences can be suppressed. The commander of the army needs to be popular to do his job, even though this is a danger to the sovereign (L 550–551, 30.28). Hobbes suggests that the sovereign can minimize the danger from the popularity of a subject by itself being popular (L 550–551, 30.29). But a sovereign will have to be very careful how it seeks to become popular if that status is not already secured; for as already discussed, granting benefits extorted by fear is a highly dangerous political strategy, and pandering to the people does just this (L 496–497, 28.25). While a sovereign can take measures to try to deflate and level out such powers, this will be an ongoing task for which success is uncertain.[56]

[55] To be sure, Hobbes says the Parliament also actively desired to usurp sovereignty.

[56] Shapin and Schaffer argue that for Hobbes, the need for social order determines his scientific method; in particular, his materialist monism and his geometrical conception of civil science (Shapin

Thus, the new political ontology shows that the sovereign will face a constant need to maintain its power in the face of spontaneously emergent powers in the populace; such powers are a threat even when they have no seditious intent.[57] On top of this, Hobbes does not display such confidence as previously that deliberately formed seditious unions can be contained (L 370–373, 516–517, 22.29–30, 29.20). The result is that it is a challenge for the sovereign to achieve actual effective capacity *potentia* commensurate to its entitlement *potestas*; peace is not so easily or definitively achieved as it was in the earlier texts. If the image of Hobbes's early science of politics was a unifier over a fragmented field, the late image is of the sovereign as imperfect hegemon, competing on a plane of *potentia* with emergent groups.

In the face of Hobbes's authoritarian politics, some readers might celebrate the emergence of popular groups putting up resistance to the sovereign's unfettered rule. Surely this represents the resurgence of unmediated popular power, despite Hobbes's best efforts to repress it?[58] Hobbes does not admit this himself. Even granting associations their own power *potentia*, Hobbes denies that they might have agency. For despite having their own power, a fundamental difference still remains between associations and unions: associations lack a single will (L 248–251, 16.13–14).[59] But it does not take much effort to think around this requirement: just as the process of an association's formation endows it with a coherent power, it simultaneously establishes a robust de facto convergence of wills. Certainly, the association does not have the formal juridical authority to speak for its members, and correspondingly individuals can dissent from the collective view without doing wrong. But in practice, all might largely find themselves in concurrence, through the processed outlined in Section 4.2. And surely there is something meaningful in this, such that it is possible to attribute a de facto mass agency to this group according to its de facto convergence of wills.

and Schaffer, *Leviathan and the Air-Pump*, 14–15, 21, 81, 99). My argument draws attention to a reverse process: an (unexpected, unwelcome) corollary of Hobbes's materialist science when extended to human collectivities generates difficulties for the efficacy of the civil science.

[57] I concede that *De Cive* already displays an incipient worry with emergent powers even when they are not deliberately for the purpose of sedition (DC 10.7). However, *De Cive* awkwardly analyses this still in the language of formal unions, which is unconvincing for examples such as popularity and wealth (DC 13.13).

[58] Montag, *Bodies, Masses, Power*, 90–103. Also suggestive are May's examples of the masses storming the Bastille, of the Arab Spring (May, *Limiting Leviathan*, 167–173).

[59] Skinner, 'Hobbes on Persons', 162–163.

The crucial question is, what shape does this concrete collective power take, and is this de facto agency of the people necessarily appealing? It is a mistake to focus on the easy case of the multitude rising up against an unequivocally wicked tyrant. In virtue of the specific exigencies of that case, popular agency is unified and has a good aim, uncontroversially advancing the common good.[60] But putting aside the easy case, what is the character of the concrete power and de facto agency of the people more generally? Frost attributes to Hobbes an appealing picture of 'people power'. If power is truly relationally constituted, then the restless pursuit of power after power needn't be conflictual; even in trying to secure their own self-interest, people should seek cooperative and peaceful forms of coexistence. People should help one another because everyone's power is interdependent and socially constituted.[61] But Frost herself is clear that she is sketching a mere rational possibility, and not what is in fact likely to obtain; Frost upholds the Hobbesian view that in real life, without a sovereign, social groups fall into conflict with one another.[62]

Indeed, Hobbes's own analysis draws attention to two highly unsatisfactory features of this de facto mass agency. First, the multitude is not likely to produce a single association encompassing all its members; the more standard picture would be the emergence of multiple and competing power blocs, sometimes compounding but other times in competition and conflict with one another. Second, even if there is an association encompassing much of the membership of the multitude, this mass agent is no pure domain of prepolitical equality.[63] For the grounds of association are not horizontal convergence. The mass agent emerges and finds it stability in the layered patterns of assistance and deference amongst power-seeking individuals; and there is nothing to ensure that this process has symmetrical egalitarian results. Rather, as established in Section 4.2, there are oligarchic tendencies in the formation of associations: power blocs form around the wealthy, the mighty, the seductive orator. The de facto will of an association reflects the

60 Even Hobbes recognizes that a very wicked tyrant fails against the normative standard of the common good, although for him it does not follow that such an uprising is rightful (L Ch 30).

61 Frost, *Lessons from a Materialist Thinker*, 135, 140, 146, 169–170.

62 Ibid., 146–148. The commentator who takes the appealing picture of a Hobbesian 'people power' the furthest is James R. Martel, *Subverting the Leviathan: Reading Thomas Hobbes as a Radical Democrat* (New York: Columbia University Press, 2007), 3, 13. Unlike Frost, Martel doesn't recognize any difficulty for the realization of this popular power.

63 Hoekstra hints at this problem ('Lion in the House', 217). Similar ideas find a classic exposition in the quite different context of 1960s US feminism: Jo Freeman, 'The Tyranny of Structurelessness', *Berkeley Journal of Sociology 17* (1972): 151–164.

degree of hierarchy in the group, as lesser members defer to the opinions and preferences of those whom they hope to propitiate. There is no natural convergence of the will of an association with the egalitarian common interest of its members.

In this chapter and the previous one, I have traced the changed conceptualization of human power *potentia* from a proper individual power to a relational power. The changed conceptualization of *potentia* changes the stakes of the political game. Rather than there being an originary prepolitical domain with each human individual in possession of their own *potentia*, and the alienation of this *potentia* only occurring juridically through contract, on the new picture, our *potentiae* are always already more or less imbricated with the powers of others in more or less hierarchical ways. Against this backdrop, the shift to politics represents a change of the forces to which we are subordinated rather than a radical break; sovereignty appears not as an imposition on a prior absence of power relations, but rather an attempt to reorder them.

The transformation of Hobbes's treatment of power has far-reaching consequences for his science of politics. Juridical arguments may generate an account of right and authority, but a cursory appeal to punitive incentives is insufficient to establish the possibility that political order under such a juridical model could stably exist. In the later texts, establishing the correct doctrine of juridical *potestas/imperium* now needs to be distinguished from and supplemented by a difficult and quite separate analysis of how the concretely causal *potentia* to which the sovereign is entitled is to be achieved and sustained. The political problem presses, with the sovereign continually combatting the spontaneous associational dynamics of the social field. Nor is capitulation to these associations an option: the associations are conflictual amongst themselves, and in any case, they are unappealingly oligarchic. In the next chapter, I trace out Hobbes's own solution.

5

Repressive Egalitarianism

5.1. Introduction

How should popular power be understood? One straightforward way is to focus on power as formal juridical authority, then to judge its popularity by asking whether the designated holder of that authority formally includes everyone. Such an approach can reasonably claim Hobbesian filiation. But Hobbes's late sharpening of the distinction between power as authority *potestas* and power as *potentia* points to an alternative Hobbesian possibility: to understand political power as *potentia*, concerned with the actual durable production of effects. This alternative possibility offers a superior analysis of both power and of popularity in politics. First, regarding power, the focus on juridical structure illuminates little if the juridical holder of power does not substantively govern the workings of society, whereas a focus on *potentia* addresses this substantive functioning directly. Second, regarding popularity, a juridical account of popularity is unable to identify or recognize emergent hierarchies and dependencies amongst formal equals, whereas the late Hobbesian analysis of power as *potentia* systematically makes such dependencies visible.

To this point, I have established that Hobbes himself becomes acutely attentive to the question of concrete power *potentia* in his later writings, and that he puts forward a relational, socially embedded conception of that power. Furthermore, I have established that this new analysis of power reveals a previously downplayed problem, which I have called the political problem: that sovereign *potestas* might lack the *potentia* to which it is entitled. In his later texts, juridical Hobbesianism cannot stand without attention to the underlying dynamics of power (*potentia*).

But I have not yet established (a) Hobbes's solution to the political problem, nor (b) what positively the popularity of this power as *potentia* might involve, and Hobbes's own attitude towards such popularity. In the present chapter, I address these two remaining issues, and thereby complete my investigation of late Hobbesian understanding of popular power. First, in Sections 5.2 and

Potentia. Sandra Leonie Field, Oxford University Press (2020). © Oxford University Press.
DOI: 10.1093/oso/9780197533864.001.0001

5.3, I reconstruct Hobbes's own solution to the political problem, including its critical implications for democratic forms of decision-making. Second, in Sections 5.4 and 5.5, I argue that Hobbes's late writings evince a certain minimal conception of and commitment to the popularity of *potentia*, insofar as he offers what I will call a repressive egalitarianism. Previous scholarship has drawn attention to Hobbes's hostility towards the independent power of churches; repressive egalitarianism represents a generalization of this hostility. Repressive egalitarianism identifies the primary obstacle to popular empowerment to be informal oligarchic distortions to the *potentia* of the sovereign; correspondingly, it commits itself to crushing informal power structures in the polity.

Hobbes's resultant positive political program is highly ambivalent to contemporary sensibilities. But even if unpersuaded by this program, the reader can still appreciate the critical insight that Hobbes offers: that any vote or measure of mass opinion in a commonwealth that has not eliminated the informal oligarchic structure of the social body can only have very weak claim to be meaningfully popular. I conclude that Tuck's Hobbesian plebiscitary democracy, far from being the exemplary expression of the power of the people, is likely to be neither popular nor powerful.

5.2. Internal and External Motivations of Subjects

Hobbes's new attention to concrete power *potentia* is deeply unsettling for his science of politics. For Hobbes, the fundamental purpose of politics is to avoid war; absolute sovereign power *potestas* is offered as the unique means to that end. Subjects in the disorderly and conflictual multitude hand over all their right to a sovereign whose unified absolute authority commands total obedience and thereby eliminates war. What I have called the political problem is the problem of a divergence between the sovereign's juridically entitled power and its concrete capacity, between (in the terms of the later texts) sovereign *potestas* and sovereign *potentia*. The incipient form of the problem is faction and sedition; its full expression is the dissolution of the commonwealth and civil war. In the later texts, there is a new political ontology of spontaneously emergent oligarchic groups. Sovereign power *potestas* finds itself vulnerable in the face of emergent concrete powers of the multitude: garnering the obedience to which it is entitled is no longer straightforward.

Let me now reconstruct Hobbes's own solution to the political problem. In his later texts, I argue, Hobbes envisages stabilizing the sovereign's *potentia* by transforming the internal motivations of both subjects (Section 5.2) and sovereign (Section 5.3) to align better with the duties specified by his civil science; this is done through a program of political rhetoric and education.

Duty and obligation are important to Hobbes's civil science, early and late. As outlined in Chapters 2 through 4, natural law is reason's recommendations for pursuing the ultimate good of self-preservation (DC 3.26, 3.33; L 242–243, 15.41). There is an obligation, or duty, to abide by natural law.[1] The central political obligation posed by natural law is the obligation to establish and uphold a commonwealth endowed with certain essential rights (EL II.1; DC Ch 6; L Ch 18). Duty requires that subjects within commonwealths should recognize these rights; in particular, they should submit totally to the sovereign such that they obey its commands regardless of their content, and they should not arrogate any rights to themselves.[2] For the sovereign, duty requires that it should rule for *salus populi*, for the good of the people (EL II.9.1; DC 13.2; L 520–521, 30.1). From the juridical point of view, once direct threats to individuals' self-preservation are removed, then duties must be performed (DC 3.27; L 240–241, 15.36). But from the concrete point of view, there remains the question of how the conformity of conduct with duty is actually brought about. Free moral choice is not a sufficient explanation, because Hobbes denies free will; rather, Hobbes needs to account for the concrete causality that generates volitions to act in accord with duty (EL I.19.7; DC 5.8; L 326–327, 21.4). The question of the causality of acting in accord with duty is especially pressing when it comes to subjects. If a significant proportion of the population fails to do their duty, then this amounts to insubordination. In this case, the sovereign faces the political problem and peace is not secure.

Suppose we make a distinction between two components of volitional[3] human behaviour: what I will call internal motivation and external

[1] Warrender's classic exegesis drives home the centrality of duty and obligation, even if his thesis about the divine grounding of that duty remains highly controversial. Warrender, *Political Philosophy of Hobbes*.

[2] Except retaining the right of self-defence in extremis (DC 6.13; L 336–343, 21.11–21); see Sreedhar, *Hobbes on Self-Defence*, for an extended discussion.

[3] That is, behaviour that is mediated by a desire or appetite of the will. Hobbes's own term is 'voluntary'; but Pettit suggests substituting 'volitional'. For in Hobbes's use, the term 'voluntary' is expansive, excluding only physically forced behaviour such as bodily movement from being pushed or enchained (EL I.15.13; L 92–3, 6.54); whereas in common use, 'voluntary' refers to a subset of will-mediated action, namely, where the will is formed under fair conditions. Pettit, *Made with Words*, 67–68.

motivation respectively, a distinction I will characterize in detail later.[4] Over this and the next section, I make explicit the limitation of my earlier analysis, which considered only external motivation. I now ask, was this an accurate rendition of Hobbes's civil science? Does internal motivation by duty play any role in avoiding the political problem and sustaining peace? And if so, how is such motivation brought about? I argue that Hobbes's early texts provide a primarily external account of subject and sovereign motivation to generate action in conformity with duty, and this external motivation is presumed to be politically sufficient. Across his oeuvre, however, there is an evolution in Hobbes's views such that his later texts increasingly demand the internalization of duties, by both subjects and sovereign, if the political problem is to be resolved. Subjects' internal grasp of duty renders their allegiance to the sovereign more resilient and less vulnerable to capture by the lure of seditious leaders (this section); the sovereign's internal grasp of duty improves the quality of its rule (Section 5.3). The means of this internalization is pedagogical and persuasive: the populace is to be educated; and the sovereign is to receive good counsel.

I start by specifying my distinction between internal and external. By the internal components of volitional action, I mean the individual's moral psychology, including passions, desires, and understanding. By external components of action, I mean incentives and threats, or in other words, those external goods and bads that connect with the individual's moral psychology to generate action. My exegesis in the previous chapters has so far accounted for variations in human behaviour exclusively through change in external incentives and threats. Specifically, subjects' political behaviour is modelled as being generated primarily by the imposition of sovereign punishment; in the later texts I have also stressed the availability of social support and status. Of course these external incentives and threats generate action only when they encounter an individual's moral psychology. But to this point, I have simply presumed a certain average moral psychology, in which the internal components of motivation are taken as more or less static, and which (in particular) lacks any internalization of duty.

According to this average moral psychology, there are desires for external goods: in the early texts, there are underlying desires for glory and advantages and fear of their loss; in the later texts, it is desire for power and

[4] This is a distinction between kinds of motivation for action and must not be confused with the contrast *in foro interno* versus *in foro externo* (EL I.17.10; DC 3.17), which is a distinction between intention and action.

fear of its loss, as established in Chapter 4, Section 4.2. Duty is not essentially opposed to these desires: after all, on Hobbes's view, complying with the duty posed by natural law (and therefore by reason itself) is the only means to secure any durable advantages or power.[5] But in practice, desires do not order themselves in a coherent way; in result, duty has no inherent motivational traction. To the contrary, average moral psychology displays a characteristic short-sightedness and is deeply biased towards the present. 'Men cannot divest themselves of the irrational desire to reject future goods for the sake of present goods (which inevitably entail unexpected evils)' (DC 3.32). People pursue their desires in a moderately but imperfectly rational way, as the urgency of present passions obscures the means to longer-term satisfaction (L 254–255, 17.2, 282–283, 18.20). Hobbes does allow the in-principle possibility of changing internal motivations, in particular, of subjects more or less thoroughly internalizing their duty. For a subject might come to feel the connection between doing their duty and achieving the future goods that they desire; if this connection is sufficiently vivid, they might be able to conduct themselves in the dutiful way even without the pressure of immediate incentives or threats. For instance, a philosopher, blessed with a complex combination of natural wit and suitable life experiences, might have a heightened capacity to focus on long-term consequences (EL I.10; L 104–105, 110–111, 8.2, 8.14). But for the average moral psychology that I have presumed to this point, there is no such internalization of duty. If conformity with duty is to be achieved, it will be in response to short- to medium-term external goods and bads.

In my preceding chapters' exegesis of Hobbes's texts, was I right to ignore internal motivation by duty? In Hobbes's early texts, I claim, the internalization of duty by subjects is not central to the good functioning of the commonwealth. To be sure, it is essential that subjects' wills be materially shaped to conform their conduct with their duty of obedience. But as I argued in Chapter 3, Section 3.3, the shaping of wills is amply achieved through external incentives, principally terror of the sovereign's sword (EL I.19.7; DC 5.8); for all subjects are powerfully motivated by a fear of imminent death.[6] In a properly established commonwealth where the sovereign claims correct rights of sovereignty, the sovereign's overwhelming punitive threat will

[5] The desire for glory, by contrast, always appears to be opposed to duty (DC 1.2).

[6] The worry that a fear of punishment in the afterlife might be greater than the fear of imminent death is absent in *The Elements of Law*, but it does start to emerge in *De Cive*: compare EL II.8.5 with DC 12.2.

generally conform subjects' behaviour to their duties even without subjects having any internal appreciation of the logic of the rights of sovereignty, or any internal attachment to the corresponding dutiful behaviour.

It is true that Hobbes identifies subjects holding seditious beliefs and incorrect political doctrines as one risk factor in the breakdown of the commonwealth, because these beliefs encourage subjects to deny their duties and challenge the sovereign's rights (EL II.8.4–10; DC 12.1–8). But without hope of success, incorrect doctrine is insufficient to generate rebellion (EL II.8.11; DC 12.11); and as I argued in Chapter 3, Section 3.4, the social ontology of fragmented equality makes it easy to neutralize this risk. Each subject has no hope of success alone; nor are there any enduring associations; and it is easy to eviscerate any seditious unions. As a result, it is just not so important to the functioning of the commonwealth that everyone understand and have a deep sense of their duty. Correspondingly, while Hobbes does briefly discuss the teaching of doctrine, he does not dwell on it (EL II.9.8; DC 13.9).

Any internalization of the duties of subjects in Hobbes's early civil science is important, not so much to establish the functioning of the commonwealth, but instead to moralize the political relationship. In the Epistle Dedicatory to *The Elements of Law*, Hobbes outlines the significance of his civil science: '[T]he conclusions thereof are of such nature, as, for want of them, government and peace have been nothing else to this day, but mutual fear' (EL Ep). In other words, he does not deny that government and peace are possible without explicitly knowing his doctrine. They are possible, but prior to his doctrine, subjects in such an (unknowingly) well-ordered polity understood their obedience and deference as mere fearful responses to violent threats. Learning Hobbes's doctrine allows individuals to rationally and morally affirm what they are (within a well-constituted commonwealth) driven by fear to accept in any case.[7]

Now turning to *Leviathan*, I do not deny that external incentives, notably the fear of punishment, remain essential in conforming subjects' wills to meet with their duty of obedience as stipulated by natural law.

> For if we could suppose a great Multitude of men to consent in the observation of Justice, and other Lawes of Nature, without a common Power to keep them all in awe [*sine Potentia communi quae posset omnes cogere*]; we

[7] DC stands as a transitional text: mass knowledge of duty has a greater practical role in its civil science than in EL. Compare EL Ep with DC Ep.6, Pref.5.

> might as well suppose all Man-kind to do the same; and then there neither would be, nor need to be any Civill Government, or Common-wealth at all; because there would be Peace without subjection. (L 256–257, 17.4)

External incentives are necessary, certainly. But are they sufficient? I argue that they are not. Within the insufficiency of external incentives, I distinguish two components, and I offer a novel explanation of the second. The first component of the insufficiency of external incentives is developed at length by Johnston. Johnston argues that Hobbes comes to recognize in his later writings that subjects do not reliably fear death as the greatest evil. If only they held an enlightened theology that supported such a fear of death, then they would submit to the sovereign; but as it is, they are superstitious and therefore captive to the threats of otherworldly punishment from their religious leaders.[8] Johnston focusses on Hobbes's lengthy theological discussions in Parts III and IV of *Leviathan*, interpreting them as an attempt to displace religious beliefs that conduce to insubordination. The project of *Leviathan* is to educate the nation in a more civilly suitable theology.[9]

This theological diagnosis is surely correct as far as it goes, but it is only half of the challenge facing the Hobbesian sovereign. Taken by itself, the theological diagnosis suggests that if only subjects could come to have the proper fears, if only they could come to have (what I have called) the average moral psychology, then they could be properly motivated by external punitive incentives. In other words, it would suggest that the success of Hobbes's civil science requires only a change in the internal composition of desires and appetites, but not necessarily an increase in internalization of duty. To the contrary, however, in *Leviathan* there is ample textual evidence of a new concern for subjects' internalization of secular civil duties, quite apart from theology. *Leviathan*'s Chapter 30, 'On the OFFICE of the Soveraigne Representative', devotes extensive and detailed attention to proper education.[10] The office

[8] Johnston, *The Rhetoric of 'Leviathan'*, 50–54, 92–113. See also Arash Abizadeh, 'The Representation of Hobbesian Sovereignty: Leviathan as Mythology', in *Hobbes Today: Insights for the 21st Century*, edited by S. A. Lloyd (New York: Cambridge University Press, 2013), 116–124.

[9] Johnston, *The Rhetoric of 'Leviathan'*, 67–70, 114–184. Johnston correlates the rise of the problem of superstition with Hobbes's changed conception of reason. In the early texts, reason is natural, but may be clouded by deceptive and superstitious rhetoric; all that is necessary is to clear away that rhetoric. In the later texts, superstition naturally emerges from the human condition; reason is a difficult and rare achievement (ibid., 106–108).

[10] The corresponding chapter in *The Elements of Law* features only one section on doctrine, at the end of the chapter, and only as an afterthought to its core discussion of topics such as population, wealth, tax (EL II.9.8). The discussion of education is similarly brief in *De Cive* (DC 13.9).

of the sovereign is to attend to the safety of the people, and fully half of the chapter's pages are devoted to 'publique Instruction' (L 520–521, 30.2) in the doctrine of the rights of sovereignty. Hobbes makes explicit that sovereign punishment is insufficient to motivate subjects' compliance; positive knowledge of rights and duties is required.

> And the ground of these Rights [of the sovereign], have the rather need to be diligently and truly taught; because they cannot be maintained by any Civill Law, or terrour of legall punishment. (L 522–523, 30.4)

Similarly, in *De Corpore*, Hobbes argues that war is prevalent because people do not know their duties (DCo 1.7).

Thus, there is a second component to the insufficiency of the sovereign's punitive incentives to motivate subjects' obedience.[11] It is common to observe that in *Leviathan*, public instruction in civil duty is important to secure a peaceful commonwealth. What is less clear, even in explicit discussion in the secondary literature, is exactly why.[12] Hobbes's own direct explanation is that the motivation to obey needs to be supported and stabilized by a sense of duty:

> [I]t is against his [the sovereign's] Duty, to let the people be ignorant, or mis-informed of the grounds, and reasons of those his essentiall Rights; because thereby men are easie to be seduced, and drawn to resist him, when the Common-wealth shall require their use and exercise. (L 520–521, 30.3)

This brief explanation demands elaboration. Why exactly is people's seduction by incorrect doctrines now perceived to be more of a problem than previously?

Johnston contextualizes Hobbes's new demand for public education in duty within the larger social changes underway in seventeenth-century England: the rise of mass education and literacy, the emergence of

[11] Even though Johnston's primary theme is the problem of fear of otherworldly punishment, he does not deny that instruction in duty is also important. Johnston, *The Rhetoric of 'Leviathan'*, 77–91, 211–213.

[12] Macpherson, *Political Theory of Possessive Individualism*, 97–99; Mary G. Dietz, 'Hobbes's Subject as Citizen', in *Thomas Hobbes and Political Theory*, edited by Mary G. Dietz (Lawrence: University Press of Kansas, 1990), 91–119; Sreedhar, *Hobbes on Self-Defence*, 166; Teresa Bejan, 'Teaching the Leviathan: Thomas Hobbes on Education', *Oxford Review of Education* 36, no. 5 (2010): 607–626; May, *Limiting Leviathan*, 122–138.

newspapers. The masses held political opinions and were enticed into political arguments in an unprecedented way. Correspondingly, Johnston shows that the intended audience of *Leviathan* is much wider than the narrow scholarly and elite readership of the earlier texts.[13] Education in the rights of sovereignty is required because the rights will be idle unless they are met with the corresponding submission and cooperation of the political community, and this political community now robustly includes the masses.[14] But this doesn't yet explain why the internalization of duty is required. For if subjects' submission to the sovereign were already externally overdetermined by fear of sovereign punishment, then political education would still not be necessary.

My analysis of Hobbes's new social ontology offers a new answer: subjects may have hope of success from collective power. If subjects can have hope of success in rebelling against a sovereign, then even a powerfully felt fear of death is not sufficient to shore up Hobbes's absolutist state.[15] As I established in Chapter 4, Section 4.2, in Hobbes's later works he offers a changed political ontology, whereby the multitude is populated by spontaneously emerging oligarchic groups, associations with *potentiae* of their own. Moderately durable associations emerge constantly and unavoidably, the result of individuals' pursuit of power. To be sure, the sovereign must make continuing direct efforts to reduce power blocs in the multitude, but as I argued in Chapter 4, Section 4.4, this is a difficult and delicate task. Any power blocs that the sovereign cannot contain furnish ready hope of success for sedition should the intention arise; and also by their very existence they dilute the sovereign's *potentia*. Relying only on external incentives applied against a background average moral psychology that fears death above all, I have argued that the political problem emerges and may become pressing: sovereign *potestas* may fail to garner the obedience to which it is entitled by right. Even within a commonwealth with the correct array of juridical rights, if the sovereign is not fully successful in limiting the growth of power blocs, external incentives will be insufficient to conform subjects' behaviour to the duties of obedience stipulated by natural law.

The attention of Hobbes's later writings to education and persuasion can be understood as his attempt to partially insulate the commonwealth from

[13] Johnston, *The Rhetoric of 'Leviathan'*, 24–25, 62–91.
[14] Ibid., 84–85.
[15] A related account is provided by Frost, *Lessons from a Materialist Thinker*, 158–163.

the political danger that the power blocs represent, by cultivating subjects' internalization of their duties. Private power blocs provide temptations and opportunities for subordination. But if subjects have a resiliently and robustly internalized respect for the rights of the sovereign and an understanding of their corresponding duties, then they may have some greater inclination to maintain their submission to the sovereign despite the temptation to shift their allegiance to seditious unions. With the newly fragile sovereign, in order for the rights of sovereignty to be effective, they must be believed and upheld by the masses. This inner motivation of duty does not merely moralize government and peace, which could be achieved without recognition of duty. Rather, it substantially assists government and peace.

Indeed, the content of public instruction foregrounds deference to the sovereign and non-deference to all other powers. Hobbes models his presentation of the public lessons of civil duty to defer to the sovereign alone on the monotheistic duty to glorify God alone in the Ten Commandments. Corresponding to the first commandment to follow the one true God and have no other gods, Hobbes asserts that subjects must not be jealous of governments of other countries; and that they should recognize that prosperity in any country comes from obedience to existing powers. Corresponding to the second commandment, not to make graven images, Hobbes asserts that subjects are not to admire popular or powerful subjects. Corresponding to the third commandment, not to take the Lord's name in vain, Hobbes asserts subjects are not to speak irreverently of the sovereign nor to dispute his power *potentia*. Hobbes's justification of this rule links to his earlier relational analysis of power: disputing or questioning power *potentia* brings the sovereign 'into Contempt with his People, and their Obedience (in which the safety of the Commonwealth consisteth) slackened' (L 527–528, 30.7–9).

This pedagogy may be necessary; but how is it possible?[16] I noted earlier that some individuals might spontaneously comprehend the connection of duty with true self-interest. This class of individuals, presumably including philosophers such as Hobbes, sounds likely to be small. But it is essential for all, even the vulgar, to appreciate and internalize the civil science, regardless of whether they have any taste or aptitude for philosophy. Fortunately, as Hobbes makes clear, all that is necessary for internalizing the duty is to know

[16] Hampton argues it is impossible; but her conclusion relies on a highly stylized characterization of the change required, as actually replacing subjects' own judgement with the sovereign's. Hampton, *Social Contract Tradition*, 212–213.

the content of the duty, and to come to feel forcefully and vividly its connection with self-preservation. This does not require understanding the full scientific derivation and rational explanation of the duties. Hobbes thinks that the experience of civil war should naturally sharpen people's appreciation of the importance of duty, but when the horrors of war have been forgotten, the role of deliberate education of 'the vulgar' in the indivisible and absolute rights of sovereignty comes to the fore (L 278–279, 18.16). He is optimistic about the possibility of educating the masses in this way:

> [T]he Common-peoples minds, unlesse they be tainted with dependance on the Potent, or scribbled over with the opinions of their Doctors, are like clean paper, fit to receive whatsoever by Publique Authority shall be imprinted in them. . . . [I]n the instruction of the people in the Essentiall Rights (which are the Naturall, and Fundamentall Lawes) of Soveraignty [*Iuribus Summae Potestatis*], there is no difficulty (whilest a Sovereign has his Power entire [*dum illi, qui Summam habet Potestatem, manet Potentia integra*],) but what proceeds from his own fault. (L 524–525, 30.6)

He offers some considerations to address the logistics of mass pedagogy, of how to teach a mass of people who may not be particularly interested in learning the truth of civil science for its own sake.

First, he targets universities. Students from universities go on to be influential leaders of popular opinion. 'It is therefore manifest that the Instruction of the people, dependeth wholly, on the right teaching of Youth in the universities' (L 532–533, 30.14). To stem the seditious ideas that may arise from reading the ancients or the schoolmen, he proposes control of permissible doctrines to be taught; if seditious doctrines are not taught or published in universities, they will not reach the masses.[17]

Second, he proposes systematic organized mass teaching from the pulpit: at the end of each church service, subjects should be reminded of the correct doctrines of civil science (L 528–529, 30.10). Beyond merely being informed of the content of their duties, Frost argues, the theatrics of collective pedagogy enacts and reinforces the correct internalization of duties. At these services, when they sit together collectively in church, they display

[17] Bejan, 'Teaching the Leviathan', 607–626. Admittedly, this represents a point of increased emphasis rather than a radical break with earlier texts: see EL II.9.8; DC 13.9.

their submission to these doctrines, and witness others' submission.[18] This optics of power constitutes a real power for the sovereign and consolidates its supremacy.

Third, consider *Leviathan* itself as a pedagogical instrument. As already noted, *Leviathan* has a much wider intended audience than the narrow scholarly and elite readership of Hobbes's earlier texts. Hobbes complains that his true civil science needs to compete with other books of politics that are essentially histories retold for entertainment (DCo 1.7). In order to grab the attention of this wider audience, Hobbes makes a marked change in style between his early and late texts: from austere rational demonstration in *The Elements of Law* and *De Cive* to florid and evocative rhetorical persuasion in *Leviathan*.[19] For his broader audience will not properly imbibe their duties in an efficacious way by simply being told or demonstrated. One prominent example mentioned earlier is the modelling of the contents of public instruction on the Ten Commandments, thereby tapping into deeper-rooted moral commitments and habits of thought of subjects of the commonwealth.[20]

5.3. Internal and External Motivations of Sovereigns

To this point I have focussed on subjects' education in duty. Subjects' conformity with duty is central for considering the success of civil science: for it is when subjects fail to do their duty that the political problem emerges. But Hobbes also enumerates duties for the sovereign, to rule for the safety of the people. In this section, I ask, how important is it for the success of Hobbes's civil science that the sovereign conform its behaviour to duty? And how is that conformity brought about, through internal or external motivations?

[18] Frost, *Lessons from a Materialist Thinker*, 158–163. Similar themes are developed in Tarlton, 'Creation and Maintenance', 313–324.

[19] Johnston, *The Rhetoric of 'Leviathan'*, 24–25, 84–91. Skinner grants that rhetoric may serve for persuading the masses, but he argues it is not only for the masses: the elite sections of the population may equally have difficulty grasping civil science, because their understanding is clouded by (immediate) self-interest. Quentin Skinner, *Reason and Rhetoric in the Philosophy of Hobbes* (Cambridge: Cambridge University Press, 1996), 426–437. Across Hobbes's oeuvre, Evrigenis finds not an increase in rhetoric, but a shift in rhetorical strategy. Ioannis D. Evrigenis, *Images of Anarchy: The Rhetoric and Science in Hobbes's State of Nature* (New York: Cambridge University Press, 2014), 44–155. Evrigenis does note that *Leviathan*'s use of the biblical story of Cain and Abel draws new attention to the problem of relapse from political order (159–178).

[20] For a broader discussion of the theological parallels in Hobbes's doctrine of sovereignty, see Abizadeh, 'Representation of Hobbesian Sovereignty', 124–135.

I will argue that in Hobbes's later view, strong conformity is required, and it is to be brought about by a change of sovereign internal motivations. In this context, I draw out Hobbes's analysis of the difficulty with democratic assemblies: far from enabling equal consideration of the needs and desires of the whole population, the very structure of democratic assemblies thwarts such consideration, due to corrosive oligarchic dynamics in both entry to, and the everyday operation of, the assembly.

The foundation of Hobbes's civil science is the enumeration of true rights of sovereignty; a sovereign needs to claim and insist upon these rights, and this will centrally involve demanding subjects' obedience with threat of punishment. But this is not the full extent of the requirements that natural law imposes on the sovereign; it is just one component of the larger duty of the sovereign to serve the safety and prosperity of the people (EL II.9; DC Ch 13; L Ch 30). This larger duty can be understood in a weak or strong sense. First, the weaker sense of duty sets a floor on acceptable sovereign conduct: the sovereign must not rule oppressively or wickedly. But second, Hobbes insists that safety should be understood expansively, 'So that this is the general law for sovereigns: that they procure, to the uttermost of their endeavour, the good of the people' (EL II.9.1). The stronger sense of duty comprises a suite of more specific duties in various policy domains, which collectively amount to a model of virtuous rule. In *The Elements of Law*, Hobbes asserts that the sovereign needs to maintain high population; minimize unnecessary restrictions on subjects' liberty; make regulations for labour and commerce to support economic prosperity; establish clear and equitable property law and tax policy; support a fair system of courts; punish the ambitious for insubordination; regulate doctrine in the universities; and maintain a military for external defence (EL II.9); a similarly detailed list is repeated in *De Cive* and *Leviathan*.[21]

In the early texts, it is not necessary to Hobbes's civil science that the sovereign perform its stronger duties. I argued in Chapter 3, Section 3.4 that, if the sovereign claims its essential rights and if it also keeps an eye out for ambitious subjects fomenting sedition, then the commonwealth will be robust. I didn't make explicit that this also presupposes that the sovereign fulfils its weak duty not to be grossly and systematically wicked. For even abject and isolated subjects with no hope of success will not comply with a sovereign who threatens their lives or the things most dear to them (DC 6.13).

[21] See discussion in Baumgold, *Hobbes's Political Theory*, 101–119.

Happily, the requirement of the sovereign performing its weak duties is easy to meet: Hobbes thinks that frank wickedness will be so obviously counterproductive as to be a marginal occurrence (DC 6.13). But beyond this fulfilment of weak duty, positively good rule is not required. If the sovereign does act as a model ruler to serve the public safety in the fullest and most virtuous way (EL II.9.3–9; DC 6.6–17), then its subjects will be happier, and indeed, the sovereign itself will share in the resultant prosperity. But it is not fatal to peace if the sovereign fails to carry out these stronger duties. For due to the political ontology of fragmented equality, even unhappy subjects lack the hope of success in rebelling.

In the later texts, it is no longer the case that merely avoiding frankly wicked rule would be sufficient to achieve a robust commonwealth.[22] As I established in Chapter 4, Section 4.4, Hobbes now conceives sovereignty as more fragile than earlier. There are continually emergent power blocs in the multitude, meaning subjects may have hope of success for any rebellion; the margin for the sovereign to rule poorly is understood to be much more narrow than previously. In order to retain individuals' obedience and allegiance, the sovereign would be well advised to dampen all three component causes of rebellion: hope of success (power blocs), pretence of right (seditious doctrine), and popular discontent. Addressing the problem of power blocs, the previous chapter argued that the sovereign must exercise extreme and sustained prudence to ensure that both the power and the seditiousness of these groupings are reduced rather than inflamed. Addressing the problem of seditious doctrine, the previous section discussed the importance of subjects being educated in civil duties, and noted that the text of *Leviathan* itself plays some role in this education. But there is a large ongoing role for the sovereign itself in carrying out a pedagogical program for subjects, as part of its duty (L 30.3–14). Addressing the problem of discontent, the duties of the sovereign include ruling in a manner that is transparently fair, with a particular emphasis on the dignity and legal equality of the poor (L 30.15–24). These three elements of good rule do not merely constitute a morally required duty; they are imperative for the success of Hobbes's civil science.

[22] See also Lazzeri, *Droit, pouvoir et liberté*, 355–360. Sreedhar is unclear regarding the threshold quality of rule required to achieve stability. Despite first outlining the detailed list of the sovereign's strong duties, in her summary she asserts that merely not starving or killing the population will be sufficient (Sreedhar, *Hobbes on Resistance*, 166–167). I argue that in *Leviathan* the stronger requirement on conduct applies.

Given that the conduct required of the sovereign is demanding, how is it concretely brought about? Let us start by modelling sovereigns as having an average moral psychology of moderately rational pursuit of desires. This modelling is supported textually. The sovereign as a 'politic person' is at the same time also either a natural individual or an assembly of natural individuals with their own private interests. Hobbes is clear that the natural person(s) of the sovereign do not act from perfect far-sighted reason; he remarks that 'for the most part, if the publique interest chance to crosse the private, he preferrs the private; for the Passions of men, are commonly more potent than their Reason' (L 288–289, 19.4).[23] Hobbes's default modelling of human motivation as short-sighted and externally driven should extend to these natural individuals forming the sovereign.

Are there external mechanisms, incentives or threats, that can bring such a sovereign's conduct to align with duty? Hampton provides the following pessimistic analysis of the efficacy of positive incentives:

> [A] shortsighted sovereign likely would believe that ruthlessness and substantial domination are the ways to self-satisfaction. And this belief does not seem obviously wrong, because the supposed benefits from moderate rule are not clearly greater than the benefits (in the short and the long run) from tyrannical rule.[24]

Indeed, even though Hobbes himself suggests that there are positive incentives for the sovereign to conform its behaviour with duty, the incentives do not have traction within the sovereign's presumed motivational structure. Good rule may well lie in the long-run interest of the sovereign, both as public and as private person, because the wealth and flourishing of the commonwealth is simultaneously the wealth and flourishing of the sovereign: '[T]he good of the Soveraign and People, cannot be separated' (L 540–541, 30.21). But ruling well requires difficult judgement and sustained focus and self-discipline to implement. A sovereign impatient to accumulate quick wealth and power would instead enrich those near and dear, or court the favour of the wealthy. Indeed, Hobbes identifies nepotism as a perennial

[23] Moller Okin argues that the duality of interests is an innovation of Hobbes's later writings. Susan Moller Okin, '"The Soveraign and His Counsellours": Hobbes's Reevaluation of Parliament', in *Thomas Hobbes: Critical Assessments*, Vol. 3, edited by Preston King (London: Routledge, 1993), 789–790. But to the contrary there are prior hints of a similar analysis (EL II.5.5–7).

[24] Hampton, *Social Contract Tradition*, 194; see also Baumgold, *Hobbes's Political Theory*, 118–119.

problem, especially in democracies. He suggests that democracies tend to siphon public funds into sectional interest more flagrantly than other regimes, because in democracy each faction has its own friends and allies to enrich, whereas in monarchy or aristocracy the number of personal contacts to enrich is limited (L 288–291, 19.4, 19.8).[25] Whether or not this analysis of the relative intensity of nepotism in different regime types is correct,[26] it hardly provides any robust mechanism for achieving virtuous rule: at most it accounts for differential degrees of bad rule across the regime types.

Where positive incentives do not succeed, might the sovereign's fear of punitive or other sanction bring it to perform its strong duties? I have argued that if the sovereign fails to perform its strong duties, subjects are likely to become non-compliant and rebel. Might it follow that the fear of subjects' non-compliance and rebellion constitutes an efficacious motivation for a sovereign to perform its duty?[27] To the contrary, even if a sovereign does have such a fear, the behaviour motivated by the fear, in a sovereign with average moral psychology, does not conform to duty. The idea that the threat of imminent rebellion could neatly motivate good rule rests on the image of an undifferentiated multitude from which emerge an egalitarian band of rebels speaking the true and wise heart of the people. But as discussed in Chapter 4, Section 4.4, the multitude is not an undifferentiated domain of equality, and correspondingly, rebellion is often fomented by oligarchic groups or interested factions in the multitude. This can be the case even if there is a genuine and worthy underlying grievance. The most direct means to appease their immediate threats is to buy off the power bloc's factional interest: '[t]o buy

[25] This line of defence of monarchy is also established in the earlier texts (EL II.5.5–7; DC 6.13, 10.18). But it is less significant there because, as I have argued, in the early social ontology, the commonwealth can successfully achieve peace even when the quality of its rule is poor.

[26] It is not obviously correct. For is it not possible that a sovereign monarch, being merely a single weak human individual, would need to buy the allegiance of many supporters in order to retain power and fend off usurpers?

[27] Hoekstra hints at this possibility ('Lion in the House', 217). Hampton entertains the possibility, only subsequently to raise difficulties relating to technological inequalities in the multitude (*Social Contract Tradition*, 247–248 versus 254–255). The idea that the masses might be efficacious in putting pressure on the sovereign to rule should not be confused with the stronger claim, advanced by Curran, that subjects have a right to put pressure on the sovereign in this way. Eleanor Curran, *Reclaiming the rights of the Hobbesian subject* (New York: Palgrave Macmillan, 2007), 112–116. But the rights retained by subjects are carefully described such that they do not lead to or licence collective destabilizing rebellion against any but the most wicked sovereign (L 336–341, 20.11–18). What is at stake in my discussion is not the case of extreme wickedness, but the more common case of a middle-of-the-road sovereign who rules poorly. Indeed, while May is 'tempted' to argue that laws that do not conform with the sovereign's duty do not deserve subjects' respect, he ultimately concedes that there is still an obligation to obey (*Limiting the Leviathan*, 126). My point is to consider whether the threat of rebellion might constitute an efficacious concrete restraint on sovereign conduct, regardless of the situation with respect to right.

with Mony, or Preferment, from a Popular ambitious Subject, to be quiet, and desist from making ill impressions in the mindes of the People' (L 544–545, 30.24). This is directly contrary to duty. There are two aspects to the harmfulness of this course of action: it compounds the power of factions, and it fails to carry out the harder work of acting for the public good by addressing the deeper grievances underlying the rebellion. Hobbes remarks that 'though sometimes a Civill warre, may be differred, by such wayes as that, yet the danger growes still the greater, and the Publique ruine more assured' (L 546–547, 30.24).

In sum, the external incentives of hope of reward and fear of punishment are not sufficient to conform sovereign behaviour to duty: to the contrary, both can press a sovereign away from good governance. But such dutiful behaviour is required if the political problem is to be overcome. Might the sovereign internalizing its duty offer a solution?

Indeed, such a solution is implicit in Hobbes's theory of counsel. Counsel is a new and prominent topic in *Leviathan*, with a whole chapter devoted to it (L Ch 25). Counsel was a common feature of political practice and theory of early modern England, whereby monarchs would rely on trusted counsellors to guide their rule. Hobbes recommends that expert counsellors have the sovereign's ear and provide serious, careful, and direct advice. There was some controversy in Hobbes's period whether rulers are under obligation to follow the counsel that they receive.[28] Hobbes strongly denies any such obligation. Counsellors do not impugn the absoluteness of sovereignty, because counsel is not command, but mere advice. Its recipient adopts its recommendations not because of the will of the counsellor, but at their own discretion, insofar as they see the advice to serve their interests (L 398–401, 25.2–4). Counsellors have a subordinate status; they have no right to counsel, much less to have their counsel accepted.

Despite counsellors' subordination to the sovereign, nonetheless counsel influences the sovereign. Whereas much of Hobbes's politics is concerned to insist on the subjects' deference to the judgement of the sovereign, the role of the counsellor is to challenge the sovereign's prior understanding and motivation and seek to change them (L 400–401, 25.5). Good counsel consists 'in a deducing of the benefit, or hurt that may arise to him that is to be Counselled,

[28] Joanne Paul, 'Counsel, Command and Crisis', *Hobbes Studies 28* (2015): 103–131; Thomas Alexander Corbin, 'The Role of Counsel in Hobbes's Political Thought' (MRes thesis, Macquarie University, 2016), 62–73.

by the necessary or probable consequences of the action he propoundeth' (L 404–405, 25.11). In the case of counsel to the sovereign, a good counsellor will recommend courses of action that will 'preserve the people in Peace at home, and defend them against forraign Invasion', including educating the sovereign in civil science, as well as advising on more specific details of good policy (L 406–407, 25.13). But what is this but assisting the sovereign to be motivated by duty? The sovereign is not externally enticed or compelled to perform its duty; rather, it receives good counsel, which allows it to perceive the longer-term stakes of the situation, and choose the path of duty even in the face of other temptations.[29] It thereby provides the desired solution to the political problem.

There is one major stumbling block for this solution: the counsel must be of sufficient quality. The difficulty is to ensure that the counsellors are wise and good; that their advice clear, accurate, and well communicated; and that their advice is offered genuinely for the public safety and not covertly for their own interest (L 404–409, 25.11–14). If counsel is bad, it compounds rather than solves the political problem. Hobbes understands one of the key determinants of the quality of counsel to be the institutional format within which it is offered. One might have thought that counsel from a public assembly might best serve the safety of the people. Hobbes vehemently opposes such an idea, even at the same time as granting some of the considerations that normally motivate the turn to collective counsel. He grants that there is no reason to expect good counsel from the rich and noble (L 548–549, 30.25). He acknowledges the importance of diverse counsel from many different experts (L 406–407, 410–413, 25.13, 25.16); he also explicitly endorses taking counsel widely across the population. Right in the context of opposing counsel from an assembly, he argues:

> The best Counsell, in those things that concern not other Nations, but onely the ease, and benefit the Subjects may enjoy, by Lawes that look onely inward, is to be taken from the generall informations, and complaints of the people of each Province, who are best acquainted with their own wants, and ought therefore, when they demand nothing in derogation of the essentiall Rights of Sovereignty, to be diligently taken notice of. (L 548–549, 30.27)

[29] Gabriella Slomp, 'The Inconvenience of the Legislator's Two Persons and the Role of Good Counsellors', *Critical Review of International Social and Political Philosophy* 19, no. 1 (2016): 68–85; Corbin, 'Role of Counsel', 74–90.

But he stresses the multiple perverse effects of having those many counsellors form a public assembly, whether the sovereign assembly of a popular (democratic) commonwealth, or equally a parliament counselling a sovereign monarch (L 288–289, 402–403, 408–411, 546–549, 19.5, 25.8, 25.14–16, 30.25–27).[30]

Assemblies offer poor counsel because of how their membership is defined; and because of the interpersonal dynamics of those members when they meet. Given the new centrality of counsel, Hobbes makes explicit that it is part of the duty of the sovereign to choose good counsel; but only a monarch (who is furthermore not tightly bound by a parliament) is able to discharge this duty. For in aristocracy and democracy, the sovereign assemblies constitute their own counsel and are unable to make this choice (L 288–289, 546–547, 19.5, 30.25). Far from the membership of such assemblies being selected according to expertise, Hobbes notes that the kinds of individuals in such assemblies tend to be those who know a lot about tending their own private fortunes, but who may have no insight into public policy: they 'have beene versed more in the acquisition of Wealth than of Knowledge' (L 288–289, 19.5).

Assemblies also offer poor counsel because of their interpersonal dynamics.[31] Two kinds of problems emerge. The first problem is impaired or obstructed cognition. Members of an assembly may not pay proper attention to the reasoning of the advice and instead be swayed by the rhetoric of others in the assembly; they may be confused and dazzled by the many digressions and interruptions to the discussion; the full picture cannot be put forward before the assembly if it includes sensitive information (L 288–289, 408–409, 548–549, 19.5, 25.14–15, 30.26). The second problem is distortion by power dynamics. The public meetings of an assembly provide a forum that is eminently susceptible to the formation, consolidation, and reconfiguration of power blocs, according to the dynamics of spontaneous competition of relational power outlined in Chapter 2, Section 2.4 and Chapter 4, Section 4.2. The members of an assembly of counsellors are worried about their status, power, and favour with respect to their peers. They worry about looking stupid, or contradicting another assembly

[30] Paul, 'Counsel, Command and Crisis', 171.

[31] These concerns are famously shared by Rousseau, who only promotes popular decision-making when it is conducted by vote of a sufficiently informed populace with no communication amongst voters. Jean-Jacques Rousseau, *On the Social Contract*, translated by Donald A. Cress (Indianapolis: Hackett, 1987), Book 2, Chapter 3.

member whose favour they seek to curry. They seek safety and patronage by allying themselves with the opinions of the wise or influential; they heap scorn upon non-conformers; they embrace conflict with partisans of another patron in order to prove their loyalty to their own side. These interpersonal dynamics lay open the assembly to being hijacked by private interests. Whether because they are too confused and inattentive to identify the underlying agendas of speakers in the assembly, or whether because they are motivated by considerations of power and status to collaborate in giving poor advice, the assembly does not serve its purpose (L 408–413, 25.15–16).

Hobbes places great stock in private counsel for monarchs; he recommends a best practice of the sovereign doing its business 'by the help of many and prudent Counsellours, with every one consulting apart in his proper element' (L 410–411, 25.16). To start with, the selection process is the choice of the sovereign and can be conducted according to expertise (L 546–547, 30.25). Furthermore, the problematic dynamics of group counsel are eliminated. When a monarch holds private court with a counsellor, cognitive confusion is stemmed, and the optical power effects are neutralized. Poor reasoning and ulterior motives can be probed. The monarch 'may interrupt [the counsellor], and examine his reasons more rigorously, than can be done in a Multitude, which are too many to enter into Dispute, and Dialogue with him that speaketh indifferently to them all at once' (L 402–403, 25.7–8).

In result, Hobbes finds different forms of government differentially able to overcome the political problem. Hobbes remarks sharply that democratic commonwealths survive in spite of the open consultations of their assemblies, not in virtue of them (L 412–413, 25.16). Considering a monarch counselled by a parliament, Hobbes offers the memorable image of a tennis player in a wheelbarrow pushed by many hands (L 412–413, 25.16). The contrast with a sovereign taking private counsel is sharp: such a sovereign does not need to respond to whims of populace, but Hobbes is optimistic that at the same time such a sovereign actually rules for subjects' benefit.

Hobbes's overall weighing of the merits and demerits of different forms of counsel are highly contestable. He pays little attention to possible perversities of private counsel, and he doesn't address whether the problems he identifies in assemblies might be overcome. Even by his own standards, he may have been too swift in his condemnation of collective forms of counsel: Moller Okin shows that favourable experience with the 1661 Cavalier Parliament roused Hobbes to a late sympathy for government by assembly.[32] But the evaluative discussion of the different regime forms in relation to the quality of their counsel clarifies what is at stake in some of Hobbes's most explicit anti-democratic polemic: its capacity or incapacity to deliver sovereign conduct in conformity with duty. The sovereign's duty includes stifling the emergent formation of oligarchic powers in broader society; but Hobbes worries that these very powers may corrupt and subvert the counselling process, wherever the sovereign's counsel is delivered via popular assembly. The discussion forcefully raises the possibility of a well-intentioned democratic form having perverse oligarchic effects; in the second half of the book, I will demand that any Spinozist account of popular power take such perversities seriously.

In this section, I have established counsel to the sovereign as one element of Hobbes's own response to the political problem. Facing the problem of sovereign *potentia* insufficient to *potestas*, due to emergent power blocs, I have argued that Hobbes's solution is to maintain his absolute model of politics, and to conform the behaviour of the political actors within it through a program of political pedagogy and persuasion in duty. This has two halves. In Section 5.2, I showed that Hobbes seeks to educate subjects in their duty; in this section I have shown that the other half of the solution is counselling sovereigns. But it is important to see that despite Hobbes's appeal to duty, his solution is not a moralism that purports to transcend the informal powers *potentiae* in society; rather, the solution amounts to proposing detailed institutional forms that can manage, channel, and reduce those powers. The simplicity and clean juridical lines of Hobbes's early science of politics are now thoroughly muddied by a persistent worry about informal collective power.

5.4. Repressive Egalitarianism

What does it amount to, Hobbes's absolutism reinforced by duty; and how does it relate to the question of popular power? Hobbes's writings display a curious ambivalence in relation to popular power. On the one hand, Hobbes's civil science takes a theoretical starting point shared with the radical egalitarians and democrats of his day.[33] Hobbes's model of the state of

[32] Moller Okin, 'Soveraign and His Counsellours', 800–805.

[33] Curran, *Reclaiming the Rights*, 26–62. See Zagorin for an overview of the Levellers' beliefs. Zagorin, *History of Political Thought*, 8–42.

nature places everyone in equal juridical status; it is from this equal right of everybody that political authority emerges. But on the other hand, Hobbes takes this radical egalitarian starting point to different ends. First, he is consistently and polemically hostile to the possibility of the mass of individuals in a society (the multitude) exercising agency. Hobbes polemically redefines the people to be (or to be personated by) the sovereign, even if a monarch. Second, in defining group agency of the people through the will and authority of the sovereign, Hobbes takes pains to deny that the sovereign is in any way required to be responsive to the expressed demands of the multitude. Third, he argues vigorously in favour of a monarchical sovereign against a democratic sovereign. In result, Hobbes appears to endorse a commonwealth retaining formal popular ground without any institutional popular influence.

In taking the reasoning of radicals and using it to shore up sovereign power, Hobbes scandalized his contemporaries. Is the popular element of Hobbes's civil science purely rhetorical, cynically harnessing the language of his political opponents contrary to their intentions?[34] Or is the truth just the opposite? Martel argues that the ambiguities of Hobbes's texts subvert their own official authoritarianism in favour of an underlying anti-authoritarian democracy.[35] Does any of the foundational commitment to equality and popular power remain in the model ultimately endorsed by Hobbes's civil science, and if so, in what form?

In this section, I characterize Hobbes's absolutism as repressive egalitarianism, and I argue that it represents a commitment to a certain conception of the popularity of political power. I argue that the Hobbesian combination of authoritarianism and democracy is not cynical; rather it is a coherent political position that genuinely shares some elements with radicals, even as it diverges in other respects. This much is perhaps not original.[36] But I offer a novel account of the radicalism at stake, arguing that the popular commitment remains not merely in the formal juridical modelling of rights, but also,

[34] Skinner, 'Hobbes on Persons', 161.

[35] Martel, *Subverting the Leviathan*, 1–13.

[36] Lee shows that the doctrine of popular sovereignty has historically been open to widely varying ideological interpretations (*Popular Sovereignty*, 317–318). More specifically, in a prominent debate between Tuck and Hoekstra, both authors agree that Hobbes is genuinely and non-cynically committed to the popular grounding of political authority, and at the same time that this commitment leads to a defence of despotic sovereignty. They disagree only over how to characterize Hobbes's institutional recommendations: insofar as Hobbes discusses democratic sovereignty and endorses democracy without an assembly or administrative power, is this really a democracy at all, or is it instead a de facto (and therefore substantive) a monarchy? Tuck, 'Hobbes and Democracy', 171–190; Hoekstra, 'Lion in the House', 191–218.

more significantly, in the preferred arrangement of the concrete power *potentia* of the multitude. I argue that Hobbes's absolutism seeks (to the extent possible) to diminish all forms of inequality of power *potentia*, except that between the sovereign and the multitude. To be sure, this raises critical worries that Hobbes is insufficiently sensitive to excesses of sovereign power. But what is often overlooked is his intense sensitivity to the excesses of powers that exist in the multitude apart from the state. The key element in common between Hobbes and the radicals of his time is an antifeudal opposition to old power blocs, freeing the individual from non-state powers; in Hobbes's hands, this extends beyond mere traditional power blocs such as the church also to emergent new ones. I argue that Hobbesian repressive egalitarianism represents an early attempt to think a non-hierarchical society. If the multitude is a domain of oligarchic power blocs, then even from the most egalitarian and popular perspective it is not desirable to conform the state to its will. Hobbes views any collective formation within the political body with great suspicion, and he is convinced that only through the state actively atomizing and disempowering the multitude can equality and popular power worthy of the name be achieved. Some institutional forms may run contrary to this goal of eliminating insidious oligarchic influences; I suggest that Tuck's popular plebiscite is just such a form.

I start to vindicate these suggestions by considering *Leviathan*'s treatment of church structure, which is a microcosm of the larger dilemma. Hobbes offers an extended sympathetic discussions of the primitive Christian church (L 774–851, 42.2–66). Hobbes's discussion emphasizes the non-despotic character of the early church, focussing on two of its striking features: its flat and non-hierarchical structure, and its free and plural treatment of its members. First, it was non-hierarchical: he characterizes it as an association or congregation lacking coercive power (L 778–781, 42.5–8). The Apostles, and after them the ministers, were only teachers; and they were answerable to their flock, by whom they were selected (L 828–860, 42.46–60). Even the ultimate power of the church, excommunication, was weak: merely a non-authoritative recommendation not to keep company with the excommunicated person. Second, the early church was free and plural in its relation to individual members. The flock were free to read independently and advance scriptural interpretations contrary to their teachers (L 812–813, 42.35); and excommunication was possible only for actions, not for errors of opinion (L 804–805, 42.27). In sum, members of the primitive church followed the Apostles only out of free reverence for their moral virtues (L

1114, 47.19). The democratic flavour of Hobbes's reflections on church structure is not limited to the distant past. After centuries of false and ambitious claims of a hierarchical church to coercive authority, Hobbes celebrates the demise of papal and episcopal power. He expresses sympathy for the religious Independents in his own time, whose churches were conceived as mere congregations of coreligionists, rather than authorities over their flocks, and as such most closely resembled the desirable free and flat structure of the early church (L 1116, 47.20).

This celebration of democratic association is striking against *Leviathan*'s larger insistence upon the absolute power of the civil sovereign. Even Hobbes's conception of sovereign democracy, laid out in clarity by Tuck,[37] is despotic; whereas the early church's insistence on the absence of coercive power and toleration of internal plurality offers a radically non-despotic conception of democracy. Martel claims that Hobbes's positive portrait of the flat structure of the early church is simply incompatible with Hobbes's official authoritarianism and the antidemocratic elements of his political philosophy.[38] He reasons that opposing church authority should entail also opposing state authority.[39] But Hobbes himself sees no contradiction; and Collins's extended study of seventeenth-century English ecclesiology provides historical context to understand the compatibility, or even more strongly, the mutual support, between the apparently conflictual elements of Hobbes's system. Collins shows that Hobbes sympathized with the 'magisterial Independents'.[40] As Independents, they opposed religious authority. The problem of freeing individuals from church power is central. But the magisterial independents took the Erastian view that the conditions of possibility of this form of non-hierarchical religious association is best secured through strong state power that can enforce equality in the structure of a religious community.[41] Like the magisterial Independents, Hobbes is not separately considering two different forms of social organization: one flat, democratic, and free; the other authoritarian. Rather, he is putting forward a theory in which the two domains are intimately connected. A non-hierarchical structure of church governance relies on an authoritarian state as its condition of existence.

37 Tuck, 'Hobbes and Democracy', 172.
38 Martel, *Subverting the Leviathan*, 6.
39 Ibid., 103–134, 205.
40 Jeffrey R. Collins, *The Allegiance of Thomas Hobbes* (Oxford: Oxford University Press, 2005), 124.
41 Ibid., 88–114.

On Collins's account, Hobbes's combination of egalitarianism and authoritarianism is not an anomalous and incoherent combination, but rather fits with a clear and prominent strain in early modern English political thought.[42] Collins stresses the ambitious modernism of Hobbes's text. Even as *Leviathan* emphatically opposes rebellion against effective rulers, Collins characterizes the book as 'a revolutionary text, not composed to re-establish a traditional monarchical order but, rather, one emerging out of the forward-looking state-building and religious reform projects of the English revolution'.[43] Collins groups Hobbes along with republicans such as Harrington and liberals such as Locke as proponents of the modernization of the state, opposed to the separate political authority of the church, preferring a model in which 'the monolithic state presided over a polity of atomized individuals'.[44] *Leviathan* is 'driven by an obsessive fear of the independent power of the Christian church, and by a sympathy with one of the central political goals of the English Revolution: securing an Erastian church settlement under the aegis of the modernizing state'.[45]

Collins's analysis is limited to questions of church power. But now I generalize the schema that it provides. Collins's account shows that when it comes to religion, the citizen's status as a free and equal individual was achieved through power of the state. The juridical egalitarianism that lies at the foundation of Hobbes's theoretical structure is brought into concrete reality through the application of state power. Lesser state power would amount to being more deferential to the power of the various churches, thereby leaving their congregations captive to the domination of the church hierarchy. But the power of the church is just one specific, albeit central, case of a more general phenomenon. Recall my presentation of Hobbes's deromanticized view of the popular multitude in Chapter 4, Sections 4.2 and 4.4: power congeals around any form of eminence: wealth, oratory, or most alarmingly, even the bare fact of appearing to have others' allegiance. The multitude is not in a state of innocence or equality: Hobbes's analysis of emergent associations

[42] See also Zagorin, who insists that Hobbes is 'no monstrous birth without a counterpart in its time. The case is just the reverse'. European consciousness at the time was characteristically antifeudal, anticlerical, bourgeois, and ambitious to remake society; Hobbes's absolutist egalitarianism fits right in. Zagorin, *History of Political Thought*, 187. See also Kinch Hoekstra, 'Early Modern Absolutism and Constitutionalism', *Cardozo Law Review 34*, no. 3 (2013): 1079.

[43] Collins, *Allegiance of Thomas Hobbes*, 116.

[44] Ibid., 279. But see Arash Abizadeh, 'Publicity, Privacy, and Toleration in Hobbes's *Leviathan*', *Modern Intellectual History 10*, no. 2 (2013): 288–291, who argues that Hobbes's Erastianism is compatible with the existence of (tightly regulated) non-public churches.

[45] Collins, *Allegiance of Thomas Hobbes*, 5; similarly, Johnston, *The Rhetoric of 'Leviathan'*, 185–213.

shows that there is such a thing as private power. This power is in itself morally indeterminate: there is nothing necessarily innocent about forms of dependency in private association that involve stark hierarchical and oligarchic tendencies; civil society is not by itself a realm of freedom and equality.[46]

Thus, putting aside Hobbes's juridical egalitarianism of right, Hobbes also offers a concrete egalitarianism of power.[47] Given the relational understanding of power, the challenge for politics is subjects' involvement in collective associations. Equality is achieved by neutralizing and diminishing the power of collective organization to the extent possible; and this is exactly what Hobbes's late absolutism seeks to do. This Hobbesian program has resonance with Richelieu's absolutist centralization of political power in France. Indeed, England had already progressed some distance in this direction in the century prior to Hobbes's writing: dissolving monasteries, revoking grants of crown land, and subordinating provinces, to a greater degree than its European counterparts.[48] In *Leviathan*, Hobbes includes a new chapter about political systems (associations), in which he counsels the sovereign to oppose the institutional solidification of the power blocs of the multitude, whether the church, the social classes, clans, or anything else (L 372–373, 22.32); subjects are also to be prohibited from holding more servants than necessary (L 372–373, 22.31). Any assembly that cannot give an account of the reasons for its existence is to be disbanded and punished as seditious (L 374–375, 22.34). Related recommendations are peppered through the text. For instance, he recommends the sovereign not accept claims of right to press counsel, whether from popular parliaments or from hereditary nobility (L 25.4, 30.25, 400–401, 546–549). Furthermore, as discussed at length in Section 5.2, the sovereign is to indoctrinate its subjects to bolster its own power through an optics of public displays of worship and submission, and to do everything it can to reshape its subjects such that they recognize and act upon their primary obligation to obey the sovereign, ahead of any other allegiances they may have. It may be that the reshaping cannot in fact reach full equality, instead needing to make some concessions to existing power relations, for fear of backlash. That is, sometimes co-optation, rather than

[46] For similar ideas outside of a Hobbesian context, see Freeman, 'The Tyranny of Structurelessness'.

[47] Hobbes's concrete egalitarianism is primarily political, by which I mean it is concerned with power and allegiance. It is not a twenty-first-century economic egalitarianism: money is only one amongst many possible grounds of accumulation of power; and Hobbes does not countenance radical economic redistribution. His view of fair economic policy is charitable but anti-redistributive (L 536–541, 30.17–19).

[48] Zagorin, *Rebels and Rulers*, 1–50, 133.

destruction, of oligarchic forces may be a tactical necessity.[49] But the ideal is to reduce such forces to a minimum.

Once the private power of associations is recognized, absolute sovereignty comes to be viewed not as an imposition of power on a previously equal social domain devoid of power relations, but as an intervention and reshaping of a field of highly layered and hierarchical power relations. Pettit stresses Hobbes's rejection of the key republican goal of non-domination: being protected against arbitrary interference; not depending on the good favour of another. Quite rightly, Pettit observes that Hobbesian subjects are dominated by their sovereign.[50] But what this analysis omits is Hobbes's frontal assault on the pervasive informal domination that occurs within the multitude. In Hobbes's later civil science, he strives to create secondarily what was presumed in his earlier works to exist naturally: a political ontology of fragmented equality. An all-powerful sovereign does not immediately preside over such a sphere of undifferentiated equality; it must create it.

The result is reminiscent of Rousseau's later proposal for a state in which the horizontal independence of citizens is held together by their absolute vertical subordination to the state as subjects. In Rousseau's ideal political community, '[E]ach citizen would be perfectly independent of all others and excessively dependent upon the city. This always takes place by the same means, for only the force of the state brings about the liberty of its members'.[51] To be sure, there are differences: for Rousseau, equality is the direct motivation, whereas Hobbes's interest in egalitarianism is often expressed as instrumental to the larger program of avoiding war and sedition. But even if instrumental, the demand for equality is intense and pervasive.

Why exactly is equality so important? Hoekstra's discussion of Hobbes's egalitarianism focuses on the resentment that inequality rouses.[52] In asserting natural human equality, 'Hobbes's priority is not to reveal an underlying ontology of equality, but to mitigate the disastrous effects of pride, contempt, and open disagreement about comparative worth'.[53] Hobbes's ninth law of nature rules that 'every man acknowledge other for his Equall by

[49] Zagorin notes that even Richelieu, centralizer extraordinaire, regretfully recognized the impossibility of entirely eliminating the power of the nobility, and contented himself with domesticating it (Zagorin, *Rebels and Rulers*, 87–121). And even the degree of centralization that Richelieu achieved was precarious, provoking the counterreaction of the Fronde (ibid., 188–222).

[50] Pettit, *Made with Words*, 132–140.

[51] Rousseau, *On the Social Contract*, Book 2, Chapter 12.

[52] Kinch Hoekstra, 'Hobbesian Equality', in Lloyd, *Hobbes Today*, 76–112.

[53] Ibid., 112.

Nature' (L 234–235, 15.21). People will not peaceably accept unequal status—'[M]en that think themselves equall, will not enter into conditions of Peace, but upon Equall terms' (L 234–235, 15.21)—therefore all should recognize one another as equal. Correspondingly, the duty of the sovereign includes not giving preferential treatment to the mighty, in order not to arouse the resentment of the masses (L 534–534, 542–543, 30.15–16, 30.23).

On Hoekstra's analysis, it is unequal treatment that is destabilizing; and it is destabilizing because subjects resent it: the villains in this story are the elite who wish to assert their superiority.[54] Surely there is a problem with elite desire, but Hobbes's analysis reveals that the masses are hardly innocent. In light of my exegetical emphasis on Hobbes's relational conception of power, we can see that popular desire does not simply or consistently oppose inequality. As *Leviathan*, Chapter 10, explains in detail, people curry favour with the powerful, hoping to benefit or at least avoid harm from that power. As I argued in Chapter 2, Section 2.4 and Chapter 4, Section 4.2, this behaviour consolidates and amplifies the power of the powerful: indeed, human power is relationally constituted. Thus, even if people do wish to be formally respected as equals, so many aspects of their everyday behaviour have valence as honour and unintentionally contribute to the emergence of great inequalities of power. People's attitudes towards these emergent inequalities are ambivalent: they may resent the special privileges that the great enjoy at the hands of the sovereign, and they may resent the might of the great if they suffer under it. But at the same time, they may accept or enthusiastically endorse the power of their own patron and accept their subservience to that patron. A sovereign may act contrary to duty and grant privileges to a mighty person not because it wants to treat subjects unequally, but out of fear of the mighty person's power (L 146–147, 10.51, 496–497, 28.25), which in turn rests on the person's popular following. It is a key threat to the commonwealth that the masses celebrate the impunity of the powerful with whom they are allied: '[T]he popularity of a potent subject . . . is a dangerous disease, because the people . . . by the flattery and by the reputation of an ambitious man, are drawn away from their obedience to the laws' (L 516–517, 29.20). As I argued in Chapter 4, Section 4.4, power blocs in the multitude are problematic because their very existence diminishes the absoluteness of sovereign power and lays the groundwork for the destabilization of the political order. The problem of equality is not only the arrogance of the mighty;

[54] Ibid., 110.

it is the pervasive willingness of everyone else to defer to and ally with the mighty. If only subjects were so consistent in their egalitarianism as Hoekstra portrays.

I have characterized this repressive egalitarianism as expressing a certain conception of and positive commitment to popular power, where its popular character is seen most vividly in its opposition to informal private oligarchy. I now turn to consider the implications of this repressive egalitarianism for the formal institutions of government. Hobbes urges sovereigns to take into account information and demands sourced in detail from across the entire country:

> The best Counsell, in those things that concern . . . the ease, and benefit the Subjects may enjoy . . . is to be taken from the generall informations, and complaints of the people of each Province, who are best acquainted with their own wants, and ought therefore, when they demand nothing in derogation of the essentiall Rights of Soveraignty, to be diligently taken notice of. (L 548–549, 30.27)

But what is the institutional means to this end? As foreshadowed earlier, Hobbes is triply hostile to democratic solutions. He is sceptical regarding claims to speak in the name of the people; he rejects any need for a sovereign to be responsive; and he is hostile to governance by democratic assembly. Martel argues that beneath Hobbes's official hostility towards popular expression not mediated by the sovereign, *Leviathan* in fact endorses the spontaneous unmediated expression of the people's will.[55] But to the contrary, I will show that Hobbes's repressive egalitarian conception of popular *potentia* makes sense of his anti-democratic commitments.

Hobbes's explicit reason for scepticism regarding claims to speak in the name of the people is part of his juridical theory of collective agency: without formal personation, the multitude remains just a collection of separate individuals (L 248–251, 16.13–14). Martel's suggestion sidesteps this argument and invokes a non-juridical emergent voice of the multitude. But what would this be? The actual de facto expressed will of the people? As I outlined in Chapter 4, Section 4.4, and elaborated earlier in this present section,

[55] Martel, *Subverting the Leviathan*, 3, 242. In what follows, I do not address Martel's highly contentious interpretive strategy, instead focussing my criticisms on the coherence of the substantive view that he develops.

Hobbes's account of the concrete power *potentia* of informal associations poses its own obstacles to identifying a will of the people distinct from the state. First, there is no reason to think that the expressed will of the people will be a single coherent thing; there may be two or more identifiable emergent wills corresponding to different groupings within the multitude. And second, even the expressed will of a given grouping does not necessarily display the egalitarian shape that might render it normatively and politically appealing. If the *potentia* of the masses is oligarchic, then so too will be the de facto expressed will: people conform their speech and conduct to secure their favour and protection within informal power blocs in the multitude. It can be the impure result of interested parties capturing the popular imagination for their own self-interested purposes.[56] A Hobbesian analysis of the multitude's power foreshadows Schumpeter's famous argument centuries later that there is no natural object 'the will of the people'.[57]

Hobbes is not merely sceptical about the credentials of a natural de facto will of the people; he is also sceptical about the people's will as expressed by public assemblies. One might have thought that democratic or parliamentary institutions offer a proper gauge of popular will, because the formal political equality of those institutions overcomes and overrides the power blocs of the multitude. In a common way of thinking about popular power, amongst the radicals of Hobbes's time as well as more recently, the key question is who holds formal power and franchise; it is implicitly presumed that this will be a good guide to political outcomes.[58] Rulers tend to rule for themselves; it is necessary to have the people rule. But for Hobbes especially in his later works, far from democratic institutions being sufficient to establish political equality, they in fact run contrary to this goal. At best, the formally egalitarian structure might simply reflect the background power inequalities;[59] but Hobbes argues that an even worse outcome is likely. Recall the discussion of counsel in Section 5.3: Hobbes believes that democratic institutions

[56] A sharp topical example is provided by political events in Australia in 2011. The Australian mining industry mounted a public relations campaign that unseated the ruling prime minister, as a fairly transparent retaliation for his attempts to tax mining companies at a greater rate. Mark Davis, 'A Snip at $22m to Get Rid of PM', *Sydney Morning Herald*, 2 February 2011.

[57] Schumpeter, *Capitalism, Socialism and Democracy*, 250–268.

[58] Indeed, this is the key question underlying *De Cive*'s conception of the sleeping democratic sovereign, recently celebrated by Tuck, *The Sleeping Sovereign*, 86–106.

[59] Similarly, Marx observes that a formally popular constitution may not challenge the underlying oligarchic social relations with the social body; to the contrary, it may perpetuate and solidify it. Marx, 'Contribution to the Critique', 61. The Hobbesian framework offers the advantage that it can understand power beyond its economic forms.

perversely compound the problem, by providing a stage on which undesirable hierarchical power blocs in the multitude can be magnified.

This brings us back to Tuck's proposal for despotic democratic sovereignty. Tuck's proposal is distinct from rule by a democratic assembly: he imagines a non-assembled, non-deliberative mass plebiscitary vote. For now, put aside the problem already discussed in Chapter 4 for this kind of 'sleeping sovereign' to maintain its real power. Presuming this despotic sovereign is effective (that is, its votes make a difference and are respected and obeyed), is it a good gauge of popular will? Even Rousseau, arch-democrat, expresses grave reservations: Rousseau promotes popular decision-making only when it is conducted by the vote of a sufficiently informed populace with no communication amongst voters. Tuck emphasizes Hobbes's Rousseauvian worry about mass deliberation, and it is for precisely this reason that Tuck argues that democratic sovereignty finds its most meaningful expression via plebiscitary vote.[60] But it is unclear how Rousseau imagined voting could be insulated from communication amongst voters; and certainly, the plebiscitary voting that Tuck recommends invites a period of campaigning in which there is ample room for opportunistic political competition. Witness the 2016 Brexit vote, in which there was ample campaigning, a fair part of which was arguably driven by factional struggles for power.[61] Furthermore, even supposing there could be truly non-deliberative voting, Rousseau does not believe that the good operation of sovereignty is automatic: on his account, it presupposes a small and equal population.[62]

Hobbes grants that it is in principle possible that a public assembly in a large country might operate as it should, as an egalitarian and reliable measure of interests. But this would depend on certain particular conditions: members should be united by fear of a foreign enemy, or by 'mutuall feare of equall factions' (L 412–413, 25.16). Presumably the same applies to the de facto will

[60] Tuck, *The Sleeping Sovereign*, 5–6.

[61] The popular credentials of plebiscites are further diminished when we consider the process by which the plebiscitary question is set in the first place: this process offers ample opportunity for cynical shaping of the plebiscitary outcome. For two particularly egregious examples, consider the 1999 Australian Republican Referendum, and the 1962 Singapore Referendum on Merger. In 1999, polling suggested high levels of support for no longer having the queen of England as Australian head of state, but the referendum question (set by a pro-monarchy prime minister) offered only a choice between an American-style presidency or retaining the status quo. Entirely predictably, Australians voted against the American system. In 1962, all three options on the ballot, as well as all spoilt ballots, effectively supported the government's favoured policy of Singapore's merger with Malaysia. Melanie Chew, *Leaders of Singapore* (Singapore: Resource Press, 1996), 92.

[62] In particular there must be minimal economic inequality, and no separate powerful towns. Rousseau, *The Social Contract*, 2.11, 3.13.

of the popular multitude even prior to its entry into parliament. But short of these exceptional circumstances, private power stands as a problem; Hobbes's solution is equal treatment via repressive egalitarianism. Popular power worthy of the name is only to be had through the state that aggressively manages the informal power dynamics of the social body. Simply appealing to the will of the people, even as channelled through democratic process, is not enough, unless private power is tackled. This analysis reveals the fundamental inadequacy of juridical readings of Hobbes.

This analysis of Hobbesian politics from the point of view of concrete power provides a solution to a dilemma, originally posed by Hobbes's contemporary critics, and recently resurrected by Hoekstra.[63] Hoekstra claims there is a dilemma for Hobbes's conception of the unity of sovereignty. Either it is possible to unify distinct entities into a single sovereign, or it is not. But Hobbes appears to want it both ways: he allows that the multitude can be unified into a single democratic sovereign, but he rejects the possibility that the various political bodies of a mixed constitution could together constitute a single sovereign. Hoekstra does not see a convincing distinction between the two cases. However, analysing through the lens of relations of *potentia*, the distinction between the cases becomes clear. In asking whether a collection of parts can constitute a collective with a single will (a sovereign will), the key question is whether the parts have the power *potentia* to challenge or destabilize the sovereign so formed. When the parts are the various political bodies of the mixed constitution, some of them may well have hope of success from their private power *potentia* to challenge the collective decision. But when the parts are mere isolated individuals, with their possibility of collective action with their fellow citizens stymied by a thoroughgoing policy of repressive egalitarianism, then they do not have sufficient *potentia* to mount any such challenge. In result, only under a despotic (non-mixed) sovereign can there be any hope to generate a sovereign with power *potentia* proportional to its right.

Hobbes's late absolutism can be seen as an attempt to break down the conflictual oligarchy of the multitude and recombine it as disempowered equality. This amounts to an attempt to achieve, but now through deliberate effort, the social domain of fragmented equality that was blithely presupposed in his early civil science. In his commitment to eviscerating private power, Hobbes crushes expressions of public will as mediated by

[63] Hoekstra, 'Early Modern Absolutism and Constitutionalism', 1092–1094.

traditional and emergent communities and groupings, whether in the public sphere or in political assemblies. He views civil society as fractious and oligarchic. But through this repression, Hobbes also takes subjects out of the power of private power blocs and establishes equal standing for the entire populace. No doubt Hobbes's analysis takes too sanguine a view of aristocracy and monarchy's credentials. No doubt there is something perverse about insisting on human equality, only then to be most happy to hand over the reins of absolute power to a single individual or small aristocratic assembly. No doubt the ruling class of the state represents the most privileged site of hierarchy, and entrenches unequal power. But what remains valuable in Hobbes's analysis is his withering scepticism of claims to speak for the people. Hobbesian analysis poses challenges to a politics that fears state power, but which turns a blind eye to the non-state powers that shape and control individuals' lives.

5.5. The Conditions of Success of Hobbes's Politics

For Hobbes, a proper science of politics should explain the causes of war in such a way that human industry can in the future prevent it (DCo 1.7). Indeed, Hobbes claims to have found out principles of reason (expressed in his account of the rights of sovereignty) such that a commonwealth organized according to those principles may be everlasting (barring external violence) (L 522–523, 30.5). In that spirit, accepting the regime of rights and duties that Hobbes claims reason gives us, I ask whether the resultant model of politics concretely offers peace. In my discussion, I have identified and analysed a threat to peace, what I have called the political problem. If a commonwealth is correctly constituted according to the principles of Hobbes's civil science, is it possible for the sovereign to garner concrete obedience commensurate to absolute *potestas*? Will subjects in fact durably submit to such a sovereign? Does Hobbes's absolutism account for the genesis of the concrete behaviour of both subjects and sovereign that it relies upon? Many commentators do not consider this concrete standard of success. Traditionally it has been more common to focus on juridical questions of the rationality and justification of the system of rights and obligations. The secondary literature emphasizing rhetoric and education does obliquely consider concrete success, and is generally optimistic that, given sufficient education of the subjects and sovereign in their civil duties, peace will be secured. The model works, not in virtue of fear of punishment alone, but only through fear of punishment when supplemented with civil indoctrination.[64]

I grant that for the most part, Hobbes himself appears optimistic about possibilities of indoctrination in civil duties for the masses and sovereign, as detailed in Sections 5.2 and 5.3. However, the upshot of my discussion over the last four chapters is to bring into view the broader organizational and interpersonal determinants of compliance or non-compliance with duty. Thus, Hobbes's civil indoctrination must operate in tandem with persistent and farsighted efforts to minimize the size and strength of power blocs. For there is a limit to the efficacy of rhetorical and educational strategies taken alone to overcome the political problem, due to the indocibility of some and the excess docibility of others.

Hobbes himself complains that unlike the masses, powerful individuals tend to be insubordinate and refuse to accept his doctrine, often instead spreading seditious counterdoctrines. The elite and the educated are resistant to his educational and rhetorical program. He diagnoses possible grounds for their resistance in the most unflattering of terms: far from being interested in understanding true civil science, they do not even work to achieve the practical prudence that they cultivate in their private business. For in public affairs, they are more interested in maintaining a reputation for wit and do not care if the public business goes to ruin (L 76–77, 5.22). Hobbes reflects most on these problems in the case of democracy, where there is an assembly in which these powerful individuals seek to capture allegiance. But equally in monarchies a related problem presses: for the universities and churches continue to exist as forums in which insubordinate individuals promote their doctrines. 'Potent men, digest hardly any thing that setteth up a Power to bridle their affections; and Learned men, any thing that discovereth their errours, and thereby lesseneth their Authority' (L 524–525, 30.6). In other words, the powerful uphold seditious civil doctrines because they hope better to preserve their own private power, wealth, and status thereby. Certainly, a prudent sovereign seeks to suppress such doctrines and promote the correct doctrine of rights of sovereignty, but these elites are ex hypothesi already powerful, so effort to force their compliance is fraught.[65]

[64] Frost, *Lessons from a Materialist Thinker*, 165–169; Sreedhar, *Hobbes on Self-Defence*, 163–167; Johnston, *The Rhetoric of 'Leviathan'*, 163; MacPherson, *Political Theory of Possessive Individualism*, 97–99; Tarlton, 'Creation and Maintenance', 313–324; Pettit, *Made with Words*, 111. By contrast, Garsten argues the model will not be successful. Bryan Garsten, *Saving Persuasion: A Defense of Rhetoric and Judgment* (Cambridge, MA: Harvard University Press, 2006), 17–18, 184–185.

[65] Frost emphasizes that Hobbes does make some allowance for special strategies to neutralize powerful subjects—bestowing titles of honour and corresponding privileges on ambitious people,

Hobbes himself identifies the problem on the side of the elite; but one might wonder whether there is an opposite difficulty on the side of the masses: the problem of excess docibility. As discussed earlier, given the insufficient public interest in philosophy, the masses are taught their duty without necessarily understanding its rational grounding. Their duty is impressed on them through religiously imbued imagery and ritual; they are encouraged in habits of deference to authority, including deference to the sovereign's authority over religion and scriptural interpretation. But as Qudrat argues, this is in itself risky, because deference to authority is achieved at the expense of judgement and understanding. With the capacity to think critically about religion dampened, the masses become vulnerable to any false prophet claiming religious sanction for their political projects.[66] This point might apply equally to secular political pretenders: in hard or tumultuous times, subjects who have imbibed the lesson of uncritical submission to authority in return for promised security might be tempted by strong usurpers.

Thus indoctrination alone is not sufficient to solve the political problem: rather, what is required is indoctrination combined with the substantive weakness of would-be usurpers. At the foundation of good Hobbesian politics lies the multitude of fragmented equality, maintained through a persistent labour to diminish and disband potential counterpowers in the social body. If the power of associations is repressed in this way, the sovereign, as sole bearer of the person of the people, acts freely for the population's interests, guided by the prompting of good counsel and without grassroots pressure. In the English *Leviathan*, Hobbes expresses confidence that a commonwealth properly constituted according to his account of the rights of the sovereign will be everlasting. Perhaps this confidence falters a little: by the time of the later Latin edition, the corresponding passage is more chastened: 'Whether the principles which I have set forth above can produce this result, I do not know' (L 522–523, 30.5). It is possible that the practical deliverances of Hobbes's civil science may be less perfect than he initially expected, but they are far from absurd or incoherent. Indeed,

in order to enlist them as allies of the sovereign (L 138–139, 146–147, 10.35–36, 10.52; Frost, *Lessons from a Materialist Thinker*, 161–163). But such a strategy requires caution, because it risks sliding into appeasement of the powerful; it emboldens them and threatens the sovereign's supremacy (L 494–496, 536–537, 28.24–25, 30.16).

[66] Maryam Qudrat, 'Confronting Jihad: A Defect in the Hobbesian Educational Strategy', in *Hobbes Today: Insights for the 21st Century*, edited by S. A. Lloyd (New York: Cambridge University Press, 2013), 229–240.

Singapore might offer an instance of Hobbesian government: government is via expert counsel for the public good, including comprehensive and (at least in the early decades post-independence) egalitarian public provision of the citizenry's needs; formally democratic but organized so as to crush all non-governmental collective organization.[67]

A striking feature of Hobbes's solution is the imperfection of the mechanism ensuring sovereign action in accord with duty. The two extreme cases are easy. On the one hand, suppose the sovereign receives good counsel and acts appropriately on this counsel: suppose it prudently and justly discharges its duty to serve the people, all the while repressing the emergence of counterpowers. Then it will have solved the political problem, and will enjoy peace and prosperity. On the other hand, suppose the sovereign entirely ignores the good counsel it receives, and rules in a self-serving and reckless manner. Then it will incur the political problem, and will suffer dissent, turmoil, and eventually, collapse. The challenging case is the intermediate one. Suppose the sovereign listens selectively to the good counsel it receives: it carefully represses counterpowers, it rules well enough not to arouse immense indignation, but its manner of rule remains self-serving. Such a sovereign avoids the political problem and secures its own stability. But it can simultaneously quite contentedly enrich itself and fail to advance the common good, because it faces no challenge to its poor rule.

Hobbes is untroubled by this feature of his proposal: for if his civil science is correct, then there are no other alternatives for achieving peace apart from repressive egalitarianism. In this case, the lack of insurance against the stably unjust regime must be borne, as the price of peace: this just attests to the imperfection of human existence in general. But might there be a different way to deal with the power blocs of the multitude? Rather than crushing those groups, is it possible instead to think about their positive political potentiality? Rather than weakening and fragmenting, might it be possible to strengthen and integrate them, such that they can improve rather than ruin

[67] See Chua Beng Huat, 'Towards a Non-liberal Communitarian Democracy', *Communitarian Ideology and Democracy in Singapore* (New York: Routledge, 2006), 184–202; Chua Beng Huat, *Liberalism Disavowed: Communitarianism and State Capitalism in Singapore* (Singapore: NUS Press, 2017), 176–194; Cherian George, *Freedom from the Press: Journalism and State Power in Singapore* (Singapore: NUS Press, 2012), 93–116. Chua sharply identifies some supplementary mechanisms containing elite indocibility in Singapore. Elite dissent is readily dissipated by permitting its expression through subversive theatre productions. Chua Beng Huat, 'Disavowing Liberalism: Political Development in Singapore since 1980s', talk delivered at Yale-NUS College, 12 October 2017. Chua also emphasizes the aspiration of the elite to state-sector employment. Chua, *Liberalism Disavowed*, 182.

the state's commitment to the common good? I will return to consider this possibility in my discussion of Spinozan popular power in Chapter 9.

With this section, I draw now to the end of my consideration of Hobbes's politics, and with it, I come to the end of the first half of the book. Hobbes has laid down a fundamental provocation: there is nothing good about the prepolitical multitude itself. The multitude is fractious and oligarchic, and something needs to be done to overcome its tendency to internal conflict. Focussing on the *potentia* of the multitude leads us decisively away from Tuck's radical democracy, as a proposal reflecting an inadequate analysis both of popularity and of power. If popular power is reconceived as collective *potentia* that has eliminated capture by private interests, then Hobbes's own model for realizing popular power is what I have called a repressive egalitarianism: a levelling-down equality that seeks to weaken and fragment the multitude in order to bring it to submit to sovereign rule and thereby constitute itself as a peaceful commonwealth. Repressive egalitarianism eliminates grassroots collective pressure as much as it can: without the disproportionate influence of particular factions, the sovereign is freed to rule according to its best, well-counselled judgement. In the second half of the book, I turn to Spinoza's analysis of the multitude's *potentia*, which is alleged to provide a rather different grounding of radical democracy. But for this to succeed, it must address the worry about informal oligarchy that Hobbes so insistently raises.

PART II
SPINOZA

6

Ethics and Efficacy

6.1. Introduction

The core concern of this book is power and popular politics. If there is such a thing as popular power, what precisely is it? Radical democrats attempt to locate popular power somehow more authentically in the power of a population, rather than in the regular institutions of the state: the agent of this popular power could be a Hobbesian-inspired, plebiscitary, absolute, democratic sovereign, or a Spinozist-inspired spontaneous multitude.[1] But these attempts raise critical questions. Are plebiscites and social movements themselves always so pure? In what sense are their decisions and actions more truly reflective of popular power, whatever that might mean, than the institutional forms of politics? This book uses a novel reading of Hobbes's and Spinoza's philosophies to establish and defend a new conception of popular power. The new conception still facilitates a critical attitude to institutional politics, but it does so without relying upon a romanticized view of non-institutional politics.

Having discussed Hobbes in the first half of the book, now in this second half of the book I turn to his slightly younger contemporary Spinoza. Notwithstanding Tuck's promotion of a 'democratic Hobbes', to most readers Hobbes remains a deeply anti-popular thinker. Spinoza's practical political prescriptions appear more pro-popular and less authoritarian than Hobbes's; this is often explained as a consequence of his focus on concrete power. On the standard interpretations, Hobbes, theorist of juridical power *potestas*, is the proponent of repressive political forms; Spinoza, theorist of concrete power *potentia*, promotes liberal or even radically liberatory democracy. This is because the concrete *potentia* of the popular multitude constitutes a

[1] *Multitudo*, multitude or crowd, is a term found in both Hobbes and Spinoza. Hobbes contrasts *multitudo*, as a mass of individuals without reference to juridical organization, to *populus*, the people as a juridically defined mass agent (DC 6.1; see my Chapter 3, Section 3.2). In Spinoza's hands, the term appears to have a similar meaning, but it does more positive work in his politics even as its precise conceptual structure remains elusive. This has generated disagreement amongst interpreters, as I will elaborate subsequently.

Potentia. Sandra Leonie Field, Oxford University Press (2020). © Oxford University Press.
DOI: 10.1093/oso/9780197533864.001.0001

limit on sovereign power *potestas*, a limit that juridical projections of *potestas* ignore at their peril. On the view of radical democratic Spinozists, popular power is the power *potentia* of the multitude, and it finds its exemplary expression in social movements and mass insurgencies.

These standard accounts are not entirely false, but they rest on an unsustainably romantic theory of concrete popular power. In the first half of the book, I demonstrated that Hobbes not only theorizes juridical power, but in his later writings also provides an account of concrete power *potentia* of emergent groupings. Collectivities can have concrete power, but this power is not necessarily normatively appealing: for the internal dynamics of the multitude often spontaneously generate oligarchy and conflict. Insofar as the multitude's *potentia* does not sufficiently support sovereign *potestas* (or in the terms of my preceding chapters, insofar as the political problem arises), then Hobbes's solution is not to defer to the multitude, but to the contrary, to overcome its oligarchic and conflictual tendency by deepening its fragmentation and disempowerment. I have labelled Hobbes's proposal repressive egalitarianism, focussed on crushing non-state powers, and I have claimed that it reflects a commitment to a useful (albeit thin) conception of popular power.

If Spinoza's account of the concrete power *potentia* of the multitude appears so different in its political implications, what accounts for these differences? Does Spinoza mean something different by power than Hobbes, or does he offer some different analysis of concrete power's dynamics that allows it to overcome its undesirable features? Does the Spinozist perspective truly support conceiving social movements as exemplary of popular power? And if not, what should replace that conception? My answer to these questions unfolds over the four chapters of the second half of the book. Regarding popularity: I criticize the idea that there is anything innocent or necessarily wholesome about the concrete power *potentia* of Spinoza's multitude. Just as for Hobbes, the multitude's power may harbour antisocial and hierarchical tendencies; it can break apart in conflict, or (depending on your perspective) even worse, it can hold together to maintain and entrench its own inner hierarchical forms. And regarding power: for Spinoza just as for Hobbes, I argue that all power must be judged within its actual social and relational context; and that any overall characterization of the power expressed in a given political order should be determined at the level of systematic outcomes. In result, a Spinozist account of popular power does not rely on appeal to a naturally existing mass democratic subject, nor even on a great faith in the democratic process per se. Rather, Spinozist popular power is expressed when the entire ecology of a political order durably generates equality and participation. Spinoza's difference from Hobbes lies not primarily in the fundamental conception of popular power as *potentia*, but in his estimation of the means best adapted to this end: Spinoza grants the possibility of good and civic forms of pressure on the holder of sovereignty, which can consolidate the orientation of the state to the common good. Against Hobbesian repressive egalitarianism, Spinoza offers a model of civic strengthening: the meticulous institutional cultivation and consolidation of non-oligarchic forms of citizenly action.

More specifically, I carry out my argument in the following steps. For this chapter, I schematize two broad interpretive approaches to Spinoza's political philosophy: what I call the radical approach; and the constitutionalist approach. Against the sunny romanticism pervading both these interpretations' conceptions of popular power, I pose three Hobbesian problems: the problem of the multitude's inner oligarchy; the problem of nonideal endurance; and the problem of democracy's perverse effects. In Chapter 7, I establish a new interpretation of Spinoza's political conception of *potentia* from within his broader metaphysical framework. Centrally, I distinguish between, on the one hand, *potentia operandi* (power of producing effects), which I argue corresponds closely to Hobbes's late notion of power (*potentia*); and on the other hand, *potentia agendi* (power of acting), associated with a thing's essence and virtue. Politically, this manifests as a distinction between merely having right, versus being in control of one's own right (being sui juris); it raises but does not answer the question of the relation between the sui juris status of a political collectivity and the sui juris status of the members making up that collectivity. In Chapter 8, I establish a more precise way to characterize a thing's own proper power of acting, building on an interpretation of being sui juris as homeostasis. I then use this analytical frame to explain how and in what sense Spinoza acknowledges both the Hobbesian problem of the multitude's inner oligarchy, and the problem of nonideal regime endurance. In Chapter 9, I establish a neo-Spinozist criterion of popular power, whereby popular power is judged at the level of systematic effects and outcomes of a political order. I provide a taxonomy of organizational elements that might best address the Hobbesian problem of democracy's perverse effects and thereby express meaningful popular power. In this frame, social movements and insurgencies are decentred: they are no longer the exemplary expression of popular power as the radical Spinozist would have it, but rather are one partial element within a larger political ecology that may or may not have an overall popular character.

Before starting my substantive argument, let me offer a note on the texts. Spinoza's political philosophy is primarily to be found in his *Theological-Political Treatise* (1670) and his *Political Treatise* (1677), then also to a lesser extent in his *Ethics* (1677).[2] The comparison of Hobbesian and Spinozist concepts has a strong historical rationale: Spinoza's *Theological-Political Treatise* transparently takes Hobbes's writings as a starting point, modelling itself on Hobbes's terminology, and developing its anti-Hobbesian conclusions from within a robustly Hobbesian theoretical frame, leading Curley to characterize Spinoza as being on the surface nothing more than an 'eccentric Hobbesian'.[3] Spinoza was in a good position to engage with Hobbesian ideas: he owned Hobbes's *De Cive* in his private library; and it is possible that Spinoza had access to *Leviathan*.[4]

Even though I will ultimately argue that Spinoza's *potentia operandi* is similar to the *potentia* of Hobbes's later writings, I am not arguing that he necessarily cribbed it from *Leviathan*. For first, as I have argued in Chapter 4, Hobbes's non-juridical conception of power, especially of non-juridical collective power, remains submerged in *Leviathan*, subordinated to the dominant discussion of juridical power; second, Spinoza himself makes a strongly juridical characterization of Hobbes's philosophy; and third, Spinoza's theory

[2] Only the *Theological-Political Treatise* was published during Spinoza's lifetime. By Curley's estimation, the first two parts of the *Ethics* were written by around 1665; the *Theological-Political Treatise* was completed in 1669; the remaining three parts of the *Ethics* were written by 1675; and the *Political Treatise* was still in progress at the time of Spinoza's death in 1677, resulting in an incomplete discussion of democracy (as I will consider in detail in Chapter 9). Benedict de Spinoza, *The Collected Works of Spinoza*, Vol, 1, translated by Edwin Curley (Princeton, NJ: Princeton University Press, 1985), 405–406; Benedict de Spinoza, *The Collected Works of Spinoza*, Vol. 2, translated by Edwin Curley (Princeton, NJ: Princeton University Press, 2016), 59, 491.

[3] Curley offers this only as a provisional characterization, before subsequently emphasizing deeper differences between the two thinkers and outlining Spinoza's similarities to Machiavelli. Edwin Curley, 'Kissinger, Spinoza, and Genghis Khan', in *The Cambridge Companion to Spinoza*, edited by Don Garrett (New York: Cambridge University Press, 1996), 315–318, 328–333.

[4] The inventory of Spinoza's library on his death includes Hobbes, *Elementa Philosophica* (Jacob Freudenthal, *Die Lebensgeschichte Spinoza's in Quellenschriften, Urkunden und Nichtamtlichen Nachrichten* [Leipzig: Verlag von Veit & Comp., 1899], 163). *Elementa Philosophica* is the title of Hobbes's three-volume systematic presentation of his philosophy, including *De Corpore, De Cive*, and *De Homine*. It is not clear from the somewhat telegraphic inventory whether Spinoza held all three volumes; but commentators presume he held at least *De Cive*. Spinoza did not read English, but it is likely he had access to *Leviathan*: a Dutch translation appeared in 1667, and the Latin *Leviathan* was republished in Amsterdam in 1668. Noel Malcolm, 'Hobbes and Spinoza', *Aspects of Hobbes* (Oxford: Oxford University Press, 2002), 41, 47. Schoneveld claims that Spinoza had access to the in-progress Dutch translation of *Leviathan* while he was writing the *Theological-Political Treatise*. Cornelis W. Schoneveld, *Intertraffic of the Mind: Studies in Seventeenth-Century Anglo-Dutch Translation* (Leiden: Brill, 1983), 40.

of political *potentia* has organic connection to Spinoza's larger systematic philosophy. Thus, my thesis about similarities between their theories does not rely on strong claims of whether Spinoza read *Leviathan* or not.

Whereas Hobbes's three core political works are essentially revisions of the same text, by contrast Spinoza's two political treatises are substantially different documents. I gave a stylized account of the relation between these treatises in my Chapter 1, Section 1.2. However, I grant that that account was somewhat reductive. There are numerous differences of structure, topic, emphasis, terminology, and concepts,[5] and there is debate in the secondary literature about what exactly these differences might amount to. Furthermore, between the two texts, there was a period of great political turmoil in the Dutch republic, including the lynching of Republican leader Jan de Witt by an angry mob, and the resurgence of a quasi-monarchical stadtholder;[6] there is debate regarding the degree to which the changes were prompted by political events.[7] In my arguments, I make use of both political texts, in combination with the *Ethics* for systematic background. However, given (as I will argue in Chapter 7, Section 7.3.2) its superior conceptualization of *potentia*, the *Political Treatise* will emerge as the authoritative text.

6.2. Spinoza's Immanent Critique of Hobbes

The standard account of the core conceptual difference between the political philosophies of Hobbes and Spinoza is that Spinoza understands politics through concrete power *potentia*, whereas Hobbes understands it through

[5] Prima facie differences include a significantly diminished theoretical prominence of a social contract; the emergence of the concept of the multitude; the greater consideration of monarchy and aristocracy; the lesser attention to imagination, religion, faith; and the more minute focus on institutional design.

[6] For an overview of the historical and political context of Spinoza's writing, see footnotes 27 and 28 in Chapter 1.

[7] There is a considerable literature that limits itself exclusively to the earlier *Theological-Political Treatise*. But of those commentaries that read the two texts together, notable accounts of the change in the texts include Balibar and Negri, who (in different ways) find a deepening of the theory of democracy; and Feuer and Prokhovnik, who argue that Spinoza becomes more favourable to aristocracy. Étienne Balibar, *Spinoza and Politics*, translated by Peter Snowdon (New York: Verso, 1998), 51–75; Antonio Negri, 'The *Political Treatise*, or, the Foundation of Modern Democracy', in *Subversive Spinoza: (Un)contemporary Variations*, edited by Timothy S. Murphy (Manchester: Manchester University Press, 2004), 22–24; Feuer, *Rise of Liberalism*, 136–197; Raia Prokhovnik, *Spinoza and Republicanism* (Houndmills: Palgrave Macmillan, 2004), 75, 181. For a recent account of the relation between the texts that does not find any strong difference in regime preference, see Justin D. Steinberg, *Spinoza's Political Psychology* (Cambridge: Cambridge University Press, 2018).

juridical power *potestas*. In this section, I lay out the standard account, but I argue that it rests on an uncharitable characterization of Hobbes's mature political philosophy.

The prima facie puzzle posed by the political texts of Hobbes and Spinoza is how, from a very similar starting frame, they end up with such pointedly different political prescriptions.[8] Spinoza, like Hobbes, moves from a state of nature, via a transfer of right, to an absolute state (TTP III/190, 16.8, III/193, 16.25; TP 2.15–17). But even a brief glance at the texts reveals Spinoza frequently evincing a greater sympathy for popular political forms and a greater hostility to absolute rule than does Hobbes.[9] Whereas Hobbes grants the sovereign right over religion and requires subjects to comply outwardly, Spinoza supports free expression and freedom of religious affiliation (TTP III/239–240, 20.1–9). Whereas Hobbes denies the possibility of popular right apart from its authoritative expression through the state (DC 6.1–2), for Spinoza, the terms are reversed: the state is defined in terms of the right and power of the multitude, and he allows that that power might be withdrawn and turned against the state (TP 2.17, 3.9). Whereas Hobbes appears to approve of democracy only insofar as it minimizes popular participation and contestation, for Spinoza a monarchical state becomes more absolute insofar as royal power is mediated by strong laws and a strong popular assembly (TP 6.8, 7.1). Regarding the relative merits of the three forms of sovereignty, Spinoza expresses a preference for rather than against democracy (TTP III/74, 5.23–25, III/194–195, 16.30, 16.36; TP 8.3, 9.1).

An obvious starting point for understanding the differences between the thinkers is their divergent conceptions of right *jus*. In a letter to his friend Jelles, Spinoza explicitly identifies this as the crux of his political difference from Hobbes.

[8] The classic framing of this problem is found in Curley, 'Kissinger, Spinoza, and Genghis Khan', 317–318.

[9] There are genuine differences between the thinkers, even without going so far as Israel, who poses Spinoza as the founder of the modern values of egalitarianism, democracy, secularism, and universalism. Jonathan Israel, *A Revolution of the Mind: Radical Enlightenment and the Intellectual Origins of Modern Democracy* (Princeton, NJ: Princeton University Press, 2010), 241. For a polemical criticism of the anachronism of such characterizations of Spinoza's political views, see Yitzhak Y. Melamed, 'Charitable Interpretations and the Political Domestication of Spinoza, or, Benedict in the Land of the Secular Imagination', in *Philosophy and Its History: Aims and Methods in the Study of Early Modern Philosophy*, edited by Justin Smith, Mogens Laerke, and Eric Schliesser (Oxford: Oxford University Press, 2013), 258–277.

> As far as Politics is concerned, the difference you ask about, between Hobbes and me, is this: I always preserve natural Right unimpaired, and I maintain that in each State the Supreme Magistrate has no more right over its subjects than it has greater power over them. This is always the case in the state of Nature. (Ep 50, IV/239b)[10]

Indeed, in the state of nature, the philosophers are in broad agreement. For Spinoza,

> [T]he Right and Established Practice of nature [*Jus & Institutum naturæ*], under which all are born and for the most part live, prohibits nothing except what no one desires and what no one can do: not disputes, not anger, not deception. Without qualification, it is not averse to anything appetite urges. (TTP III/190, 16.9)

Similarly, Hobbes claims that 'nature has given each man a right to all things' (DC 1.8), and each individual's rights do not generate any corresponding duties in others (DC 1.10; L 198–199, 14.4). But this superficial agreement rests on a divergent underlying understanding of right. Whereas Hobbes conceives of rights as juridical permissions to exercise power (*potentia*) (DC 1.7; L 198–199, 14.1–2), for Spinoza rights are not mere permissions. At the foundation of his political philosophy is his notorious[11] assertion that right, *jus*, is coextensive with power, *potentia* (TTP III/189, 16.3–4; TP 2.3–4). Juridical right can be handed over, but for Spinoza, 'No one will ever be able to transfer to another his power, or consequently, his right [*suam potentiam & consequenter neque suum jus*], in such a way that he ceases to be a man' (TTP III/201, 17.2): each thing always keeps its *potentia* (and thus any right corresponding to that *potentia*) (TTP III/201, 17.1–5). This underlying divergence generates distinct analyses of the state's right. On the one hand, we have Hobbes, theorist of sovereign power *potestas* constructed out of absolute

[10] I provide the passage in English, not in Latin, because the original letter was composed in Dutch, and only subsequently translated into Latin. Furthermore, Curley argues that the Latin translation was probably not at Spinoza's own hand: for he argues Spinoza probably meant to write *Staat* (= state = *civitas*) not *Stat* (= city = *urbs*), but the Latin provides *urbs* (Spinoza, *Collected Works*, Vol. 2, 406 n. 70). Given the unreliability of this letter's Latin, when I reconstruct the systematic relation of Spinoza's terms, I will not attach much weight to the letter's translation of power as *potestas* rather than *potentia*, focussing instead on Spinoza's own Latin presentation in his treatises.

[11] Now notorious, but not unusual in Dutch intellectual life of the time. For a discussion of Dutch attempts to de-juridify Hobbes in this period, especially in the works of the De La Courts, see Malcolm, 'Hobbes and Spinoza', 40–46.

transfer of juridical right *ius*, leaving subjects lacking in any right against the sovereign; on the other hand, we have Spinoza, theorist of *potentia*, where *potentia* remains bound to those human subjects whose *potentia* it is, refusing to acknowledge any right *ius* that parts company from that *potentia*. This appears to explain the philosophers' differing political preferences: because Spinoza recognizes non-juridical power, he can acknowledge non-state popular agency; because Spinoza recognizes non-juridical power, he prefers forms of juridical power that cleave as closely as possible to their non-juridical underpinnings.

It is clear that Hobbes has an elaborate system of juridical right that is lacking in Spinoza's political writings. But what exactly follows from this? Do we merely have a case of two parallel but different ways of classifying and evaluating political phenomena?[12] To the contrary, it is commonplace to understand the Spinozist conception of right as effecting an immanent critique of Hobbes. The Spinozist analysis is taken to serve as a critique that Hobbes by his own lights would need to accept.[13] Hobbes's position is not merely innocently different from Spinoza's: rather, the Spinozist analysis is alleged to show Hobbes's position to be self-defeating.

The immanent critique runs as follows. Hobbes's politics is focused on juridical power and right and is committed to central tenets: that the sovereign has the right to rule with impunity, and that the sovereign has the right to demand total subjection of subjects. But in taking this focus, Hobbes stands accused of ignoring concrete power. Spinoza points out that a functioning

[12] There are a few scholars who do not position the Spinozist position as superior to Hobbes, but instead simply chart divergences: where Hobbes claims a certain act or mode of governance to be rightful but Spinoza denies it; or where Spinoza attributes right to a collective as such but Hobbes grants it only to individuals who happen to be collected together. See, for instance, Malcolm, 'Hobbes and Spinoza', 50; Jonathan Havercroft, *Captives of Sovereignty* (Cambridge: Cambridge University Press, 2011), 53–75.

[13] Spinoza scholars almost universally position Spinoza as a political thinker superior to Hobbes. The reason most often given is this alleged self-defeating character of the focus on *potestas*. See Aurelia Armstrong, 'Natural and Unnatural Communities: Spinoza beyond Hobbes', *British Journal for the History of Philosophy 17*, no. 2 (2009): 281–283, 293; Balibar, *Spinoza and Politics*, 103–104; Curley, 'Kissinger, Spinoza, and Genghis Khan', 327–331; Israel, *Radical Enlightenment*, 258–262; Lazzeri, *Droit, pouvoir et liberté*, 215; Alexandre Matheron, *Individu et communauté chez Spinoza* (Paris: Éditions de Minuit, 1988), 221–222, 464–465; Michael A. Rosenthal, 'Spinoza's Republican Argument for Toleration', *Journal of Political Philosophy 11*, no. 3 (2003): 334; Montag, *Bodies, Masses, Power*, 67–71, 90–103. There are also other reasons offered for Spinoza's superiority. For Negri, there is absolutely an opposition between Spinoza and Hobbes—Spinoza is 'the anti-Hobbes'. But the problem with the Hobbesian focus on *potestas* is not that it is (immediately) self-defeating, but that it dominates and blocks *potentia* (Negri, *The Savage Anomaly*, 110–113). For Den Uyl, Spinoza is superior to Hobbes because Hobbes relies on an excessively pessimistic model of human behaviour. Douglas J. Den Uyl, *Power, State, and Freedom: An Interpretation of Spinoza's Political Philosophy* (Assen, The Netherlands: Van Gorcum, 1983), 158–159.

juridical model depends on concrete power. All the juridical specifications of sovereign *potestas* are idle unless *potestas* is effective in the world; if concrete efficacy is too far eroded, then *potestas* itself collapses. Implicitly, Hobbes accepts some form of this observation: he repeatedly notes that the sovereign maintains its right only so long as it is able to provide security (DC 8.8, 9.4; L 344–345, 21.21–22, 1133–1134, Review and Conclusion.6). But what is the ground of this ability? Spinoza points out that the power that either supports or destroys *potestas* is the concrete power of the multitude, and (so the accusation goes) Hobbes's juridical approach, obsessed with parsing contractual obligations, prevents him from understanding this power and remains merely and perniciously theoretical (TTP 17.1, III/201). Spinoza, by contrast, focuses on popular *potentia* and its problematic relation to sovereign efficacy. He denies that it is possible for individuals fully to subject themselves to a sovereign, and he thinks that demanding total subjection is destabilizing (TTP III/201, 17.1–4; TP 3.8). Spinoza twice quotes Seneca: no one continues violent rule (*violenta imperia*) for long (TTP III/74, 5.22, III/194, 16.29); this is taken as a riposte to Hobbes's formidable and terrifying sovereign. The idea central to Hobbes's absolutism, that allowing a ruler to rule with impunity conduces to stability, is roundly rejected (TP 7.14, 7.23, 7.29). Spinoza's most prominent example concerns free expression: against Hobbes's ambitious control of speech and teaching, Spinoza denies the sovereign has the power *potentia* or the right to such control, because humans cannot simply hand over their power of thought or speech; thus the sovereign lacks the power to put the control into effect. More precisely, the capacity of a sovereign to control speech will have differential efficacy across a population: in insisting upon that course of action, it antagonizes citizens of principle and elevates sycophants, thereby undermining the state (TTP 20.1–9, III/239–240, 20.27–31, III/243–244). So Hobbes's political model of absolute *potestas* will be prone to undermine its own concrete power, and thereby undermine itself. By contrast, Spinoza's politics is not self-defeating, because he allows *potestas* only insofar as it is a name for *potentia*, and he assiduously concerns himself with the concrete popular grounds of *potentia*. He clearly recognizes that any attempt to assert *potestas* beyond what is supported by the people's power is doomed to failure.

The standard account of the relation between the political philosophies of Hobbes and Spinoza is unfair to Hobbes. I do not deny that this account is encouraged by Spinoza himself: in his letter to Jelles, quoted previously, he does attribute to Hobbes a purely juridical discussion of politics.

Furthermore, it is true that in Hobbes's early writings, discussion of individual concrete power is quickly superseded once we move to the juridical discussion of state: the core of the early civil science is a purely juridical account of collectivities. But as I have argued at length, in Hobbes's later work we have a clear theory of concrete *potentia*, including collective *potentia*.[14] Nor is it sustainable to accuse Hobbes of lacking the conceptual resources to grasp the problem of overweening *potestas* unsupported by *potentia*: for this problem is nothing other than the political problem, which, as I have argued, Hobbes makes vigorous efforts to solve. Perhaps Spinoza is correct that extreme tyranny and extreme repression of speech are politically unsustainable. But this is something that Hobbes himself can readily grant. Despite affirming the in-principle rightfulness of such rule, those are not modes of government that Hobbes recommends. Indeed, his detailed concrete measures are crafted to minimize wicked rule. Rather, as I argued in Chapter 5, Hobbes brings the collective *potentia* of the people to match entitled *potestas* through what I have called repressive egalitarianism, in which counterpowers are eliminated, and the resultant regime of fragmented equality is stabilized by well-counselled sovereign rule and the moralized obedience of individual subjects. This repressive egalitarianism is not obviously unworkable; although to be sure, it is possible to raise doubts as to how profoundly it will advance the common good.

In result, Spinoza's alleged immanent critique of Hobbes is not a resounding success, and the divergence of the philosophers' respective political prescriptions cannot simply be explained by accusing Hobbes of not recognizing *potentia*.

[14] Why does Spinoza not remark on the theory of concrete collective *potentia*? First, he may only have been working from *De Cive*, in which the theory is not yet developed (see footnote 4). Second, even if he is working from *Leviathan*, Hobbes's theory of collective *potentia* is submerged in the text and less prominent than the juridical theory of *potestas*, as I have argued in Chapter 4, Section 4.3. In characterizing the relation between the thinkers, Spinoza scholars, especially scholars in a more Marxist tradition, have not only drawn on the actual content of Hobbes's texts, but have also been unduly swayed by MacPherson's interpretation of Hobbes. Already in my Chapters 2 and 4, I have criticized central aspects of MacPherson's reading of Hobbes: notably, although MacPherson does concern himself with concrete power in Hobbes, he alleges that Hobbes fails to conceive *collective* concrete power. MacPherson does not himself discuss Spinoza, but MacPherson's (mis)characterization of Hobbes is regularly relied upon in order to defend the superiority of the Spinozist alternative. See Armstrong, 'Natural and Unnatural Communities', 280–281; Balibar, *Spinoza and Politics*, 55; Eugene Holland, 'Spinoza and Marx', *Cultural Logic 2*, no. 1 (1998): §23; Matheron, *Individu et communauté*, 86, 222; Negri, *The Savage Anomaly*, 69–71, 206, 220. Indeed, Negri wrote the preface to the Italian edition of MacPherson's book. Antonio Negri, 'Prefazione all'edizione italiana', in Crawford B. MacPherson, *Libertà e proprietà alle origini del pensiero borghese: La teoria dell'individualismo possessivo da Hobbes a Locke* (Milan: Istituto Editoriale Internazionale Milano, 1961), 13–22.

6.3. Combining Ethics and Efficacy: Two Standard Approaches

To understand why Spinoza is more enthusiastic than Hobbes about popular political forms, despite both authors recognizing *potentia*, perhaps it is a mistake to fixate upon the textual presence or absence of this term *potentia* in the authors' respective texts. After all, *potentia* is a term of art, and there is no reason to think Hobbes and Spinoza should use it with the same meaning and theoretical structure. Indeed, Spinoza's conception of *potentia* appears just fundamentally different from Hobbes's, textually linked to an entirely different constellation of terms. In particular, in his later texts, Hobbes's power is a pure question of effects within a flat-footed mechanistic non-normative frame. But while Spinoza does retain some sense of efficacy, Spinoza's power appears deeply ethical. In this section, I sketch out key textual indications of an ethical structure to Spinoza's *potentia*. I delineate two main interpretive strategies in the literature for making sense of this combination of ethics and efficacy, in particular as it bears upon Spinoza's politics. In the following section, I articulate three problems that cast these two interpretive strategies into doubt.

In my Chapters 2 and 4, I insisted on the relational and de-essentializing character of Hobbes's late conception of *potentia*, and correspondingly its determination in social context; I made this argument both with respect to Hobbes's natural scientific treatment of natural bodies and also with respect to human beings. I argued that there is no normative grain to *potentia* on this late conception; a thing's *potentia* is not a normative tendency, nor does greater *potentia* necessarily match with greater normative appeal. In particular, I demonstrated that collective human *potentia* is layered and hierarchical, conceived as teeming with oligarchic power blocs.

Spinoza is not unconcerned with efficacy: he prides himself on offering a realistic political philosophy, in contrast to the utopian fantasies of other philosophers (TP 1.1), in particular, one that can account for the security and stability of the political orders that it sketches.[15] Nonetheless,

[15] Whatever else a political order must achieve, it must be stable and secure. The *Political Treatise* asserts that the virtue of the state is its security (TP 1.6); the *Theological-Political Treatise* still requires security (TTP 3.20), but additionally states that the 'end' of the state is individual freedom (TTP 20.12; see also TP 5.2, 5.5). I will return to the question of freedom in Chapter 8, Section 8.3.

his conception of power *potentia* itself seems to build in a deeply ethical grain. In the previous section, I outlined in a general way the connection between Spinoza's power analysis and his commitment to normatively appealing forms of politics. The concept of *potentia* developed in the *Ethics* shows these combined characteristics of efficacy and ethics even more forcefully. In a series of enigmatic but crucial propositions in Book 3, Spinoza connects *potentia* with essence, striving *conatus*, and perseverance (E 3p4–3p8); throughout Book 4, *potentia* is linked to virtue (E 4d8, 4p20d, 4p36s2, 4p54). I now draw attention also to a more specific feature of Spinoza's political philosophy: against Hobbes's hierarchical layering, there are suggestions that the structure of collective power is horizontal. In the *Political Treatise*, Spinoza introduces the concept of a multitude, on whose power *potentia* rests the state, by explaining that human collective right (*ius*, which has already been equated with power *potentia* [TP 2.3]) is constituted from individuals joining together and thereby being able to do more together than they could individually (TP 2.13, 2.17; see also E 4p35c2s). A similar idea can be read back into a similar passage in the *Theological-Political Treatise*, although the term *potentia* is not specifically used: Spinoza claims that democracy is the most natural form of government because it reflects the natural equality of the state of nature (TTP III/74, 5.23–25, III/195, 16.36).

Any reconstruction of Spinoza's conception of *potentia* needs to account for its distinctive amalgam of ethics and efficacy. But at the same time, it will need to escape the charge of political naivete: in particular, it must account for ethically unappealing yet efficacious regimes, examples of which impose themselves on any student of history. I divide the literature into two stylized strands. The first group, whom I will label the radical interpreters, celebrates the people's power *potentia* against sovereign power *potestas*. Popular power *potentia* is normatively appealing, but its intrinsic tendency to express itself can be thwarted by external obstacles of *potestas* (understood as political institutions and the political power of rulers). The radical interpretation can take either liberal or democratic form. The second group, whom I will label the constitutional interpreters, does not insist upon a strong distinction between *potentia* and *potestas*: the sovereign's *potestas* is just one emergent feature of the people's collective *potentia*. Their distinction is instead between fragile and enduring power. Tyrannically structured collectivities tend to collapse; therefore, ultimately, greater normative appeal and greater efficacy go hand in hand.

6.3.1. The Radical Approach

Consider first the radical interpretations of Spinoza. According to the radical liberal interpretation,[16] the power *potentia* of natural individuals is their essence, and an essence is something that cannot be separated from the individual whose essence it is. By contrast, a state is not a natural individual, so it lacks any *potentia* of its own.[17] In consequence, the state and its *potestas* should avoid infringing on a libertarian sphere of individual self-determination, within which the individual can exercise and develop *potentia*. The state's proper role is minimal: just warding off 'bothersome hindrances' to individual human development, such as famine, invading armies, and harm from other citizens,[18] perhaps paired with some checks and balances on rulers.[19] This is what should occur; but what will actually be efficacious? For radical liberals, on the one hand, states regrettably can and often do trespass on subjects' freedom and power.[20] On the other hand, if the state reaches so far as to grossly oppress its subjects' freedoms, it will not succeed because the people will rebel.[21]

The radical democratic interpretation[22] finds its canonical expression in Antonio Negri's 1981 book *The Savage Anomaly*.[23] Negri grants that the

[16] Stephen Barbone and Lee Rice, 'Introduction', in Benedictus de Spinoza, *Political Treatise* (Indianapolis: Hackett, 2000), 1–30; Den Uyl, *Power, State, and Freedom*, 67–80, 117–118, 128; Stephen Barbone, 'Power in the *Tractatus Theologico-Politicus*', in *Piety, Peace and the Freedom to Philosophize*, edited by Paul J. Bagley (Dordrecht: Kluwer, 2000), 91–109.

[17] Barbone and Rice, 'Introduction', 12–19, 26–27; Barbone, 'Power', 97–99; Den Uyl, *Power, State, and Freedom*, 67–80. There has been a lively controversy in Spinoza studies regarding the individuality of the state and its possession of a *potentia* of its own. Radical liberal interpretations have been the main focus of the controversy, but insofar as radical democrats deny *potentia* to the state, they are also implicated. For overviews, see Justin D. Steinberg, 'Spinoza's Political Philosophy', in *The Stanford Encyclopedia of Philosophy*, Winter 2013 ed., edited by Edward N. Zalta (http://plato.stanford.edu/archives/win2013/entries/spinoza-political/), §5; Andre Santos Campos, 'The Individuality of the State in Spinoza's Political Philosophy', *Archiv für Geschichte der Philosophie 92* (2010): 1–9. See also my Chapter 8, Section 8.2.

[18] Barbone, 'Power', 108; also 103–104; Den Uyl, *Power, State, and Freedom*, 117–118, 128.

[19] Barbone and Rice, 'Introduction', 27–28; Den Uyl, *Power, State, and Freedom*, 112–118, 126.

[20] Den Uyl, *Power, State, and Freedom*, 86, 126.

[21] Ibid., 82.

[22] The label 'radical democratic' is also claimed by some interpreters who count as 'constitutionalists' (Section 6.3.2) by my taxonomy, for instance, Martin Saar, 'The Immanence of Power: From Spinoza to "Radical Democracy"', *Mededelingen Vanwege Het Spinozahuis 106* (Uitgeverij Spinozahuis, 2014). However, I will use the term only to refer to the Negrian conception.

[23] Negri, *The Savage Anomaly*. Originally published in Italian as *L'anomalia selvaggia: Saggio su potere e potenza in Baruch Spinoza*. I rely on the English translation. Negri's reading of Spinoza's politics has been reiterated in his essays through the subsequent three decades; he also frequently calls upon it as the theoretical ground for the concept of the multitude in his immensely popular collaborations with Michael Hardt. Antonio Negri, '*Reliqua Desiderantur*: A Conjecture for a Definition of the Concept of Democracy in the Final Spinoza', in *The New Spinoza*, edited by Warren Montag and Ted Stolze (Minneapolis: University of Minnesota Press, 1998), 219–247; Negri, 'The

Theological-Political Treatise toys with liberalism. However, he claims that this is superseded in Spinoza's mature view, which is to be found in the later *Political Treatise*,[24] where Spinoza introduces a new third element between individual and state: the 'multitude' (*multitudo*), a non-juridically conceived collectivity of human beings (TP 2.17, 3.2, 3.7, 3.9). Spinoza's politics still lies in his affirmation of power as *potentia* rather than *potestas* of state—'the defining struggle is that of power [*potentia*] against Power [*potestas*]'[25]—but instead of tying *potentia* to individuals as in the *Theological-Political Treatise*, Negri claims the entity holding *potentia*, and therefore right, is the collective mass subject, the multitude.[26]

In the first half of the book, I discussed radical democracy in a Hobbesian context: Tuck's celebration of plebiscitary democratic despotism. Tuck reads Hobbes as a radical democrat insofar as his absolutism refuses any limit on a democratic sovereign's power.[27] Tuck's Hobbes is suspicious of the oligarchic machinations of any complex established system of government, and refuses to subordinate the sovereign people to such a system. But from the point of view of the radical democracy of Negri's Spinoza, Hobbesian democracy—whether Tuck's plebiscitary democracy or Hobbes's own democracy via representative assembly—counts as a 'democratic monarchy',[28] because of its juridical conception of the mass popular agent as 'the people'. The Hobbesian 'will of the people' is really a decision of the sovereign that is then aggressively imposed upon the populace. Even when the sovereign decision is defined by democratic vote, the juridical and impositional character of the popular will remains: dissenters are obliged to acknowledge the sovereign will as their own.[29] Negri argues that Spinoza's non-juridical perspective allows him to understand popular mass agency without juridical mystification: or in other words, the multitude.

What exactly is the multitude? Negri makes a distinction between the multitude in its historical shape and the multitude in its ontological foundation.

Political Treatise'; Hardt and Negri, *Empire*, 73–91, 184–185; Hardt and Negri, *Multitude*, 184–194, 221–222, 240, 311–330; Hardt and Negri, *Commonwealth*, 43–53, 171–195, 235–236; Michael Hardt and Antonio Negri, *Assembly* (New York: Oxford University Press, 2017), 14, 78.

[24] Negri, *The Savage Anomaly*, 114, 194; Negri, 'The *Political Treatise*', 9, 23.

[25] Negri, *The Savage Anomaly*, 196.

[26] Ibid., 190–197, 226–229; Negri, 'The *Political Treatise*', 15–20. By contrast, liberals vigorously oppose the attribution of *potentia* to collectivities. Rice and Barbone, 'Introduction', 18 n. 61; Barbone, 'Power', 103.

[27] See my Chapter 4, Section 4.3.

[28] Negri, '*Reliqua Desiderantur*', 222.

[29] Negri, *The Savage Anomaly*, 68–73, 112–113, 139.

On the one hand, Negri interprets Spinoza's multitude as the population in its historical actuality. In all cases, instances of command, *potestas,* emerge only from the actual historical configuration of the collective power *potentia* of the multitude (a ruler has power *potestas* only if and to the extent subjects actually obey). But on the other hand, Negri understands the multitude as an (in principle) entirely non-hierarchical and unalienated combination of human singularities of productive force. The two aspects of the multitude are related through what Negri calls 'constitutive process'. The ontological tendency of the multitude to equality plays itself out over the ages in actual historical experience: through the historical succession of state forms, conflict and hierarchy gradually overcome themselves in a 'constitutive advance of power'.[30]

On Negri's analysis, giving Hobbesian right to 'the people' cramps and overrides the naturally plural *potentiae* of individuals in the multitude. The ideology of Hobbesian juridical *potestas* might effectively allow the consolidation of an actual alienated political form of *potestas* for a period of time; sometimes a similar effect can be produced by religious superstition. But ultimately the juridical illusion faces the concrete limits of the power of the multitude.[31] When Spinoza defines the state by the power of the multitude, he removes the possibility of this mystification and debunks the claim of any institution whatever to authority, even forms of democratic right of the people. *Potentia* is inevitably temporarily consolidated into successive historical forms of *potestas*, but any particular *potestas* should be and will be disrupted to match the underlying dynamic tendency of the multitude's *potentia* toward horizontality.[32] Radical democrats present Spinoza as a proto-Marxian; Negri's interpretation is replete with the language of revolution and counterpower, and he considers insurgent mass movements against the political status quo as the paradigmatic manifestation of the multitude.[33]

[30] Ibid., xviii–xxiii, 119, 226–229; Negri, '*Reliqua Desiderantur*', 229–237; Negri, 'The *Political Treatise*', 15–20.

[31] Negri, *The Savage Anomaly*, 69–71; Negri, 'The *Political Treatise*', 17, 24.

[32] Negri, *The Savage Anomaly*, 108–119. A pressing problem for the Negrian view is how a multitude can act without forsaking its nature as multitude. For a detailed reconstruction both of the problem and of Negri's answer, see Sandra Leonie Field, 'Democracy and the Multitude: Spinoza against Negri', *Theoria* 59, no. 131 (2012): 21–40.

[33] Negri, *The Savage Anomaly*, xxi, 112, 119, 141, 190–191, 221. The Marxian frame of Negri's interpretation is explicit and pervades his analysis, including the core distinction of *potestas* versus *potentia*. Negri maps the multitude's *potentia* onto the productive force of the proletariat, whereas the structure of *potestas*—obligation generated by consent—is shared by both the capitalist market and the state. But in both cases, *potestas* mystifies the human productive force that is their underpinning; indeed these two forms of mystification are intertwined. Negri, *The Savage Anomaly*, 68–73, 136–143, 218, 229.

For both radical liberal and democratic interpretations of Spinoza's politics, minimizing or removing the state doesn't reveal individual human subjects who are already ethically virtuous. But they both display optimism regarding *potentia*'s 'ontological force':[34] both radical views believe human virtue has its own tendency to increase if not prevented by the external force of the state. Furthermore both radical views share a horizontal non-hierarchical interpretation of the natural structure of human collectivities. The radical liberals acknowledge the need for a minimal state to prevent harm between imperfectly virtuous subjects. But within this space cleared by the state, individual virtue can gradually increase of itself.[35] And between these individuals there is no natural hierarchy: *potestas* is understood as a deliberate imposition on a field previously free of power relations, as an assertion of 'control over'.[36] For radical democrats, individuals cannot increase their virtue alone; but in collective existence in the multitude, and when not distorted by pressure from a state claiming transcendental right, there is an upward spiral of increasing virtue and freedom amongst members of the multitude.[37] Negri recognizes that the still imperfectly virtuous and rational individuals in any actual multitude may have hostile relations amongst themselves. But he claims that even human antagonism and conflict are a manifestation of an ontological movement towards 'horizontality' and 'beautiful and animated flatness'.[38] Hierarchical relations of *potestas* are viewed as contingency, aberration, or even non-being: '[U]nreality . . . rises up to pose relationships of slavery'. But in all cases they are transient, to be swept away by the underlying ontological force of equality.[39]

The result, in slightly different ways for the liberals and radicals, is a politics hostile to complex institutional forms. Both groups attribute to Spinoza a normative vision in which the ethical *potentia* (of individuals or of the multitude) ought to and does tend to resist the encroachments of *potestas*.[40] *Potestas* is acceptable only if it 'flattens onto' the *potentiae* of the multitude or of the collection of individuals, and not if it puts pressure on them.

[34] Negri, 'The *Political Treatise*', 20.
[35] Den Uyl, *Power, State, and Freedom*, 112–118, 125; Barbone, 'Power', 104.
[36] Barbone, 'Power', 100.
[37] See footnotes 31 and 32.
[38] Negri, *The Savage Anomaly*, 119.
[39] Ibid., 194, 226.
[40] This is a curious rapprochement. In terms of gross political orientation, the two groups are poles apart: autonomist Marxists against American right-libertarians. Nonetheless, their underlying philosophical framework is not so divergent.

Both these radical lines of interpretation are somewhat dated with respect to the cutting-edge anglophone literature. Yet both have had an enduring influence. The radical liberal interpretation is forcefully stated in the introduction to the widely used Hackett (2000) edition of the *Political Treatise*.[41] The radical democratic interpretation represented an important voice within the vibrant francophone Spinozist milieu of the late twentieth century. At publication, Negri's book included laudatory prefaces and introductions by luminaries of French Spinozism.[42] Outside of mainstream anglophone political philosophy narrowly conceived, it is common to find representations of Spinoza's political philosophy resting on Negrian understandings of insurgent democracy and the multitude.[43] Some authors merge a Negrian reading of the contrast between *potentia* and *potestas* with a left-Schmittian contrast between constituent and constituted power.[44] And at a further remove, Negri's radical democratic reading of Spinoza has been taken up in a general way in other domains of the humanities.[45]

6.3.2. The Constitutionalist Approach

I now turn to the 'constitutional' interpretation, which offers a different way to bring together the ethical and effective elements of Spinoza's *potentia*. *Potentia* is interpreted as efficacy, producing effects. This conception is ontologically permissive and normatively ambivalent. It is ontologically permissive: where the radicals denied that the sovereign has

[41] Barbone and Rice, 'Introduction', 1–30.

[42] Gilles Deleuze, Alexandre Matheron, and Pierre Macherey wrote prefaces to the French edition: Antonio Negri, *L'anomalie sauvage*, translated by Alexandre Matheron (Paris: Presses Universitaires de France, 1982). Of course, writing a preface does not entail substantive agreement on particular arguments or points of exegesis. The strong endorsements can partly be understood in relation to the historical context. The book was published shortly after Negri's release from being a political prisoner (Negri, *The Savage Anomaly*, xxiii); philosophers rallied to defend the merit of his research.

[43] Montag, *Bodies, Masses, Power*, 66–85; Michael Hardt, 'Translator's Foreword: The Anatomy of Power', in Negri, *The Savage Anomaly*, xi–xvi. Holland is critical of Negri's teleology, but accepts his account of horizontal *potentia* against vertical *potestas* ('Spinoza and Marx', §§26–29).

[44] Del Lucchese objects to the abstract, dehistoricised flavour of Negri's discussion of constituent power, but his own more historical interpretation retains the crucial idea of a real tendency to equality. Filippo Del Lucchese, 'Spinoza and Constituent Power', *Contemporary Political Theory* 15, no. 2 (2015): 184–204; Filippo del Lucchese, *Conflict, Power, and Multitude in Machiavelli and Spinoza: Tumult and Indignation* (New York: Continuum, 2009), 109–166.

[45] Paolo Virno, *A Grammar of the Multitude: For an Analysis of Contemporary Forms of Life*, translated by Isabella Bertoletti, James Cascaito, and Andrea Casson (Los Angeles: Semiotext(e), 2004), 21–26; Dussel, *Twenty Theses on Politics*; Nick Nesbitt, *Universal Emancipation: The Haitian Revolution and the Radical Enlightenment* (Charlottesville: University of Virginia Press, 2008).

potentia of its own, the constitutionalist interpretation is less restrictive. The sovereign does have *potentia*, which is nothing other than the *potentia* of the multitude. It is normatively ambivalent: whereas the radicals built a normative grain into *potentia* itself, the constitutionalists do not. Certainly, virtue is power, but this is merely a stipulative definition of virtue. In proportion to their efficacy, all regimes have *potentia* and virtue, whether good, bad, popular, or tyrannical, and no matter how the individual *potentiae* are combined to form collective *potentia*. In both these respects, the constitutionalist interpretation of *potentia* is closer to that found in Hobbes's later work. Correspondingly, it faces the Hobbesian political problem: how to constitute a sovereign with sufficient *potentia* not to fall apart? How to constitute a stable political order? Spinoza's solution combines efficacy and ethics in the long run, because greater efficacy is achieved in a normatively appealing[46] liberal democratic political order; in turn, this is so because such an order best secures the loyalty of subjects. Less normatively appealing political orders are prone to collapse: tyrannies never last long.[47]

Della Rocca puts forward such a line in clarity. The right of the state is coextensive with its power, and power is just producing effects; but there is an important qualification: the relevant power is only power in the long run. And tyrannies never last long. So power is just efficacy, but the regimes that endure are the normatively appealing ones.[48] Similarly, Rosenthal asks, '[O]nce Spinoza has identified right with power in his social contract theory, then does not anything that we have the power to do make it right?'[49] He answers in the negative, by appeal to an idea of stability: 'A state is stable to the extent that it can foster broad and deep participation among its citizens';[50]

[46] I provide a fuller analysis and taxonomy of being 'normatively appealing' in Chapter 8, Section 8.3.

[47] As well as Della Rocca and Rosenthal quoted subsequently, see also Armstrong, 'Natural and Unnatural Communities', 269–299; Étienne Balibar, 'Spinoza, the Anti-Orwell: The Fear of the Masses', *Rethinking Marxism 2*, no. 3 (1989): 121–125; Balibar, *Spinoza and Politics*, 51–75; Susan James, *Spinoza on Philosophy, Religion and Politics: The Theologico-Political Treatise* (Oxford: Oxford University Press, 2012), 251–260; Matheron, *Individu et communauté*, 287–514 but especially 428; Israel, *Radical Enlightenment*, 258–262; Lazzeri, *Droit, pouvoir, et liberté*, 347, 364; Saar, 'The Immanence of Power', 12; Hasana Sharp, 'Violenta Imperia Nemo Continuit Diu: Spinoza and the Revolutionary Laws of Human Nature', *Graduate Faculty Philosophy Journal 34*, no. 1 (2013): 133–148; Justin D. Steinberg, 'Spinoza on Being *Sui Juris* and the Republican Conception of Liberty', *History of European Ideas 34* (2008): 239–49.

[48] Michael Della Rocca, *Spinoza* (New York: Routledge, 2008), 206–215.

[49] Michael A. Rosenthal, 'Spinoza's Political Philosophy', in *The Oxford Handbook of Spinoza*, edited by Michael Della Rocca (New York: Oxford University Press, 2018), 431.

[50] Ibid., 428.

so, 'While oppression might in the short term produce stability, in the long term it will not'.[51]

For the constitutionalists, the state plays an active role in the development of human virtue. Recall that the radicals disagreed. For the radical liberal view, state institutions should simply prevent gross harm and restrain rulers; for the radical democratic view, the state should simply channel the current voice of the multitude: then the natural unfolding of human virtue can proceed. But for the constitutionalists, while states sometimes repress individual development and enforce hierarchy, human virtue and freedom cannot be advanced simply by winding back the state. For humans have both sociable and unsociable tendencies. Individual virtue and power are not an inner essence waiting to be expressed; nor can the horizontal relation of imperfectly virtuous individuals be taken for granted. Rather, equality and virtue need to be generated, and this is done through the scaffolding of external supports, especially the institutional structures of the state.[52]

6.4. Three Hobbesian Problems for Spinoza's Political Philosophy

I have presented two interpretations of Spinoza's political philosophy that both interpret *potentia* to reconcile efficacy and ethics and, correspondingly, offer a rosy picture of popular power. To deal with apparently unappealing political regimes, both make some kind of distinction between two senses of the word 'power', whether *potestas* against *potentia*, or fragile *potentia* versus durable *potentia*. For the radicals, so long as external distortion from an overbearing state is kept at bay, popular power tends to have a normatively

[51] Ibid., 430. Rosenthal recognizes that for some societies, the appropriate form will be aristocratic rather than democratic (due to low levels of rationality). But he claims that the principle isolated through analysis of democracy—maximizing the rationality and participation of the populace—guides the models of other forms of state (ibid., 427–428). See also Steinberg, *Spinoza's Political Psychology*, 163–189. Matheron argues that in conditions of modernity, there are four possible stable types of regime: liberal monarchy, centralized aristocracy, decentralized aristocracy, or democracy. Democracy is the most ideal, even if it is not always the most suitable. Matheron, *Individu et communauté*, 465–467.

[52] Armstrong, 'Natural and Unnatural Communities', 297–305; Balibar, *Spinoza and Politics*, 76–95; Matthew J. Kisner, *Spinoza on Human Freedom* (Cambridge: Cambridge University Press, 2011), 215–234; Matheron, *Individu et communauté*, 281–283, 505–513, and more generally 287–514; Mugnier-Pollet, *La philosophie politique de Spinoza*, 84–89; Steinberg, *Spinoza's Political Psychology*, 101–128, 163–189; Ericka Tucker, 'The Multitude', in *Spinoza: Key Concepts*, edited by André Santos Campos (Exeter: Imprint Academic, 2015), 129–141.

appealing horizontal structure, within which individual virtue tends to increase. For constitutionalist readers, popular power is collective efficacy, and that efficacy increases in proportion to the good organization of the state. But from the late Hobbesian point of view, if Hobbes's analysis of the emergence of oligarchic power blocs within the multitude is correct, then the alleged Spinozist view, on either interpretation, looks romantic and naive. I sketch three specific ways in which Hobbesian analysis poses problems to the alleged Spinozist reconciliation of ethics and efficacy. I also show elements in Spinoza's own texts that render support to the Hobbesian political scepticism. Insofar as Spinoza's philosophy imposes on itself a requirement of realism, the Hobbesian accusations must be answered and the sceptical textual elements must be integrated. In the subsequent chapters, I will offer a new characterization of the distinction between two kinds of power within Spinoza's politics, which better meshes both with the sceptical textual passages and with Spinoza's systematic philosophy, and which relieves Spinoza of Hobbesian accusations of naivete. This lays the groundwork to provide a new characterization of the stakes of the disagreement with Hobbes on democracy and mass popular power. Ultimately, my interpretation counts as a variant of the constitutionalist interpretation of power, insofar as it will insist on the institutional scaffolding of human *potentia*, but it diverges insofar as it rejects the pervasive political romanticism which near-universally characterizes extant constitutionalists.

The first critical point is *the problem of the multitude's inner oligarchy*, and it applies most pointedly to the radical interpretation. I noted that for the radicals, the structure of collective power is normatively appealing: the multitude consists in a horizontal combination of individual *potentiae*, which are conceived as the essential possession of each individual; hierarchical human relations are the result of the imposition of *potestas*. This bears striking resemblance to Hobbes's early view of power as faculties, which generated a model of social life populated by independent actors, amongst whom the only power is either horizontal combination or full vertical domination of *potestas*[53] (with the difference that radical Spinozists are, unlike Hobbes, suspicion of *potestas*). But as I argued, Hobbes comes to reject his own early view. Human interpersonal dynamics constantly generate asymmetrical relations falling short of total domination, ramifying into emergent hierarchies and power blocs: human relations have an inner oligarchic structure. For

[53] See Chapter 2, Sections 2.2–3, and Chapter 3, Sections 3.2–4.

later Hobbes, the idea of a natural horizontal combination of powers is just a perniciously misleading abstraction.

Indeed, in Spinoza's own works, the key textual basis for the radical view of horizontal combination of powers is far more equivocal than the radicals admit. Just prior to the famous passage imagining two individuals joining together and thereby being able to do more together than they could individually (TP 2.13),[54] Spinoza discusses *potestas*. In the political discourse of the period, *potestas* was normally conceived as purely vertical domination;[55] Spinoza's discussion works to expand this definition. He initially provides a commonplace gloss, relating *potestas* to gross force or domination: a person is in control of his own right (sui juris), or equivalently, avoids being in anyone else's power (*in/sub potestate*) 'so long as he can fend off every force and avenge an injury done to him, as seems good to him, and absolutely, insofar as he can live according to his own mentality' (TP 2.9). But Spinoza then expands the definition of *potestas*: A has power over B (*sub potestate habet*) if (1) A binds B in chains; (2) A deprives B of arms; (3) B is frightened of A; or (4) B hopes for some benefit from A. Thus, even if physically unbound and unthreatened, B only escapes A's *potestas* if B has neither hope nor fear in relation to A (TP 2.10). Even this specification is too loose: for A can have power over B if A is more knowledgeable than B; the only way to be truly sui juris is to be perfectly guided by reason (TP 2.11). Thus, *potestas* includes any kind of human dependence whatsoever, however slight.[56] *Potestas* need not be a perfectly vertical relation of domination; rather, it is a matter of degree.[57]

Now consider the implications of this analysis for conceiving human combination and for conceiving the multitude. The multitude is the collection of diverse human singularities. From the *Ethics*, we know that being perfectly guided by reason is impossible for human beings (E 4p2–4p4);[58] and even

[54] The passage is regularly cited by Negri at critical points of his argument. Negri, *The Savage Anomaly*, 194; Negri, '*Reliqua Desiderantur*', 225; Negri, 'The *Political Treatise*', 16.

[55] For an overview, see Steinberg, 'Spinoza on Being *Sui Juris*', 242–243.

[56] Here I am claiming a conceptual congruence between Hobbes and Spinoza, but not a terminological congruence. Under the heading of *potestas*, Spinoza illuminates the complex inner structure of collective *potentia*, in a manner similar to Hobbes. But Hobbes himself does not use the term *potestas* to analyse concrete power, reserving it for the juridical relation of vertical domination.

[57] One interesting implication of this conception is the breakdown of the conception of 'power over' as necessarily unidirectional. To combine two of the examples from above: imagine a cunning person encountering a strong person, who has the *potestas*? On Spinoza's analysis, it seems natural to say that both do: in different respects, they are each hopeful and fearful in respect of one another (although not necessarily equally).

[58] On this point, the two texts use the same technical language. In the *Political Treatise*, Spinoza explains that we are maximally sui juris and avoid relations of *potestas* insofar as we are guided by reason, because to that extent we are determined to action by causes that can be understood adequately through our own nature alone (*quæ per solam ejus naturam possunt adæquatè intelligi*) (TP

achieving the status of a sage who is maximally guided by reason takes lifelong effort of cultivation and reflection (E 5p42s; TTP 16.7, III/190; TP 1.5). Thus the multitude will not predominantly be composed of sages. For a diverse collection of people, who have mostly not achieved sagehood, it is hard to see how there could fail to be relations of *potestas* between them. Each person will have some kind of hope or fear in relation to the other, and in general, there will be differences of knowledge. Thus *potestas* is pervasive and natural, and internal to the multitude. The multitude is not a horizontal plane of unhierarchized *potentiae*: to the contrary, juxtapositions of *potentiae* always already involve *potestas*.[59] On this reading, the point of Spinoza's discussion is to dissolve the strict analytical distinction between vertical and horizontal combinations of human *potentiae*, in favour of a continuum between the two forms of combination.

Spinoza is less explicit than Hobbes in providing a general account of how these hierarchical micro-relations might compound to constitute larger blocs. But the ingredients for such an account are already there. In the *potestas* relations (3) and (4) above, powers are joined together to form a new composite body: A binds B through B's fear of harm or hope of benefit, and B aligns B's own wishes with A's.[60] Surely this process could be iterated or compounded. For instance, Spinoza acknowledges the problem of nepotism: people tend to favour their kin and their allies (TP 8.12–15, 11.2). A different mechanism is illustrated by the case of religious enthusiasms. People

2.11). In the *Ethics*, he argues it is impossible for a person to 'undergo no changes except those which can be understood through his own nature alone [*per solam suam naturam*], and of which he the adequate cause [*adæquata causa*]' (E 4p4). This technical language will be important in Chapter 7, Section 7.3.2.

[59] See also Field, 'Democracy and the Multitude', 29–31; Freeman, 'The Tyranny of Structurelessness', 152–153.

[60] Further corroborations can be found in the *Ethics*, where Spinoza offers an affective (feelings-based) theory of affinity. We hate things that reduce our feeling of power, and love things that increase it; correspondingly, we strive to destroy the former and maintain the presence of the latter (E 3p13). Thus, we strive to maintain a relationship with those from whom we hope for benefit. Superficially, an important difference between Spinoza's and Hobbes's analysis is that Spinoza focuses on affects, whereas Hobbes offers a rational-strategic model. However, for Spinoza, the conscious desire to persevere in one's being is one of the primary affects (E 3p9–11), so he can accept the (at least partial) usefulness of an analysis of conduct in terms of strategic desires. The limitation of Hobbesian analysis might be its difficulty to account for non-strategic affective identification: explaining why it is that subjects rejoice at the joys of those they identify with, or of those who remind them of those whom they love; and conversely for hatred (E 3p15–3p24). See Matheron and Lazzeri for a useful account of the differences (putting aside their shared, unsustainable claim that Hobbes's *Leviathan* understands actual human behaviour as oriented to the end of biological preservation: see my discussion in Chapter 4, Section 4.2). Matheron, *Individu et communauté*, 153–156; Lazzeri, *Droit, pouvoir, et liberté*, 61–89.

find an outlet for their hopes and fears in superstitious allegiance, meaning that they eagerly subordinate themselves to religious visionaries. At the same time, this allegiance constitutes great power for religious leaders. Corrupted by greed and ambition, they mobilize religion and theology to win more supporters and demonize followers of other sects (TTP Pref.15, III/8).[61]

These considerations should defeat any simple claim that an actual multitude, when freed from state domination, will have a horizontal structure freed from *potestas*. But Negri's claim, in its more careful and precise articulation, is sometimes more subtle: that it is *potentia* as ontological foundation that is horizontal, even if the actual historical manifestation does not immediately match. For Negri, the reason that the *Political Treatise*'s Chapter 2 discusses *potestas* first and the horizontal combination of *potentiae* second is that this reflects the historical sequence of constitutive process: relations of *potestas* tend over time to be superseded and displaced by a horizontal combination of *potentiae*. Attempted domination provokes resistance, and this antagonism between subjects is the motor of 'constitutive progress' towards equal combination.[62] Indeed, I admit that there are some suggestive textual passages claiming that people will not tolerate inequality (TTP 5.23, III/74; TP 7.5). But there are equally numerous passages in the *Ethics* suggesting not a virtuous spiral towards horizontality but a vicious escalation of passion and oppression (E 3p40, 3p52s, 4p54s, 4p57d, 4p58s). Negri dismisses such passages as evidence of the 'unfinished character' of Spinoza's philosophy in the *Ethics*.[63] But even putting aside the *Ethics*, Negri's reading of the critical passages 2.9–11 of the *Political Treatise* is not obviously more plausible than my more pessimistic alternative account; adjudicating the case will require a larger consideration of Spinoza's metaphysics, as will be provided in Chapters 7 and 8.

I turn now to the constitutional reading. Insofar as this reading conceives power as producing effects, there is no presumption that individuals possess an essential power independent of the relations in which they find themselves. Thus, they can readily accept that there may be inner oligarchy within

[61] I am not claiming that such power blocs are sufficient as government. My claim is merely that human capacities and behaviours need to be understood not through individual endowments, but through interpersonal structures of dependence, as in later Hobbes.

[62] Negri, *The Savage Anomaly*, 194–195. Even some readers that I classify as constitutionalist share some version of this idea: for instance, Matheron offers an evolutionary explanation of the improvement of politics, driven by the self-interest of sovereigns witnessing the collapse of tyrannical regimes (*Individu et communauté*, 428).

[63] Negri, '*Reliqua Desiderantur*', 237–238.

the multitude. Indeed, as I noted in Section 6.3.2, writers in this tradition are critical of the anti-institutionalism of the radicals. Institutions are required to scaffold and shape a good multitude; this is not a need that will be historically superseded. My own approach will share this understanding of the important constructive role of institutions. However, constitutionalists combine this view with a further distinctive claim that I wish to put under scrutiny. They near-universally claim that regimes are more efficacious in proportion as their structure is more normatively appealing. Democracies are effective; tyrannies never last long.

This leads to my second and third critical points. The second point is *the problem of nonideal endurance*. Do tyrannies really never last long? I grant that Spinoza makes such claims numerous times, especially in his earlier *Theological-Political Treatise* (TTP 16.28–31, III/194, 17.2–4, III/201, 17.11, III/203, 20.1–9, III/239–240; TP 3.7–9). But the claims invite scepticism. Certainly, some extreme and poorly calibrated kinds of tyranny tend to collapse; and certainly, Spinoza insists that stability requires commanding popular loyalties (TTP 17.16–17, III/203–204). But there are possibilities of stability that depart from Rosenthal's 'broad and deep' citizen participation. For starters, there is Hobbes's repressive egalitarianism, which is far from obviously unstable.[64] Curley, who otherwise takes a broadly constitutionalist view, departs from other commentators' rosy assessment of the popular credentials of Spinoza's political philosophy. For he notes that there can be very durable tyrannies; insofar as right is nothing but power, he worries that Spinoza lacks any conceptual resources to criticize such regimes.[65] Beyond Hobbes's repressive egalitarianism, we could add examples that are Spinoza's own, or readily derivable from Spinozist premises: Turkish despotism (TTP Pref.9, III/7; TP 6.4);[66] the original model of commonwealth of the Hebrews (TTP 17.101, III/218, 18.1, III/221);[67] regimes repressing a majority (women

[64] See Chapter 5, Section 5.5.

[65] Curley, 'Kissinger, Spinoza, and Genghis Khan', 333–335.

[66] Revisionist scholarship has shown 'Turkish despotism' to be an orientalist figment of the European republican imagination. Patricia Springborg, *Western Republicanism and the Oriental Prince* (Austin: University of Texas Press, 1992). My point in this context is simply that Spinoza himself upholds the standard representation of Turkish despotism as a stable yet normatively unacceptable political form.

[67] Although the secondary literature contains two quite different reasons for not classifying the Hebrew republic as an instance of nonideal endurance, neither reason is compelling. First, Mugnier-Pollet claims the Hebrew republic was not durable. He points out that in fact it collapsed; a fortiori it was unstable (Mugnier-Pollet, *La philosophie politique de Spinoza*, 152). Of course it did in fact collapse, but Spinoza's argument is that it would have been extremely stable if it had been established as it was initially planned. In fact, it was unstable because the original plan was broken, to give privileges to the Levites (TTP 17.101, III/218). Second, Rosenthal challenges the characterization of the

and/or servants) (TP 11.3–4); regimes repressing small minorities (minority as scapegoat);[68] paternalistic rule by outsiders (derived from Spinoza's discussion of smaller cities within a republic) (TP 9.2, 9.13); slave regimes from colonial conquest (TP 5.6);[69] or corrupt pyramid regimes of voluntary servitude (as I will explain later). Indeed, at the very opening of the *Political Treatise*, Spinoza acknowledges the astuteness of political practitioners: the regimes of these shrewd *politici* tend more 'to set traps for men than to look after their interests', and pose the problem of durable but normatively undesirable forms of politics (TP 1.2). Would constitutionalist interpretations have us reclassify these instances of prima facie bad rule as good, insofar and to the extent they are durable? Or should we find some other way to discriminate amongst them, regardless of their stability?[70]

I do not claim that Spinoza necessarily knew La Boétie's *Discourse on Voluntary Servitude*,[71] but the text offers an interesting model of well-calibrated tyranny, one that might be conceived as an extension of a Spinozist analysis. La Boétie asks how it is that people willingly shoulder the yoke of an oppressive ruler who has no power save what their own obedience grants him.[72] Similarly, Spinoza himself asks, in the preface to the *Theological-Political Treatise*, why people 'fight for slavery as they would for salvation' (TTP Pref.9).[73] Spinoza explains that people's fearfulness makes them

original plan as nonideal, instead emphasizing how Spinoza uses it as a positive historical example Michael A. Rosenthal, 'Why Spinoza Chose the Hebrews: The Exemplary Function of Prophecy in the *Theological-Political Treatise*', *History of Political Thought 18*, no. 2 (1997): 237–238. I do not deny that the example is in some respects a positive exemplar (in particular, its separation between religious and political authority). However, I would note that Spinoza is simultaneously critical of it in other respects, especially its reliance on the unthinking obedience of its citizens (TTP 17.88–78, III/216), and on their hatred of foreigners (see footnote 68).

[68] Spinoza remarks that a unified and powerful commonwealth can be based on a multitude united by a common fear, or by desire to avenge a common loss (TP 3.9). His classic example is the Hebrew republic, in which hatred of outsiders consolidated political unity (TTP 17.80–81, III/215). But I am suggesting the same dynamic could apply against an internal minority.

[69] Spinoza does not endorse this form of rule (TP 9.13). But what is at stake here is not its desirability, but its possible durability. Matheron's example of Genghis Khan conquering a small Spinozistic republic (Alexandre Matheron, 'Le 'droit du plus fort': Hobbes contre Spinoza', in *Études sur Spinoza et les philosophies de l'âge classique* [Lyon: ENS Éditions, 2011], 154; Curley, 'Kissinger, Spinoza, and Genghis Khan, 333–334), is often dismissed as being unstable in the long run. But this is far from clear. In the history of colonialism, some conquests have been unstable, but others rather durable.

[70] An obvious route to investigate is Spinoza's distinction between free and slave regimes (TP 5.4). I will return to discuss this in Chapter 8, Section 8.3. But for present purposes, the important point is that the non-democratic and repressive regimes, however we label them, can be durable.

[71] Étienne de la Boétie, 'Discourse on Voluntary Servitude', in *Michel de Montaigne: Selected Essays*, translated by James B. Atkinson and David Sices (Indianapolis: Hackett, 2012), 284–312.

[72] Ibid., 285.

[73] This is Curley's older translation. Benedictus de Spinoza, *A Spinoza Reader: The Ethics and Other Works*, translated by E. M. Curley (Princeton, NJ: Princeton University Press, 1994), 6. In the

susceptible to superstition; both he and La Boétie note a history of tyrants investing themselves with divine grandeur to capture these fears politically. But they both think that this strategy will only constitute a robust governmental structure with a very stupid or barbarous population (TTP Pref.8–10, III/6–7, 17.20–24, III/204–205).[74] The constitutionalist reading of Spinoza would leave us thinking that this is the end of the matter: tyrannies never last long, at least when we presume modern levels of education.[75] But this is not La Boétie's conclusion. Instead, La Boétie identifies the true 'source and secret of domination' amongst more sophisticated populations as a pyramidical structure of capture of desire.[76] In La Boétie's preferred model of voluntary servitude, society is stabilized by being segmented into multiple hierarchical layers, each layer of the population hoping to retain the favour of their superiors and the mastery of those below them; citizens are crafted into voluntary sycophants by the well-designed structure of incentives. Subjects find themselves 'clutching at servitude with both hands and embracing it'; and even the upstanding characters amongst them often find themselves unable to resist.[77] In this spirit, Lordon constructs an explicitly Spinozist model of joyful hierarchical submission in order to understand neoliberal employment relations: rather than a Marxian enmity between capitalist and worker, between whom there is an ever-widening gulf, instead in neoliberalism each level of managers internalizes capitalist imperatives and imposes them on its subordinates.[78]

Let me apply this model to reassess Spinoza's argument for the self-defeating character of restrictions on free expression. When Spinoza claims in the *Theological-Political Treatise* that the sovereign lacks power to restrict expression, recall (from Section 6.2) that it is not strictly impossible. The law can be made, and it may be reasonably effective: for many people can be led to believe and say all manner of things. Rather, the problem with a such a law is its practical ramifications: it has the effect of elevating sycophants and

Collected Works, Curley translates *salus* as survival rather than salvation; the newer translation blunts the rhetorical sharpness of the paradox.

74 La Boétie, 'Discourse on Voluntary Servitude', 305.

75 Matheron, *Individu et communauté*, 465–466; Steinberg, *Spinoza's Political Psychology*, 159–160.

76 La Boétie, 'Discourse on Voluntary Servitude', 305–308.

77 Ibid., 307–309. In this light Matheron's attempted exhaustive taxonomy of stable regimes (see footnote 51) appears inadequate; the difficulty is that Matheron does not consider layered forms of power (*Individu et communauté*, 446, 502).

78 Frédéric Lordon, *Willing Slaves of Capital: Spinoza and Marx on Desire*, translated by Gabriel Ash (London: Verso, 2014), 1–104.

antagonizing citizens of principle, thereby indirectly reducing the durability of the state (20.27–31, III/243–244). One way to stave off this instability, Spinoza's own, is to permit free expression. But another response would be possible: try to increase the proportion of sycophants in a population. Maybe there will always be some citizens of principle who cannot be co-opted, but with sufficient incentives, might their number be reduced so as not to be politically troubling? Certainly, the La Boétie model is not perfectly stable; in particular there can be problems of succession and praetorian struggles at the top.[79] But on the other hand, if well calibrated, such a regime could have moderate success.[80]

The third critical point is *the problem of democracy's perverse effects*. Are democracies effective? As detailed in Chapter 5, Sections 5.3–4, Hobbes is sceptical. He argues that popular regimes and religiously tolerant regimes corrupt themselves. Indeed, they are acutely subject to the political problem: for democratic assemblies may unintentionally allow and even encourage the formation of power blocs, as may a policy of toleration of religious sects. The rise of these power blocs means that liberal democracies, even if stable, do not necessarily rule for the common good; and sectarianism and poor rule mean that they may lead themselves into instability.

Spinoza himself oscillates in his assessment of democracies. The *Theological-Political Treatise* initially appears to view a democratic constitution as a political panacea, as something which by its very structure overcomes all political problems. Spinoza argues that since in a democracy laws are by common consent, they preserve freedom and express equality (TTP 5.25, III/74). Furthermore, he argues that a large assembly is unlikely to agree to anything very stupid (TTP 16.30, III/194). But on the other hand, in the later *Political Treatise*, he acknowledges that of all regimes, 'none have been less lasting' than popular or democratic regimes (TP 6.4). Already in the earlier text, Spinoza remarks that democracy is inappropriate for societies accustomed to a monarch (TTP 18.30–33, III/226–227); but this hardly entails that democracy will run smoothly for those who are accustomed to it. He observes that everyone, both rulers and ruled, tends to be governed by affects rather than reason; they are 'easily corrupted' by the pursuit of profit. He identifies the fundamental political challenge: to bring everyone to put public good over private interest (TTP 17.14–16, III/203). One wonders how

[79] Matheron, *Individu et communauté*, 309–312.

[80] See Chapter 5, footnote 67.

such destructive dynamics are to be kept at bay within the democratic assembly: for even though a democratic constitution establishes formally equal status and removes private violent threat, this far from exhausts power relations between democratic subjects, as per the earlier discussion of *potestas*.[81] Furthermore, the confidence in democratic governance exists in some tension with his liberal commitments. Spinoza famously argues that sovereigns lack the right to oppress citizens, or to treat as enemies those who disagree; they should allow the people the freedom to say and teach as they please (TTP 20.1–9, III/239–240). But what ensures a democratic assembly will not be oppressive in these ways towards political or other minorities?

Thus we are left with three Hobbesian criticisms of Spinoza's political philosophy, which are not well answered by existing interpretations; and there are textual hints that Spinoza himself could acknowledge their force. In the following chapters, I will develop a new interpretation that makes analytical space for a fundamental divergence between ethics and efficacy, and thereby can accommodate these criticisms. This new interpretation will give rise to a new conception of popular power that conceives a collective's own *power* as its ongoing robust self-driven efficacy in determining social and political outcomes, and its *popularity* in terms of its elimination of oligarchic and hierarchical affronts to equal status. Social movements and popular plebiscites will be resituated as possible contributing elements within a larger complex ecological conception of popular power, rather than its defining and exemplary instances.

[81] As a Marxian perspective also reveals: see Chapter 5, footnote 59.

7

The Power of Producing Effects

7.1. Introduction

The two common and influential interpretations of Spinoza's political *potentia* linking efficacy and virtue, laid out in Chapter 6, paint an altogether too rosy picture of popular political power. Their respective attempts to distinguish between two senses of power each fail to redeem Spinoza from accusations of political naivete. In this chapter, I present a different distinction: between *potentia operandi* and *potentia agendi*. To sketch the distinction that I will develop more fully as I proceed, in Spinoza's hands *potentia operandi* is the power of doing or (in Curley's translation) producing effects (not making a distinction whether what is done is active or passive); whereas *potentia agendi* is the power of acting (in contrast to passive undergoing). *Potentia operandi* accounts for whatever actually occurs, including fractious and oligarchic behaviour, and is fundamentally normatively ambivalent. By contrast, *potentia agendi* is the source for the positive readings of power in Spinoza: it is *potentia agendi* that is linked to essence, striving, and virtue. *Potentia operandi* is little analysed as such; but it is crucial for understanding Spinoza's political philosophy and its relation to Hobbes; and more broadly for understanding Spinoza's theory of popular power and democratic mass agency.

In this chapter, I offer a brief precis of Spinoza's metaphysics. In particular, I explain the place of *operari*, producing effects, within this system, and establish the metaphysical contrast between *potentia agendi* and *potentia operandi* (Section 7.2). I then argue that the *Political Treatise*'s distinction between having a right and being in control of one's right (being sui juris) offers a far more adequate political rendering of this metaphysical distinction than do the concepts of the earlier *Theological-Political Treatise*. I show how the conception of being in control of one's right applies separately to individual persons and to a political collectivity (Section 7.3). In both sections of this chapter, I show that *potentia operandi* is similar to Hobbes's late relational conception of *potentia*, concerning the actual production of effects within a

Potentia. Sandra Leonie Field, Oxford University Press (2020). © Oxford University Press.
DOI: 10.1093/oso/9780197533864.001.0001

complex network of causal influences; this lays the groundwork for the three Hobbesian problems outlined in Chapter 6 to have purchase on Spinoza's political thought.

In the following chapters, I will argue that my new interpretation relieves Spinoza's politics of accusations of naivete, insofar as it allows for a stark divergence between ethics and efficacy; I will bring to the fore the strong antinomian current of Spinoza's philosophy. But at the same time, I will show how Spinoza's *potentia agendi* lays the groundwork for a distinctive conception of popular power that, while not hostile to social movements and popular plebiscites, decentres them and no longer counts them as popular powers' exemplary expression.

7.2. *Potentia Agendi* and *Potentia Operandi*

Spinoza's philosophical system reflects his intellectual context within early modern substance metaphysics, within the milieu of early modern encounters between scholastic and mechanical philosophy.[1] As discussed in Chapter 2, within the earlier scholastic hylomorphic metaphysics, a substance is something that exists in itself, and is not dependent as a part or a predicate of some other thing. So for Aquinas, humans, animals, plants, and rocks are all substances. It is these substances that each have a *potentia*. Science involves identifying substances and investigating their *potentiae*, as inherent qualitative tendencies proper to the particular substance in question. In Spinoza's time, new philosophers such as Descartes worked ambivalently within the frame of substance. On the one hand, Descartes still identifies various substances: God, human souls, and extended substance.[2] But on the other hand, when we focus on the natural sciences, the substance metaphysics recedes into the background. For extension as a whole is a single

[1] For a general overview, see Steven Nadler, *Spinoza's Ethics: An Introduction* (Cambridge: Cambridge University Press, 2006), 52–121. For readers interested in Spinoza's proximate sources beyond the immediate Hobbesian/Cartesian context, see Julie R. Klein, 'Spinoza's Debt to Gersonides', *Graduate Faculty Philosophy Journal 24*, no. 1 (2003): 19–43; Yitzhak Y. Melamed, 'Teleology in Jewish Philosophy: Early Talmudists To Spinoza', in *Teleology: A History*, edited by Jeff McDonough (New York: Oxford University Press, forthcoming); Charles Harry Manekin, 'Spinoza and the Determinist Tradition in Medieval Jewish Philosophy', in *Spinoza and Medieval Jewish Philosophy*, edited by Steven Nadler (Cambridge: Cambridge University Press, 2014), 36–58.

[2] René Descartes, 'The Principles of Philosophy', in *The Philosophical Writings of Descartes*, translated by John Cottingham, Robert Stoothoff, and Dugald Murdoch, Vol. 1 (Cambridge: Cambridge University Press, 1984), 1.48, 1.51–52.

substance; the animals, plants, and rocks that are parts of extension do not have their own distinct substantial existence, and are instead understood in their mechanistic causal interaction within extended substance.[3]

Spinoza starts the *Ethics* with a definition of substance: 'By substance I understand what is in itself [*in se est*] and is conceived through itself [per se *concipitur*]' (E 1d1). He argues that there is a single unique and infinite substance, otherwise known as God, which encompasses all of nature. His argument can be read against the backdrop of Cartesian metaphysics.[4] By Descartes's own admission, only God is strictly independent; whereas human souls and extension are dependent on God, relying on his 'concurrence'. Nonetheless, Descartes still calls them substances, as they are independent of everything else apart from God.[5] This is unsatisfactory for Spinoza: in accord with his definition of substance, the conceptual dependence of everything on God means that in fact, only God is substance (E 1p14). Everything that is, is in God; God is not a creator standing outside creation, but the 'immanent' cause of all things (E 1p18). Human beings, along with all other finite things, are not substances, but instead modes within substance (E 1p10, E 2p10). Spinoza replaces the contrast between God and his creation with a contrast between two aspects of God: *natura naturans*, which is God considered as the cause of himself, uncaused by anything else; versus *natura naturata*, which is everything that follows from God's nature. This is God considered as the sum of his modes, or in other words, nature as a whole (E 1p29s).[6]

In result, Spinoza's metaphysics offers a radicalization of the Cartesian mechanistic account of the natural world. Like Descartes and Hobbes, natural bodies exist in a causal network, such that each thing within this network, and the effects it produces, is the result of the causal effects on it by infinite other things (E 1p28). This causality is deterministic: if an effect is caused, it cannot be rendered uncaused; but against Descartes,[7] this applies to humans as much as anything else, removing free will (E 1p29). And

[3] Ibid., 2.23–64, 4.199. For his part, Hobbes is less ambivalent, more hostile to retaining any robust notion of substance. He imagines an extended void with bodies placed in it. The bodies are *subsistens* per se only in the sense that they are not dependent on our thought; their motions are mechanistically understood within nature as a whole (DCo 8.1, 8.19; see also my Chapter 2, Section 2.5).

[4] Spinoza was intimately familiar with Descartes's works; indeed, he composed a geometrical reconstruction of Cartesian metaphysics. See Spinoza, *Collected Works*, Vol. 1, 221–348.

[5] Descartes, 'Principles of Philosophy', 1.51.

[6] For a more precise presentation and defence of this interpretation, see Yitzhak Melamed, 'Spinoza's Metaphysics of Substance: The Substance-Mode Relation as a Relation of Inherence and Predication', *Philosophy and Phenomenological Research* 78, no. 1 (2009): 17–82.

[7] René Descartes, 'The Passions of the Soul', in *Philosophical Writings of Descartes*,, Part 1.

against both Descartes and Hobbes, Spinoza also argues that nature is necessitarian: a different chain of causal effects could not have been put in play. For God, *natura naturans*, being uncaused, acts from the necessity of his own nature and could not have acted any other way (E 1p33).

Let me now situate the concepts of power *potentia*, acting *agere*, and producing effects *operari*, in relation to my sketch of Spinoza's metaphysics. At the very start of *Ethics*, Spinoza links action to a thing's causality from its own nature alone; whereas producing an effect is linked to causality by another:

> That thing is called free which exists from the necessity of its nature alone, and is determined to act by itself alone [*à se solâ ad agendum determinatur*]. But a thing is called necessary, or rather compelled, which is determined by another to exist and produce an effect [*ab alio determinatur ad existendum, & operandum*] in a certain and determinate manner. (E 1d7)

In Book 1 of the *Ethics*, it is substance that acts, whereas finite modes only produce effects. Spinoza constantly links action with substance: God acts from his own nature alone, and as such is free. Towards the end of Book 1,[8] Spinoza also links action with power *potentia*: God's power *potentia*, by which he acts, is the same as his essence, which is the same as his nature (E 1p34–36, 1App). By contrast, there is no discussion of action or power in relation to finite modes: they merely produce effects. All finite things are 'determined from the necessity of the divine nature to exist and produce an effect in a certain way [*ad certo modo existendum, & operandum*]' (E 1p29; see also 1p26–28). This determination does not come directly from God's absolute divine nature, but rather, indirectly within the infinite causal network of all other finite things (E 1p28). In sum, action and producing effects both ultimately pertain to God, but in different ways. As *natura naturans*, or as cause of himself, or as substance, God acts. But as *natura naturata*, as an infinite collection of his modes, God is necessarily caused to exist and produce effects (E 1p29).

Even if nature as a whole can be said, from different perspectives, to act or to produce effects, on the basis of *Ethics* Book 1 there is no hint that singular things (finite modes) themselves have any activity. Each finite thing

[8] Perhaps Spinoza delays in deploying the term *potentia* systematically due to the volume of misconceptions he needs to clear before claiming the term for his own purposes: in several scholia in the earlier part of Book 1, he tentatively makes use of it without defining it, primarily in the context of criticizing other mistaken understandings of God. See E 1p9s, 1p15s, 1p17s, 1p31s, 1p33s2.

is, emphatically, determined by another to produce effects (E 1p26–1p29). Indeed, amongst his contemporaries, Spinoza had good precedents for a view of a passive nature of deterministic causal relations. In Descartes's metaphysics, human beings are active because they have substantial souls;[9] but within extended substance, there is no active power for individual natural bodies. Animals are conceived as elaborate mechanical machines.[10] Notwithstanding his retention of the word 'power', Hobbes's later metaphysics offers an even more passive picture of nature: including human beings also as part of nature and denying them Cartesian free will.[11]

But against such precedents, the continuation of Spinoza's *Ethics* takes the idea of action, and especially human action, as absolutely central. Book 3 is organized around the notion of human *potentia agendi*, power of acting. The technical definition of virtue is power of acting, and the project of the *Ethics* is its increase (E 3p11–13, 3p15). How is this possible within his deterministic single-substance metaphysics? In sketch, the solution is as follows.[12] Only God is perfectly self-caused. But amongst other things, despite being entirely immanently caused by God's power and entirely deterministically integrated in the network of efficient causes of *natura naturata*, it is still possible to identify a thing's own nature. Undisputably, anything an individual in fact does is deterministically caused, ultimately by another. But proximately, to what degree is it caused from the individual's own nature, and to what

[9] Descartes, 'Passions of the Soul', Part 1.

[10] René Descartes, 'Discourse on the Method of Rightly Conducting One's Reason and Seeking the Truth in the Sciences', in *Philosophical Writings of Descartes*, Part 5. Descartes allows that such extended things might have power, understood as persistence in rest or motion ('Principles of Philosophy', 2.43, 4.37). However, the term is not prominent in his works; furthermore, he is emphatically opposed to attributing particular powers to gross individuals (stones, rocks, animals) as such (ibid., 4.187).

[11] The concept of 'active power' in Hobbes's later work has no particular importance attached to it. A thing's active power is simply its efficient causality with respect to a particular effect; this power itself is understood as the result of prior causes, without distinction as to whether those prior causes are external or somehow internal (see Chapter 2, Section 2.5).

[12] For more detailed and comprehensive reconstructions, see Matheron, *Individu et communauté*, 9–24; Don Garrett, 'Spinoza's Conatus Argument', in *Spinoza: Metaphysical Themes*, edited by Olli Koistinen and J. I. Biro (Oxford: Oxford University Press, 2002), 127–156; Valtteri Viljanen, 'Spinoza's Actualist Model of Power', in *The World as Active Power: Studies in the History of European Reason*, edited by Juhani Pietarinen and Valtteri Viljanen (Leiden: Brill, 2009), 213–228. Garrett organizes his exegesis around the concept of inherence, being '*in se*', which characterizes substance absolutely. Inherence is correlated with Spinozistic activity, adequacy, and freedom ('Spinoza's Conatus Argument', 134–141, 149–150). Garrett shows that for Spinoza, finite individuals are conceived as finite approximations to substance: 'finite things can have, in varying degrees, characteristics that only infinite substance possesses absolutely' (139). See also Don Garrett, 'Representation and Consciousness in Spinoza's Naturalistic Theory of the Imagination', in *Interpreting Spinoza: Critical Essays*, edited by Charles Huenemann (Cambridge: Cambridge University Press, 2008), 10–14.

degree from an external cause?[13] Spinoza offers a technical language for this distinction: adequate versus inadequate causation.

> D1: I call that cause adequate whose effect can be clearly and distinctly perceived through it. But I call it partial, *or* inadequate, if its effect cannot be understood through it alone. (E 3d1)

Action is defined as adequate causation.

> D2: I say that we act [*agere*] when something happens, in us or outside us, of which we are the adequate cause, i.e. (by D1), when something in us or outside us follows from our nature, which can be clearly and distinctly understood through it alone. On the other hand, I say that we are acted on [*pati*] when something happens in us, or something follows from our nature, of which we are only a partial cause. (E 3d2)

The distinction between causation from one's own nature alone (adequate causation) and causation with another (inadequate causation) recurs in Spinoza's so-called *conatus* doctrine. Spinoza stipulates that an individual's own power of acting, its *potentia agendi*, is its striving (*conatus*) by which it does something, either by itself or with another (E 3p7s). This scholium allows us to articulate the connection between the adequacy of causation and *potentia agendi*. If a thing is the adequate cause of an effect, the effect is generated from its *potentia agendi* alone, and the thing is active; if a thing is an inadequate cause of an effect, the effect is generated from its *potentia agendi*, not taken alone, but only in combination with other powers, and to that extent, the thing is passive. Note that despite the apparently binary cut suggested by the opposed terms of action and passivity, in fact there is a continuum. Any causation of effects involves the causing individual's own nature; or in other words, even passivity involves some degree of active power. The question will be merely how partial or complete that causality is.[14]

While Spinoza's analysis is entirely general in its scope, it can be more vividly illustrated by considering its application to human behaviour and its bondage to the passions. In the face of an adverse event or loss, consider

[13] Of course, the tricky thing will be characterizing what exactly is one's own nature; I will return to this in Chapter 8, Section 8.2.

[14] Garrett, 'Spinoza's Conatus Argument', 139–140, 144–145; Matheron, *Individu et communauté*, 11–24.

three kinds of human response. Some people may be devastated or enraged, finding the event debilitating or lashing out. Intense affects (emotions) toss them about 'like waves on the sea, driven by contrary winds' (E 3p59s). Other people, with better emotional self-regulation, will be able to weather the event, still retaining their serenity and unswayed from their characteristic temperament. Others again may maintain their serenity, but not through their own self-regulation. For instance, consider a child who is able to endure a frightening event with equanimity, due to the support of a parent, blankie, and pacifier; or the adult who can avoid exploding in rage only when their partner is there to keep that rage in check. Now, a person acts insofar as they are an adequate cause of effects, or in other words, insofar as the effects can be understood through their own nature alone. I have not yet specified precisely what this own nature might be, but already a rough intuitive contrast can be made to plainly external forces. The sadness or anger of the first group can be understood in relation to external events that trigger these passions; accordingly, sadness and anger are passive undergoing (*pati*, or passion *passio*) and are attributed partially to the power of those other things (E 3d3, 4p2–4p6). But not all human experience is equally captive to fate. The serenity of the second group is more understood through their own nature than through the external cause: thus, they are more active, they have greater *potentia agendi*. Finally, the third group, the intermediate case, illustrates that it is not the particular kind of conduct that constitutes activity, but its causality. For in these cases, the outcome is qualitatively similar to the second group, but with different causality. The individuals have been spared subjection to one kind of external cause (the adverse event) through dependence on a different one (their external resources for staying calm) (E 4p23–4p24). Perhaps they are more active than the first case of people overcome by passion, but they still fall short of those who regulate their emotions for themselves (E 4p59d).

Spinoza stipulatively defines virtue as power of acting:

> D8: By virtue and power [*potentia*] I understand the same thing, i.e. (by IIIP7), virtue, insofar as it is related to man, is the very essence, or nature, of man, insofar as he has the power of bringing about certain things [*potestatem habet, quædam efficiendi*], which can be understood through the laws of his nature alone [*per solas ipsius naturæ leges*]. (E 4d8)[15]

[15] The definition does not explicitly include *agere*, but bringing things about through the 'laws of his nature alone' clearly corresponds to adequate causation, or, in other words, action. See also E 4p20. Spinoza's understanding of power of acting as adequate causation is intertwined with his

While Spinoza's overall ethical view is highly idiosyncratic, a virtuous person in his technical sense of the word would conform to some degree to common understandings: for they would not lash out in anger, nor hate anyone, and they would recognize the fundamental importance of bringing a similar serenity to those human beings amongst whom they live (E 1p49s). Furthermore, like some common-sense accounts of virtue, Spinoza's human virtue is not something simply fully achieved or lost. For as I emphasized earlier, there is not a binary division between activity and passivity; rather, activity and virtue admit of degrees. The project of the *Ethics* is the increase of this human virtue and power.

In commentators' enthusiasm to grasp *potentia agendi* and virtue, less discussed is a different way of analysing an individual finite mode's conduct: answering the question, what kind of efficacy the individual has, what sum of effects it produces, regardless of whether that efficacy is active or passive (adequate or inadequate). Indeed, we already have the terminology for this: it is the finite mode's operation, or production of effects. The terminology of *operari* is most prominent in Spinoza's explanation of *natura naturata* in *Ethics* 1, but it recurs subsequently. For instance, when specifically not discussing the essence of a body, but instead its duration, Spinoza notes that the body is caused to exist and produce effects (*ad existendum, & operandum*) by an infinite chain of other finite causes (E 2p30d, 2p31d).

I now raise the question: is power *potentia* associated with a singular thing's producing of effects? Is there such thing as *potentia operandi*? This would be the power of a finite cause to produce effects, without regard to whether those effects are fully understood through it: a power encompassing adequate and inadequate causation. Or does a singular thing only have power to the extent it is active?

In the *Ethics*, by and large, power is only attributed to a finite mode to the degree it is an adequate cause; in other words, there is no such thing as *potentia operandi*. Indeed, sometimes Spinoza associates inadequate causation not with power, but with lack of power *impotentia* (E 4App2). So, if someone flies into a rage, this is an expression more of the power of other things than of that person's own power. Thus, they are better seen as powerless than powerful, even if they successfully bring about many effects in their

understanding of reason as having adequate ideas; in the *Ethics*, the key threat to both is the affects (emotions) (E 2p38–40, 3p59s). However, as I will argue in Section 7.3.2, the threats to active power cannot be managed by individual emotional self-regulation alone without regard to broader external political conditions.

rage (smashing things, pursuing a vendetta).[16] Even where an individual's conduct is good, but understood through an external cause, on this analysis we can deny that conduct is from the individual's own power alone. Recall the child or irascible adult who is calm through external supports: can we say that they have the power to keep calm? It would appear that the answer is no, not straightforwardly: they have power to do so only when their power combined with that of others. The effect is not fully accounted for by their power, because power is only *potentia agendi*.

But on one occasion, the *Ethics* uses the phrase *potentia operandi*. In a difficult passage answering the question of what can increase or decrease power of acting, Spinoza distinguishes human *potentia agendi* from a different power, human *potentia operandi*, or more precisely, 'the power of each singular thing . . . by which he exists and produces an effect [*potentia, quâ existit, & operatur*]' (E 4p29d). The particular argument of this passage[17] is not important at this point; I merely wish to draw attention to the fact that *potentia operandi* is used in contrast to *potentia agendi*.

This concept of *potentia operandi* links neatly to Hobbes's late conception of power. Recall my exegesis and arguments from Chapter 2, Sections 2.3–4. For Hobbes, an act happens if and only if there is plenary power, or equivalently, an effect happens if and only if there is an entire cause. Secondarily, we can individuate actors and stipulate 'their' power to be a subset of the plenary power, but this is done without any interest in connecting their power to some conception of their nature. In particular, an entity's power could very

[16] The secondary literature commonly fails to take into account examples such as the one just given, instead just equating the powerfulness of the *Ethics* (correlated with activity, rationality, and freedom) with powerfulness in the sense of producing many effects. (See, for instance, Steinberg, 'Spinoza on Being *Sui Juris*', 34, 246–248.) But people may successfully produce many effects without any particular ethical or rational warrant, as becomes clear when considering human action in social context. For a sharp example, consider the unethical official shielded from accountability within an oligarchic regime. Chapter 8, Section 8.3 will offer a broader discussion of this point.

[17] In brief, Spinoza is arguing that, because a person's power of producing effects is determined by other things, therefore the person's power of acting (which is a component of this larger power of producing effects) can be affected by other things; in particular, the power of acting may be increased or decreased through external supports. This invites a prima facie objection: even if external forces can render me more capable, can this really count as an increase in my own power? That is, in the case of the person with the anger problem, when they become more capable insofar as their temper is kept under control by another, is there any increase in their own power? E 4p59d and 5p39s suggest that under some circumstances, there is an increase in power; similar ideas are developed in Steinberg's discussion of the role of the state in individual ethical development, and in Deleuze's account of the progress from joyful passions to active joys. Gilles Deleuze, *Expressionism in Philosophy: Spinoza*, translated by Martin Joughin (New York: Zone Books, 1992), 239–246, 257–265, 273–288; Justin D. Steinberg, 'Spinoza on Civil Liberation', *Journal of the History of Philosophy 47*, no. 1 (2009): 35–58; Simon Duffy, 'The Joyful Passions in Spinoza's Theory of Relations', in *Spinoza Now*, edited by Dimitris Vardoulakis (Minneapolis: University of Minnesota Press, 2011), 51–64.

immediately be the result of the act of some other entity upon it. A white billiard ball has power with respect to the act of hitting the red ball, even if that power itself is merely the act with respect to the prior power of the cue stick. Similarly, for Spinoza, an effect is produced when and only when the infinite web of deterministically connected causes in nature combine to bring it about. But secondarily, we can separate out a particular thing's *potentia operandi*, thereby naming its contribution to the effect, without reference to whether the contribution flows from its own nature, or whether it is better understood as the knock-on effect of the impact of some other nature. The child and the angry person whose passions are restrained do have the power to remain calm, on equal footing with the sage (producing the same effects), even though the causal pathways are different; the angry person flying into a rage may be very powerful (causing many effects), even though the person is dominated by the passions.

Despite the neat systematic fit of the concept of *potentia operandi*, if the *Ethics* were Spinoza's only text, I would have to admit that there is only a slender textual basis for that particular terminology. But I will argue that this category, not prominent in *Ethics*, becomes explicit in politics.

7.3. From Metaphysics to Politics

With the distinction between *potentia agendi* and *potentia operandi* in hand, I turn to the politics. When Spinoza refers to power *potentia* in the political texts, is it merely *potentia agendi*, or is it also sometimes *potentia operandi*? Recall in Chapter 6, Section 6.3, I showed how both groups of commentators find a way to account for the apparent combination of ethics and efficacy in Spinoza's politics. For both groups, this reading is supported, with greater or lesser explicitness, by linking power in the *Theological-Political Treatise* and *Political Treatise* to human *potentia* in the *Ethics*, which (as I have shown) is *potentia agendi*.[18] For instance, Rosenthal appeals to the *Ethics*' account

[18] In what follows, I discuss Rosenthal and Melamed, but see also Barbone and Rice, 'Introduction', 12–18; Barbone, 'Power', 91–99; Negri, 'The *Political Treatise*', 14–15; Negri, *The Savage Anomaly*, 157, 190; Della Rocca, *Spinoza*, 208–209; Steinberg, 'Spinoza on Being *Sui Juris*', 247. On this point, Curley is an outlier: he interprets Spinoza's political power without any ethical grain ('Kissinger, Spinoza, and Genghis Khan', 315–342). Indeed, the turn to active power sometimes arises as an explicit critical response to Curley's piece, for instance, Rosenthal, 'Spinoza's Political Philosophy', 431; Moira Gatens, 'Spinoza's Disturbing Thesis: Power, Norms and Fiction in the *Tractatus Theologico-Politicus*', *History of Political Thought 30*, no. 3 (2009): 456.

of virtue as power *potentia* in order to understand the political texts' identification of a thing's power *potentia* with its right. He argues that the result is normatively discriminating, and not some blunt view of 'might is right'.[19] Commentators often acknowledge that not all discussions of power in the political texts fit perfectly with the concept from the *Ethics*, but they put this down to the less precise and less philosophical nature of the political texts. For instance, Melamed draws attention to Spinoza's contrast between a state with a skilled mercenary army and a state with a civilian army (TP 7.12, 7.17, 7.28): the key difference is that the former kind of state has greater military prowess, but the latter kind of state is better at avoiding war in the first place.[20] For Melamed, there is some common-sense 'colloquial' way of talking about power according to which the state with a skilled mercenary army is more powerful. But Melamed argues that Spinoza is able to deny the mercenary state has the greater power by bringing in the more technical and more philosophically significant notion of the state's *potentia agendi*.[21] This exegetical strategy is fairly directly suggested by Spinoza's own discussion in Chapter 20 of the *Theological-Political Treatise*: Spinoza initially asserts the repressive state has great power (the colloquial sense), but then is quick to revise his analysis to deny it holds genuine power (presumably *potentia agendi*) (TTP 20.7, III/240).

This account raises two sets of questions. First, what is this 'colloquial power'? Is there a technical or non-colloquial analysis? Are interpreters right to minimize its significance? Second, granting the existence of a distinct and more normatively discriminating conception of political power in the texts, how well does the political discussion fit with the metaphysics of *potentia agendi*?

[19] Rosenthal, 'Spinoza's Political Philosophy', 409–411, 418–419, 428.

[20] Yitzhak Y. Melamed, 'When Having Too Much Power Is Harmful: Spinoza on Political Luck', in *Spinoza's 'Political Treatise': A Critical Guide*, edited by Yitzhak Y. Melamed and Hasana Sharp (Cambridge: Cambridge University Press, 2018), 164–167. The republican tradition also found other reasons to worry about mercenaries: in war, a mercenary army lacks any patriotic commitment to the republic, and can turn against it (TTP 17.74–75, III.214; similarly Niccolò Machiavelli, *Discourses on Livy*, trans. Harvey Claflin Mansfield and Nathan Tarcov [Chicago: University of Chicago Press, 1996], II.20).

[21] Melamed, 'Having Too Much Power', 171–173; see also Mugnier-Pollet, *La philosophie politique de Spinoza*, 96. Della Rocca makes a similar move. Della Rocca accepts that, at first, right is equated with power without qualification; but he claims that the more precise and accurate statement is that right is equated with power in the long run (Della Rocca, *Spinoza*, 206–208). He explicitly links (208–209) this claim to his earlier discussion (175–205) of power of acting in the *Ethics*, associated with essence and adequate causation. He grants that something wrong in the long term may be right in the short term, but the privileged perspective is the long-term one (222–223).

7.3.1. 'Colloquial' Power as *Potentia Operandi*

In answer to the first question, I will argue that the 'colloquial' power is in fact *potentia operandi*, readily and robustly grounded in Spinoza's metaphysics. Furthermore, this 'colloquial' power is of fundamental importance in Spinoza's politics: for it is this conception of power that is at stake in the key passages establishing Spinoza's doctrine of right.

In both the *Theological-Political Treatise* and in the *Political Treatise*, Spinoza begins his consideration of politics by laying out his doctrine of right. Notoriously, he links right to power. But what power is at stake? In both texts, right is explicitly connected, not to *acting* (*agere*), but to *producing effects* (*operari*).

> [E]ach individual has the supreme right [*jus summum . . . habere*] . . . to exist and have effects as it is naturally determined to do [*ad existendum & operandum prout naturaliter determinatum est*]. (TTP 16.4, III/189)

> [E]ach natural thing has as much right by nature as it has power to exist and have effects [*tantum juris ex naturâ habere, quantum potentiæ habet ad existendum, & operandum*]. (TP 2.3)

This terminological choice is repeated throughout the presentation of the doctrine of rights (TTP 16.2, III/189, 16.7, III/190, 16.10, III/191; TP 2.2).

Beyond mere terminology, I claim that the substantive claims of the passages also map onto the concept of *potentia operandi* as I sketched it in Section 7.2. Admittedly, Spinoza's discussion does appeal to the nature of the individual.

> By the right and established practice of nature I mean nothing but the rules of nature of each individual. (TTP 16.1, III/189)

This appeal to rules of nature might superficially be reminiscent of the *Ethics*' notion of adequate causation and action: the production of effects that can be understood through laws of an individual's nature alone, or equivalently, from the individual's *potentia agendi* alone. Furthermore, the appeal to rules suggests the possibility of violation: surely if right corresponds to rules of nature of each individual, then when those rules are not observed, right is lost?

Such a reading of this passage finds apparent corroboration in Spinoza's later denial of right to sovereigns who govern in a way that contributes to their own downfall (TTP 20.7, III/240).

To the contrary, in the foundational passages laying out the doctrine of right, it is clear that in fact the power to which right corresponds is *potentia operandi* as I described it in the previous section. For nothing that actually occurs lacks right. Spinoza takes pains to insist that various wicked and irrational human behaviours cannot be faulted from the point of view of right.

> [T]he Right and Established Practice of nature, under which all are born and for the most part live, prohibits nothing except what no one desires and what no one can do: not disputes, not hatreds, not anger, not deception. Without exception, it is not averse to anything appetite urges. (TTP 16.9, III/190)[22]

Thus, right is not aligned exclusively with an individual's active power and adequate causation, but instead it is attributed to any production of effects at all.[23]

In result, it is not acceptable to appeal to the *Ethics*' *potentia agendi* to understand Spinoza's political conception of right. In the *Ethics*, the very same wicked and irrational human behaviours are considered exemplars of impotence, evidencing a subject overwhelmed by the power of other things (E 3Pref, E 4p20d). But ethically impotent behaviour can have an oversized impact on human social existence. A person whose behaviour is understood through the power of other things may be extremely effective and in this sense may have very great power (*potentia operandi*): to return to my earlier example, an angry person may bring about many effects (smash things, pursue vendettas), even though only a very inadequate cause of those effects. Spinoza contrasts the political and ethical ways of assessing behaviour: he explicitly grants that problematic human behaviours may not properly count as actions (*actiones*) (TP 2.5), but he asserts that this observation is irrelevant to the question of right. All varieties of human behaviour without exception are in accordance with the right of nature, because all arise as effects of nature

[22] See also TTP 16.5–11, III/189–191; TP 2.5–8.

[23] Matheron makes this claim very explicitly; however he also presumes that a regime (and its right) will only be enduring if its power is active (*Individu et communauté*, 287–289). For criticisms of this presumption, see the discussion in Chapter 8, Section 8.3.

(*effectûs naturæ*) (TP 2.5). If I give rise to an effect that is not from my active power alone, then it must have involved the active power of other things. But Spinoza's nature broaches no privilege for my active power over the powers of other things.

> Nature is not constrained by the laws of human reason, which aim only at man's true advantage and preservation. It is governed by infinite other laws, which look to the eternal order of the whole of nature, of which man is only a small part. It is only by the necessity of this whole order that all individuals are determined to exist and have effects [*ad existendum & operandum*] in a definite way. (TTP 16.10, III/190–191)

The 'rules of nature of each individual' cited earlier (TTP 16.1, III/189) can be understood as local rules of the production of effects, within the totality of the laws of nature as a whole; unlike laws of human advantage and preservation, they are never violated. This concurs with the initial claim in the *Theological-Political Treatise,* Chapter 20, where Spinoza asserts that. strictly speaking, 'by right sovereigns can rule with the utmost violence, and condemn citizens to death for the slightest of reasons' (TTP 20.7, III/240), even though this is gravely unwise.

Perhaps Melamed is correct to identify a 'colloquial' sense of power in Spinoza's political texts. But this 'colloquial' sense also has a rigorous place in Spinoza's metaphysics as *potentia operandi*, and is critical for Spinoza's account of right. And furthermore, *potentia operandi* fits more closely with prevalent contemporary uses of the word 'power' than does *potentia agendi*. A powerful conqueror is said to be powerful even if that power is hardly at all understood through their nature alone, but primarily in terms of the soldiers and weapons that they can deploy. A church is said to be powerful even if its power is not understood through its nature alone, but in virtue of its role in harnessing wider economic and racial grievances. A wicked official can be very powerful, even if their power is understood through the official's place in a corrupt oligarchic institutional system. To return to Melamed's example from the *Political Treatise*, a state with a mercenary army is said to be powerful, productive of mass effects, even if it may destabilize itself in the long term. This matches with Hobbes's late treatment of power as purely a question of effects; it is not important whether those effects are properly due to the actor's own nature alone.

7.3.2. Being Sui juris

I now turn to consider the second question, the question of the fit between the normatively discriminating conception of power in the political writings and the metaphysics of *potentia agendi*. Certainly, after getting past the initial antinomian presentation of the doctrine of right as coextensive with power, Spinoza's political writings often appear to discuss political power *potentia* with an ethical grain. Nature may not care about the preservation and flourishing of any particular thing, but as humans, we must. As noted, many commentators understand this ethical power in the politics as corresponding to *potentia agendi*.[24] But against a uniform theory of ethical power *potentia agendi* across Spinoza's political writings, I will distinguish two variants, representing two different attempts to translate power *potentia agendi* into right. The translation is difficult because of the poor match between the structure of the respective concepts. I argue that the first attempt, in the *Theological-Political Treatise*, is problematic, because it relies on a binary cut between having right and power and lacking right and power, whereas the version in the *Political Treatise* fits better with Spinoza's underlying metaphysics, because it allows gradualism. The *Political Treatise*'s translation of metaphysics into politics relabels the degree to which an entity produces effects from its own active power alone as the degree to which it is in control of its own right (sui juris). From this analytical frame, in principle one can inquire separately into the sui juris status of the political order as a whole versus that of the individual persons making up that order; in the present chapter I do not establish the relationship between these statuses. It is the *Political Treatise*'s analytical frame, centred on being sui juris, that I will deploy in Chapters 8 and 9, to criticize the romanticism of extant interpretations of Spinoza, and to put forward a new conception of popular power.

The much-discussed Chapter 20 of the *Theological-Political Treatise* gives the most explicit statement of the first approach to translating *potentia agendi* into politics. In that chapter, Spinoza initially asserts that whatever the sovereign in fact does, it has the power and consequently the right to do. But then Spinoza immediately retracts his initial assertion, denying that it makes sense to attribute power to self-destructive behaviour.

[24] See footnotes 18–21.

> Indeed, because they can't do these things[25] without great danger to the whole state, we can also deny that they have absolute power [*absolutam potentiam*] to do such things. So we can deny also that they can do them with absolute right [*absolutum jus*]. For we've shown that the right of the supreme powers [*jus ... summarum potestatum*] is determined by their power [*potentia*]. (TTP 20.7, III/240)

Notwithstanding Spinoza's reference back to his own earlier demonstration, this passage clearly represents a shift of perspective. For as argued in Section 7.3.1, on the earlier analysis in Spinoza's Chapter 16, all actual occurrences, including the destruction of any particular thing, occur by right.

The shift of perspective involves Spinoza focussing his analysis on a particular thing's own proper power, as opposed to the power of other things. The idea that self-destructive behaviour cannot flow from a thing's own power is certainly reminiscent of some propositions of the *Ethics* regarding *potentia agendi*. In setting up his *conatus* doctrine (discussed in Section 7.2), Spinoza asserts:

> No thing can be destroyed except through an external cause. (E 3p4)

He goes on to connect a thing's own power of acting with its perseverance: a thing's power is

> the striving [*conatus*] by which [each thing] (either alone or with others) does anything, or strives to do anything [*agit, vel agere conatur*]—i.e. . . . the power, *or* striving [*potentia, sive conatus*], by which it strives to persevere in its being. (E 3p7d)

But I will now argue that despite the superficial compatibility, the analysis in the politics does not fit well with this metaphysics.

As I argued in Section 7.2, in Spinoza's metaphysics a thing entirely lacks *potentia agendi* only insofar as it produces no effects whatsoever, or in other words, insofar as it ceases to exist. Any effect that an individual is involved in causing arises in part from its *potentia agendi*. Nor, at the other extreme, is it possible for any finite thing to act fully and exclusively from its own nature

[25] 'These things' being to 'rule with utmost violence, and condemn citizens to death for the slightest of reasons' (TTP 20.7, III/240).

(E 4p2–4p4). Perfect activity is reserved for God alone. Thus, for finite existing things, activity is a matter of degree, and any classification of acts as definitively active or passive, or as definitively possessing or lacking power, will be irredeemably arbitrary. Notwithstanding his use of terminological contrasts between activity and passivity, or between power and impotence, Spinoza's metaphysics does not support a sharp binary division amongst actually occurring behaviours.[26]

Turning to the *Theological-Political Treatise*'s passage 20.7, what is at stake is a certain imprudent mode of governance, where the self-destructive effect is not instant. Accordingly, in denying right and power to this mode of governance, the passage demands a sharp binary division amongst actually existing behaviours—precisely what Spinoza's metaphysics does not support. To be sure, if we were speaking of the instant a state ceases to exist, then at that moment the state is entirely lacking in active power. But that is not what is in question in the case at hand. The repressive state is said to lack power and right because its mode of governance may undermine the state's existence in the longer term. But what exactly is the relevant timescale of destruction to determine whether a policy is sufficiently imprudent to count as lacking in right? What if in fact the regime manages to kick along for a fairly long time despite its restrictions on speech? According to Spinoza's metaphysics, insofar as it doesn't immediately collapse, it expresses some degree of its own active power.[27]

The *Theological-Political Treatise*'s attempt to relate right to active power problematically collapses together two different questions: first, whether a state continues to exist and cause effects; and second, how active it is. The first question fits well with a binary cut of having or lacking right. But the second would be served better by a gradual scale, recognizing (metaphysically) that

[26] This is reflected in the prominent use of qualifiers in the *conatus* doctrine: 'Each thing, insofar as it is in itself [*quantum in se est*], strives to persevere in its being' (E 3p5, translation modified). The qualifier is necessary because nothing apart from God is ever fully 'in itself' or active. When a thing does something self-destructive without actually ceasing to exist, this simply means that its active power and striving were combined with other forces inimical to that striving. See Garrett, 'Spinoza's Conatus Argument', 139–145.

[27] Perhaps a student of the *Ethics* might hope to map the binary division from the politics onto a different metaphysical distinction: the distinction between behaviour that increases the active power of the state and behaviour that decreases it, or in Spinoza's technical language, between its joyful and sad affectations (E 3d3, E 3p11s). That is, might we attempt to gloss passage 20.7 as granting the state a right to joyful but not sad governance? But such a proposal cannot succeed. Every single instance of imprudent governance decreases the state's active power, but Spinoza emphatically upholds the right to moderately poor governance: he clearly states that citizens should continue to obey unreasonable laws (TTP 20.15, III/15).

activity is a matter of degree and (politically) that political decisions and governance exist on a spectrum of prudence and imprudence. Indeed, in the *Political Treatise*, Spinoza offers a new way of mapping active power onto right, in which these two questions are sharply separated, offering an analysis of right and power that coheres much better with Spinoza's underlying metaphysics.

The first dimension of analysis of any political situation is the question of possession of right. Early in the *Political Treatise*, Spinoza links possession of right to *potentia operandi*, as I have argued. This is maintained throughout the text. Whatever occurs, occurs by right; regarding whatever does not occur, right is lacking. Thus, any state, insofar as it exists and produces effects, does so with full right. Attributing right to a state does not involve any discrimination between better and worse ways in which it might exist and produce effects. The name for the state's right is *imperium* (translated by Curley as sovereignty) (TP 2.17); Spinoza also uses it to refer the entity unified by that right (TP 3.1 and *passim*). This right is binary, in the sense that there either is *imperium* (the state exists and produces effects) or there is not (the state has fallen apart and thus no longer exists as such).

As an aside, let me draw attention to a striking feature of the *Political Treatise*'s analysis of the production of political effects: its analytical privilege to the political order as a whole. *Imperium* is defined by the power of the multitude (TP 2.17); and the term is used more or less interchangeably with commonwealth, *civitas*, the 'whole body' of the state (TP 5.1–2). By contrast, the central term to analyse political order and its right in the earlier *Theological-Political Treatise* was *summa potestas*, which referred more narrowly to the holder of sovereign power (whether a monarch or an assembly) (TTP 16.24–35, III/193–195 and *passim*). If (as Spinoza asserts) the power of rulers rests on and emerges from the power of the populace, these two concepts turn out to be coextensive: the right of the rulers must be understood in terms of the power and right of the political order taken as a whole. Indeed, Spinoza tends to equate the two quite freely (TP 3.1–2). Nonetheless, *imperium* is a superior analytical and explanatory term, because the conduct of the formal holder of sovereignty is not free-floating. Rather, it is itself generated within a network of determinate causes, most centrally the social and institutional structures of the polity.[28]

[28] See also Balibar, *Spinoza and Politics*, 69–70.

The second dimension of analysis supplies normative discrimination. Just as in Spinoza's metaphysics, there is a question, for any thing's causation of effects (for any thing's *potentia operandi*), to what degree is that causation adequate (to what degree does it arise from its own *potentia agendi* alone); so too in Spinoza's politics, there is a question, for any right, to what degree is this right the thing's own right alone. Or, to introduce new equivalent terminologies, to what extent is the thing sui juris, in control of its own right.[29] The concept of being sui juris is laid out in two key textual passages in the *Political Treatise*. First, Chapter 2 addresses individual right; then Chapter 5 addresses the state's right. Loosely speaking, Spinoza's normative criterion for a good state is both that the state itself be sui juris, and also that the subjects of the state within it be maximally sui juris. I will develop this claim in my own Chapters 8 and 9, with various qualifications and caveats. For now, my purpose is merely to characterize each of these conditions separately; in Chapter 8 I will argue that they can readily come apart.

I start by characterizing what it is for an individual to be sui juris, establishing an equivalence with the metaphysical concept of being active or virtuous (producing effects more from one's own *potentia agendi* than from external causes); but equally with the more familiar political concept of independence.[30] The connection with independence has obvious textual support. The idea of being sui juris is initially introduced in opposition to *potestas*. Recall the analysis of *potestas* discussed in Chapter 5, Section 5.4: to whatever extent a person is dependent on another, they are in that person's power, *in/sub potestate*. Insofar as a person is in the power of another, they are *alterius juris*, subject to another's right. By contrast, to the extent a person is not subjected to the *potestas* of another, or in other words, to the extent they are independent, they are in control of their own right, sui juris (TP 2.9–11). At face value, there is also a patent connection between being sui juris and the *Ethics*' discussion of action and adequate causation, insofar as the key passages use the exact same technical language.[31] Being sui juris corresponds to being adequate cause of one's actions, with producing effects from one's *potentia agendi* alone, which amounts to rational self-determination.[32]

[29] I grant that the terminological distinction is not perfectly respected in the text. For instance, consider the case of an individual in a collective, whose conduct is subject to the control of the collective. Spinoza oscillates between saying that such conduct lacks right altogether, and saying that it does have right, but that right is not its own (TP 2.16, 3.2).

[30] Balibar, *Spinoza and Politics*, 61.

[31] See footnote 58 of Chapter 6.

[32] The connection with the metaphysics of the *Ethics* suggests that the scope of dependency at stake in being *alterius juris* encompasses non-human dependencies.

Being *alterius juris*, by contrast, means that one's conduct is understood not through one's nature alone, but through that nature in combination with the nature of other things.[33]

However, this dual equivalence has troubled commentators, because they do not see how ethical activity and political independence can be equated, and they see textual suggestion that Spinoza himself does not make such an equation. Steinberg articulates the puzzle as follows. The sage is said to be most sui juris (TP 2.11), but any sage will also fully submit themselves to be *in potestate* of the state (TP 3.5–6): that is, they will simultaneously be not sui juris.[34] Steinberg's solution is simply to separate the ethical-metaphysical and political meanings of being sui juris. The apparent contradiction of Spinoza's claim is dissolved: it reduces to the claim that a sage, sui juris in the metaphysical sense, will not want to be sui juris in the political sense.[35]

Against Steinberg, distinguishing two separate and unrelated senses of 'being sui juris' is unnecessary and unhelpful. For being sui juris is a gradualist concept, and it always makes reference to a relevant contrast class. These two features of the concept allow it to encompass both of its supposedly distinct meanings of being sui juris in the case of Steinberg's sage, but also allow it to account for the ambivalent status of the mad person, which would remain unexplained on Steinberg's account.

As argued in Chapter 6, Section 6.4, Spinoza's analysis of being *in potestate / alterius juris* is concerned to include all ways in which one's conduct is dependent on that of others, whether this is overwhelming or only slight. Thus, being sui juris and being *sub potestate / alterius juris* need to be understood on a continuum, and Spinoza speaks of being more or less sui juris (TP 2.9–11, 3.7, and *passim*). The gradualist character of dependency necessitates using these concepts with respect to particular contrast classes. For if dependency is not total and exclusive but admits of degrees, then a given individual may be dependent in different respects on different things.[36] Spinoza's

[33] A similar idea can be seen already in the *Theological-Political Treatise*'s discussion of obedience: 'So whatever a subject does which answers to the commands of the supreme power—whether he's been bound by love, or compelled by fear, or (as indeed is more frequent) by hope and fear together, whether he acts from reverence (a passion composed of fear and wonder) or is led by any reason whatever—he acts by the right of the state, not his own right [*ex jure imperii, non autem suo agit*]' (TTP 17.7, III/202).

[34] Steinberg, 'Spinoza on Being *Sui Juris*', 239–240, 243–244.

[35] Ibid., 24–248.

[36] See footnote 57 in Chapter 6. This idea of differential and contextual dependency also allows that a person might be both *sub potestate* of the state and also *sub potestate* of another individual or group within the state; for instance, a servant is subject to both their master and the political order as a whole.

use of the term reflects this contextual specificity, as is seen most sharply in the case of the mad person (TP 3.8). Why is a mad person sui juris? They are sui juris with respect to the state, for insofar as (*eatenus*) they are unresponsive to the state's incentives and punishments, their conduct cannot be understood through the power of the state.

> [T]hose who neither fear nor hope for anything are to that extent their own masters [*eatenus sui juris sunt*]. (TP 3.8)

But they are profoundly *alterius juris* to other human beings: the mad are extremely vulnerable to others' violence, exploitation, domination, insofar as they are less able to navigate the social domain. Indeed, they also are paradigmatically *sub potestate* of the state: for they are often captured, punished, and constrained by the state. Steinberg's distinction is inadequate to resolve this paradox, because the mad are simultaneously sui juris and not sui juris in Steinberg's second (political) sense of the term.

With these considerations in hand, we can return to Steinberg's case of the sage.

> I call a man completely free just insofar as he is guided by reason, because to that extent he is determined by causes which can be understood through his own nature alone. (TP 2.11)

Is a sage (one who has approached intellectual perfection) completely free? To be sure, their high degree of reason allows them optimally to negotiate the predicaments they find themselves in, and to avoid some bad predicaments altogether. A sage is sui juris with respect to other human beings, insofar as the sage is not swayed by collective passions, and conducts themself as well as possible to encourage virtuous and sociable conduct in others. But it does not follow that they are perfectly sui juris, determined exclusively by causes that can be understood through their own nature alone. Insofar as they can be threatened by others, or insofar as they need material goods in order to live, or need others not to steal their material goods or attack them, they are still very much *alterius juris* and dependent on other human beings. Even the hermitic sage is not sui juris: they are subject to famine and attack and are at the mercy of nature should they fall ill (TP 3.11).[37] The state has an important

[37] Matheron, *Individu et communauté*, 282.

role in reducing these acute kinds of dependency, albeit in favour of a more diffuse dependency on the political order as a whole (TP 3.3).[38] In result, the sage within a state is subject to the state's power, just like any other member of the political community. This framework of subjection to the state allows the sage to remain sui juris with respect to their fellows (TP 3.5–6). Thus, in saying the sage is both sui juris and not sui juris, Spinoza is not making use of two different conceptions of being sui juris. Rather, he is pointing to two different contrast classes of dependency.[39]

The discussion in Chapter 2 of the *Political Treatise* concerns a human individual's status as sui juris, for which we have a series of Spinozist equivalences: an individual is sui juris, or in control of their own right, to the degree that they are active, or to the extent they produce effects from their *potentia agendi* alone, which is the same as producing effects that can be understood through their own nature alone. In Chapter 9, I will flesh out the broader political import of this conception of individual sui juris status: I will characterize a social order in which citizens are maximally sui juris, not as what would be impossible (a community of sages), but as a social order that simultaneously allows individual ethical development and also eliminates overwhelming relations of dependency between citizens. But for now, I turn to showing how the concept of being sui juris can separately be applied to the political order as a whole.[40]

Whenever a state produces effects, then it has power (*potentia operandi*) and right to do so. This right and power are defined by the power of the multitude (*multitudinis potentia*) composing the state. But it is an open question, is the state sui juris in the production of these effects? Indeed, throughout the *Political Treatise*, the dominant concept for normatively evaluating the state (*imperium*) is being sui juris; Spinoza explicitly contrasts this, the best way for a state to run, with the merely rightful operation that characterizes any state whatsoever (TP 5.1). Later in the *Political Treatise*, he redefines political absoluteness as being maximally sui juris (TP 8.3–7, also TP 5.2).

[38] Ibid., 327. See also Balibar: 'To be in the power of others, to depend upon their power, can also constitute a positive condition through which one can, up to a point, preserve and affirm one's own individuality' (*Spinoza and Politics*, 61).

[39] This analysis is structurally similar to the late Hobbesian analysis from Chapter 5, Section 5.4: far from individual freedom being intrinsically opposed to the state, individual freedom relies on a good state as its condition of possibility (to eliminate private and informal domination).

[40] Armstrong and Matheron usefully distinguish between active and passive power, mapping onto my distinction between *potentia agendi* and *potentia operandi*. But whereas Armstrong applies this analysis only to individual human subjects, Matheron also extends it to the state as a whole. Armstrong, 'Natural and Unnatural Communities', 269–299; Matheron, *Individu et communauté*, 330–348.

One might have thought that a state sui juris just is one that maximally secures the sui juris status of its subjects, but I emphasize that this needs to be demonstrated and is not built into the concept of being sui juris itself. To be sure, just as an individual human being is maximally sui juris when their behaviour is determined by reason, so too is the state most sui juris when it is founded on reason (TP 5.1). But being determined by reason is equivalent to being determined by one's own nature alone (producing effects that can be understood through one's own nature alone); thus a precise application of the concept of being sui juris will need to wait until I have provided a clear characterization of what the state's nature might be (Chapter 8, Section 8.2). For now, I will merely sketch two paradigmatic and intuitive cases of a state failing to be determined by its own nature alone and hence failing to be maximally sui juris. The first is when the political unit as a whole finds itself subjected to or dependent on a gross external force (TP 3.12): for instance, in Melamed's example of a bellicose state suffering counterattacks from its neighbours;[41] or states uneasily allied through royal marriage (TP 7.24); or a small city requiring another's protection (TP 7.16). The second case is where there is some fragility internal to the state, such that the component parts do not constitute a resilient whole: the effects produced by the state are understood not through its unified nature, but through the natures of its disparate parts. This could take the form of general lawlessness (TP 5.2); or more interestingly, in a division between groups. If rulers (patricians, or the ruling clique in a monarchy) are terrified of the masses, then their rule is not absolute, even and especially if this terror is the result of their own tyrannical rule.

> The greater reason for fear [the Commonwealth] has, the less it is its own master [*eò minùs sui juris*]. (TP 3.9)

From this point of view, the apparently most absolute monarchy (in the conventional/Hobbesian meaning of absoluteness) is actually revealed to be the least sui juris and the least absolute, because of the monarch's fear of the masses who resent the monarch's formally unchallengeable supremacy (TP 6.5–8).[42] But equally, other kinds of divisions are also possible, as, for

[41] Melamed, 'Having Too Much Power', 164–167.

[42] Steinberg's account of a state's absoluteness has some similarities with mine: a state is absolute to the extent 'it will beget civic harmony, or establish a common *ratio*'. However, Steinberg emphasizes the role of the holder of sovereignty: 'The onus for maintaining order and indeed its own authority is placed squarely on the sovereign' (Steinberg, *Spinoza's Political Psychology*, 172). In order to support this claim, Steinberg interprets away Spinoza's use of *civitas* rather than *summa potestas* at critical

instance, the hostility between the Levites and the other tribes of the ancient Hebrew republic (TTP 17.3, III/201, 17.13–18, III/203–204, 17.96–101, III/217–218; TP 6.5–8, 8.3–7).

7.4. Conclusion

In this chapter, I have offered a new distinction between two senses of power, *potentia operandi* and *potentia agendi*. I sketched it conceptually and I grounded it textually in the *Ethics*. Translating these senses of power to politics, I have privileged the *Political Treatise*'s two-dimensional account of right as more faithful to the metaphysical frame than the more familiar one-dimensional account in the *Theological-Political Treatise*.

Spinoza's two-dimensional account of right allows us to parse out various critical distinctions in analysing political power. First, we can ask what right a collectivity has, that is, how powerful it is in terms of exercising a capacity to produce effects. But second, we can ask how much its effects can be understood through its own nature alone, how much it acts by its own power, or equivalently in Spinoza's redefinition of the terms, how absolute or sui juris it is. And third, we can ask whether the inner structure of the collective power involves citizens being sui juris or being dependent on one another. With this two-dimensional analysis of right, I open the possibility of an interpretation of Spinoza's politics that emphasizes its antinomian themes: recognizing and accommodating a possible gulf between political efficacy and ethics. Over the next two chapters, I will deploy this analysis to characterize the Spinozist response to the three Hobbesian problems outlined in Chapter 6, but also to build a positive conception of popular power that escapes accusations of political naivete or romanticism, and which has critical consequences for how we view the democratic credentials of social movements and popular plebiscites.

points in TP (ibid., 172 n. 36; TP 5.2–3). But on my account, the focus on the determinate causes of good or bad rulerly behaviour, reflected in the shift away from a focus on *summa potestas*, is a distinctive and appealing feature of the later text's analysis. Already in the TTP, there is brief mention of the need to constrain rulers (TTP 17.14, III/203), but the theme is developed only in relation to the Hebrew republic, not more generally. By contrast, TP makes explicit that it is no use simply to stipulate correct rulerly behaviour outside of an account of its determinate causes: '[I]t's necessary to set up a state, so that everyone—both those who rule and those who are ruled—does what's for the common well-being, whether they want to or not' (TP 6.2). Undue focus on *potestas* inappropriately narrows our focus onto the holder of power rather than the power-holder's function within the whole ecology of the political body.

8

Nature's Indifference

8.1. Introduction

The larger purpose of the book is to understand popular power. Are radical democrats correct to identify popular plebiscites or social movements as exemplary expressions of popular power? If not, how should popular power worthy of the name be conceived? In Part I of this book, I have used Hobbes to construct a conception of popular power as the durable production of political effects not distorted by oligarchic private powers. I examined Hobbes's withering scepticism towards romantic conceptions of the spontaneous equality and goodness of the popular multitude; on his view, democracy tends to suffer from the political problem, and does so the more acutely, the more open and participatory it is, due to the continuous oligarchic generation of power blocs within the multitude. Hobbes overcomes the political problem through an institutional proposal that I have called repressive egalitarianism, a proposal that is highly ambivalent to contemporary sensibilities.

Now, in Part II, I have turned to Spinoza in pursuit of a more inspirational vision of popular power. On the standard presentations, Spinoza offers a view of politics that I have referred to in shorthand as the 'combination of ethics and efficacy': for it holds that genuinely effective political power in fact coincides with what is ethically desirable. In Chapter 6, I showed that this optimism is shared by both camps of contemporary Spinoza interpreters: on the one hand, the radical democratic interpreters, for whom popular power is an underlying insurgent force disrupting unjust rule; but equally the more mainstream 'constitutionalist' interpreters, who are less inclined to grant the existence of a prepolitical popular power, but for whom nonetheless the only possibility of a stable political order is one that meets the ethical desiderata of equality and participation. This view needs to face a three-part Hobbesian accusation of naivete: the problem of the multitude's inner oligarchy; the problem of nonideal endurance; and the problem of democracy's perverse effects.

Potentia. Sandra Leonie Field, Oxford University Press (2020). © Oxford University Press.
DOI: 10.1093/oso/9780197533864.001.0001

In Chapter 7, I offered a new interpretation of Spinoza's political philosophy, resting on the distinction between two fundamental concepts: on the one hand, having right and power; on the other hand, being in control of one's right, and acting from one's own proper power. Everything that happens, happens by right, and there is no right to anything that does not in fact occur; a thing's right is coextensive with its *potentia operandi*. But there remains an open question of whose right and power: are the effects produced by a right and power that are properly that thing's own, or in other words from that thing's nature and active power *potentia agendi* alone? Or are the effects produced from its nature and active power only in combination with the nature and active power of another? If the effects are produced from its own nature alone, then it is sui juris, and by a series of Spinozist equivalences, it is free, absolute, active, and virtuous. The question of sui juris status can be posed both to a political order and to the subjects who make it up.

In the present chapter, I will use this framework to argue that there is a separation between the ethics and the efficacy of popular power in Spinoza's politics, thereby relieving him of the accusation of naivete with respect to the first and the second Hobbesian criticisms from Chapter 6 (I hold over the third for Chapter 9). First, I claim that Spinoza accepts *the problem of the multitude's inner oligarchy*. I establish a characterization of being sui juris as homeostasis: thus, I argue that for any horizontality of a collectivity's inner structure to be attributed to the collectivity's own power, it needs to be established as a homeostatic self-perpetuating feature of the collectivity over time. I show that for Spinoza any horizontality of a collectivity's inner structure is neither a natural ground nor the *telos* of a natural tendency, but something that needs to be established. The upshot is that oppositional social movements cannot constitute exemplars of a multitude sui juris. Second, I claim that Spinoza accepts *the problem of nonideal endurance*. Virtuous political organization that cultivates individual human virtue, freedom, and equality may conduce to stability, but stability is also possible in other ways, whether from durable external causes, or from non-egalitarian homeostatic forms of collective organization (whereby the state is itself sui juris, but the subjects within it find themselves in hierarchical relations of dependency or subjection).

This chapter underscores the deep antinomianism of Spinoza's philosophy. Spinoza insists that

> [n]ature is not constrained by the laws of human reason, which aim only at man's advantage and preservation. It is governed by infinite other laws, which look to the eternal order of the whole of nature, of which man is only a small part. (TTP 16.10, III/190–191)

The positive upshot of my analysis will be twofold. First, Spinoza's analysis poses an understanding of human collectivities as neither inherently popular nor powerful. A good and strong horizontal multitude needs to be constituted, not merely through removing the obstacles of oppressive institutions, but also through positive structuring of good civic institutions. Second, a Spinozist analysis does not licence any democratic complacency that only good states will endure; regimes may endure that bear little relation to any appealing republican liberal-democratic model.

8.2. Accepting the Problem of Inner Oligarchy

A goal of Spinoza's politics is for a political community to be sui juris and absolute. Paying attention to Spinoza's grounding of state power (*imperium*) in the power *potentia* of the multitude (TP 2.17), the goal of absoluteness then amounts to the goal of a multitude sui juris, a multitude governed by its active power alone. What is controversial is to understand what it takes to achieve a multitude sui juris. In particular, supposing that a multitude sui juris displays a horizontal equal shape internally,[1] is this 'natural' and spontaneous, the result of removing bad institutions? Or does it require positive institutional structure of its own? Radical democrats conceive of the multitude as naturally good, but their view has already been amply criticized in the literature for its romanticism;[2] indeed, the group of commentators I designated 'constitutionalist' is defined by their shared rejection of any natural goodness of the multitude (see Chapter 6, Section 6.3). However, in this section, I consider

[1] In Section 8.3, I will argue that there are also hierarchical multitudes sui juris, or in other words, multitudes that are themselves sui juris, but whose internal structure features subjects who are not sui juris with respect to each other. For now, I focus only on the standardly presumed horizontal multitude sui juris.

[2] Notably by Balibar. Balibar, 'Spinoza, the Anti-Orwell', 123–125; Balibar, *Spinoza and Politics*, 61–70, 88; Étienne Balibar, 'Potentia Multitudinis, Quae Una Veluti Mente Ducitur', in *Current Continental Theory and Modern Philosophy*, edited by Stephen H. Daniel (Evanston, IL: Northwestern University Press, 2005), 92–93. Matheron proposes that unmediated human relations, far from being democratic and equal, resemble the anarchic inequality of medieval society (*Individu et communauté*, 158–159).

a phenomenon that greatly interests proponents of the radical democratic view, and which might appear to confound the constitutionalist commitment to institutional mediation of mass power: namely, social movements.

Recall from Chapter 6, Section 6.3.1, that radical democratic readers of Spinoza understand the multitude as a horizontal collection of unhierarchized human singularities, opposed to the state. To be sure, some actually existing multitudes are distorted from this natural shape, but this is explained by pressure from state power *potestas*. (Or in some more cautious formulations, the multitude has a tendency towards horizontality, a tendency that can be temporarily thwarted by state power.) Such a view is diametrically opposed to the late Hobbesian understanding of power developed in the first half of the book: as argued, in Hobbes's later writings, there is nothing naturally horizontal about the multitude, neither its actual state nor its tendencies, even if state power is removed. Already in Chapter 6, Section 6.4, in my exegesis of Spinoza's expansive conception of *potestas*, I provided a preliminary argument that Spinoza would agree with Hobbes. Human social existence is pervaded by microhierarchical relations that may tend to compound to generate oligarchical power blocs in the multitude.[3]

I can imagine that my preliminary argument might be contested by radical democratic readers of Spinoza. For it is possible to grant that human relations feature micro-*potestates*, and yet deny that they tend to compound. Indeed, Spinoza asserts that people hate inequality (TTP 5.23, III/74; TP 7.5), a claim that appears to corroborate the radical democratic view. While sometimes oligarchical power blocs emerge and compound themselves, we also have striking real examples of the opposite. Negri celebrates '[c]enturies of struggle by oppressed minorities, by the exploited proletariat'; he interprets social movements as harbingers of the multitude's constituent progress towards equal combination.[4] Social movements against state power are often internally horizontal, equal, and plural; in them, the compounding tendencies worried about in Chapter 6 do not eventuate. Furthermore, note the distinctive thing about social movements: far from being part of the state

[3] This argument departs from the more common characterization of the deficiencies of the preinstitutional multitude. Most constitutionalist readers of Spinoza characterize the preinstitutional multitude as pervasively unstable: although individuals attempt to establish hierarchical relations, the larger problem is that nothing, neither these relations of domination nor any larger unity, can have even mid-range stability prior to the establishment of the state. In the terms of my discussion from Chapters 2 through 4, the analysis remains early Hobbesian. This lack of consideration of stable forms of emergent hierarchy and domination results in an inadequate understanding of domination within the state; see my discussion in Section 8.3.

[4] Negri, *The Savage Anomaly*, 221; Hardt and Negri, *Multitude*, xi–xvi, 67–88, 213–222.

apparatus, they are opposed to it. They appear to give grounds for reasserting the natural democratic goodness of the multitude's active power, its power from its own nature as opposed to distortions from external causes.[5] Negri concludes *The Savage Anomaly* by prophesying the rise of an independent multitude, 'the independence of productive force,' which has moved beyond the antagonistic struggle between *potentia* and *potestas*.[6] Other radical democratic readers of Spinoza take a more tragic interpretation of the trajectory of history: the multitude rises up to express its natural equality, but is regularly crushed or co-opted, without any necessary progressive increase in its success over time. But even here, they still share Negri's idea of equality as the natural or authentic condition of the multitude.[7]

Might social movements be a manifestation in miniature of the entire multitude's active power, as radical democrats suggest? Are they exemplars of a multitude sui juris? Do they support the radical democratic idea of a natural horizontal shape for the multitude? In this section, I will argue that social movements cannot be exemplary cases of a multitude sui juris. For just as individual being sui juris is a relational concept (as I elaborated in Chapter 7, Section 7.3.2), so too is a collectivity's sui juris status relational, in a sense that I will explain. Social movements ordinarily exist in relation to the source of injustice that they oppose, and as such, they are deeply *alterius juris* and do not act from their own active power alone; to understand them as sui juris rests on an abstraction that is impermissible within Spinoza's approach to politics. The Spinozist challenge is to take these appealing features displayed in collectivities when they are *alterius juris*, and find a way to sustain them in a non-oppositional situation. Only then can they be said to give rise to effects from their own power alone. The challenge is a difficult one: but any successful response will require collectivities to establish a positive institutional structure of its own.

[5] Negri's reading of Spinoza echoes the autonomist Marxist insistence on the primacy of the power of the working class. Tronti, 'The Strategy of Refusal,' 28–35; Weeks, *The Problem with Work*, 92–96.

[6] Negri, *The Savage Anomaly*, 229. Similarly, Montag celebrates the 'politics of permanent revolution' (*Bodies, Masses, Power*, 84–85). Dussel claims that his position is opposed to Negri's, because Dussel holds that popular *potentia* must inevitably be expressed as *potestas*, not as pure *potentia* (*Twenty Theses on Politics*, 16–28). For Dussel, the critical question is whether the *potestas* is 'obediential' (good, delegated) or 'fetishistic' (bad, alienated/corrupted) (ibid., 26, 30–31, 39–41). However, Dussel's frame overall remains very similar to Negri's. For first, he insists on popular power *potentia* as a hidden ontological level of political life, linked to the common good (ibid., 14–15, 20). And second, he claims that excessively fetishistic *potestas* is inherently unstable and tends to be disrupted by a democratic and egalitarian '*hyperpotentia*' of the masses, expressed through social movements (ibid., 54–57, 78–95, 135).

[7] Holland, 'Spinoza and Marx,' §§26–29.

I prosecute this argument in several steps. First, I lay out Spinoza's theory of individuality, and I offer an account of what each individual's nature is. Second, I build on this theory of individuality to establish a clear account of being sui juris, acting from one's own nature alone, by appeal to the idea of homeostasis. This provides a more precise analytical content to my preliminary discussions of being sui juris from Chapter 7. Finally, I apply this framework to understand social movements opposed to the state, concluding that the exemplary multitude sui juris is not an unstructured social movement, but an institutionally structured collectivity.

Spinoza's metaphysics involves a theory of weak individuality.[8] Individuals are not distinguished by difference of substance: for there is only one substance, the unique infinite substance of nature as a whole. Rather, all it is to be an individual is to be a concrete entity composed of parts that maintain a characteristic ratio of speed and slowness, motion and rest (Lemma 1 after E 2p13). A set of parts constitute an individual over time to the extent they 'keep the same ratio of motion and rest to each other', even if particular parts are substituted in or out (E 2p13d, Lemmata 4–7 after 2p13). On this definition, a rock is an individual (with a very simple rigid characteristic ratio of motion and rest); an animal is an individual (with a much more complex and composite characteristic ratio of motion and rest), and remains the same individual even as its body experiences cellular turnover. Furthermore, each individual has its own active power. For Spinoza, the individual's nature is nothing other than its characteristic pattern of movement and rest. To the extent that an individual maintains its characteristic ratio at all, it produces effects that are at least to some degree understood through its own nature, and that is what Spinoza means by power.[9]

On Spinoza's account, individuality is emergent and nested.[10] Individuality is *emergent*: Positively, if a thing maintains a certain ratio, that is all that is

[8] For detailed accounts, see Étienne Balibar, *Spinoza: From Individuality to Transindividuality* (Delft: Eburon, 1997), 6–22; Matheron, *Individu et communauté*, 37–71; Yitzhak Melamed, 'Acosmism or Weak Individuals? Hegel, Spinoza, and the Reality of the Finite', *Journal of the History of Philosophy 48*, no. 1 (2010): 77–92; Garrett, 'Spinoza's Conatus Argument', 127–156; Garrett, 'Representation and Consciousness', 10–14; Daniel Garber, 'Descartes and Spinoza on Persistence and Conatus', *Studia Spinozana 10: Spinoza and Descartes* (1994): 43–67. For an account of the Hobbesian origin of Spinoza's physics, see Daniel Garber, 'Natural Philosophy in Seventeenth-Century Context', in *The Oxford Handbook of Hobbes*, edited by A. Martinich and Kinch Hoekstra (Oxford: Oxford University Press, 2016), 107–130.

[9] Matheron, *Individu et communauté*, 43, 89. The only way that it would entirely lack active power is if its nature did not figure in the causation of effects at all, but this could only be the case if its characteristic ratio were lost, or in other words, the thing ceased to exist.

[10] These two features loosely correspond to Matheron's two dimensions of individuality: integration and complexity (*Individu et communauté*, 57–58). See also Balibar's discussion of complexity

required for it to count as an individual with a certain nature. Negatively, if it does not maintain such a ratio, then it is to that extent less individuated.[11] Each thing may be more or less individuated, depending on how robustly it maintains its characteristic ratio of motion: a clump of wet sand is less individuated than a rock. And individuality *displays a nested structure*: for the parts of any given individual themselves are individuals,[12] and any given individuals may combine together to comprise a higher-order, more complex individual (Lemma 5s after E 2p13). It is possible to recognize individuals at one level without precluding that they should simultaneously combine to form a genuine individual at a higher level, nor is there privilege to any particular level in the nesting of individuals. Spinoza illustrates this point by imagining 'a little worm living in the blood' (Ep 32, IV/171a-173a). From my human point of view, the most crucial level of individuation is the human level: I observe my own characteristic motions as they interact with those of other humans. But from the point of view of a worm in my blood, this greater individual hardly registers; the most salient individuals that it observes are the clumps of chyle and lymph in the blood that float along with it in the bloodstream.

Spinoza's expansive view of individuality dissents in some crucial aspects from the scholastic frame, and I claim that it is just these antischolastic aspects that are missing from the radical democratic reading of his political philosophy. First, recall that for the scholastics, only proper entities are endowed with form, essence, or power; a mere accidental collocation or heap of parts lacks any power of its own (Chapter 3, Section 3.3). This scholastic attitude toward individuality is on display in the radical Spinozists. They uphold a restricted sense of what counts as a proper entity, refusing that a juridical union counts as a proper individual with its own nature, and on that

and the exchange of parts (*Spinoza: from Individuality to Transindividuality*, 21). See also Hasana Sharp, *Spinoza and the Politics of Renaturalization* (Chicago: University of Chicago Press, 2011), 35–40; Hasana Sharp, 'Spinoza's Commonwealth and the Anthropomorphic Illusion', *Philosophy Today 61*, no. 4 (2017): 833–846; Genevieve Lloyd, *Part of Nature: Self-Knowledge in Spinoza's 'Ethics'* (Ithaca, NY: Cornell University Press, 1994), 10–16.

[11] See Deleuze, *Expressionism in Philosophy*, 236–239. Spinoza defines a 'singular thing' as any set of parts that combines to cause an effect (E 2d7). On this definition, every individual is also a singular thing, but a purely instantaneous singular thing without any durable characteristic motion would not count as an individual (or would represent the limit case of individuality).

[12] In Spinoza's presentation, individuation bottoms out with 'simplest bodies', which have no further parts and which are characterized by simple speed and slowness, motion and rest (E 2p13A″). It is an open question in the literature whether Spinoza is asserting that such simple bodies exist or are merely a theoretical heuristic. See Matheron, *Individu et communauté*, 25–26, 51–52.

basis denying a state has *potentia*. The radical liberals press this anti-state ontology most vigorously, especially Barbone.[13] As indicated in Chapter 6, Section 6.3.1, often the radical democrats find themselves in agreement on this point: Negri characterizes state power *potestas* as 'nonbeing'.[14] But strictly speaking, this anti-state ontology is unsustainable. To be sure, juridical stipulation of authority alone will not constitute a Spinozist individual. But regular patterns of behaviour do. Any actually existing state is a concrete entity, comprising structured patterns of behaviour of its component human parts. In other words, it has a characteristic ratio of motion and rest, and to this extent it is a genuine individual and has some active power.[15] Indeed, this is reflected in Spinoza's mature preference to conceive the state as the whole social body, and not more narrowly as rulerly action and institutional practices taken in abstraction from the social body in and on which they operate (see Chapter 7, Section 7.3.2). Far from diminishing the concrete reality of the state, Spinoza's conception of individuality allows it to be robustly acknowledged.

Second, recall the scholastic frame conceives *potentia* as potential, not actual. When an individual displays nonideal behaviour (compared to some qualitative standard), the individual's full *potentia* exists but has been thwarted. The rock has a *potentia* to fall, but may be thrown up; the seed has a *potentia* to grow but withers instead. This conception is shared by the radical Spinozists: the multitude may manifest itself in a hierarchical way, but its underlying nature and *potentia* is asserted to be equal combination of human singularities.[16] But to the contrary, for Spinoza there is no unactualized

[13] Barbone, 'Power', 102. See also Den Uyl, *Power, State, and Freedom*, 115. In making his argument, Barbone relies excessively on the *Theological-Political Treatise*: he uses the absence of the phrase *potentia imperii* in the *Theological-Political Treatise* as evidence that the state does not have *potentia* of its own, without remarking on the presence of that exact term in the *Political Treatise* (TP 7.18).

[14] Negri, *The Savage Anomaly*, 226; see also Hardt and Negri, *Empire*, 76, 360–369.

[15] Matheron, *Individu et communauté*, 42, 58, and *passim*. Although Montag denies that the state has power (*Bodies, Masses, Power*, 92), Montag's account of collectivities as individuals (69) could be extended to account for state power.

[16] This is also commonplace amongst radical democrats more generally. For Dussel, *potentia* is 'the ultimate foundation of all power'. But in a very Aristotelian analogy, he explains that it may be unexpressed: 'The merely feasible consensual will of the community remains initially indeterminate and in-itself, that is, it lacks roots, a main stem, branches, and fruit. It could have them, but as yet it does not. The seed is a tree in-itself, prior to having manifested itself, realized itself, grown, and appeared in the light of day'. Just as a seed stands in relation to a future tree, Dussel claims, *potentia* is the foundation of all politics, but needs to be actualized (*Twenty Theses on Politics*, 18). Within the Spinoza scholarship, this conception of *potentia* as a non-hierarchical potentiality is central to the radical democratic interpretation, but it is also found more broadly, for instance, in Lazzeri, whom I nonetheless counted as a constitutionalist because of his positive attitude towards the institutional facilitation of human *potentia* (Lazzeri, *Droit, pouvoir et liberté*, 276–283). Some radical democratic Spinozists take this view without drawing any conclusion about what actually is likely to

potentia: each individual has precisely the degree of power that it displays.[17] A *potentia agendi* that did not actually produce determinate effects is not conceivable for Spinoza.[18] Certainly, the determinate effects that an individual causes sometimes may not be understood through that individual's own *potentia agendi* exclusively, but rather in combination with an external cause. But such a situation merely attests to the individual's low degree of *potentia agendi*.[19] Thus, an individual human being who is behaving irrationally is not suffering the thwarting of a naturally given human power of rationality. Rather, irrationality shows that nature did not sufficiently give such power in that case: '[Not all men are naturally determined to operate according to the rules and laws of reason . . . [Nature] has denied them the actual power

occur (see footnote 7). But Negri links the view to a further idea familiar from scholastic natural scientific understandings of *potentia*: a tendency to actualize. Scholastic natural science holds that each proper natural thing tends or strives to actualize its power, and this accounts for its behaviour for the most part. In Negri's hands, *potentia* (as an inner property of certain kinds of proper entities) is a tendency that explains what happens for the most part, except when a violent external force thwarts it. This idea of real tendency made especially clear in Negri's rendering of the *conatus* doctrine. Negri characterizes active ('constitutive' or 'constituent') power as something with a real tendency to express itself. '*Conatus* tends to realise itself in adequacy (P9S)' (Negri, *The Savage Anomaly*, 146). *Conatus* is 'fundamentally linear' and 'progressive' (Negri, 'The *Political Treatise*', 12). Specifically, he puts forward the idea that the multitude becomes more active over time, unless thwarted by the state (Negri, '*Reliqua Desiderantur*', 237–238). This interpretation is unsustainable; the *conatus* doctrine licences no presumption of increase in activity for the most part. I grant that the *conatus* doctrine bears some similarities to scholastic teleology. See detailed discussion in Don Garrett, 'Teleology in Spinoza and Early Modern Rationalism', in *New Essays on the Rationalists*, edited by Rocco J. Gennaro and Charles Huenemann (Oxford: Oxford University Press, 2003), 311–312, 330. But I would make two observations: First, there is nothing here about the increase of power, only about perseverance. Second, even regarding perseverance, the doctrine includes a critical qualification: *quantùm in se est* (E 3p6). As indicated in Chapter 7, Section 7.2, each thing strives to persevere in its being only *to the extent that it is in itself*, that is, to the extent it produces effects that can be understood through its own nature alone. But the striking feature of Spinoza's metaphysics is that things are not fully 'in themselves' (see Garrett, 'Spinoza's Conatus Argument', 144–145). A finite thing generally causes effects through its own power along with the power of other things, and depending on the character of those others, it may or may not maintain its own activity, let alone increase it. There is no general tendency of increase in activity. Nor is there any deficiency when activity does not persevere or increase: the universe not ordered to human reason and human purposes, so nature does not privilege the striving of human individuals or collectivities over that of any other thing in nature, nor does the thwarting of human striving constitute a defect in nature (E 1App).

[17] Deleuze, *Expressionism in Philosophy*, 28; Viljanen, 'Spinoza's Actualist Model of Power', 222–228. This feature is not unique to Spinoza: recall that Hobbes also offers a resolutely actual account of power in his later works (see Chapter 2, Section 2.5), including a purely actualist conception of *conatus*/endeavour (DCo 15.2, 22.1, 25.12). The result, for both Hobbes and Spinoza, is a commitment to understand power within a complex ecology of human relations, and a refusal to read political power abstractly.

[18] See an illuminating discussion in Garrett, 'Spinoza's Conatus Argument'.

[19] Put into the language of the metaphysical terms of Chapter 7, *potentia agendi* is always part of *potentia operandi*, not something opposed to it: a thing must first produce effects (express *potentia operandi*) before the question can be asked to what degree these effects can be understood in terms of its own nature alone (express *potentia agendi*).

[*actualem potentiam*] to live according to sound reason' (TTP 16.7, III/190). Similarly, if in fact humans relate in hierarchical and dependent ways, rather than independently and equally, this merely shows that they lack the power to do otherwise. It follows that, as Balibar explains, human equality of rights and power exists only when it is actually achieved.[20]

Can the radical democratic view of the natural goodness of the multitude be redeemed in spite of these two points? The existence of social movements might appear to offer a path, as I will now explain. In response to my first criticism of radical democratic scholasticism, suppose it is acknowledged that the state, when it is taken as a whole political body displaying a certain characteristic ratio of speed and motion of parts, counts as an individual with its own nature. In all cases, the nature of the state is defined by a particular configuration of the multitude, as the entire actual population of the state. Also, in response to my second criticism of radical democratic scholasticism, suppose it is granted that the multitude has no counterfactual power or nature; rather, its power must be understood from its actual manifestation. But recall that individuality has a nested structure. It is possible that sometimes, within the concrete body of the state, two distinct individuals can be identified: on the one hand, the rulers, on the other hand, the multitude conceived in a narrow sense to exclude the rulers. This will be particularly clear when the government is disliked: the multitude (in the narrow sense) understands itself in opposition to the elite political class. Such a fractured state is not very sui juris: it is understood through its disparate parts rather than through the whole. Radical democratic readers of Spinoza are often interested in the multitude in this narrower sense, and its possibilities as a political actor, for instance, oppositional social movements displaying an appealing internal structure (flat, equal, responsive).[21] Such a social movement's appealing power structure is not counterfactual, but is actually displayed. The critical question is: is such a social movement an exemplar of the free powerful multitude, the multitude sui juris? Far from being part of the unified state, it is defiantly insubordinate to the state. Might the state be removed, allowing this multitude to flourish free and sui juris?

[20] Balibar, *Spinoza and Politics*, 62. What, then, is the status of ideals of equality? Rosenthal provides a useful account of political ideals as fictions, enabling political agents to reflect upon how to behave. Michael A. Rosenthal, 'What Is Real about 'Ideal Constitutions'? Spinoza on Political Explanation', in Melamed and Sharp, *Spinoza's 'Political Treatise'*, 12–28.

[21] See footnotes 4–7. Indeed, Spinoza himself sometimes uses the term 'multitude' to refer to the non-ruling portion of the population in an aristocracy or a monarchy (TP 7.31, 8.4–5).

I now will argue that this manoeuvre is also impermissible from a Spinozist point of view: for being active and being sui juris are not merely qualitative but also relational terms. Thus, taking social movements as exemplars of a multitude sui juris relies on an impermissible form of abstraction.

Recall that being sui juris is equivalent to being active. Already in Chapter 7, Section 7.2, I insisted on the relational character of Spinoza's active power. I offered an example to illustrate this point, of three kinds of human response to an upsetting event. The latter two responses were qualitatively similar: the serenity of the child with the blankie and parent, or the serenity of the sage who has excellent autoregulation of passions. But the two cases are not equally active. For activity is adequate causation: producing effects that can be understood from a thing's own nature alone, without others. The sage's autoregulation is part of their own nature, whereas the child's blankie and parent are straightforwardly not part of the child's own nature. The relationality of Spinoza's conceptual frame is made even more patent in its political translation, in the discussion of individuals and collectives sui juris. A person who relies on a patron for their livelihood is to that extent *alterius juris*, whereas a person who does not rely on the goodwill of any particular citizen or part of society is to that extent sui juris (TTP 17.5–7, III/202; TP 2.9–11; see discussion in Chapter 7, Section 7.3.2). Imagine these two people undertaking qualitatively the same activities, say contributing to charity or helping out for a good cause. Nonetheless, their behaviour may remain very unequally sui juris, insofar as the former does so to curry favour or to avoid the displeasure of the patron.

However, at this stage the distinction between being sui juris and being *alterius juris* remains undertheorized. For it remains unclear whether a social movement does or does not act from its own nature. Suppose we take the distinguishing principle to be the following: insofar as a thing interacts only with hostile external causes, its endurance must be understood through its own nature alone. On this principle, the child with respect to their blankie or the client with respect to their patron will count as *alterius juris* because they receive help, whereas the social movement counts as sui juris because it does not receive any help from the state, only hostility. However, this is not the correct distinguishing principle: for Spinoza repeatedly analyses activity and being sui juris from the point of view of what commentators have dubbed homeostasis, self-correction, or autoregulation.[22] And as I will explain, a social movement opposed to an oppressive state is not homeostatic.

Homeostasis is an individual's maintenance of its characteristic ratio of motion and rest across a wide range of external encounters. Homeostatic bodies certainly rely on their external environment to persevere: but the key point is that they are not dependent on any particular thing within that environment. By contrast, a non-homeostatic body is one that maintains itself only in relation to particular causes. It relies on particular external supports without which it could not persevere, and it can be said to be dependent on these supports. For instance, a heating system with thermostat is moderately homeostatic: on the one hand, it can maintain its set temperature even as the weather fluctuates warmer or colder, but on the other hand, it cannot if the thermostat is blocked or if there is a power outage. Animate things display a higher degree of homeostasis, insofar as they have even more resources to deal with external pressures: they are able to register and identify external sources of threat or assistance, and avoid them or seek them out accordingly.

The idea of activity as homeostasis is fairly directly supported by Spinoza's account of the highest form of human ethical development and control of the passions. Spinoza is interested in the proportion to which 'the actions of a body depend more on itself alone, and . . . other bodies concur with it less in acting' (E 2p13s). Such a body can 'be affected in a great many ways' without losing its own nature (E 4p38; see also E 5p39). This formulation focusses on the diversity of affects that can be accommodated; elsewhere, Spinoza emphasizes the diversity of action that can be undertaken: 'He who has a Body that is capable of doing a great many things is least troubled by evil affects' (E 5p39, see also E 2p13s). But this amounts to the same thing: being capable of doing many things facilitates accommodating the blows of fortune without being swayed.[23]

[22] Matheron provides the classic development of these ideas. Matheron, *Individu et communauté*, 43–51. See also Deleuze, *Expressionism in Philosophy*, 225; François Zourabichvili, *Le conservatisme paradoxal de Spinoza: Enfance et royauté* (Paris: Presses universitaires de France, 2002), 262; Garrett, 'Representation and Consciousness', 12–13; Garber, 'Descartes and Spinoza', 43–67. The concept is most useful for complex individuals. Complex individuals interact with their environment in many ways, and here the question of degrees of homeostasis, as a question of self-maintenance in response to diverse stimuli, seems appropriate. For low-complexity things, it is still possible to answer the question of self-maintenance in response to diverse stimuli (a clump of sand is less good at it than a rock). But the rock is so inert as to be homeostatic only in the most trivial sense of the word (Garrett, 'Representation and Consciousness', 11).

[23] The concept of homeostasis helps to illuminate another aspect of the Spinozist conception of active power: the impossibility of a finite thing being perfectly active, or equivalently, the impossibility of being perfectly sui juris (see Chapter 7, Section 7.3.2). For similarly, nothing is perfectly homeostatic. There are always some impacts that cannot be accommodated. Even the most emotionally

The physical characterization of activity and being sui juris as homeostasis provides a sharp analytic frame for understanding the relationality of human action. The question of whether a thing is dependent on external causes amounts to the question of whether it concurs with particular things in acting (E 2p13s). Here, the quality of that concurrence is not relevant. Certainly, in my previous examples of human dependence, the dependency is made clear by the positive contribution of the external cause (the parent and the blankie are helpful to the child, and are intended as such; similarly the patron is helpful to the client). But helpfulness is inessential to relationality: a thing can have concurrence of movement even with a hostile external cause. For instance, if people do community service for fear that their failure to do so will give their enemies a pretext to denounce them, their behaviour concurs or correlates with aspects of their enemies' behaviour, rather than being independent of it. Their conduct is understood through the relation to those enemies, and they are not homeostatic.

The general consequence of this discussion is that sometimes forms of conduct can be held in place in relation to an external cause, and when that external cause is removed, the forms of conduct find they do not have sufficient internal structure to sustain themselves. Spinoza remarks 'how imprudent many people are to try to remove a Tyrant from their midst, when they can't remove the causes of a prince's being a Tyrant' (TP 5.7; see also TP 7.26). This concern about internal structure is evident in his discussion of the English Revolution and the Restoration. Spinoza observes that the English people rallied together to dethrone their king, but despite all the collective effort to do so, they ended up reinstating a monarchy a short time later (TTP 17.33, III/227). On Spinoza's analysis, this is because removing the king revealed two weaknesses in the inner constitution of the English people, weaknesses that were not concretely overcome. First, the people did not have sufficient familiarity with democratic forms of relation, and still desired a king above them (TTP 17.28, III/226). Second, they lacked a total unanimity of opinion in the community; there were still partisans of the old overthrown regime amongst them (TTP 17.30–33, III/226–227).

Let me apply this conceptual framework to oppositional social movements. It may be true that protest movements against oppression often

stable person cannot persist in their characteristic motion without food or sleep, or when ill or grievously injured. Nor are the limits on homeostasis merely grossly physical: the most emotionally stable person may lose bearings if betrayed by someone trusted. And in a political vein, even the most sagely individual cannot maintain serenity and characteristic motion once physical security is lost.

have an egalitarian and horizontal structure, of 'free singularities' on a plane of equality. Unlike the English of the seventeenth century, social movements may have a deep commitment to values of equality and democracy. Nonetheless, often their structure is consolidated by the movement's oppositional status. Internally diverse coalitions may put aside their disagreements for the sake of pursuing a shared cause, but if the oppressor is removed, these disagreements then resurface. Social movements may have direct democratic internal organization, but the intense temporal and interpersonal demands of this form of organization are sustained by the excitement of a particular moment of struggle: in steady state, this commitment may be eroded by members' other extra-political life obligations and aspirations.[24] Furthermore, in most real political cases, the challenge is also not merely to subtract the oppressor: for partisans of the oppressor do not disappear, but need to be integrated into the new political order.[25] In sum, the good shape of social movements has to be understood in part through the power of the oppressors that they oppose, and to this extent, these movements are *alterius juris* with respect to their oppressor.

Other authors sympathetic to social movements come to a similar sceptical assessment of the spontaneous goodness of popular association. Walzer's *Spheres of Justice* develops at length the idea that one must not be complacent regarding the continued appeal of the inner character of oppositional movements once the oppressor that they oppose is removed. Walzer argues that a singular focus on destroying the monopoly on a society's dominant good can often merely facilitate the emergence of a new dominant good.[26] For instance, a society might eviscerate religious power, only to find a new elite formed by those with wealth; a society might equalize wealth, only to find that a new elite is formed from those with political connections.

[24] Hardt and Negri have been criticized for valorizing struggle, which is so often evanescent; they make some belated recognition of this criticism in their most recent books. Hardt and Negri, *Commonwealth*, 356–374; Hardt and Negri, *Assembly*, xviii, 7, 233, 289. Their substantive response appears to be support for a universal basic income (UBI) and direct democracy (*Commonwealth*, 310; *Assembly*, 288). However, for scepticism regarding the presumed radical egalitarian potential of a UBI, see Elizabeth S. Anderson, 'What Is the Point of Equality?', *Ethics 109*, no. 2 (1999): 298–299; Alex Gourevitch and Lucas Stanczyk, 'The Basic Income Illusion', *Catalyst 1*, no. 4 (2017): 151–178. For scepticism regarding direct democracy, see my Chapter 9, Sections 9.3–4.

[25] Indeed, Hardt and Negri constantly talk of 'enemies' of the multitude; it is not clear how they fit these enemies and their behaviour into their vision of the all-inclusive multitude. Rather, they tend to lapse into rather un-Spinozistic moralism: 'May the gods, wherever they are, curse and plague the sad perpetrators of violence in all these hidden and overt forms! The racists, misogynists, transphobes, destroyers of the earth, warmongers—may the putrid rot of their souls gnaw at them from within!' (Hardt and Negri, *Assembly*, 263; compare TP 1.1–4).

[26] Michael Walzer, *Spheres of Justice* (New York: Basic Books, 1983), 3–30.

The critical question regarding social movements is whether homeostasis will be possible when they are not ranged against an oppressor. Is there textual evidence that Spinoza supports an intrinsic tendency of the non-elite to organize themselves democratically? Spinoza famously considers and rejects commonplace accusations against the plebeians, such as the accusation that 'there's no moderation in the common people; that they're terrifying, unless they themselves are cowed by fear' (TP 7.27). However, rejecting these common accusations does not entail that he believes the plebeians are spontaneously virtuous. Spinoza makes very clear that what worries him is the attribution of vice *exclusively* to plebeians. His conclusion is not that these commonplace accusations are untrue, but rather, that 'everyone has the same nature' (TP 7.27): the plebeians are no worse than the patricians. The challenge is to determine institutional conditions under which vice is reduced. Similarly, although Spinoza asserts that people desire equality, he equally recognizes a range of non-egalitarian desires, such as ambition, and hostility to people with different customs and opinions.[27]

Indeed, Spinoza quite explicitly understands the quality of the multitude's conduct to be institutionally determined. 'Men aren't born civil; they become civil': subjects' virtue or vice is attributed to the quality of the fundamental laws (TP 5.2–3). All virtue, including the virtue of relating to one another as equals, has its determinate causes, which are best understood at the level of the state. It is instructive to consider Spinoza's own analysis of a very equal society: the Hebrew republic. Spinoza introduces his analysis of the ancient Hebrew republic as a response to the problem of how 'to establish things so that everyone, whatever his mentality, prefers public right to private advantage' (TTP 17.16, III/203). Spinoza argues that the Israelites were brought to uphold public advantage and the common good of their nation through a mix of internal and external causes. An external cause of the internal equality of the Hebrew political order was their religiously elevated hatred of other nations, which was also reciprocated by those other nations (TTP 17.76–82, III/214–215).[28] But there was also comprehensive internal structuring: Spinoza draws attention to the whole suite of regulations (agrarian,

[27] As indicated in Chapter 6, Section 6.4; see further discussion in Chapter 9, Section 9.3. See also Matheron, *Individu et communauté*, 150–179.

[28] There has been some controversy as to whether Spinoza's portrayal of the ancient Hebrews is antisemitic. See, for instance, Emmanuel Lévinas, 'Le cas Spinoza', *Difficile liberté: Essais sur le judaïsme* (Paris: A. Michel, 1976), 142–147. Without taking a view on that controversy, my point is simply to draw attention to his analysis of the determinate causes of political order as illustrated by this case.

economic, theological, political) that were also required in order to achieve the internal, equal, flat structure (TTP 17.42–92, III/208–217).

If the goal is the democratic self-organization of the multitude, the challenge will be to understand and manage the determinate causes of non-egalitarian desire.[29] Zourabichvili characterizes Spinoza's focus on stability as a paradoxical conservatism: the challenge is not to preserve what exists, but to bring into existence what will be able to preserve itself.[30] Often there is a lament that bureaucratic structures re-emerge even in initially pure popular movements, stifling the free spontaneity of the multitude. And certainly, sometimes development of bureaucratic structures reflect a capture of power by self-serving elite. But from a Spinozist point of view, anyone claiming a natural equality of human relations needs to supply an account of the determinate causes of this mode of interaction in the first place.[31] Perhaps enthusiasm and ideological commitment can do some work for some period of time. But what could sustain this in the longer term?

> It's not enough to have shown what ought to be done; it's necessary especially to show how it can be done in such a way that men may still have firmly established rights and laws, whether they're led by affect or reason. (TP 7.2; see also TP 1.6)

The ancient Hebrew way is no longer possible,[32] but a modern replacement is required. In Chapter 9, I will offer a sketch of the institutional structure appropriate to maintain a democratic multitude. But for now, the point is that the good form of a social movement cannot serve as evidence for the claim that the natural state of the multitude lacks the compounding power blocs that worried me in Chapters 5 and 6; nor is it evidence for the claim that it is the natural human condition to relate to one another as equals.

[29] Hardt and Negri come to a belated recognition of the possibility of democratically unappealing collective forms of the multitude, which they dub 'corrupt love' (*Commonwealth*, 167–196). However, they believe that contemporary changes in the mode of production—the rise of 'biopolitical' labour, which requires cooperation, autonomy, and networking—will resolve the problem (ibid., 353). This strikes me as extraordinary techno-optimism; isn't biopolitical labour entirely politically ambivalent, equally capable of generating new forms of domination, division, and subordination? Indeed, the effort to account for the determinate causes of 'non-corrupt love' is somewhat in tension with Hardt and Negri's glee in identifying and condemning enemies: see footnote 25.

[30] Zourabichvili, *Le conservatisme paradoxal de Spinoza*, 262.

[31] Balibar, *Spinoza and Politics*, 62.

[32] Due to its reliance on the low degree of education and the isolation of the population (TTP 17.92, III/217, 18.2, III/221).

In a way, left-Schmittian readers of Spinoza embrace this point, and correspondingly do not seek to eliminate the state. They recognize the mutual determination between formal holders of political power and informal oppositional forces. On their view, a good political order flourishes in conflictual opposition between rulers and multitude. The locus classicus for this view is Machiavelli's *Discourses on Livy*: Machiavelli diagnoses the interminable conflict between the Roman plebs and patricians as the structural guarantee of the goodness of the Roman republic.[33] Spinoza was avowedly influenced by Machiavellian republicanism. The left-Schmittian reading of Spinoza foregrounds the productive role of popular uprisings in keeping the state on its toes, without making the mistake I criticized earlier of imagining the multitude standing on its own.[34]

Nonetheless, in a different way Schmittians still romanticize the multitude, insofar as they presume that conflict is always constructive. This presumption is not shared by Machiavelli. For Machiavelli, whether conflict is good or bad depends on what kind of cleavage and what kind of conflict:

> It is true that some divisions are harmful to republics and some are helpful. Those are harmful that are accompanied by sects and partisans; those are helpful that are maintained without sects and partisans.[35]

In his view, the Roman conflict was good, but the Florentine conflict was simply destructive. Where conflict takes the form of power blocs vying amongst themselves for supporters, harmful possible outcomes include a breakdown of social trust, or an increase in oligarchy. For while popular energies channel themselves into intergroup conflict, they can be distracted away from checking the self-aggrandizement of elites on all sides.[36] I will return to consider different kinds of conflict in Chapter 9, Section 9.4.

[33] Machiavelli, *Discourses on Livy*, I.4–6; John P. McCormick, 'Machiavellian Democracy: Controlling Elites with Ferocious Populism', *American Journal of Political Science 95*, no. 2 (2001): 297–313.

[34] Del Lucchese, *Conflict, Power, and Multitude*, 109–166; Filippo Del Lucchese, 'The Revolutionary Foundation of Political Modernity: Machiavelli, Spinoza, and Constituent Power', in Melamed and Sharp, *Spinoza's 'Political Treatise'*, 190–203. Indeed, Hardt and Negri's later work heads in this direction, increasingly celebrating conflictual institutions (Hardt and Negri, *Commonwealth*, 356–374; Hardt and Negri, *Assembly*, 258).

[35] Niccolò Machiavelli, *Florentine Histories*, translated by Laura F. Banfield and Harvey C. Mansfield (Princeton. NJ: Princeton University Press, 1988), 276. See also Machiavelli, *Discourses on Livy*, I.17.2, I.55.2, I.58.2.

[36] Consider the phenomenon of racialized anxieties undermining working-class solidarity. On Feuer's telling, Spinoza became more cautious regarding popular movements between his two texts. Early on, Spinoza was sympathetic to Masaniello, the fishman who led a popular uprising against

For Spinoza, it is necessary to understand the determinate causes of human behaviour. There is no reason to think that spontaneous popular expression is of itself good, unless it is a community of sages, which is impossible. Certainly, social movements can be powerful (producing many effects), certainly they can display a spontaneous and unstructured horizontal form. But this form is not understood from their own nature alone. Rather, it is understood from their nature along with the nature of the state that they oppose.[37] In result, the features that would characterize a multitude properly sui juris cannot be read off the features of a multitude that actually exists in opposition to the state, simply by abstracting from this opposition. For a social movement's egalitarian structure may be a product of individuals' shared antipathy to the state, and may not be stable once it loses its target. When the determinate causes of a social movement's shape include its opposition to an oppressor, it is counterproductive moralism to appeal to that shape as natural. There needs to be a new account of the determinate supports of maintaining that shape once the oppressor is removed. A multitude that exists sui juris will require internal structuring; a multitude sui juris will be intertwined and coextensive with an institutional form of its own. In Chapter 9, I will return to consider what precise form this will need to take.

8.3. Accepting the Problem of Nonideal Endurance

Now I turn to *the problem of nonideal endurance*. Is Spinoza committed to the claim that ethically unappealing regimes will not endure? The view finds apparent support in the *Political Treatise*:

Hapsburg rule in Naples in 1647. However, later, having witnessed the mob ferocity of the lynching of the Dutch republican leader Jan de Witt, Spinoza reportedly had to be restrained from posting a sign *ultimi barbarorum* (worst of the barbarians) in the public square (Feuer, *Rise of Liberalism*, 38–39, 119, 151–152, 197).

[37] To be clear, my point is not to argue that the real agency lies on the side of the state and to situate social movements as merely and necessarily reactive. First, in all cases, for Spinoza each actually existing thing produces effects at least to some degree from its own power and nature; and second, in the case of a state and a social movement opposed to one another, the two entities reciprocally determine one another's action. Nor do I hold that oppositional social movements cannot increase their activity, or even achieve sui juris status. Patently they can, as in the case of successful decolonization movements. What I mean to stress is the conditions of possibility of such an achievement: it relies on the movement developing the internal self-regulation to maintain its structure once external pressure is removed. I thank Hasana Sharp for pressing me on these two points.

> For the Right of a Commonwealth is determined by the power of a multitude which is led as if by one mind. But there is no way this union of minds can be conceived unless the Commonwealth aims most at what sound reason teaches to be useful for all men. (TP 3.7)

But against this, I have already provided examples of nonideal enduring regimes in Chapter 6, Section 6.4. Now I provide a philosophical analysis and taxonomy of these same examples. In Chapter 7, Section 7.3.2, I established the key Spinozist concept of being sui juris, equivalent to producing effects from one's own active power alone, and thus also equivalent for Spinoza to being free and virtuous. I suggested that Spinoza's normative ideal for politics is that a commonwealth be itself maximally sui juris, as well as maintaining the maximal sui juris status of its subjects. I defer a more precise and positive account of the second part of this condition until Chapter 9. But even without a precise account in hand, it will already be possible to show that durability and power of producing effects need not track this dual condition. I claim that Spinoza's politics accommodates the possibility that a commonwealth may have great and durable *potentia operandi* without being sui juris; furthermore, it accommodates the possibility that a commonwealth may be sui juris without political participation, or the other desiderata of ethically appealing free politics. That is, I will argue that Spinoza accepts the problem of nonideal endurance. This brings out more sharply the antinomic aspect of Spinoza's politics that troubles Curley and which others are too swift to dismiss: Spinoza attributes right to ethically unappealing states, which may well endure.

My interpretation of Spinoza's politics rests on a distinction between a state's *potentia operandi* (its power of producing effects) and its *potentia agendi* (its active power), or equivalently, between a state doing many things by right and a state being in control of its right (being sui juris). It is in principle possible to have *potentia operandi* extending far beyond *potentia agendi*: a tyrannical state rules by right, but it may be very little in control of its right. In this case, the state perseveres through factors external to its own nature. But as I indicated in my precis of the constitutionalist view (Chapter 6, Section 6.3.2),[38] it is common to presume that such a perseverance from external causes cannot endure for long. In the context of his discussion of politics, Della Rocca glosses active power as power (producing

[38] See footnotes 47–52 in Chapter 6.

effects) in the long run.[39] Melamed provides a more precise gloss of *potentia agendi* as causal self-sufficiency. But when considering politics, just like Della Rocca, he uses stability or endurance as a proxy.[40] That is, on the common view, a state's endurance implies that it is sui juris and that the effects it produces can be attributed to its own active power; furthermore, it is presumed that any state sui juris is also ethically appealing.[41]

This common view is strange and unjustified, both against a consideration of historical examples (see my discussion of examples in Chapter 6, Section 6.4) but also against the background of the Spinozist metaphysics that I have sketched. Let me first focus on the idea that a thing's endurance testifies to its own active power. Certainly, if something falls apart, then it is not active, and its demise must be attributed to an external cause.[42] But if a thing stays together, it does not follow that this endurance is to be attributed to its own nature.[43] A thing's endurance must be attributed to some degree to its own nature, but this internal contribution to endurance could be low if there are significant external causes holding it together. For external causation can still be very stable. So long as the external cause persists, so too can the individual, even if it is very poorly internally organized.[44]

To illustrate this metaphysical point, let me provide some examples. Recall Spinoza's worm in the blood. The worm may endure very well in its host. But this endurance is not understood through its own nature alone, but through its own nature in combination with that of the nature of its host: it will die if it is extracted from the bloodstream. Think of a person with anger management problems, who is an exemplar of Spinozist passivity. Perhaps sometimes such a person may die as a consequence of poor emotional regulation

[39] Della Rocca, *Spinoza*, 206–209. Della Rocca is explicit that his political discussion of power is an extension of his discussion of active power from the *Ethics* (ibid., 175–205).

[40] Melamed, 'Having Too Much Power', 172–174 versus 162, 165. Similarly, Matheron is clear on the distinction between active power and producing effects from an external cause, but he presumes that external determination cannot be durable (*Individu et communauté*, 47). Steinberg is more cautious, noting that a state's endurance does not testify to its goodness ('Spinoza on Civil Liberation', 47–50). But he actually does not think corrupt endurance is a very real possibility (Steinberg, *Spinoza's Political Psychology*, 90, 159–160, 177–179).

[41] Radicals also often take the view that tyrannies never last long, although as noted, their account of the underlying metaphysics of *potentia* differs from the constitutionalists. See Chapter 6, Section 6.3.1; also Montag, *Bodies, Masses, Power*, 59.

[42] Remembering that a cause external to a thing's nature could be physically internal to it—for instance, a thing could have had an insufficiently integrated nature in the first place.

[43] Indeed, this explains why '[n]o singular thing can be called more perfect for having persevered in existing for a longer time' (E 4Pref).

[44] See also E 1p31: finite things are determined to exist and produce effects by the infinite web of other things, so we can only have very inadequate knowledge of any given thing's duration.

(for instance, by getting into a fight). More frequently, though, such a person may muddle through life in an unsatisfactory way, for approximately the same duration as any other human being. And occasionally such a person may be very successful in life, despite their lack of self-regulation, through one of two possible pathways. First, external causes might regulate their emotions for them, for instance, if they have a partner who calms them. But second, such a person could also be successful even without any emotional regulation at all. Lashing out in anger is no obstacle to success if a person also has a large inheritance, or lackeys, or other resources and supports that shield them from bearing the consequences of their poor behaviour.[45] We thus have a variety of possibilities of endurance, where endurance is very little understood through the person's own nature.

These examples show that endurance has no particular relation to being active, free, and in control of one's right. This has important implications for thinking about politics. As laid out in Chapter 7, Section 7.3.2, there are two loose (and overlapping) classes of states not sui juris: those dependent on a gross external cause; and those lacking sufficiently strong internal integration. The claim made by the many interpreters noted earlier is that any state that is not sui juris will not endure in the long run. But what about stability through an external cause, where that external cause is itself enduring? Possible external causes of political stability include fear of enemies, or fear of war, or paternalistic foreign rule (TP 3.12).[46] Recall the ancient Hebrew republic: Spinoza thinks that its constitution was moderately well constituted internally (TTP 17.62–92, III/212–217), but as discussed earlier, it was held in place by the Hebrews' unifying, shared hatred of foreigners. Matheron denies that it was truly stable, because it was in principle at the mercy of circumstances (if there were a rise in commerce, then it would collapse).[47] But the 'in principle' modality is not relevant here: for the point is that under the prevailing circumstances—circumstances that were themselves stable and not likely to change for some time—the state was also very stable.[48]

[45] At the time of writing, the Harvey Weinstein scandal had just unfolded. Weinstein is alleged to have practised systematic bullying, sexual harassment, and sexual assault, for decades; his capacity to make or break careers in film bought him impunity for his conduct. To be sure, when the scandal was broken, his career was ruined. But what is striking is how long his conduct went on unchecked; this suggests that there may well be others who carry out their whole life in a similarly reprehensible way and never face a comeuppance.

[46] Matheron considers external pressures on states, but only as a source of instability, not a source of stability (*Individu et communauté*, 350–357).

[47] In fact, he equivocates: at first he says it is very stable, but says it is in principle unstable (ibid., 447–460 versus 503).

[48] See footnote 67 of Chapter 6.

Similarly, a state could endure through paternalistic colonial rule by a more powerful imperial state.[49] This externally achieved durability is not only a possibility for well-ordered states, and it does not rely on the benevolence of the external rule: it is also possible for bad and fractious internal organization to be held together by external force.[50] One might think of the modern-day Israel and Palestine, and in particular the Israeli occupation of Palestine, which is possible through foreign support for Israeli action.[51]

Prima facie, this argument sits uncomfortably with the claim made in *Political Treatise* that the virtue of a state is its security (TP 1.6). Recall that the technical meaning of having virtue is being active, producing effects from one's active power alone. If it is possible to equate virtue with security, surely this requires that states driven by external causes, by definition not virtuous, do not endure.[52] How can Spinoza acknowledge the kind of unethical endurance just described (regimes that are stable and in that sense secure, but which are not sui juris, active, or virtuous), and yet claim that the virtue of a state is its security? However, this problem is only apparent. The virtue of a state is its security, but it doesn't follow that the robustly stable and secure state is virtuous. I argued previously that sui juris status is relational and not merely qualitative; the same holds for being virtuous. If the state's security is understood through its own nature, then the effects it produces are understood through its own nature, and it is sui juris, active, and virtuous. But if the state's security is understood through another, then any security is not attributable to its own virtue, but to the power and virtue of other things.

I grant that sometimes durable external determination is self-effacing: and when this is the case, the endurance of the state really does testify to the state's own power and virtue. For instance, hostile parties are sometimes forced to reach a modus vivendi: their powers are so precisely balanced that they have no choice but to cooperate with their enemies. In result, they reach some pattern of characteristic behaviour and operation without being deeply unified: each side would take any opportunity to crush the other, should the opportunity arise. But over time, they may come to endorse the terms of their coexistence as inherently valuable. This is Rawls's account of the emergence of a value of liberal toleration from the European wars of religion: in

[49] Spinoza does not consider this explicitly, but it has the same structure as his proposed rule of greater cities over lesser cities (TP 9.2, 9.13).

[50] See footnote 69 of Chapter 6 above.

[51] Melamed observes that Israeli colonial rule over Palestine is bad for Israel's power, but contra Melamed, it is not for that reason any less enduring. See Melamed, 'Having Too Much Power', 172.

[52] Rosenthal, 'Spinoza's Political Philosophy', 431.

his terms, a mere modus vivendi is transformed into an overlapping consensus.[53] This scenario may be plausible for some cases, where a state fails to be sui juris not because of gross external pressure but because of an internal lack of integration. But in the (more common?) cases where the failure to be sui juris involves some degree of gross external pressure, there is ample room for non-self-effacing external causation. For instance, colonial powers often justify their external rule as part of a process of teaching those ruled to become self-organizing. But colonialism may entrench the colony's dependency on the imperial power, and may prop up bad internal governance practices.[54]

So we have the first break between ethics and efficacy: enduring states may nonetheless not be sui juris; instead, they can be sustained by a durable external cause. Now consider the next class of dissonance between ethics and efficacy: states that are sui juris and enduring, which fully integrate their subjects' desires, but which do not match with our image of a good participatory state.

It is trivially true to say that a state sui juris is also a free state: Spinozist metaphysics establishes a definitional equivalence between an entity being sui juris, being active, and being free. But what about the subjects of that state? Are they themselves sui juris and free? We cannot expect everybody in a whole population to have reached the highest levels of human freedom (the sage who is rationally self-determining and therefore maximally sui juris). But there are less exalted notions of freedom that might apply to the population of a state. In Chapter 9 I will reconstruct and defend a systematic conception of maximal sui juris status for a population (combining the mutual independence of citizens with the possibility of their individual ethical development),[55] but for now, I follow the various notions of freedom that are to be found scattered throughout Spinoza's political texts. Commentators

[53] John Rawls, *Political Liberalism, with a New Introduction and the 'Reply to Habermas'* (New York: Columbia University Press, 1996), xl–xli. Thus, when a state is not under pressure from a particular gross external cause, then its endurance may well be a good indicator of its being sui juris. But more often, states do find themselves under such external pressure.

[54] At the level of individual persons, the analogous good case would be the pedagogical process: a child is subjected to a parent, only in order to build the child's own capacities to be an independent adult. The bad case is when the parent and child establish an enduring relation of domination or co-dependency. Perhaps there is greater likelihood of self-effacing external dependency in the human rather than the state case: for an individual can physically move away from a parent, whereas a state is stuck with the geopolitical situation in which it finds itself.

[55] It is not clear how strongly Spinoza himself is committed to achieving maximal sui juris status for the *entire* population of a state: see my discussion of the limits of Spinozist democracy in Chapter 9, Section 9.2, and of Spinoza's celebration of aristocracy in Chapter 9, footnote 8.

variously seize upon five other meanings of freedom that can be located in Spinoza's political writings, although often not explicitly distinguishing them. A state that is sui juris and enduring might also be a free state

(i) in the sense that it is a non-slave state, where the distinguishing difference between free and slave is the dominant affect of its subjects (hope versus fear) (TTP 5.22–24, III/74; TP 5.6);
(ii) in the sense that it permits free expression (TTP 20.7–9, III/240; TP 6.40, 8.46);
(iii) in the sense that it features extensive political participation from its subjects (TTP 5.23–25, III/74, 16.25–26, III/193; TP 6.15–16, 7.4);
(iv) in the sense that it supports the development of individual ethical freedom (individual self-determination by reason) of its subjects (non-slavery in a different sense than (i) above) (TTP 20.12, III/241; TP 5.4–5);
(v) in the sense that its governance is oriented to the common good (TTP 16.32–34, III/194–195; TP 3.7).

Commentators often presume that states sui juris must be at least moderately free in these five additional senses, and that a state's degree of control of its own right increases in proportion to the increase of these freedoms.[56] But I will now argue that there is such thing as a sui juris slave state (slave in sense (i)); and that there can be a sui juris non-slave state (free in sense (i)) that lacks various of the freedoms (ii–v). All these varieties of states sui juris are stable and enduring, but they are not ethically appealing in the sense initially promoted.

First, I will articulate more fully the criteria of and challenges for a state to be sui juris. This builds upon the idea of homeostasis provisionally laid out in Section 8.2. Just like any other actually existing individual, each state has its own characteristic motion, or law of its own nature: if it did not, it would be a fantasy, not a natural thing (TP 4.4). In a more political language, the

[56] The idea of proportionality is used to accommodate Spinoza's clear acceptance of virtuous aristocracy: interpreters understand Spinoza's call for broad councils as a reflection of the principle that the less exclusionary and the more participatory the state becomes, the more sui juris it will be; a virtuous aristocracy is acceptable because and insofar as it approaches democracy. Rosenthal, 'Spinoza's Political Philosophy', 19; Steinberg, *Spinoza's Political Psychology*, 184–186; Mugnier-Pollet, *La philosophie politique de Spinoza*, 153; Lazzeri, *Droit, pouvoir et liberté*, 364. I criticize this representation of the logic of aristocracy in Sandra Leonie Field, 'Political Power and Depoliticised Acquiescence: Spinoza and Aristocracy', *Constellations 27*, no. 1 (2020), https://doi.org/10.1111/1467-8675.12486.

characteristic motion of a state is its fundamental law or fundamental principles (so long as we are careful to conceive these terms broadly)[57] (TP 7.1–2). For the state to be sui juris, these laws must be maintained homeostatically. The requirement for the state to be sui juris is a requirement to bring about a cohesive self-maintaining political order. A state that is maximally sui juris in the Spinozist sense is a state whose Hobbesian power (*potentia*) is enduring, not through external supports but through its own internal structure; in other words, a state that has solved the Hobbesian political problem. The difficulty of achieving this lies in the fact that the state, as a complex individual, has subparts: its human subjects. The integration of the state requires that its laws continually generate and maintain in subjects the kinds of passions that will tend to uphold its fundamental laws (TP 5.2–3, 10.9).[58] In Matheron's formulation, the criterion of a state enduring from its own nature alone is that it inspires its subjects to patterns of conduct that reproduce the state in perpetuity.[59] But here lies the difficulty: individual human subjects each have their own range of characteristic motions, which may not conform neatly with this political project.

Spinoza is far from thinking that humans are unmalleable (TTP 17.5–7, III/201, 20.4, III/239; TP 2.16); and far from thinking that it is desirable for the state to leave human conduct unshaped, given the imperfectly moral character of human behaviour (TP 3.3–4, 6.3). Nonetheless, Spinoza explains the limits on state power through a memorable analogy:

> If I say, for example, that I can rightly do whatever I wish concerning this table, I surely don't mean that I have the right to make this table eat grass. Similarly, even though we say that men are not their own masters, but are subject to the Commonwealth, we don't mean that they lose their human nature and take on a different nature. (TP 4.4)

[57] The concept of the 'fundamental law' of a state is equivocal. At one point Spinoza makes the equivocation explicit, contrasting fundamental law as *jus civile*, the explicit legal foundations of the state, with fundamental law as *jus naturale*, its characteristic motion as an actually existing individual (TP 4.4–5). However, outside of this passage, only context reveals which sense of law *jura* is at stake (TP 3.4–6, 4.4, 7.1). It is the second sense of fundamental law that is at stake in my preceding discussion.

[58] Rawls similarly is concerned to account for the 'stability' or 'equilibrium' of the just society that he models: for a conception of justice to meet the stability requirement, a society with its basic structure conforming to that conception of justice 'must engender in human beings the requisite desire to act upon it [the conception of justice]'. John Rawls, *A Theory of Justice*, rev. ed. (Cambridge, MA: Belknap Press, 1999), 398. He argues that his own conception of justice meets this criterion better than other conceptions (ibid., §§75–76, 81).

[59] Matheron, *Individu et communauté*, 460; Lazzeri, *Droit, pouvoir et liberté*, 10, 388.

Balibar dubs this the 'incompressibility' of human nature,[60] and it can be analysed into two categories. First, some kinds of conformity are impossible to obtain: it is not possible[61] to make human subjects torture themselves, or not strive to avoid death, or kill their parents (TTP 17.2, III/201; TP 3.8). Second and more interestingly, some kinds of conformity can be superficially obtained, but they are poorly integrated with the rest of the characteristic motions of the individual human subjects. For instance, a state may use threats of harm to bring subjects to act against their better judgement. If a state relies on too much of this superficial conformity, the state itself is poorly integrated. For if such a state suffers a shock and is no longer able to enforce conformity so vigorously, its subjects may cease to coordinate in the required way, or may even coordinate in a way hostile to the state.

The question will be, how far does this 'incompressibility of human nature' constrain the possible forms of states sui juris? The standard view is that this 'incompressibility' is significant, such that for a state sui juris to be achieved, it is necessary to accommodate human characteristic motion via the five types of freedom articulated previously.[62] Rosenthal explains that even the most public-minded citizens

> will not identify their goods exclusively with those that the state can provide.... The fact that the scope of individual goods exceeds the scope of the political constitutes an important check on state power.

In result, '[P]rivate virtue expressed as individual freedom . . . serves as the natural check on the excesses of state power'.[63] Or in other words, the view is that Spinoza shows the Hobbesian political problem can only be solved by an ethically appealing regime (Chapter 6, Sections 6.2 and 6.3). The key mechanism underpinning the instability (and a fortiori, non-sui juris status) of states lacking these freedom is indignation (TP 4.4).[64] Recall the earlier example of a state using threat of harm to make subjects act against their better judgement. Spinoza claims that instability tends to befall states that try

[60] Balibar, 'Spinoza, the Anti-Orwell', 137; Balibar, '*Potentia Multitudinis*', 91.

[61] Beyond isolated extreme cases.

[62] Rosenthal, 'Spinoza's Political Philosophy', 430; Matheron, *Individu et communauté*, 504; Steinberg, *Spinoza's Political Psychology*, 90, 159–160.

[63] Rosenthal, 'Spinoza's Political Philosophy', 431.

[64] This idea has a Machiavellian filiation: Machiavelli views fear as politically efficacious only if hatred can be avoided. Niccolò Machiavelli, *The Prince*, translated by Harvey C. Mansfield (Chicago: University of Chicago Press, 1998), 67.

to control whole populations through fear, even if it is successful for a short period.

> Because the Commonwealth's Right is defined by the common power of a multitude, it's certain that its power and Right are diminished to the extent that it provides many people with reasons to conspire against it. (TP 3.9)

When subjects are indignant at or resentful of the rulers' command, they may superficially be brought to comply with governmental dictates, but much against their better judgement. Thus, they constantly look out for emergent weakness in the government, for an opportunity to overthrow it (TTP 17.3, III/201; TP 4.4, 5.2). When subjects are indignant in this way, they oppose themselves to their rulers, and the state does not act 'as if with one mind' (TP 2.16). The problem is self-intensifying: as rulers fear overthrow, they rule in an even more oppressive way, seeking to cripple popular opposition but equally contributing to further rises in indignation.[65]

I now scrutinize this conclusion regarding the possibilities of regime organization sui juris. First, I consider slave states (lacking freedom (i.)). Spinoza distinguishes between free and slave states, according to whether the predominant affect of the state's subjects is hope or fear. (TP 5.6)

> For a free multitude is guided by hope more than by fear, whereas a multitude which has been subjugated is more guided by fear than by hope. The first want to cultivate life; the second care only to avoid death. The first are eager to live for themselves; the second are forced to belong to the victor. So we may say that the second are slaves, and the first are free. (TP 5.6)

It is common to claim that a state can only be sui juris if it is based more on hope than on fear in the sense just specified. For in the slave state, the people are not content with their lot, and their indignation constitutes a source of disruption and instability (TP 5.7).

But are state mechanisms of fear always subject to this instability? To the contrary, consider Spinoza's treatment of Turkish despotism. Spinoza conceives the Turkish state as a slave state, and he characterizes its

[65] Here I discuss the destabilizing function of indignation. Indignation can also under some circumstances have a stabilizing function, as I will discuss in Chapter 9, Section 9.3.

population as motivated by fear (TTP Pref.9–10, III/7; TP 6.4).[66] Matheron claims that the Turkish state is not truly stable or durable: it could readily be overwhelmed, because its subjects have no patriotism and would not defend it in case of attack.[67] A fortiori, it is not sui juris and does not display a high level of activity. But this reading does not fit well with Spinoza's own discussion: he considers the Turkish state to be remarkably durable.[68] Can we say it is only durable from an external cause, not from its own nature? This would require that the state is not strongly self-reproducing, and in particular, that it fails to bring about the passions and conduct in its subjects that would tend to its own perseverance. Other slave states fail this criterion because they generate indignation. But what is so shocking to Spinoza about the Turkish case is precisely the lack of indignation. He remarks the subjects 'lack spirit'; they are 'led like sheep, and know only how to be slaves' (TP 5.4). In other words, unlike the case of the unstable slave state discussed previously, the population is said to have a properly internalized fear; hence, the state endures from its own nature.

Commentators have argued that the Turkish state is not stable and that it is not characterized by the active power and virtue of a state sui juris, by appeal to Spinoza's assertion that slave states are not at peace.[69] Slave states are said to be 'without war, but not at peace. Peace isn't the privation of war, but a virtue which arises from strength of mind' (TP 5.4). But I claim that this passage (TP 5.2–5.5) has been misread.[70] Spinoza's point in this discussion is precisely that he does recognize the Turkish state to be sui juris.

[66] I take it that TP 5.4, 5.6 also refer to the Turkish state. It bears repeating that this discussion concerns Spinoza's conception of the possibility of a slave state, rather than the historical reality of the Turks. Spinoza simply presents standard orientalist accounts of the Turkish state; see a revisionist discussion in Springborg, *Western Republicanism*.

[67] Matheron, *Individu et communauté*, 419–420. Referring to the same passages, Balibar argues that in such regimes 'any apparent unanimity cannot long survive so much latent antagonism' (*Spinoza and Politics*, 95).

[68] In his argument, Matheron appeals to an 'in principle' source of instability. But this 'in principle' modality is problematic (see also footnote 47). Spinoza states baldly that the Turkish state was extraordinarily stable over a long period of time: surely if it is stable under a broad range of external conditions, it cannot count as relevantly unstable.

[69] Mugnier-Pollet, *La philosophie politique de Spinoza*, 152.

[70] Indeed, neither of the pieces of textual evidence that Matheron provides to support his reading relate to the case at hand: his citation about lack of virtue is part of Spinoza's opposition to sumptuary laws in a commercial republic; his quotation that 'tyrannies never last long' only features in the *Theological-Political Treatise* and is not repeated in the *Political Treatise*, where Spinoza's most explicit discussion of the Turkish regime as a lasting tyranny occurs (Matheron, *Individu et communauté*, 419–420).

> When we attend to the general right of each state [of free and slave states], *there is no essential difference* between one created by a free multitude, and one acquired by the right of war. (TP 5.6; emphasis added)

And this poses a problem: for in order to determine the best state, it is not sufficient to determine which states solve the Hobbesian political problem and achieve sui juris status. For not all states sui juris are humanly desirable: there are both slave and free states sui juris. Spinoza's purpose is to distinguish between these categories.

> When we say, then, that the best state is one where men pass their lives harmoniously, I mean that they pass a human life, one defined not merely by the circulation of the blood, and other things common to all animals, but mostly by reason, the true virtue and life of the Mind. (TP 5.5)

The standard of the best state is not merely a state sui juris, but a state sui juris built with the possibility of human development. Thus, the lack of virtue relating to the slave state, cited earlier, concerns not the state itself, but the individuals who compose the state: subjects in a slave state, preoccupied by the threat of death, cannot develop virtue and strength of mind, and for this reason the state is humanly undesirable. Indeed, when Spinoza asserts that such a slave commonwealth 'would more properly be called a wasteland' (TP 5.4), it is because of the passivity of its subjects (the absence of freedom (iv)), not because of the passivity's fearful genesis (TP 5.4). Could a state be a wasteland in this sense even without being driven primarily by fear? I will return to this later.

Perhaps a regime like the Turkish despotism is not possible anymore, for perhaps modern levels of education prevent such a total and stultifying fearful convergence of desire (TP 17.24, III/205). Perhaps any contemporary slave regime would either conform to the picture Spinoza paints of a fickle population pinning their hopes on one false prophet after another, pinning their blame on one false enemy after another; or alternatively, they would achieve stability only through external causes, for instance, colonial domination. Either way, perhaps modern slave states (in the sense (i)) are not sui juris.[71]

[71] Matheron, *Individu et communauté*, 447–466; Steinberg, *Spinoza's Political Psychology*, 159–160.

Consider now non-slave states: that is, states in which subjects are motivated more by hope of living than by fear of dying. There will still be some fear: for that is true in some degree of all political orders whatsoever (TP 4.4). But the category I am interested in is regimes that are simultaneously built around facilitating behaviour of individuals who are 'eager to live for themselves' (TP 5.6). It is commonly presumed that only when such a state features all the other ethically appealing elements (free in the remaining four senses) can it effectively channel subjects' passions to uphold the state. But now I will show that various kinds of unfreedom are possible in a modern state sui juris. I will not exhaustively consider all possible permutations and combinations of features, but content myself with two cases: Hobbesian repressive egalitarianism and La Boétie's voluntary servitude. They operate through a comprehensive harnessing of the desires of subjects, and as such, they can be enduring, and I propose that they count as sui juris.

First, consider Hobbesian repressive egalitarianism.[72] As I characterized it in Chapter 5, it is far from the standard caricature of a Hobbesian regime as a regime governed by fear alone. To the contrary, it is organized for the sake of the flourishing of the people. However, it is certainly repressive: incipient collective formations in the multitude are to be minimized and disempowered, such that the possibility of resistance to sovereign rule (whether the sovereign is an assembly or a monarch) is minimized. Accordingly, there is not robust political participation, especially in Hobbes's preferred non-democratic regimes. Also, both democratic and non-democratic forms are sharply hostile to public expression of political views contrary to sovereign determination. According to the standard Spinozist criticism, this repressive Hobbesian regime should face difficulty. To start, there is Rosenthal's observation that humans will always resent state intrusions on their freedoms because they care about goods that the state cannot provide (relevantly for this case, friendship and truth). But beyond this, there is also the problem of diversity. Each individual human has an *ingenium* ('mentality', or character) that is peculiar to that person alone (TP 10.8). If a regime does not allow political participation and free expression, it will have to push against this diversity in its population, and can only ever have superficial success.

Against this criticism, I suggest that these potential sources of instability can be contained within Hobbes's model, consistent with his prohibition on

[72] In terms of my earlier taxonomy, such a regime has freedoms ((i), (iv), (v)), lacks freedom (ii), and in Hobbes's preferred form, lacks freedom (iii).

political participation and free expression. Recall that Hobbesian repressive egalitarianism conceives the safety of the public expansively, and seeks to support a rich and contented life to subjects of the state, including their own pursuit of individual goals and individual ethical and intellectual development.[73] That is, it accommodates and permits many human desires and endeavours. The limit is simply that these are not to be pursued collectively. To be clear, I am not assessing the question of whether this is the optimal regime for individual development, only whether it is sui juris qua political order. And on this score, it seems to succeed. In Chapter 5, Section 5.5, I characterized the regime as reasonably robust through its own internal self-reproducing mechanisms. Although the state is repressive of groups, so long as the sovereign takes wise counsel and attends to the complaints of its populace, it is not experienced as grossly oppressive, and it largely avoids widespread indignation. At the same time, even if it should stray towards self-serving rule, this is not too grievous for its stability, so long as the populace lacks inner collective organization. Accordingly, it should count as reasonably sui juris in the Spinozist sense.

Second, consider political orders featuring a pyramid structure of voluntary servitude, as analysed by La Boétie.[74] I gave two examples earlier: La Boétie's own tiered political regime in which individuals at each level of responsibility are provided positive incentives to conform themselves and others below them with state narratives and rulings; and Lordon's Spinozist, neoliberal, industrial model in which each level's pursuit of positive incentives leads them to enforce their own and others' conformity with corporate goals.[75] What is striking is the degree to which such regimes

[73] It might be puzzling how freedom of speech and the possibility of ethical development can come apart. Perhaps there cannot be ethical development in the total absence of free speech: but recall, restriction of speech admits of degrees. Speech is far from unfettered even in Spinoza's own preferred regimes (TTP Ch 20).

[74] In terms of my taxonomy above, such a regime has freedoms ((i), (ii)), and may or may not have freedoms ((iii), (iv), and (v)). Steinberg briefly acknowledges the possibility of Lordon's regime (Steinberg, *Spinoza's Political Psychology*, 99). But he mischaracterizes its structure: Steinberg takes it that unless systematically duped, people will not willingly uphold laws contrary to their own long-term interests (Steinberg, 'Spinoza on Civil Liberation', 54); hence people in Lordon's regime must have been brainwashed to cooperate with their own self-destruction. To the contrary, for a well-calibrated system of voluntary servitude, the key is breaking down any connection between individual and collective self-interest. With the narrow parameters afforded to them, each subject pursues their own individual interest, even when the collective result is regrettable. To be sure, the systematic result is often to discourage critical reflection on the entire structure, in favour of focussing each individual on their own immediate incentives. But this does not amount to brainwashing or duping.

[75] A third example, from Spinoza himself, is a king currying favour with his military, in order for the military to control the masses (TP 7.12). However, it appears Spinoza anticipates this form would

can be organized around hopeful desires, yet simultaneously depart from the common good.[76] Indeed, Lordon explicitly takes the point that is central to Rosenthal's argument—the supposed impossibility of merging individual and collective goals and desires—and argues that this convergence is achieved in contemporary corporate pyramids of voluntary servitude, to a previously unimaginable degree. From a Spinozist point of view, the difficulty posed by such regimes is not only their failure to promote the common good, although that certainly is a central concern.[77] The problem is also that they inculcate individual ethical slavishness (unfreedom in the sense (iv)): turning people into 'beasts or automata' (TTP 20.12, III/241) who do not cultivate their own independent judgement. Sometimes ethical slavishness is associated with the overwhelming domination by fear, as in the case of the Turkish despotism already discussed. But Spinoza himself freely grants the possibility of a hopeful but slavish existence. The ancient Israelites underwent an 'extreme training in obedience':

> To those who had become completely accustomed to it, this regime must have seemed no longer bondage, but freedom. The inevitable result was that no one desired what was denied, but only what was commanded. (TTP 17.88, III/216)

While a regime like the ancient Hebrew republic may no longer be possible, perhaps Lordon's layered corporate incentive structures provides a modern institutional matrix within which ethical slavishness can be cultivated.[78]

Now I turn to the final set of cases breaking down the presumed impossibility of enduring but ethically unappealing regimes. This is the case of enduring regimes with a division of political status.[79] First, consider societies in which a sizeable part of the population, perhaps even a majority, have unequal political status: for instance, women, servants, or foreigners. Certainly,

not be stable, because it is prone to embroil itself in unnecessary foreign combat, and because the loyalty of the military is limited.

[76] The pyramidical regime does not necessarily depart from the common good: it would be possible to make use of a pyramidical structure precisely in order to achieve the common good (to overcome principal-agent problems). Rather, my point is that the robust self-reproduction of such a regime is not dependent on this connection to the common good.

[77] See footnote 76.

[78] This appears to be Arendt's view: the failure to think and to take responsibility for one's actions is facilitated within modern bureaucratic structures. Hannah Arendt, *Eichmann in Jerusalem: A Report on the Banality of Evil* (New York: Penguin Classics, 2006).

[79] Steinberg denies divided hierarchical regimes can be stable (Steinberg, *Spinoza's Political Psychology*, 90, 177–179). One piece of evidence is Spinoza's treatment of Spanish Jews, which on Steinberg's gloss, shows that exclusion of a group generates resentment. However, Spinoza's own

if the subordinate group protests and resists its inferior status, then the state will not count as sui juris, because the state will be divided. But sometimes the subordinate group is so dominated that they are resigned to their status, or even affirm it. For example, consider any European state in Spinoza's period or earlier: in all cases, women were subordinated. But these women broadly and for the most part performed their roles and did not anticipate the possibility of equality, far less organize effectively to demand it.[80] For another example, household servants' personal dependency undermines any effective solidarity, removing hope of successful revolt. These subordinate subjects accept their status, or even if they are unhappy about it, they do not make any politically efficacious expression of their indignation. I claim that a state featuring such inequality can count as sui juris: it does not feature an internal division of parts that threatens its own self-perpetuation.[81] The desire of the population is effectively channelled into one unified mind, even when portions of the population are neither politically participating nor free to develop their own individuality.

Second, consider societies where a small part of the population has unequal political status: for instance, an ethnic or religious minority. Such a state may be politically stable even as it metes out intense oppression on the minority group. Indeed, such oppression may be used to shore up the unity of the rest of the population: the minority may be used as a scapegoat, channelling and discharging the sad passions of the population. Minority groups in such a position may resist and protest, expressing their indignation; or

point is somewhat different: that the Jews' social exclusion sustained their distinct communal identity and non-assimilation, without any suggestion that this is an unstable arrangement (TTP 3.54, III/56).

[80] This is not to deny that some individuals actively protested their subordination. In sixteenth century Venice, a city state that was an exemplar of republican virtue and unity, there was a lively literature defending the nobility and excellence of women. See Virginia Cox, 'The Single Self: Feminist Thought and the Marriage Market in Early Modern Venice', *Renaissance Quarterly 48*, no. 3 (1995): 513–581. My point is that historically, such dissent remained entirely unthreatening to the existing political system. Gatens provides a contemporary Spinozist account of the domination of men over women in terms of the mutual support of social imaginaries and real subordination. Moira Gatens, *Imaginary Bodies: Ethics, Power, and Corporeality* (New York: Routledge, 1996), 108–145; see also Susan James, 'Democracy and the Good Life in Spinoza's Philosophy', in Huenemann, *Interpreting Spinoza*, 128–146.

[81] It is common to claim that such regimes have democracy as their inner truth, meaning that if they are to retain stability, they will tend towards greater inclusion. The history of the expansion of franchise over the past three centuries is cited in support of this view. However, I have argued elsewhere that the democratizing tendency does not universally hold, and that the reverse process of exclusion is equally possible. See Field, 'Political Power'. See also Susan James, 'Politically Mediated Affects: Envy in Spinoza's "Tractatus Politicus"', in Melamed and Sharp, *Spinoza's 'Political Treatise'*, 61–77, for an account of the elimination of envy.

alternatively they may accede to their unequal lot in society (out of a lack of hope for anything better, or from fear of the extreme penalties resistance would incur?). But in neither case does this situation necessarily impugn the state's status as moderately sui juris. For it is not difference or even conflict alone that prevents a state from being sui juris, only when division generates passions tending to interrupt the characteristic motion of the state.[82] I discussed earlier how indignation can destabilize regimes. But indignation is a double-edged sword: it can also be a force of consolidation and stabilization. For the most sui juris regime is one where its fundamental law 'can't be undermined without arousing the indignation of the greater part of an armed multitude' (TP 7.2). In the case at hand, an unequal society, the greater part of the armed multitude may well be opposed to, rather than supportive of, the minority.[83]

In conclusion, I have argued, against the constitutionalists, that the endurance of a state is not always matched with ethical appeal, and I have shown that this is readily accommodated within Spinoza's metaphysics. The point is not that Spinoza doesn't value the five kinds of freedom previously articulated: to the contrary, he evidently does; and he thinks they are important for a fully flourishing human collective life.[84] The question is rather whether the desiderata of political endurance or (even more demandingly) political homeostasis can be achieved in the absence of the full complement of the five. I have argued that they can. I have schematized three cases: states durable but not sui juris (durable through an external cause); states that are durable and sui juris, but which lack various of the other desiderata of political freedom (durable through thoroughly integrating the desires of their subjects); and finally states that are durable despite internal inequality of political status (durable through subordinate groups not having hope of success). Thus, Spinoza's metaphysics upholds the *problem of nonideal endurance* introduced in Chapter 6, Section 6.4. Political endurance is possible without being sui

[82] Certainly, such a society is not necessarily sui juris. For it depends on how strategically the scapegoating is performed. If scapegoating of a minority served to unify the majority population only superficially, and allowed underlying grievances within the majority population to remain unaddressed, then the state would not count as sui juris. But is scapegoating part of a broader repertoire of effective (albeit morally regrettable) rule? Consider Spinoza's suggestive discussion of one kind of minority: he claims that just because a few devotees of a particular religion are opposed to the state, the laws of the state are not thereby undermined because most citizens abide by them. Those who do not respect the laws of the state count as enemies of the state (TP 3.8). Spinoza does not spell it out, but I take it that this state counts as reasonably (albeit not maximally) sui juris.

[83] See for instance TTP 20.31, III/244.

[84] Steinberg offers a comprehensive argument for the connection between Spinoza's substantive ethical goals and his political goals (*Spinoza's Political Psychology*, 101–128, 190–216).

juris, and being sui juris possible without wide political participation and orientation to the common good. This conclusion underscores the antinomianism of Spinoza's system, which so often is downplayed in his discussions of politics: nature is not ordered to human purposes.

I can imagine a possible response to my argument that ethically unappealing regimes may endure and consequently have right. My objector could grant that any regime, no matter how bad, has right to the extent that it endures. But my objector might claim that this need not be troubling, because it is always true that the oppressed multitude can rise up against the state; and when it does so, it will have the right![85] This is La Boétie's own conclusion to his analysis of voluntary servitude;[86] and a similar move often crops up in discussions of popular power beyond Spinoza studies: for instance, Gandhi claims that people always have the power to resist oppression if only they make the decision to do so, through the collective exercise of *satyagraha* (truth force, or equivalently, passive resistance).[87] However, for Spinoza, this cannot really be any consolation. For what is the modality of this claim? In a logical sense, it is always possible that a multitude might rise up and refuse to be oppressed any more. But this is the wrong modality for considering human affairs (or indeed, nature more generally). Spinoza has no sympathy for voluntarist accounts of human agency, considering them (at best) misleading, or (at worst) pernicious vehicles for philosophers to feel superior to the masses. Spinoza complains that philosophers 'conceive men not as they are, but as they want them to be' (TP 1.1). Rather, it is essential to grasp the determinate causes of human behaviour. There will be determinate conditions that lead to the formation of collective resistance, and determinate causes that dissipate any such formation. Gandhi conceives the motivation to stake everything on the joint effort to overcome injustice as merely a moral choice that ought to be taken. But the real question is conditions under which such motivation can arise. Certainly sometimes in history it has been sufficiently achieved (for instance, in union organizing, or in the Indian struggle against the British). But these are particular situations, rather than the underlying tendency of human collective power.[88] The opposite situation

[85] See, for instance, Matheron, 'Le "droit du plus fort"', 153–154; Balibar, *Spinoza and Politics*, 103; Hardt and Negri, *Empire*, 204.

[86] La Boétie, 'Discourse on Voluntary Servitude', 287–289.

[87] M. K. Gandhi, *Hind Swaraj and Other Writings*, Centenary Edition, edited by Anthony J. Parel (Cambridge: Cambridge University Press, 2014), 91–97.

[88] Indeed, even in the most propitious cases, there are considerable contrary pressures: Gandhi notes that people with families cannot be effective satyagrahis because their particular attachments interfere with their commitment to the cause (ibid., 95). But most of the population in any society will

just as common. The point of the discussion of ethically unappealing regimes above is that these are regimes in which a robust determination of desires can be achieved such that an uprising of the multitude does not occur, despite the unappealing features of the regime.

8.4. Conclusion

My arguments in this chapter have sought to undermine the romance of popular power in Spinoza's political philosophy. It is common to interpret Spinoza's political philosophy as putting forward an idea of collective power that is both efficacious and ethical. But to the contrary, I have used a systematic understanding of Spinoza's philosophy of power to demonstrate how and why Spinoza accepts the Hobbesian criticisms of any naive celebration of popular power. Accepting the problem of the multitude's inner oligarchy, I show that Spinoza views the multitude's horizontal form as an institutional achievement rather than an essential starting point. Accepting the problem of nonideal endurance, I show that Spinoza can and does accept that there can be enduring power out of proportion to normative appeal. There is no salvation from scorning the state and turning to prepolitical constituent power. Collective power as it actually exists is entirely ethically ambivalent, just as for Hobbes. Nor is there any room for a democratic complacency that only democratic regimes will endure. Virtuous political organization lends to endurance, but endurance is also possible from other means. In chapter 9, I will answer the remaining Hobbesian criticism: the problem of democracy's perverse effects. I lay out explicitly a neo-Spinozist criterion of popular power, and I sketch a complex vision of democracy capable of meeting this criterion and overcoming the Hobbesian worry.

feel the pull of such attachments. After the mass arrest of Singaporean opposition parliamentarians in the 1963 Operation Coldstore, the few prisoners without families refused to sign confessions that they were communists and instead maintained their innocence, even at cost of decades of imprisonment. But those with families could not afford this choice. Thum Ping Tjin, 'Living in a Time of Deception', *The History of Singapore*, http://thehistoryofsingapore.com, Podcast Episode 23 (2016), accessed 19 November 2018.

9

Civic Strengthening

9.1. Introduction

This chapter will present Spinoza's own positive vision of popular power: both a new criterion to determine whether political phenomena express popular power, and also a set of institutional proposals to meet this criterion.

In the first half of this book, I discussed Hobbes, proposing that the salient and illuminating question of power in politics lies not in the consideration of juridical authority and *potestas*, but in the consideration of concrete power *potentia* (Chapter 2). This focus on concrete power brought into view 'the political problem': how is the cohesion of the political order concretely and durably to be achieved, and more particularly, how are subjects to be brought to comply with rulerly commands (Chapters 3–4). For spontaneous social dynamics can generate oligarchic power blocs; Hobbes worries about the tendency of such power blocs to destabilize the state. However, even if stability is not threatened, these informal oligarchic power blocs distort politics from the common good and the flourishing of the people, because of their capacity to capture and influence sovereign deliberation. In this light, any meaningful definition of popular power must recognize and address the problem of informal oligarchic power; indeed, I propose a thin Hobbesian conception of popular power as the power manifested by a political order that eliminates such oligarchy. On my interpretation, Hobbes himself shows some commitment to such a conception, insofar as he determinedly works to eviscerate informal powers in the multitude, in favour of a fragmented equality of individual power blocs, unified only through their representation by the sovereign. Once informal powers have been crushed, the sovereign can wisely and freely choose to serve the common good. I have labelled this model of politics 'repressive egalitarianism' (Chapter 5). In principle, repressive egalitarian sovereignty can take monarchical, aristocratic, or democratic form. However, Hobbes argues that democracy has perverse effects: the very structures of democratic decision-making encourage the flourishing of informal oligarchic power and its striving to capture sovereign power. Thus,

Potentia. Sandra Leonie Field, Oxford University Press (2020). © Oxford University Press.
DOI: 10.1093/oso/9780197533864.001.0001

counterintuitively, Hobbes holds that democracy will remain more prone to distortion than monarchy or aristocracy. As I noted in concluding my discussion of Hobbes in Chapter 5, even if we do not share Hobbes's optimism for non-democratic forms upholding the common good, he sharply identifies a difficulty for democracies.

In the second half of the book, turning to Spinoza, I raised three Hobbesian criticisms of the celebration of popular power common in the Spinozist literature: the problem of the multitude's inner oligarchy; the problem of nonideal endurance; and the problem of democracy's perverse effects (Chapter 6). On the basis of a new interpretation of Spinoza's concept of *potentia* (Chapter 7), I have argued that Spinoza acknowledges the first and second problems: that the power of the people does not automatically take horizontal shape, that any such shape is an achievement rather than an underlying natural tendency; and that it is not exclusively ethically appealing regimes that can be stable (Chapter 8).

Now in this final chapter, I build a positive Spinozist understanding of popular power capable of addressing the Hobbesian problem of democracy's perverse effects. First, I establish a Spinozist criterion of popular power: to express popular power worthy of the name, the basic structure of a state must feature and sustain equality and participation. In more technical language, the state must itself be sui juris, but at the same time, its structure must preserve its citizens' sui juris status with respect to each other. I show that this is not so distant from the Hobbesian conception of popular power established in the first half of the book. Second, I consider what might meet this criterion, and it is here that Spinoza's differences from Hobbes become apparent. I argue that Spinoza acknowledges many elements of the Hobbesian analysis of democracy, and in consequence, he would view his own early unqualified generic support for democratic forms in the *Theological-Political Treatise* as naive.[1] But I argue that he offers a different solution than does Hobbes: not repressive egalitarianism, but what I will call civic strengthening. Hobbes hopes to secure the common good by removing any pressure on the holder of sovereignty, presuming that such pressure can only be dangerous, oligarchic, and partisan in the pejorative sense; and he does so by individualizing and atomizing subjects. By contrast Spinoza explores the determinate

[1] The privileging of Spinoza's later account of democracy is common amongst both radical and constitutionalist interpreters. See, for instance, Justin D. Steinberg, 'Benedict Spinoza: Epistemic Democrat', *History of Philosophy Quarterly* 27, no. 2 (2010): 148; Negri, '*Reliqua Desiderantur*', 220–224.

causes of constructive non-oligarchic forms of citizenly collective action. He applies these considerations both to design the inner structure of the institutional holder of democratic sovereignty, and also to establish counterpowers ranged against the holder of sovereignty.

In making this argument, I face a textual difficulty: Spinoza's final view of the institutional form of a democracy of the multitude cannot be determined directly from his texts, because the *Political Treatise* was incomplete at his death, with only a few initial introductory paragraphs on the question of democracy. This means that the theory of democracy needs to be reconstructed somewhat speculatively. To defend my view I draw both on my systematic reconstruction of his political philosophy and on aspects of the *Political Treatise*'s direct institutional proposals for monarchy and aristocracy.

9.2. A Criterion of Popular Power

I start by establishing a Spinozist criterion for judging which political phenomena count as expressions of popular power. At the very outset of the book, I considered two prevalent conceptions of popular power: popular power as that which is expressed in plebiscitary decisions; or as that which is expressed in mass movements. I posed a set of questions to these conceptions: Is such popular power inherently virtuous? Is it inherently democratic? And what is its relation to the state? On both prevalent conceptions, popular power is essentially and definitionally distinct from the ordinary institutional structures of governance; through the course of the book, I have put forward Hobbesian and Spinozist arguments that popular power so conceived is not necessarily virtuous, nor necessarily meaningfully democratic. But conceptually prior to the question of the allegedly good and popular quality of this power is the question of its status as 'power' at all. Power, from the Hobbesian and Spinozist perspective of *potentia*, is the actual determination of effects; as such, it should be judged by effects. In human society, effects are continually produced as the complex emergent result of microrelations amongst individuals throughout the entire social body. Thus, several times in the course of my arguments I have suggested that it is a category mistake to look to punctual or partial phenomena such as social movements or plebiscites as an index of popular power. I will now give this suggestion a clearer theoretical form through a Spinozist conceptual frame. In this section, I move beyond received conceptions and propose a new conception of what, from a

Spinozist point of view, ought properly to be understood as popular power. Admittedly, the term 'popular power' is not Spinoza's own; but the proposal I advance makes heavy use of Spinozist analytical frames.

I propose that the political phenomenon that expresses popular power is a state sui juris whose fundamental laws feature equality and participation, where the relevant conception of equality is cashed out in terms of the independence of citizens (or sui juris status) with respect to each other.[2] I defend this proposal first positively, by showing how it emerges out of Spinoza's general approach to analysing politics; then negatively, by showing its superior fit with an intuitively appealing notion of equality, compared to its rivals.

Despite the prominence of the phrase *potentia multitudinis* (the power of the multitude) in Spinoza's political writings, it is not actually immediately straightforward to establish a concept of popular power supplying the desired connection to equality and participation. The power of the multitude is certainly central to Spinoza's understanding of politics, but this is a general point about political analysis, not a criterion distinguishing between states. For the state is a complex individual composed of a multitude of human parts; as such, all states, whether tyrannical or free, unequal or equal, are grounded in the power of the multitude. The multitude's power in this sense is equivalent to state power, because state power refers to the systematic production of effects, not to the power of the ruling element taken alone.[3] Rather, to answer the question of whether popular power is expressed in a given political formation, it is necessary to consider the particular character of the multitude's power in that case.

For Spinoza, any individual's power can be analysed in two dimensions: qualitatively (what are the individual's characteristic motions, what effects does it characteristically produce); and relationally (can its effects be understood through its own nature alone, or only through its own nature in combination with others). Equivalently, in the political case, a state's power can be analysed in terms of its fundamental principles or laws (where law is

[2] In my earlier discussion of individual sui juris status, I emphasized its dual aspect: not only independence from determination by others, but also self-determination by reason (see especially Chapter 7, Section 7.3). I do not deny the significance of the second aspect: indeed, Spinoza insists that the good state is one in which subjects live 'a human life, one defined not merely by the circulation of the blood, and other things common to all animals, but mostly by reason, the true virtue, and the life of the Mind' (TP 5.5). However, this is amply discussed by the existing literature; by contrast, my contribution is to elaborate the first, more political, aspect of individual sui juris status.

[3] See Chapter 7, Section 7.3.2 and Chapter 8, Section 8.2.

expansively understood as the regime's basic structure); and in terms of how much it is in control of its own right (how sui juris it is).[4]

A state sui juris, in control of its own right, is one that tends to reproduce its fundamental laws homeostatically: in particular, it is one that tends to generate in subjects the passions and motivations that will lead them to uphold the political order (TP 4.4–5, 7.1–2, 10.9). Thus, a state sui juris is a state that has answered Hobbes's political problem: it has achieved concrete durable unity. Such a state, in Spinozist terms, acts from its own power (its *potentia agendi*) alone; its Spinozist *potentia agendi* corresponds to its Hobbesian *potentia*. I propose that a state expressing popular power must be sui juris in this sense. For if a state is not sui juris, it is instead either expressing the power of a gross external entity, such as a colonial power, or it is suffering internal conflict so destabilizing that it is better understood as merely the result of conflicting parts.[5]

When I say popular power, I start with an intuitive sense that any idea of popular power worthy of the name should have some connection with equality and participation. Contrary to a common view in the Spinozist literature, I have argued that equality and participation may still fail to be secured within a state sui juris.[6] For instance, Hobbesian repressive egalitarianism, in its monarchical or aristocratic form, counts as sui juris;[7] and Spinoza himself considers his own proposed virtuous aristocracy as very sui juris.[8] For a state to express neo-Spinozist popular power, I propose that it must fulfil the following compound criterion: the state must be sui juris and organized around a fundamental law that enshrines equality and participation for citizens, where citizenship is not restricted by occupation or gender.[9]

[4] Although superficially a state being in control of its own right concerns its right and not its power, in Spinoza's metaphysics, being sui juris, is equivalent to acting from one's own active power (*potentia agendi*). See Chapter 7, Section 7.3.2.

[5] As I will emphasize in Section 9.4, some forms of conflict are consistent with being sui juris; the question is the character of the conflict. Recall the Machiavellian distinction between Rome and Florence, discussed in Chapter 8, Section 8.2.

[6] See Chapter 8, Section 8.3; see also footnotes 47–52 in Chapter 6.

[7] In Chapter 5, Section 5.4, I characterized these regimes as displaying a certain commitment to popular power, albeit a very thin one: negatively, a hostility to informal oligarchic powers, but without positive political participation or formal political equality.

[8] It is a common mistake to interpret Spinoza's aristocracy as sui juris only to the extent it approximates democracy. But Spinozist monarchy is more equal and participatory than aristocracy, which by contrast entrenches the exclusion of the commoners. Nonetheless Spinoza views aristocracy as more sui juris than monarchy, the more so the more effectively it prevents commoners from engaging in politics (TP 7.3–4, 8.3–5). See Field, 'Political Power'.

[9] It is an important question whether migrants can be excluded from citizenship. However, I put this aside for the purposes of the present argument.

Note that on this definition, Spinoza's own democracy does not count as an expression of popular power. For it notoriously involves extensive political exclusions. At minimum, Spinoza excludes all women and servants (TP 11.3). There is a debate as to whether these exclusions are consistent with the structure of his political philosophy.[10] To understand what is at stake, it is useful to recall Zourabichvili's dictum: Spinoza's 'paradoxical conservatism' poses the challenge not to preserve what exists, but to bring into existence what will be able to preserve itself.[11] A state that can preserve itself is one with a fundamental law that maintains itself homeostatically. Spinoza appears to take it for granted that certain forms of intense personal dependency are ineliminable: in his view, there is no foreseeable social order in which women are not dependent on men, nor where there will be no personal servants.[12] And insofar as women and servants are subject to this intense personal dependency, they are not equal in power to independent males.[13] If individuals in positions of dependency are treated as if they are equal, then they will distort popular equality. Matheron reconstructs the mechanics of this distortion: the man with many servants ends up with de facto more voting power, but for his own oligarchic benefit, not for the common good:[14] in this way the fundamental law of equality amongst citizens would constantly corrupt itself.[15]

[10] Montag and Sharp deny that it is coherent; Matheron argues that it is. Montag, *Bodies, Masses, Power*, 84–89; Hasana Sharp, 'Eve's Perfection: Spinoza on Sexual (In)Equality', *Journal of the History of Philosophy* 50, no. 4 (2012): 559–580; Alexandre Matheron, 'Femmes et serviteurs dans la démocratie spinoziste', *Études sur Spinoza et les philosophies de l'âge classique* (Lyon: ENS Éditions, 2011), 287–304. In brief, it seems to me to be entirely possible that such a regime could be sui juris, for the reasons laid out in Chapter 8, Section 8.3. However, it is unclear whether it should count as a state satisfying Spinoza's requirement to provide for a properly human life in the sense of footnote 2. For in it, intense personal dependency precludes many subjects from developing virtue.

[11] Zourabichvili, *Le conservatisme paradoxal de Spinoza*, 262.

[12] Spinoza's confidence on this point is supported by his cyclical understanding of history: 'I am fully persuaded that experience has shown all the kinds of State which might conceivably enable men to live in harmony' (TP 1.3). A more open view, whereby the future may contain new possibilities of human collective existence, only strongly emerges with thinkers in later centuries.

[13] James, 'Politically Mediated Affects', 61–77.

[14] Spinoza makes an analogous argument in the case of a state composed of cities unequal in power: he denies that having a fundamental law that treats these cities as if they were equal would be sustainable (TP 6.9, 9.4). To see a contemporary example of such distortion, consider the phenomenon of impoverished nations voting in accord with the desires of the United States in the United Nations General Assembly: for instance, the 2017 Resolution of the General Assembly of the United Nations (ES-10/19), condemning US recognition of Jerusalem as the capital of Israel. The only countries joining the United States and Israel to vote no were seven poor nations: Guatemala, Honduras, Marshall Islands, Micronesia, Nauru, Palau, and Togo and Tonga.

[15] Matheron, 'Femmes et serviteurs', 296. The alleged mechanism of distortion is rather more compelling in relation to servants than women (presuming polygamy is not permitted) (ibid., 301); and it is rather more compelling in relation to non-secret voting. However, my purpose here is not to defend these exclusions, so much as to argue that they relate to seventeenth-century exigencies and can be put aside for the purposes of thinking about twenty-first-century popular power.

By contrast, in our contemporary age, the idea of a society of equal citizens without any classes of gross personal dependents[16] is readily conceivable and is sometimes approximately achieved. In this context, it becomes interesting to investigate the conditions of perpetuation of such a society.

At this point, the idea of equality remains underspecified. Already in my discussion of Hobbes in Chapter 5, I offered a preliminary negative specification of equality as the elimination of oligarchic dependencies amongst subjects; the above discussion suggests equality as the absence of gross personal dependency. But these accounts remain ad hoc and unsystematic, and the effort to be more systematic faces a problem: how can a conception of equality be specified, when each individual's power is qualitatively distinct, meaning that power is not a straightforwardly comparable quantitative property? However, for both later Hobbes and Spinoza,[17] power is always determined in an actual social ecology with other humans. The relevant metric for comparing power is how individual powers relate in combinations: the question of equality amounts to the question of dependency. At minimum, equality must involve not being legally dependent. But recall my discussion of *potestas* and being sui juris in Chapter 6, Section 6.4 and Chapter 7, Section 7.3.2: legal status is just one of many and diverse forms, of varying degrees of intensity, that dependency can take.[18] In light of this broader conception of dependency, equality cannot require what would be impossible, eliminating human dependency altogether, and making everyone in a society absolutely independent. Rather, I propose that democratic equality demands pluralized and cross-cutting dependency: no individual or group should find themselves overwhelmingly subjected to any other single individual or group, short of the political order as a whole.[19] This amounts to saying that citizens should be maximally sui juris with respect to one another.[20] To achieve this

[16] Except children.

[17] See Chapter 2, Section 2.4; Chapter 7, Sections 7.2 and 7.3.2.

[18] Lord's recent articles rely variously on intuitive, juridical, and economic accounts of political equality; I suggest that the concept of dependency might provide a more general theoretical frame. Beth Lord, 'The Concept of Equality in Spinoza's Theological-Political Treatise', *Epoché 20*, no. 2 (2016): 367–386; Beth Lord, 'Spinoza, Equality, and Hierarchy', *History of Philosophy Quarterly 31*, no. 1 (2014): 59–77.

[19] This criterion is demanding, but not deeply original. Walzer offers a contemporary development of the idea of pluralizing dependencies, in order to avoid dominance of any particular one (*Spheres of Justice*, 3–30). Anderson offers a contemporary development of the idea of equality as undominated status: no one needs to 'bow and scrape' to any other. Elizabeth S. Anderson, 'What Is the Point of Equality?', *Ethics 109*, no. 2 (1999): 313–314.

[20] The claim in the *Ethics* that acting by reason is the greatest human good and can be shared by all equally is suggestive of such a criterion (E 4p36–37). However, as discussed previously, Spinoza himself takes for granted the necessity of personal dependents. For reflection on the status of impossible ideals, see Field, 'Political Power'.

standard of equality, equal rights of formal political participation may be necessary, but as we will see, they are by themselves insufficient.

I will now clarify how my neo-Spinozist criterion for deciding what political phenomena express popular power differs from the criteria underlying prevalent celebrations of popular power. First, on my criterion, popular power can only be expressed by a state sui juris. A consequence of this view, which is perhaps counterintuitive but nonetheless that I wish to defend, is that forms of popular political disruption such as social movements do not count as expressions of popular power. To be clear, my criterion does not in any way rule out the causal role of popular movements in bringing such a popular regime into existence (we need not share Spinoza's own scepticism on this point).[21] Nor does it rule out the ongoing role of popular movements in keeping the regime honest and non-corrupt (to the contrary, this role will be essential, as I will discuss in Section 9.4). But my criterion does refuse to acknowledge the moment of protest as the paradigmatic expression of popular power. Instead I take the proof of popular power to lie in an ongoing state of affairs.[22] If an oppressed people rise up and overthrow their oppressors, but are unable to establish a continuing political order that speaks to their needs and aspirations, I take it that this indicates a deficiency of popular power in the Spinozist sense.

Second, on my criterion, while in any state expressing popular power there will be some role for the expressed will of the people, being governed by this will is insufficient to establish popular power. To explain why this is the case, I turn to Spinoza's reflections on the role of rulerly will in the context of monarchy. There is an apparent conflict of political authority in his account. In general, Spinoza insists that subjects must defer to the determinations of their sovereign, for without this, the political order collapses (TTP 16.25–27, III/

[21] As discussed in Chapter 8, Section 8.2, Spinoza thinks that revolutions tend not to achieve their aims. The English attempted a change of regime through civil war, but ended up with only a more corrupt version of their initial regime: Spinoza takes this experience as paradigmatic. Instead, he thinks regimes should only seek to optimize their current form. However, subsequent centuries have provided many examples of revolutions that did achieve a fundamental change of political structure, especially where underlying social and economic change lays the groundwork for the new political form. For a discussion of successful revolutionary change in Spinoza's own time, see Michael A. Rosenthal, 'The Siren Song of Revolution: Spinoza on the Art of Political Change', *Graduate Faculty Philosophy Journal* 34, no. 1 (2013): 111–132.

[22] Would Negri oppose this criterion? Sometimes Negri valorizes protest itself, but in the more subtle presentation in '*Reliqua Desiderantur*', he takes the fundamental definition of absolute democracy to be 'the political process in its complexity' ('*Reliqua Desiderantur*', 240–241). I understand this to mean that popular power is expressed in the continual readjustment of institutions to the ever-varying needs of the multitude. This is closer to my definition, with the difference that Negri holds that in fact there is an ontological tendency to the increase of popular power over time.

193; TP 3.2–5). But as argued, the defining feature of any regime is its fundamental law, and sometimes the explicit expressions of the sovereign's will do not uphold the fundamental law. For it is readily possible that a short-sighted king might make decisions that erode the homeostatic functioning of the state. Spinoza resolves the conflict by reinterpreting what counts as the monarch's will in the relevant sense. He asserts that ministers should regard the fundamental laws of the state as the king's eternal decree: just as Ulysses was bound to the ship's mast for his own good, so too will a wise king subject himself to these laws (TP 7.1). The explicit will of the king is affirmed only secondarily. In Spinoza's preferred model of monarchy, the king cannot put forward any policy proposals of his own, but he is empowered to make a final and binding decision between the possibilities laid before him by his advisory council (TP 6.25). Thus the king's decisions are authoritative, but only within the broader remit defined by the state's fundamental laws.

From this point of view, it should be clear that having a state governed by expressed popular will (regardless of whether it is expressed through equal vote in a plebiscite, in a direct democratic assembly, or in a representative assembly of elected representatives) does not necessarily guarantee that it counts as an expression of popular power.[23] For even though such expressions of popular will rest on formal equality and participation, whether they in fact express popular power depends on whether this institutional form of decision-making sustains the fundamental law of the regime.[24] If formal equality and participation in voting somehow generates substantive inequality (increasing dependency, or generating legislation for sectional

[23] I grant that Spinoza does make a distinction between individual will and the will of a large assembly: whereas not everything a king wills should be law, by contrast whatever an assembly decides should be law (TP 8.3). However, recall from Chapter 8, footnote 57, Spinoza distinguishes two senses of law: civil (law as express legal provisions) versus natural (the laws of the state's nature as a natural thing, its characteristic motion or fundamental principles) (TP 4.4–5). I understand Spinoza's claim in TP 8.3 to be that in an aristocracy, whatever the assembly wills should become civil law (unlike in the case of monarchy). However, that does not guarantee that the civil law so produced conforms to the state's fundamental law, as will be discussed in detail later: a major and non-trivial task is to structure the assembly and surrounding institutional forms such that the desired uniformity is achieved. Spinoza's discussion of the 'mind' of the multitude follows a similar dual structure. The power of the state is determined by 'the power of a multitude, led as if by one mind [*una veluti mente*]', where that mind is the 'mind of the whole state' (TP 3.2). Sometimes the 'mind' of the state refers to the express commands of the holder of sovereignty; other times it refers to the actually achieved and durably reproduced affective coordination of the multitude (the whole population being disposed to act in a way that maintains the state's fundamental principles) (TP 2.16–17, 3.2, 3.5, 3.7, 3.9, 4.1). It is possible for these to come apart; a sovereign's commands might be obeyed even as they contribute in the longer term to undermining the state's fundamental principles.

[24] This approach, focussing on effects, echoes Spinoza's account of divine law and faith. The criterion of obedience to divine law and of faith is good works and ethical action, not compliance with particular dictates or profession of particular doctrines (TTP 5.50, III/80; 14.39, III/180).

benefit, not the common good), then it wouldn't count as an expression of popular power. So on my account, it is an open question whether any particular regime directed by popular will expressed through voting does or does not maintain the fundamental laws of a state expressing of popular power. I have already argued that plebiscitary voting generally does not: both because a plebiscite has too little influence on everyday operations of governance (Chapter 4, Section 4.3), and also because it is too readily captured by oligarchic interests (Chapter 5, Section 5.4).[25] Now in the next section, I set up the question of the two other forms of mass voting.

9.3. Accepting the Problem of Democracy's Perverse Effects

In his earlier *Theological-Political Treatise*, Spinoza expresses optimism for democratic institutions as inherently and robustly equalizing without the need for further institutional specification (TTP 5.23–25, III/74, 16.36, III/195, 20.37–38, III/245). It is not clear whether he has in mind representative or direct democracy; I will now consider each of them as important contending institutional proposals, to be measured against my criterion of popular power. I will argue that both these proposals incur Hobbesian scepticism, a scepticism which Spinoza endorses and even amplifies.

As a first plausible proposal, consider a stylized model of liberal representative democracy as it is commonly conceived: that is, decisions are made by the vote of representatives who in turn are elected by popular vote, and these decisions are constrained by some legal protection of citizens' liberties.[26] I put this forward because, substantially, this book's ambition to speak to the contemporary question of popular power makes it relevant to consider

[25] The considerations raised in earlier chapters do not entirely rule out some secondary role for plebiscites, within a broader institutional scheme. But this underscores my point: whether a plebiscite expresses popular power must be judged by how it functions within an actual political milieu. This framework gives voice to the intuitive sense that some plebiscites are more meaningful than others, and that some kinds of questions are more suitable for plebiscites than others. See footnote 59.

[26] Many constitutionalist interpreters of Hobbes make generic mention of liberalism and democracy, but beyond this, they offer scant institutional details. Rocca, *Spinoza*, 219–221; Balibar, 'Spinoza, the Anti-Orwell', 124; Armstrong, 'Natural and Unnatural Communities', 301–305; Steven B. Smith, 'What Kind of Democrat Was Spinoza?', *Political Theory* 33, no. 1 (2005): 24–25; Alexandre Matheron, 'The Theoretical Function of Democracy in Spinoza and Hobbes', in Montag and Stolze, *The New Spinoza*, 207–217; James, 'Democracy and the Good Life', 137–140; Kisner, *Spinoza on Human Freedom*, 215–229. For the few notable exceptions, see footnote 37 and the footnotes to Section 9.4.

whether the familiar institutions of twenty-first-century liberal representative democracy might fit with Spinozist requirements; and because textually, Spinoza himself relies on representation in the popular assembly of his favoured model of monarchy.

As a second plausible proposal, consider direct mass participatory democracy. The idea that direct participatory democracy might provide an appropriate expression of popular power is a widespread one, and it also has some currency in Spinoza studies. Although Negri's conception of Spinozist radical democracy is often avowedly anti-institutional,[27] at other points he allows certain institutions so long as they 'flatten onto the multitude':[28] and for him, this means the institutions of direct participatory democracy.[29] Democracy is 'a council composed of the multitude as a whole', democracy as the totality of citizens assembled together.[30] There are three features of this conception to highlight. First, it is anti-representative. Representative democracy alienates the multitude's power to an assembly who can police their conduct. Second, and for the same reasons, it is against institutional delegation. And third, it is vehemently opposed to formal constitutions; it views any constraint of democratic expression as an illegitimate defence of the privileged status quo against the claims of the masses.[31]

Negri does not merely propose this form of democracy; he also claims that it is Spinoza's own view. Such a claim faces a textual hurdle: it jars with Spinoza's evident interest in representative, delegated, and constrained institutional forms. In discussion of aristocratic and monarchical regimes, as well as the theocracy of the ancient Hebrew republic, Spinoza devotes great attention to meticulously engineered rules of selection of representatives and officers, a proliferation of assemblies checking one another, and constantly invokes fundamental laws (TTP 17.16–115, III/203–221; TP 6–10). But on

[27] See Chapter 6, Section 6.3.1.

[28] I do not accept Negri's analytical characterization of the status of these institutions. I have argued that the power of the multitude is not conceptually prior to institutions; rather, it is inseparable from the institutions through which it is expressed (Chapter 6, Section 6.4 and Chapter 8, Section 8.2). Hence, I would say the institutions of direct participatory democracy shape the multitude rather than flattening onto it.

[29] In his subsequent collaborations with Hardt, Negri has developed a model of democracy of the multitude that goes beyond simple direct participation, also promoting an open network structure and facilitating internal conflict (Hardt and Negri, *Commonwealth*, 356–374).

[30] Antonio Negri, 'Democracy and Eternity in Spinoza', in Murphy, *Subversive Spinoza*, 102, 111; see also Negri, 'The *Political Treatise*', 19–21. A similar idea is promoted in Holland, 'Spinoza and Marx', §26.

[31] Negri, *The Savage Anomaly*, xxii, 196; Negri, '*Reliqua Desiderantur*', 222, 234–235; Negri, 'The *Political Treatise*', 14, 24.

Negri's interpretation, these are remedial measures only relevant for non-democratic polities, with no corollary or lesson for democracy. He anticipates that the *Political Treatise*'s chapter on democracy, had it been completed, would have eliminated this institutional complexity.[32] Even though Negri concedes the need for 'functions of control' and even though he thinks that democracy should be animated by tolerance and respect for conscience,[33] he attributes to Spinoza the view that these are self-generated by the multitude. In particular, there is no role for the philosopher to propose any forms of limitation or constraint: the power of the multitude inherently has its own limits, in the sense that oppressive laws will provoke revolt and will thus undermine themselves.[34] In other words, Negri thinks that his preferred direct democratic order, without representation, institutional delegation, or formal constitution, will self-regulate to maintain the desired equality amongst citizens.

Let me start by sketching why, on Spinozist grounds, democracy (on either of these two institutional models) might be a promising institutional model. The first reason is self-interest. The general challenge for all politics is 'to establish things so that everyone, no matter what his mentality, prefers the public right to private advantage' (TTP 17.16, III/203). Reason generated by pure philosophical reflection is in principle sufficient to lead to this public-spirited political virtue, but 'the path reason teaches to follow is very difficult' (TP 1.5). For Spinoza, humans are often driven not by reason, but by various passions and desires. The only mass basis for overcoming selfish motivations is an institutional order that generates the required virtue (TP 1.6, 5.3).[35] In this human condition, democracy appears to offer a neat solution. If all are prone to pursue their self-interest, then any form of rule resting on a ruling class will end up privileging that ruling class and not the common good. By contrast, in a democracy, a plurality of self-interested actors with formal equality in voting may generate policy decisions that fairly balance

32 Negri, 'The *Political Treatise*', 20–21.

33 Negri, '*Reliqua Desiderantur*', 227–228, 235.

34 Negri, 'The *Political Treatise*', 18. Montag similarly celebrates a 'politics of permanent revolution' and perpetual mass mobilization (*Bodies, Masses, Power*, 84).

35 Armstrong claims that Spinoza advances an ideal of democracy as a community of perfectly rational humans, and she criticizes this view as inconsistent with his broader philosophical system, recommending that he should rather advocate a system of good laws and institutions (Armstrong, 'Natural and Unnatural Communities', 301–305). My argument in here and in Section 9.4 supports her recommendation. However, she errs in offering this as a point against Spinoza. For when Spinoza asserts that people in a democracy obey 'not simply by reason of the authority of a ruler', he does not (contra Armstrong) mean that their obedience is from reason. Rather, it is 'by hope of some good that they urgently desire' (TTP 5.24–25, III/74).

individual needs and generate an outcome for the common good (TTP 5.25, III/74, 16.36, III/195, 20.38, III/246; TP 7.4).

The second reason is collective rationality. Quite apart from questions of the proper alignment of interests, there is the question of wise decision-making. Just as an individual may ardently desire to advance their own interest, yet unwittingly make decisions that contradict it, the same risk faces a political assembly even with the perfect alignment of interests with the common good. However, Spinoza expresses confidence that the assembly form itself can help to insulate against this problem: he claims that larger assemblies are less likely to agree on folly. When diverse ways of thinking about a problem are brought into conversation, a good decision is more likely (TTP 16.30, III/194; TP 7.5).

Commentators all observe Spinoza's explicit expression of concern about democracy: no states 'have proved so short-lived as popular or democratic states, nor have any been so liable to frequent rebellion' (TP 6.4). However, the comment occurs in the context of Spinoza's criticisms of despotic monarchy: it is often taken to be merely a statement of the risk of any form of non-slavish collective life, a risk that nonetheless is worth taking. But the comment also has implications for democracy. As I flagged in Chapter 6, Section 6.4, there is cause for concern: for democracy seem to face a Hobbesian problem of perverse effects. Now I lay out the Hobbesian concern, and show how and why Spinoza shares this concern; then I indicate two further distinctively Spinozist worries about democracy.

The fundamental lesson of the first half of this book is that informal powers existing beneath the juridical holder of authority can disrupt and distort that authority's function. Recall the logic of informal power. Individuals seek to safeguard their capacity to pursue their ends, now and in the future; consequently, they act so as to placate and propitiate others who might be in a position to harm or benefit them (Chapter 2, Section 2.4). The resultant forms of deference and allegiance constitute power and tend to cumulate individuals into power blocs. Deference and allegiance are generated and magnified in a heavily self-referential web of appearances: I see A and B offering allegiance to X; that constitutes power for X, so I offer allegiance also, hoping to benefit from the association. As I argued at length, the power blocs so formed are not horizontal associations of equals. To the contrary, the informal accumulation of power is highly unequal: the more needy the individual is, the more cheaply their allegiance can be secured (Chapter 4, Section 4.2).

In Chapter 5, I presented Hobbes's argument that this mechanism of accumulation of and competition for power, far from being disrupted by formal democratic procedures, actually captures democratic institutions and thrives within them. First, it is often those successful at garnering informal power (wealth, popularity) who secure election into the democratic assembly in the first place; second, powerful actors outside of the assembly seek to leverage compliance of those within; and third, members of the assembly constantly jockey for power amongst themselves, achieving the patronage of the powerful in return for servicing their needs.[36]

The result is that both of the supposed virtues of democratic organization are corrupted. First, regarding self-interest, the formal equality of a democratic institutional form does not break down unequal power in the social body, but expresses it, ruining the required alignment of interests with the common good. Second, regarding collective rationality, the assembly form also ruins the capacity to make wise decisions. The pursuit of truth and good policy is confused and derailed by individual assembly members' desire to maintain their status: speaking truth to power comes at a personal cost, for it runs contrary to efforts to flatter and not to incur the hostility of those with higher status, and contrary to efforts not to be on the wrong side of a debate (in modern terms, 'groupthink'). The more polemical the message, the easier it is for an individual to capture the disaffection of the masses to advance their own status. This has the routine result of unwise policy, sometimes to no one's advantage, but more often to the advantage of the oligarchic powers within the society.

Due to the continued influence of such oligarchic power blocs, formal democracy often becomes a confused and fractious crypto-aristocracy, inferior (in Hobbes's view) in its capacity to serve the common good than monarchy or a restricted aristocracy that is properly set up in the first place (Chapter 5, Sections 5.3–4). I offered a preliminary argument in Chapter 6, Section 6.4, that Spinoza acknowledges this concern: the accumulation of power may occur, and mass desire may vent itself on minorities. Steinberg astutely observes that for Spinoza, good government is not secured by the bare requirement of decision-making by democratic voting. Rather, the success of democracy is conditional on having a political structure that ensures the management of self-interest and ensures 'good epistemic conditions' for

[36] While the first is specific to representative forms of democracy, the other two apply equally to direct democracy.

good decisions.[37] In his discussion of superstition, Spinoza sharply identifies the mass effects of feelings of insecurity:

> If men could manage all their affairs by a definite plan, or if fortune were always favourable to them, no one would be in the grip of superstition. But they are often in such a tight spot that they cannot decide on any plan. Then they usually vacillate wretchedly between hope and fear, desiring immoderately certain goods of fortune, and ready to believe anything whatever. (TTP Pref.1, III/5)

In Spinoza's analysis, this has two interconnected consequences. First, the popular capacity for judgement is directly reduced (TTP Pref.2–4, III/5). Second, false prophets, schismatics, and charlatans thrive as the masses throw themselves into their hands (TTP Pref.6, III/6); and the intensity of mass allegiance to these groups is intensified by the elation individuals feel in crushing their perceived enemies (E 4p58s, TP 1.5). This analysis of superstition can readily be translated to the democratic context. Mass desire can ruin both Steinberg's management of self-interest and his 'good epistemic conditions'. It distorts the composition of interests in the assembly, as people may well support the candidacy and policy proposals of the popular and charismatic candidates who make unambiguous bold promises, without a critical eye to the capacity to deliver on those promises; and it undermines the quality of debate, both in public and in the democratic assembly, as political success comes to those willing to inflame these mass passions and capture them to their own advantage.

Let me pile on two further Spinozist worries.

First, Spinoza accepts Machiavelli's dictum: regimes do not tend to maintain themselves; in every day that passes, a regime accumulates defects (TP 10.1). Does this apply to democracy? Given the incompletion of Spinoza's discussion of democracy, I will consider his analysis of aristocracy. Two key threats to the fundamental laws of an aristocracy are the narrowing of its broad-based patriciate, and a rise of inequality amongst patricians. Indeed, the decline of Venice in Spinoza's time, from being the historical exemplar of the virtuous aristocratic republic, was the result of an increasingly closed and nepotistic patriciate.[38] This is driven by a collective solidarity against

[37] Steinberg, 'Benedict Spinoza', 147, 158. Specifically, fear, manipulation, and pressure for conformity need to be eliminated (ibid., 154).

[38] Haitsma Mulier, *Myth of Venice*, 201.

outsiders and by the desire to benefit one's own. For the citizenry conceives itself as a community imbued with moral significance from its shared history and experience, and does not want to extend benefits to outsiders (TP 8.2, 8.11–12). Furthermore, within the patriciate, inequality tends to arise, driven not only by the more narrow desire to benefit one's own, but also by laziness: 'All men, whether they rule or are ruled, tend to prefer pleasure to difficult work' (TTP 17.14, III/203). This can lead to patricians disengaging politically and not participating in the assembly. Those who do attend have disproportionate influence, ruining the mechanism of equal interests (TP 8.16). Is democracy somehow immune to this kind of degeneration? To the contrary, the problems of aristocracy are understood as part of a larger process of political shrinkage: even if democracies are not overcome by rebellion or war, they tend incrementally to degenerate into aristocracies and thence into monarchies (TP 8.12). Extrapolating the analysis of aristocracy to the case of democracy, the diminishing size of a citizenry compared to the total population and the diminishing of political engagement within the citizenry are perennial temptations for a democratic community, in tension with its fundamental principle of equality and participation.

Second, one of the appealing features of Spinoza's analysis of human motivation is that it goes beyond mere rational strategy to encompass the full gamut of passional drives. On Spinoza's analysis, simple desires for immediate material benefits do drive human action; but so also do more complex feelings of joy and sadness that are sparked by social life.[39] In particular, Spinoza analyses the striving to have others share our likes and dislikes, and our discomfort with those who manifest a way of thinking or living different from our own (E 3p31, 3p45–46, 4p37s1).[40] '[E]veryone wants others to live according to his mentality, so that they approve what he approves, and reject what he rejects' (TP 1.5; see also TTP 17.15, III/203; E 5p4s). This can manifest itself both in illiberality of legislation, and hostility towards minorities in a democratic community; as such, it again can threaten a departure from substantive equal status within the community.

In sum, a system of democratic voting can generate inequality and exclusion. As noted earlier, Negri takes the view that the multitude has its own inherent limits: any bad decisions will be contested and overthrown by the

[39] Indeed, even the parallel Spinozist account I provided earlier of Hobbesian power-blocs in assemblies is not so narrowly rational-strategic as Hobbes's. See also Chapter 6, footnote 60.

[40] See discussion in Steinberg, *Spinoza's Political Psychology*, 139–142.

multitude itself. But this is an inadequate response: as argued at length in Chapter 8, there are many ways in which human power can stably configure itself, and not all of them are morally appealing. Furthermore, even if they are unstable, there is no guarantee that the instability leads to improvement rather than to installation of an even more corrupt regime, or to a corrosive cycle of conflict.

These observations regarding the characteristic perversions of democratic processes are echoed three centuries later by Schumpeter. Schumpeter analyses the strategic capture of democracy by political entrepreneurs and other private interests; he observes the weakness and irresponsibility of democratic debate.[41] But his response is to offer a more 'realistic' minimalist definition of democracy:

> [T]he democratic method is that institutional arrangement for arriving at political decisions in which individuals acquire the power to decide by means of a competitive struggle for the people's vote.[42]

Schumpeter is in favour of democracy so conceived, and he believes it is a virtue of his account that it assiduously refuses to judge whether particular democracies count as more or less genuinely popular.[43] In his view, not only is there no coherent meaning to terms such as 'popular power', 'popular will', or 'common good', but worse, the appeal to such terms is the hallmark of the worst and most dangerous politics. Politicians take advantage of this

> phraseology that flatters the masses and offers an excellent opportunity not only for evading responsibility but also for crushing opponents in the name of the people.[44]

Schumpeter accepts that in his democracy, citizens do not have equal power; and he accepts that the democratic process of competing for votes could

[41] Schumpeter, *Capitalism, Socialism and Democracy*, 256–264.

[42] Ibid., 269.

[43] Schumpeter does concern himself with assessing the conditions under which democracy as he defines it might be self-sustaining (ibid., 290 n. 5; his criterion of being self-sustaining echoes the Spinozist criterion of being sui juris). He concludes that there are various presuppositions, including tolerance, non-sectarianism, and the willingness of the masses to defer to the organs of government and not to attempt political action on their own (ibid., 290–296). He identifies various historical places and times where these conditions may have been met, but he does not (as Spinoza might) consider the role of the institutional scheme itself in maintaining or eroding these presuppositions.

[44] Ibid., 268.

reasonably be characterized as one of manipulation and fraud.[45] However, he views his minimalist definition as superior to non-democratic socialism, the major perceived alternative against which he inveighs.[46]

My Hobbesian and Spinozist analysis throughout this book supports Schumpeter's scepticism regarding appeals to expressed popular will; however, in this chapter I have offered a neo-Spinozist criterion of popular power that can be deployed notwithstanding Schumpeterian concerns. My criterion for political phenomena to count as expressing popular power is that there be a system of government that enduringly generates equality and participation. But can there be a state expressing popular power in my neo-Spinozist sense? The possibility of a regime meeting this criterion is peremptorily excluded by Schumpeter's stark dichotomy between bourgeois minimalist democracy and non-democratic socialism. But even putting aside his dichotomy, the possibility is not straightforward to establish.[47] Steinberg identifies necessary good epistemic conditions for Spinozist democracy; but on Hobbes's analysis, democracy itself erodes these very same conditions, and consequently it is not an optimal regime form. In Hobbes's view, for democracy even to be barely acceptable, it needs to take a 'repressive egalitarian' form and minimize collective formations within society. The critical question now becomes, are there other, less repressive, institutional and organizational possibilities to express a popular power worthy of the name?

9.4. Schematic Elements for a Political Order Expressing Popular Power

Spinoza claims that a democratic state has the potential to be the most absolute and free of all regimes (TP 11.1). But I have argued that this is far from the automatic result of formally democratic procedures. In this section, I schematize three elements of a Spinozist institutional proposal to bring a democratic regime to express popular power. This does not represent a complete institutional portrait of Spinoza's own political vision,[48] nor do

[45] Ibid., 271–272. He remarks that everyone is free to compete for political office 'in the same sense in which everyone is free to start another textile mill' (ibid., 272 n. 6).

[46] Ibid., 297.

[47] Indeed, Feuer argues that Spinoza supported democracy and liberalism at the time of the *Theological-Political Treatise* (Feuer, *Rise of Liberalism*, 65–69), despite underlying difficulties with the model (ibid., 69, 106–107). However, by the time of the *Political Treatise*, Spinoza moved to supporting commercial aristocracy (ibid., 158–175).

[48] For a fuller discussion, see Lazzeri, *Droit, pouvoir et liberté*, 331–388.

I propose that seventeenth-century institutions are directly translatable to twenty-first-century needs. Rather, I hope to articulate three general kinds of mechanisms of autoregulation that a state might require for it to be said to express popular power.[49]

The first consideration is eliminating bad oligarchic pressure within formally democratic decision-making institutions. To start with, it is necessary to consider the relative credentials of direct democracy compared to representative democracy. Certainly, many of the problems outlined in the previous section arise equally in direct or representative democracy. But one might suspect, with Negri, that direct democracy is superior because it removes one possible mechanism of oligarchic capture. As Spinoza acknowledges, spending time in a position of political power leads decision-makers to be 'corrupted by gifts and favours' (TP 7.13). To be sure, there are grave problems with representative forms of democracy, as I will discuss, but for now I consider the conditions of success of direct democracy.

Spinoza himself is not in principle averse to direct non-representative assemblies: indeed, in an aristocracy, all patricians participate in the patrician assembly (TP 8.16). By contrast, selected representatives form the membership of the popular council in his favoured model of monarchy (TP 7.15). While Spinoza does not make the logic of the distinction explicit, I claim that the distinction supports the need for representation in a democratic assembly. Within an aristocracy, the fundamental principle is equality amongst patricians, and inequality between patricians and commoners (TP 8.47). The mere fact of having a non-representative patrician assembly does not adequately secure patrician equality. Unless all take their political duties seriously, some will reap informal advantages from the laziness and disengagement of others. For this reason, Spinoza proposes imposing fines on patricians who fail to participate in the assembly (TP 8.16). Such fines can be borne and can be viewed as reasonable because the main obstacle to political participation is mere laziness. The patricians are a leisured class whose ability to participate is supported by the commoners carrying out the productive and caring labour of society. Nor is the duty of participation without its perquisites: in return for participation, patricians are entitled to wear 'a certain decoration, granted only to them, by which they may be recognized and held in honor by everyone else' (TP 8.25).

[49] I conceive the status of these ideas as action-guiding fictions. See Rosenthal, 'What Is Real', 12–28.

Consider now what happens when the need for an assembly is transposed from the patriciate in an aristocracy onto the mass, as in Spinoza's monarchy: can a non-representative assembly be maintained? The obstacles for the mass to participate politically are much greater. Many people have jobs to keep and caring responsibilities to uphold: not all would simultaneously be able to fulfil the time commitment of participation in assembly. To overcome this difficulty but retain direct democracy, two responses are possible: make participation voluntary; or retain compulsory participation but with lesser demand for engagement (this latter option amounts to continuous plebiscitary government, not merely for occasional constitutional matters as per Tuck's proposal but for everyday legislative decisions).[50] In monarchy as in democracy, the goal is equality amongst the mass (TP 7.18–20); but both solutions to mass participation run contrary to this goal: we have already seen that self-selection of participants is directly distorting; and the vote of an unattentive public is sharply vulnerable to Schumpeterian capture by oligarchic power blocs and political entrepreneurs. Spinoza's own preferred route is to maintain compulsory participation and high demands for engagement, but only for representatives and not for the entire mass (TP 6.22, 6.28).

Now I turn to consider representative assemblies. Hobbes worries about power blocs of wealth, charisma, and sectarian allegiance perverting representative institutions; his response is to avoid democracy where possible, but if there is to be democracy, it is critical to eviscerate the distorting power of informal collectivities within the society. Spinoza does not have any naive faith in the good function of representative democracy, but his solution is different, as is shown by his proposals for the structure of the council in a well-ordered monarchy. Spinoza seeks not to destroy informal power blocs, but to mechanically eliminate the link between informal power blocs and the operation of the assembly.[51]

Spinoza stipulates that the king should choose the counsellors for his assembly (TP 6.16). This might sound like a form of royal prerogative, which would provide an open channel for power blocs in society to consolidate themselves: surely the king, mindful of the need to overcome the political problem, will be careful to curry favour with the powerful by honouring them

[50] Perhaps this was not feasible in Spinoza's time, but it is now, through internet technology. A thoroughgoing commitment to online plebiscitary decision-making on all issues constitutes the entire policy platform of a registered political party in Australia, Online Direct Democracy (https://www.onlinedirectdemocracy.org, accessed 29 May 2018).

[51] See also Mugnier-Pollet, *La philosophie politique de Spinoza*, 243–249.

with selection to the representative assembly. But to the contrary, I argue that what Spinoza proposes is essentially a process of sortition (lottery).

Spinoza proposes that the citizenry of the state should be divided into equal clans, and that the council should comprise an equal number of representatives from each clan: approximately five representatives (one of whom will be a jurist) from each of six hundred clans (TP 6.11, 6.15, 7.18). The king selects his councillors from lists of candidates provided by each clan. For each clan's five representatives, two should be replaced each year, except in the year when the sole jurist is replaced. Each representative can serve for no longer than four years; representatives cannot be immediately reselected; and they cannot even be placed back on the clan's list of candidates for five years after their term ends (TP 6.15–16, 7.13–14, 7.21). Thus, in effect, Spinoza recommends that each year, the king should choose one thousand distinct representatives.[52] Combined with the restriction on reselection, Spinoza in effect is proposing that the monarchical council should feature a rotating roster of at least eight thousand representatives, selected from the pool of male citizens over the age of fifty (TP 6.21).[53] As Spinoza observes, the result is that all men can reasonably hope to hold office at some point (TP 7.10).[54]

The sheer volume of representatives to be chosen means that the king implements what is effectively a system of broad-based sortition. This system attacks oligarchic power both in entry to and in the operation of the assembly. Prior to entry to the assembly, the perverse incentive for the powerful to build up their entourage is eliminated. There is no electoral mechanism by which individuals can leverage their following for votes; and the king cannot be influenced by offers of allegiance when he is required to select so many councillors. Furthermore, the perverse incentives to form power blocs once in the assembly are minimized: the short non-repeating terms in office prevent accumulation of power.[55] There are also elements of randomization in the assembly's procedures: clans take turns in leading the sessions of the

[52] In a given year, two-thirds of clans will replace two representatives, and one-third of clans will replace their jurist.

[53] Presuming each representative serves for three years. Textually, it is not clear whether the five-year restriction on reselection applies only to jurists or to all representatives. Even if it only applies to jurists, and other representatives only require a one-year break, the result is still an impressive forty-eight hundred minimum roster.

[54] Elsewhere, Spinoza indicates that a state of 'moderate size' would have resident population of approximately 250,000 men over the age of thirty, including all foreigners, servants, and disreputable occupations (TP 8.2, 8.13, 8.15). This is perhaps comparable with Holland, which in 1680 had a total population—inclusive of women and youth—of 883,000 (Price, *Dutch Republic*, 40).

[55] In addition to the term limits for representatives mentioned previously, military commanders and judges also have short terms (TP 7.17, 7.21).

assembly; and each session is led by the first-selected of the representatives of that clan (TP 8.23).[56] In this way, equality is maintained in the ongoing operations of the assembly.

The idea of sortition has garnered great interest within recent mainstream democratic theory. James Fishkin has identified a pathology of contemporary democracy: the pressure to win electoral contests makes serious discussion of certain difficult social problems off-limits; encourages the oversimplification of complex issues to the public; rewards the inflaming of existing prejudices and divisions; and rewards short-termism in policy. A party may put forward a robust policy platform, but then cut-throat political competition punishes nuance and rewards those that compete for power as such. Because of public inattention, any principled policy platform tends to be distorted, and there is little pressure to rule in accord with it in any case.[57] Fishkin's solution is what he calls 'deliberative polling', to operate in parallel with the standard electoral mechanisms of democracy: citizens are randomly selected by sortition, then brought together for in-depth discussion of policy issues. This removes perverse electoral incentives and overcomes inattention. Why should a population respect the outcomes of such deliberative publics? It depends how they are formed. Recently, Ireland has established a Citizens' Assembly, comprising ninety-nine members selected at random, to consider various long-term challenges facing Irish society.[58] It is endowed with official status from the state, and it enjoys popular legitimacy precisely because it overcomes the widely accepted perversities of electoral politics as normal.[59]

Now I move on to the second consideration for institutional design expressing the power of the people: addressing the gradual erosion of the

[56] Within aristocracy, Spinoza offers further mechanisms to reduce oligarchic power blocs: secret ballotting of officials (meaning the powerful cannot reward or punish allegiance, eliminating any perverse incentive to support the powerful) (TP 8.27); also secret accusations and complaints (TP 8.28).

[57] James S. Fishkin, *When the People Speak: Deliberative Democracy and Public Consultation* (Oxford: Oxford University Press, 2011), 3–28.

[58] https://www.citizensassembly.ie/en/Home/. See also Michael K. MacKenzie, 'A General-Purpose, Randomly Selected Chamber', in *Institutions for Future Generations*, edited by Iñigo González-Ricoy and Axel Gosseries (Oxford: Oxford University Press, 2016), 282–298.

[59] Indeed, the existence of such an assembly by sortition opens the possibility of less flawed plebiscitary procedures. When a plebiscite is set up by elected officials, it can be captured to those officials' particular agenda. Tactical considerations of the sitting government were widely viewed as shaping the format of both the 1999 Australian Republican Referendum and the 2017 Australian Same-Sex Marriage Postal Survey. See Chapter 5, footnote 61. This form of distortion is eliminated when a plebiscite is set up by an assembly by sortition: for instance, the 2018 Irish Abortion Referendum, established by the Irish Citizens' Assembly, retained much higher public confidence than the Australian plebiscites, even as it dealt with an intensely controversial issue.

state's fundamental principles. As outlined in Section 9.3, Spinoza takes the Machiavellian view that a state starts to degenerate from the moment it is established. In the case of the democratic order, this degeneration had three components: the tendency for a *demos* to shrink itself by excluding newcomers; the tendency for a *demos* to repress and oppress its internal forms of difference; and the tendency for political disengagement.

Analogous problems face the patriciate in an aristocratic order, and Spinoza is quite clear that the patrician assembly cannot rely on itself, as the very same body that makes the law, to uphold and maintain it (TP 8.19). His solution is to establish a permanent separate body for the purpose of maintaining the fundamental laws: a subcouncil of syndics (TP 8.20–28). This proposal raises questions: how can a separate council serve to consolidate the basic law rather than undermine it? Hobbes holds that formal institutional divisions fracture the state and lead to war. What incentive is there for syndics to focus on the common good and the state's fundamental principles where patricians fail? If they do not perform their duties, they are useless; and if they do perform their duties, disciplining and correcting patricians, why will they not rouse the patricians' ire?

Spinoza addresses these concerns in detail, through careful structuring of institutional incentives. He proposes that the syndics' duties should be very clearly defined and limited, including enforcing political participation; enforcing the induction of new members into the patriciate in order to maintain its size; and ensuring this induction is not nepotistic (TP 8.11, 8.13–16). They are motivated to perform their duties because their pay is tied to performance: they are paid such that 'they cannot maladminister affairs of state without great loss to themselves' (TP 8.24–25). They are insulated from needing to worry about displeasing powerful patrons in the course of disciplining and correcting them: their appointment for life means that they do not need to build support to be re-elected; and they present their (internally voted) decisions as the decision of the whole body, thereby protecting themselves from being pressured individually by the powerful who want to buy them off (TP 8.28, 10.2). They are limited from going beyond the proper scope of their duties: they are elderly, meaning that they do not have time to build a personal empire even if they wanted to; and in any case, at that age they are likely to be less ambitious (TP 10.2). In turn, Spinoza argues that the patricians will be disposed to support their work. The syndics' close adherence to their well-defined duties means that they 'can't be a terror to good men, but only to bad men' (TP 10.2); and every patrician has a fair chance one day to become a syndic (TP 8.28, 8.30). In sum, the syndics do their job; patricians support them; and any disagreements between them do not degenerate into hostile conflict. The result is that a delegated institutional body maintains the fundamental principles of its aristocratic form and thereby improves the credentials of the state in expressing the patriciate's power.

By analogy, I propose that in a popular state, delegated bodies may further the expression of popular power, insofar as they contribute to the homeostasis of a political system of equality and participation. They might be described as counterpowers, insofar as they seek to discipline the assembly. Contemporary institutions that might be understood in this way include appointed human rights, anti-discrimination, or equal opportunity bodies; and independent electoral commissions to determine electoral districting or to enforce voting.[60] Of course, there is always the risk that such independent bodies might become sites of oligarchic capture of power: the challenge is to monitor for this eventuality and to design them well to avoid it. The establishment of intermediate and semi-independent bodies need not be seen as a counterweight to popular power, but rather, an element of its expression, insofar as these bodies effectively serve to limit the counterproductive and self-corrupting tendencies of mass democracy.

The third and final consideration for the institutional design of a state expressing popular power is the role of informal collectivities. To this point, I have sketched a model of representative democracy including elements of sortition and delegation. But my discussion so far has focussed on formal institutions. What about the informal structure of society beneath these institutions? Both Hobbes and Spinoza hope for the holder of sovereignty (whether individual or assembly) to work for the common good and maintain equality, through their institutional structure of decision. But they disagree on the role of counterpower. Hobbes not only rules out any formal counterpower (such as Spinoza's syndics) within a good state's constitutional structure; he also holds that it is necessary to crush informal powers in society. Is Hobbes correct to think crushing informal power is necessary or desirable?

Left Schmittians assert that conflict between the popular mass and the state generates good results. But there are multiple reasons to doubt this as

[60] Australia has an independent electoral commission that both determines electoral boundaries and enforces compulsory voting; unlike the United States, for instance, where voting is not compulsory and in most states electoral boundaries are controlled by the elected politicians themselves.

a universal claim. First, there is no guarantee that informal pressure corresponds to the common good (think of the oligarchic power of the wealthy). Second, even if there is some more egalitarian popular sentiment underlying informal pressure against the sovereign, it is much easier for a sovereign to buy off leaders rather than address underlying grievances (see Chapter 5, Section 5.3). Third, sometimes the presence of informal power blocs resisting sovereign rule leads to political collapse and civil war, and the corresponding total destruction of the social fabric of society. In Hobbes's view, the better way for a sovereign to serve the public good should be to make good decisions based on extensive consultation and wise counsel, but without having to deal with any informal pressures at all. Informal pressure is eliminated in his repressive egalitarian state by sharply limiting forms of collective organization. But a repressive egalitarian democracy risks becoming a crypto-aristocracy, because should the sovereign depart from the common good, the populace has no effective constraint on it: for even if subjects feel indignant, they are individually too weak to contest state power. For Hobbes, this is an unavoidable inconvenience of the human condition, and better than any alternative (L 282–283, 18.20).

As I argued earlier, Spinoza certainly accepts the deep ethical ambivalence of informal power: informal power can be oligarchic, and sometimes indignation can destabilize equality and consolidate inequality (TTP 20.31, III/244). Even social movements of a more egalitarian aspiration (such as the English effort to eliminate the monarchy) can be destructive and inefficacious (Chapter 8, Section 8.2). Nonetheless, from a Spinozist perspective, if a sovereign is unconstrained except by its own good judgement, then the risk of its rule straying from the state's fundamental principles is very troubling.[61] As he asserts, it is necessary

> to set up a state, so that everyone—both those who rule and those who are ruled—does what's for the common well-being, whether they want to or not. That is, it's been necessary to set it up so that everyone is compelled to

[61] Equally, consider La Boétie's pyramidical structure. La Boétie himself is interested in tyrannical states (states not oriented to the common good), but it is entirely conceivable that his pyramidical structure could be deployed for the sake of the common good. For instance, in the face of principal-agent problems, some bureaucratic structures institute a chain of command, in which each individual is answerable to a superior who enforces the conduct of that individual, through motivation of the incentives that the individual faces. In such a model, the direction of action is determined from the top, and collective pressure on the pyramidical structure is viewed as negative and distorting. From my Spinozist point of view, the concern is that the decision-maker at the top will face difficulty in staying focussed on common good when not constrained to do so.

> live according to the prescription of reason, whether of his own accord, or by force, or by necessity. (TP 6.3; see also 1.6)

The force and necessity in question are not merely the pressure of formal institutions such as the body of syndics: the possibility of parts of the populace rising up is a key limit to the discretion of rulers.[62] If the fundamental laws of a monarchy 'can't be undermined without arousing the indignation of the greatest part of an armed multitude' (TP 7.2), this makes them firm and secure. However, given the normative ambivalence of mass indignation, it is a non-trivial question how to ensure that popular indignation is well directed.

To answer this question, I develop a distinction between two kinds of informal collectivities. The first kind finds its exemplar in Hobbes. In Hobbes's model, power blocs are generated by everyone seeking to placate and propitiate the more powerful, for hope of benefit or avoidance of harm, resulting in pervasive hierarchical dependency. That is, people pursue patronage of the powerful for the pure reason of their apparent power. Power blocs so formed certainly distort both the equality of interests and everyone's good judgement. However, from a Spinozist point of view, Hobbes's model is not universal. Rather, it is a form of association generated by pervasive fear and insecurity. When Hobbes himself identifies a 'perpetuall and restless desire of Power after power [*Potentiam unam post aliam*]' as a 'generall inclination of all mankind', he analyses its basis as follows:

> [T]he cause of this, is not alwayes that a man hopes for a more intensive delight, than he has already attained to; or that he cannot be content with a moderate power: but because he cannot assure the power and means to live well, which he hath present, without the acquisition of more. (L 150–151, 11.2)

[62] See Hasana Sharp, 'Family Quarrels and Mental Harmony: Spinoza's *Oikos-Polis* Analogy', in *Spinoza's 'Political Treatise': A Critical Guide*, edited by Yitzhak Melamed and Hasana Sharp (Cambridge: Cambridge University Press, 2018), 93–110; Saar, 'The Immanence of Power', 19–21. Interestingly, the positive role for informal resistance does not apply to all regimes: Spinoza is very hostile to guild activity and mass assembly within aristocracies (TP 8.4–5, 8.46). For the fundamental laws of aristocracy include the total political disempowerment of the commoners, in contrast to Spinoza's monarchy, which is essentially a system of democratic equality. Popular resistance supports only an egalitarian fundamental law, not an aristocratic one. Within an aristocratic regime, informal resistance and indignation are only welcomed from within the ranks of the patriciate. See Field, 'Political Power'.

But in Spinoza's view, anxiety is a feature of certain institutional orders, and not an existential condition of humanity. A good political structure (such as the good monarchy and aristocracy discussed previously) achieves gross political stability, but just as important, it secures equality amongst its citizens by blocking oligarchic influences from policy decisions. Living in such a state, subjects can be confident that their community will be ruled more or less for the public good, and need not be so anxious for the future. Consequently, they are less driven to affiliate with power blocs for their own sake. From a rational-strategic point of view, there is less to gain by currying favour with oligarchs; and affectively, the disabling epistemic effects of fear are reduced, diminishing subjects' tendency to throw themselves into the hands of charismatic saviours.[63]

This is not to say that a secure society lacks inner collective structure. Humans always depend on one another and tend to associate together. When groupings are not driven by Hobbesian anxiety for the future, but rather, emerge within a secure equal social order, then we have the second kind of informal collectivity: rooted less in instrumental relations of oligarchic dependency and more in deeper forms of human connection. Groups form amongst those with common interests, common faith, geographical proximity, or shared difficulties in life. Such groups, should they see problems with the political decisions being made, have power to put pressure on the holder of sovereignty. But because the perverse incentives for groups to build up beyond their 'natural' shape for the sake of capturing political power are eliminated, and because group members by and large recognize the role of the state in providing their security, there can be greater confidence that the pressure of such groups will constitute a legitimate constraint to sovereign power rather than an oligarchic threat of capturing it. Oligarchy is avoided not, as Hobbes recommends, by attacking collective power per se, but by undercutting its pernicious forms. This is reflected in Spinoza's positive attitude towards the very same power blocs in society that for Hobbes are deeply troublesome. So long as the citizens are confident the state serves the common good, and so long as religious groupings do not have access to governmental power, they can be allowed to flourish (TTP 18.22–26, III/

[63] Steinberg emphasizes the ethically rich meaning of *securitas* in Spinoza's politics (*Spinoza's Political Psychology*, 74–92). Rosenthal provides a Spinozist reconstruction of how affects of fear and ambition combine to generate intolerance, and how fear provides a fertile ground for the formation of power blocs (Rosenthal, 'Spinoza's Republican Argument', 321–326). Sharp argues that political fear erodes democracy. Hasana Sharp, 'Why Spinoza Today? or, 'a Strategy of Anti-Fear,'' *Rethinking Marxism 17*, no. 4 (2005): 591–608).

225–226, 20.40–41, III/246; TP 6.40; contrast L 732–735, 39.5); so long as citizens are confident that the state serves the common good, the power of cities can be viewed not as a threat but as a guard of freedom (TP 7.16–17, 6.9; contrast L 516–517, 29.21).

To be clear, the distinction between good and bad informal pressure on sovereign decision is not a distinction of politeness or civility. The criterion is whether the effects of the pressure support the fundamental principles of popular power. As Machiavelli insists, it may be that riotous and unruly forms of collective action sometimes serve this purpose well; as Spinoza remarks, democracies, like families, can be marked by frequent and bitter quarrels (TP 6.4). My point is that it is important to be alert in case conflict is not having this good effect, and to ascertain what the determinate causes of this failure might be.

In sum, a state expressing neo-Spinozist popular power is one that maintains its fundamental principle of political equality and participation. Achieving this outcome will require careful institutional design to eliminate creeping oligarchy and exclusionary tendencies. My Spinozist model of civic strengthening achieves these goals by embracing and cultivating the collective capacity of subjects to raise civic resistance to governmental plans, both through formal and informal channels. For counterpowers help to ensure that the democratic representative assembly more reliably maintains fundamental principles of popular power.

9.5. Conclusion

I opened this book by laying out two prevalent conceptions of popular power, both trying to give expression to a 'constituent power', conceived as the ground of legitimacy of the constituted forms of established institutional politics. Whether celebrating the neo-Hobbesian sleeping sovereign of plebiscitary democracy, or the neo-Spinozist free multitude of social movements, contemporary thinkers of constituent power oppose the oligarchic capture of this power by the state. However, I have argued that this emphatic opposition to the state comes at the cost of failing to recognize the non-state sources of oligarchy and domination, including their capture of plebiscitary votes and their spontaneous emergence within human social life, and the possible role of the state in mitigating these problems.

I have argued that whether and to what degree political phenomena express popular power must be judged at the level of the characteristic effects of a given political system. The determinate causes of these characteristic effects includes the full gamut of institutional and organizational structures, including both the formal and informal human collectivities that dwell within them. Plebiscites and social movements may play a positive role, but they are not in themselves the exemplary expression of popular power. Rather, the exemplar of popular power is a political system, taken as a whole, that durably achieves equality and participation for its citizens.

Bibliography

Primary Sources

See front matter for abbreviations and citation conventions.

Hobbes, Thomas. 'Of Liberty and Necessity: A Treatise'. In *The English Works of Thomas Hobbes of Malmesbury*, Vol. 4, edited by William Molesworth (London: John Bohn, 1839).

Hobbes, Thomas. 'On Man'. In *Man and Citizen*, edited by Bernard Gert (Indianapolis: Hackett, 1991), 33–86.

Hobbes, Thomas. 'A Short Tract on First Principles'. In *The Elements of Law, Natural and Politic*, edited by Ferdinand Tönnies (London: Frank Cass, 1984), 193–210.

Hobbes, Thomas. *Behemoth, or The Long Parliament*, edited by Paul Seaward (Oxford: Clarendon Press, 2014).

Hobbes, Thomas. *Critique du De Mundo de Thomas White* (Paris: Vrin, 1973).

Hobbes, Thomas. *De Cive*, edited by Howard Warrender (Oxford: Clarendon Press, 1983).

Hobbes, Thomas. *The Elements of Law, Natural and Politic*, edited by Ferdinand Tönnies (London: Frank Cass, 1984).

Hobbes, Thomas. *The English Works of Thomas Hobbes of Malmesbury*, edited by William Molesworth (London: John Bohn, 1839).

Hobbes, Thomas. *Leviathan*, edited by Noel Malcolm (Oxford: Clarendon Press, 2014).

Hobbes, Thomas. *Leviathan: With Selected Variants from the Latin Edition of 1668*, edited by Edwin Curley (Indianapolis: Hackett, 1994).

Hobbes, Thomas. *On the Citizen*, edited and translated by Richard Tuck and Michael Silverthorne (Cambridge: Cambridge University Press, 2014).

Hobbes, Thomas. *Thomæ Hobbes Malmesburiensis Opera philosophica quæ latine scripsit omnia*, edited by William Molesworth (London: John Bohn, 1839).

Hobbes, Thomas. *Thomas White's De Mundo Examined*, translated by Harold Whitmore Jones (London: Bradford University Press, 1976).

Spinoza, Benedictus de. *The Collected Works of Spinoza*, translated by Edwin Curley (Princeton, NJ: Princeton University Press, 1985, 2016).

Spinoza, Benedictus de. *Spinoza Opera*, edited by Carl Gebhardt (Heidelberg: Carl Winter, 1972).

Spinoza, Benedictus de. *A Spinoza Reader: The 'Ethics' and Other Works*, translated and edited by Edwin Curley (Princeton, NJ: Princeton University Press, 1994).

Secondary Sources

Abizadeh, Arash. 'Hobbes on the Causes of War: A Disagreement Theory'. *American Political Science Review 105*, no. 2 (2011): 298–315.

Abizadeh, Arash. 'Publicity, Privacy, and Toleration in Hobbes's *Leviathan*'. *Modern Intellectual History 10*, no. 2 (2013): 261–291.

Abizadeh, Arash. 'The Representation of Hobbesian Sovereignty: Leviathan as Mythology'. In *Hobbes Today: Insights for the 21st Century*, edited by S. A. Lloyd (New York: Cambridge University Press, 2013), 113–154.

Ackerman, Bruce. *We the People: Foundations* (Cambridge, MA: Belknap Press, 1991).

Althusser, Louis. *Essays in Self-Criticism*, translated by Grahame Lock (London: NLB, 1976).

Amar, Akhil Reed. 'Philadelphia Revisited: Amending the Constitution outside Article V'. *University of Chicago Law Review 55*, no. 4 (1988): 1043–1104.

Anderson, Elizabeth S. 'What Is the Point of Equality?' *Ethics 109*, no. 2 (1999): 287–337.

Aquinas, St. Thomas. *Summa Theologica: Complete English Edition in Five Volumes*, translated by Fathers of the English Dominican Province (Notre Dame, IN: Christian Classics, 1981).

Arendt, Hannah. *Eichmann in Jerusalem: A Report on the Banality of Evil* (New York: Penguin Classics, 2006).

Armstrong, Aurelia. 'Natural and Unnatural Communities: Spinoza beyond Hobbes'. *British Journal for the History of Philosophy 17*, no. 2 (2009): 279–305.

Astorga, Omar. 'Hobbes's Concept of Multitude'. *Hobbes Studies 24* (2011): 5–14.

Balibar, Étienne. 'Potentia Multitudinis, Quae Una Veluti Mente Ducitur'. In *Current Continental Theory and Modern Philosophy*, edited by Stephen H. Daniel (Evanston, IL: Northwestern University Press, 2005), 70–99.

Balibar, Étienne. *Spinoza: From Individuality to Transindividuality* (Delft: Eburon, 1997).

Balibar, Étienne. 'Spinoza, the Anti-Orwell: The Fear of the Masses'. *Rethinking Marxism 2*, no. 3 (1989): 104–139.

Balibar, Étienne. *Spinoza and Politics*, translated by Peter Snowdon (New York: Verso, 1998).

Barbone, Stephen. 'Power in the *Tractatus Theologico-Politicus*'. In *Piety, Peace and the Freedom to Philosophize*, edited by Paul J. Bagley (Dordrecht: Kluwer, 2000), 91–109.

Barbone, Stephen and Rice, Lee. 'Introduction'. In Benedictus de Spinoza, *Political Treatise* (Indianapolis: Hackett, 2000), 1–30.

Baumgold, Deborah. *Hobbes's Political Theory* (Cambridge: Cambridge University Press, 1988).

Bejan, Teresa. 'Teaching the Leviathan: Thomas Hobbes on Education', *Oxford Review of Education 36*, no. 5 (2010): 607–626.

Brandt, Frithiof. *Thomas Hobbes's Mechanical Conception of Nature* (Copenhagen: Levin & Munksgaard, 1928).

Brett, Annabel. '"The Matter, Forme, and Power of a Common-wealth": Thomas Hobbes and Late Renaissance Commentary on Aristotle's Politics'. *Hobbes Studies 23* (2010): 72–102.

Buchholz, Robert and Key, Newton. *Early Modern England, 1485–1714: A Narrative History*, 2nd ed. (Malden, MA: Wiley-Blackwell, 2009).

Campos, Andre Santos. 'The Individuality of the State in Spinoza's Political Philosophy'. *Archiv für Geschichte der Philosophie 92* (2010): 1–38.

Carmichael, D. J. C. 'C. B. Macpherson's "Hobbes": A Critique'. In *Thomas Hobbes: Critical Assessments*, Vol. 1, edited by Preston King (London: Routledge, 1993), 359–379.

Carmichael, D. J. C. 'Reply: Macpherson versus the Text of *Leviathan*'. In *Thomas Hobbes: Critical Assessments*, Vol. 1, edited by Preston King (London: Routledge, 1993), 390–392.

Chew, Melanie. *Leaders of Singapore* (Singapore: Resource Press, 1996).

Christov, Theodore. *Before Anarchy: Hobbes and His Critics in Modern International Thought* (New York: Cambridge University Press, 2015).

Chua Beng Huat. *Liberalism Disavowed: Communitarianism and State Capitalism in Singapore* (Singapore: NUS Press, 2017).

Chua Beng Huat. 'Towards a Non-liberal Communitarian Democracy'. In *Communitarian Ideology and Democracy in Singapore* (New York: Routledge, 2006), 184–202.

Collins, Jeffrey R. *The Allegiance of Thomas Hobbes* (Oxford: Oxford University Press, 2005).

Colon-Rios, Joel. 'The Legitimacy of the Juridical: Constituent Power and Democratic Reform'. *Osgoode Hall Law Journal 48*, no. 2 (2010): 199–245.

Corbin, Thomas Alexander. 'The Role of Counsel in Hobbes's Political Thought'. MRes thesis (Macquarie University, 2016).

Cox, Virginia. 'The Single Self: Feminist Thought and the Marriage Market in Early Modern Venice'. *Renaissance Quarterly 48*, no. 3 (1995): 513–581.

Curley, Edwin. 'Kissinger, Spinoza, and Genghis Khan'. In *The Cambridge Companion to Spinoza*, edited by Don Garrett (New York: Cambridge University Press, 1996), 315–342.

Curran, Eleanor. *Reclaiming the Rights of the Hobbesian subject* (New York: Palgrave Macmillan, 2007).

Davis, Mark. 'A Snip at $22m to Get Rid of PM'. *Sydney Morning Herald*, 2 February 2011.

Del Lucchese, Filippo. *Conflict, Power, and Multitude in Machiavelli and Spinoza: Tumult and Indignation* (New York: Continuum, 2009).

Del Lucchese, Filippo. 'The Revolutionary Foundation of Political Modernity: Machiavelli, Spinoza, and Constituent Power'. In *Spinoza's 'Political Treatise': A Critical Guide*, edited by Yitzhak Y. Melamed and Hasana Sharp (Cambridge: Cambridge University Press, 2018), 190–203.

Del Lucchese, Filippo. 'Spinoza and Constituent Power'. *Contemporary Political Theory 15*, no. 2 (2015): 184–204.

Deleuze, Gilles. *Expressionism in Philosophy: Spinoza*, translated by Martin Joughin (New York: Zone Books, 1992).

Deleuze, Gilles. 'Preface à *L'anomalie sauvage* de Negri'. In *L'anomalie sauvage* (Paris: Presses universitaires de France, 1982).

Della Rocca, Michael. *Spinoza* (New York: Routledge, 2008).

Den Uyl, Douglas J. *Power, State, and Freedom: An Interpretation of Spinoza's Political Philosophy* (Assen, The Netherlands: Van Gorcum, 1983).

Des Chene, Dennis. *Physiologia: Natural Philosophy in Late Aristotelian and Cartesian Philosophy* (Ithaca, NJ: Cornell University Press, 1996).

Descartes, René. 'Discourse on the Method of Rightly Conducting One's Reason and Seeking the Truth in the Sciences'. In *The Philosophical Writings of Descartes*, Vol. 1 (Cambridge: Cambridge University Press, 1984).

Descartes, René. 'The Passions of the Soul'. In *The Philosophical Writings of Descartes*, Vol. 1 (Cambridge: Cambridge University Press, 1984).

Descartes, René. 'The Principles of Philosophy'. In *The Philosophical Writings of Descartes*, Vol. 1 (Cambridge: Cambridge University Press, 1984).

Dietz, Mary G. 'Hobbes's Subject as Citizen'. In *Thomas Hobbes and Political Theory*, edited by Mary G. Dietz (Lawrence: University Press of Kansas, 1990), 91–119.

Duffy, Simon. 'The Joyful Passions in Spinoza's Theory of Relations'. In *Spinoza Now* edited by Dimitris Vardoulakis (Minneapolis: University of Minnesota Press, 2011), 51–64.

Dussel, Enrique. *Twenty Theses on Politics*, translated by George Cicciarello-Maher (Durham, NC: Duke University Press, 2008).

Evrigenis, Ioannis D. *Images of Anarchy: The Rhetoric and Science in Hobbes's State of Nature* (New York: Cambridge University Press, 2014).

Feuer, Lewis Samuel. *Spinoza and the Rise of Liberalism* (Boston: Beacon Press, 1958).

Field, Sandra Leonie. 'Democracy and the Multitude: Spinoza against Negri'. *Theoria 59*, no. 131 (2012): 21–40.

Field, Sandra Leonie. 'Political Power and Depoliticised Acquiescence: Spinoza and Aristocracy'. *Constellations 27*, no. 1 (2020). https://doi.org/10.1111/1467-8675.12486.

Fishkin, James S. *When the People Speak: Deliberative Democracy and Public Consultation* (Oxford: Oxford University Press, 2011).

Forsyth, Murray. 'Thomas Hobbes and the Constituent Power of the People'. *Political Studies 29*, no. 2 (1981): 191–203.

Freeman, Jo. 'The Tyranny of Structurelessness'. *Berkeley Journal of Sociology 17* (1972): 151–164.

Freudenthal, Jacob. *Die Lebensgeschichte Spinoza's in Quellenschriften, Urkunden und Nichtamtlichen Nachrichten* (Leipzig: Verlag von Veit & Comp., 1899).

Friedle, Simon. 'Thomas Hobbes and the Reception of Early-Modern Epicureanism'. PhD dissertation (University of Cambridge, 2012).

Frost, Samantha. *Lessons from a Materialist Thinker: Hobbesian Reflections on Ethics and Politics* (Stanford, CA: Stanford University Press, 2008).

Gandhi, M. K. *Hind Swaraj and Other Writings*, Centenary ed., edited by Anthony J. Parel (Cambridge: Cambridge University Press, 2014).

Garber, Daniel. 'Descartes and Spinoza on Persistence and Conatus'. *Studia Spinozana 10: Spinoza and Descartes* (1994): 43–67.

Garber, Daniel. 'Natural Philosophy in Seventeenth-Century Context'. In *The Oxford Handbook of Hobbes*, edited by A. Martinich and Kinch Hoekstra (Oxford: Oxford University Press, 2016), 107–130.

Garrett, Don. 'Representation and Consciousness in Spinoza's Naturalistic Theory of the Imagination'. In *Interpreting Spinoza*, edited by Charles Huenemann (Cambridge: Cambridge University Press, 2008), 267–314.

Garrett, Don. 'Spinoza's Conatus Argument'. In *Spinoza: Metaphysical Themes*, edited by Olli Koistinen and J. I. Biro (Oxford: Oxford University Press, 2002), 127–156.

Garrett, Don. 'Teleology in Spinoza and Early Modern Rationalism'. In *New Essays on the Rationalists*, edited by Rocco J. Gennaro and Charles Huenemann (Oxford: Oxford University Press, 2003).

Garsten, Bryan. *Saving Persuasion: A Defense of Rhetoric and Judgment* (Cambridge, MA: Harvard University Press, 2006).

Gatens, Moira. *Imaginary Bodies: Ethics, Power, and Corporeality* (New York: Routledge, 1996).

Gatens, Moira. 'Spinoza's Disturbing Thesis: Power, Norms and Fiction in the *Tractatus Theologico-Politicus*'. *History of Political Thought 30*, no. 3 (2009): 455–468.

George, Cherian. *Freedom from the Press: Journalism and State Power in Singapore* (Singapore: NUS Press, 2012).

Goldsmith, M. M. *Hobbes's Science of Politics* (New York: Columbia University Press, 1966).

Gourevitch, Alex and Stanczyk, Lucas. 'The Basic Income Illusion'. *Catalyst 1*, no. 4 (2017): 151–178.

Haitsma Mulier, Eco O. G. *The Myth of Venice and Dutch Republican Thought in the Seventeenth Century*, translated by Gerard T. Moran (Assen, The Netherlands: Van Gorcum, 1980).

Hampton, Jean. *Hobbes and the Social Contract Tradition* (Cambridge: Cambridge University Press, 1986).

Hardt, Michael. 'Translator's Foreword: The Anatomy of Power'. In *The Savage Anomaly* (Minneapolis: University of Minnesota Press, 1991), xi–xvi.

Hardt, Michael and Negri, Antonio. *Assembly* (New York: Oxford University Press, 2017).

Hardt, Michael and Negri, Antonio. *Commonwealth* (Cambridge, MA: Belknap Press, 2009).

Hardt, Michael and Negri, Antonio. *Empire* (Cambridge, MA: Harvard University Press, 2000).

Hardt, Michael and Negri, Antonio. *Multitude: War and Democracy in the Age of Empire* (New York: Penguin Press, 2004).

Havercroft, Jonathan. *Captives of Sovereignty* (Cambridge: Cambridge University Press, 2011).

Hindess, Barry. *Discourses of Power: From Hobbes to Foucault* (Oxford: Blackwell, 1996).

Hoekstra, Kinch. 'The *De Facto* Turn in Hobbes's Political Philosophy'. In *Leviathan after 350 Years*, edited by Tom Sorell and Luc Foisneau (Oxford: Clarendon Press, 2004), 33–73.

Hoekstra, Kinch. 'Early Modern Absolutism and Constitutionalism'. *Cardozo Law Review 34*, no. 3 (2013): 1079–1098.

Hoekstra, Kinch. 'Hobbesian Equality'. In *Hobbes Today: Insights for the 21st Century*, edited by S. A. Lloyd (New York: Cambridge University Press, 2013), 76–112.

Hoekstra, Kinch. 'A Lion in the House: Hobbes and Democracy'. In *Rethinking the Foundations of Modern Political Thought*, edited by Annabel Brett, James Tully, and Holly Hamilton-Bleakley (Cambridge: Cambridge University Press, 2006), 191–218.

Holland, Eugene. 'Spinoza and Marx', *Cultural Logic 2*, no. 1 (1998), 1–17.

Hull, Gordon. 'Hobbes's Radical Nominalism', *Epoché 11* (2006): 201–223.

Israel, Jonathan. *Radical Enlightenment: Philosophy and the Making of Modernity, 1650–1750* (Oxford: Oxford University Press, 2001).

Israel, Jonathan. *A Revolution of the Mind: Radical Enlightenment and the Intellectual Origins of Modern Democracy* (Princeton, NJ: Princeton University Press, 2010).

James, Susan. 'Democracy and the Good Life in Spinoza's Philosophy'. In *Interpreting Spinoza: Critical Essays*, edited by Charles Huenemann (New York: Cambridge University Press, 2008), 128–146.

James, Susan. 'Politically Mediated Affects: Envy in Spinoza's "Tractatus Politicus"'. In *Spinoza's 'Political Treatise': A Critical Guide*, edited by Yitzhak Melamed and Hasana Sharp (Cambridge: Cambridge University Press, 2018), 61–77.

James, Susan. *Spinoza on Philosophy, Religion and Politics: The Theologico-Political Treatise* (Oxford: Oxford University Press, 2012).

Johnston, David. *The Rhetoric of 'Leviathan': Thomas Hobbes and the Politics of Cultural Transformation* (Princeton, NJ: Princeton University Press, 1986).

Kavka, Gregory S. *Hobbesian Moral and Political Theory* (Princeton, NJ: Princeton University Press, 1986).

Kisner, Matthew J. *Spinoza on Human Freedom* (Cambridge: Cambridge University Press, 2011).

La Boétie, Étienne de. 'Discourse on Voluntary Servitude'. In *Michel de Montaigne: Selected Essays* (Indianapolis: Hackett, 2012), 284–312.

Lazzeri, Christian. *Droit, pouvoir et liberté: Spinoza critique de Hobbes* (Paris: Presses universitaires de France, 1998).

Lee, Daniel. *Popular Sovereignty in Early Modern Constitutional Thought* (Oxford: Oxford University Press, 2016).

Leijenhorst, Cees. *The Mechanisation of Aristotelianism: The Late Aristotelian Setting of Thomas Hobbes' Natural Philosophy* (Leiden: Brill, 2002).

Leijenhorst, Cees. 'Sense and Nonsense about Sense: Hobbes and the Aristotelians on Sense Perception and Imagination'. In *The Cambridge Companion to Hobbes's 'Leviathan'*, edited by Patricia Springborg (Cambridge: Cambridge University Press, 2007), 82–108.

Lévinas, Emmanuel. 'Le cas Spinoza'. In *Difficile liberté: Essais sur le judaïsme* (Paris: A. Michel, 1976), 142–147.

Lloyd, Genevieve. *Part of Nature: Self-Knowledge in Spinoza's 'Ethics'* (Ithaca, NY: Cornell University Press, 1994).

Lord, Beth. 'The Concept of Equality in Spinoza's Theological-Political Treatise', *Epoché 20*, no. 2 (2016): 367–386.

Lord, Beth. 'Spinoza, Equality, and Hierarchy', *History of Philosophy Quarterly 31*, no. 1 (2014): 59–77.

Lordon, Frédéric. *Willing Slaves of Capital: Spinoza and Marx on Desire*, translated by Gabriel Ash (London: Verso, 2014).

Lotringer, Sylvère. 'Introduction'. In *A Grammar of the Multitude: For an Analysis of Contemporary Forms of Life*, edited by Paolo Virno (Los Angeles: Semiotext(e), 2004), 7–20.

Macherey, Pierre. 'Préface à *L'anomalie sauvage*, de Negri: "Spinoza présent"'. In *L'anomalie sauvage* (Paris: Presses universitaires de France, 1982).

Machiavelli, Niccolò. *Discourses on Livy*, translated by Harvey Claflin Mansfield and Nathan Tarcov (Chicago: University of Chicago Press, 1996).

Machiavelli, Niccolò. *Florentine Histories*, translated by Laura F. Banfield and Harvey C. Mansfield (Princeton, NJ: Princeton University Press, 1988).

MacKenzie, Michael K. 'A General-Purpose, Randomly Selected Chamber'. In *Institutions for Future Generations*, edited by Iñigo González-Ricoy and Axel Gosseries (Oxford: Oxford University Press, 2016), 282–298.

Macpherson, C. B. 'Introduction'. In *Leviathan*, edited by C. B. Macpherson (London: Penguin, 1985), 9–63.

Macpherson, C. B. 'Leviathan Restored: A Reply to Carmichael'. In *Thomas Hobbes: Critical Assessments*, Vol. 1, edited by Preston King (London: Routledge, 1993), 380–389.

Macpherson, C. B. *The Political Theory of Possessive Individualism: Hobbes to Locke* (Oxford: Clarendon Press, 1962).

Malcolm, Noel. 'Hobbes and Spinoza'. In *Aspects of Hobbes* (Oxford: Oxford University Press, 2002), 27–52.

Malcolm, Noel. 'Hobbes's Science of Politics and His Theory of Science'. In *Aspects of Hobbes* (Oxford: Clarendon Press, 2002), 146–155.

Manekin, Charles Harry. 'Spinoza and the Determinist Tradition in Medieval Jewish Philosophy'. In *Spinoza and Medieval Jewish Philosophy*, edited by Steven Nadler (Cambridge: Cambridge University Press, 2014), 36–58.

Martel, James R. *Subverting the Leviathan: Reading Thomas Hobbes as a Radical Democrat* (New York: Columbia University Press, 2007).

Martinich, A. P. *Hobbes: A Biography* (Cambridge: Cambridge University Press, 1999).

Marx, Karl. 'Contribution to the Critique of Hegel's *Philosophy of Right*: Introduction'. In *The Marx-Engels Reader*, edited by Robert C. Tucker (New York: Norton, 1978), 53–65.

Matheron, Alexandre. *Individu et communauté chez Spinoza* (Paris: Éditions de Minuit, 1988).

Matheron, Alexandre. 'Le 'droit du plus fort': Hobbes contre Spinoza'. In *Études sur Spinoza et les philosophies de l'âge classique* (Lyon: ENS Éditions, 2011), 131–154.

Matheron, Alexandre. 'Maîtres et serviteurs dans la philosophie politique classique'. In *Études sur Spinoza et les philosophies de l'âge classique* (Lyon: ENS Éditions, 2011), 267–286.

Matheron, Alexandre. 'Preface à L'anomalie sauvage de Negri'. In *L'anomalie sauvage* (Paris: Presses Universitaires de France, 1982).

Matheron, Alexandre. 'Spinoza et la décomposition de la politique thomiste: Machiavélisme et utopie'. In *Études sur Spinoza et les philosophies de l'âge classique* (Paris: ENS Éditions, 2011), 81–112.

Matheron, Alexandre. 'The Theoretical Function of Democracy in Spinoza and Hobbes'. In *The New Spinoza*, edited by Warren Montag and Ted Stolze (Minneapolis: University of Minnesota Press, 1998), 207–217.

May, Larry. *Limiting Leviathan: Hobbes on Law and International Affairs* (Oxford: Oxford University Press, 2013).

McCormick, John P. 'Machiavellian Democracy: Controlling Elites with Ferocious Populism'. *American Journal of Political Science* 95, no. 2 (2001): 297–313.

McNeilly, F. S. *The Anatomy of Leviathan* (London: Macmillan; New York: St. Martin's Press, 1968).

Melamed, Yitzhak. 'Acosmism or Weak Individuals? Hegel, Spinoza, and the Reality of the Finite'. *Journal of the History of Philosophy* 48, no. 1 (2010): 77–92.

Melamed, Yitzhak. 'Charitable Interpretations and the Political Domestication of Spinoza, or, Benedict in the Land of the Secular Imagination'. In *Philosophy and Its History: Aims and Methods in the Study of Early Modern Philosophy*, edited by Justin Smith, Mogens Laerke, and Eric Schliesser (Oxford: Oxford University Press, 2013), 258–277.

Melamed, Yitzhak. 'Spinoza's Metaphysics of Substance: The Substance-Mode Relation as a Relation of Inherence and Predication'. *Philosophy and Phenomenological Research 78*, no. 1 (2009): 17–82.

Melamed, Yitzhak. 'Teleology in Jewish Philosophy: Early Talmudists Till Spinoza'. In *Teleology: A History*, edited by Jeff McDonough (Oxford: Oxford University Press, 2020).

Melamed, Yitzhak. 'When Having Too Much Power Is Harmful? Spinoza on Political Luck'. In *Spinoza's 'Political Treatise': A Critical Guide*, edited by Yitzhak Y. Melamed and Hasana Sharp (Cambridge: Cambridge University Press, 2018), 161–174.

Moller Okin, Susan. '"The Soveraign and His Counsellours": Hobbes's Reevaluation of Parliament'. In *Thomas Hobbes: Critical Assessments*, Vol. 3, edited by Preston King (London: Routledge, 1993), 787–810.

Montag, Warren. *Bodies, Masses, Power: Spinoza and His Contemporaries* (New York: Verso, 1999).

Mugnier-Pollet, Lucien. *La philosophie politique de Spinoza* (Paris: Vrin, 1976).

Nadler, Steven. *A Book Forged in Hell: Spinoza's Scandalous Treatise and the Birth of the Secular Age* (Princeton, NJ: Princeton University Press, 2013).

Nadler, Steven. 'Doctrines of Explanation in Late Scholasticism and in the Mechanical Philosophy'. In *The Cambridge History of Seventeenth-Century Philosophy*, edited by Daniel Garber and Michael Ayers (Cambridge: Cambridge University Press, 1998), 513–552.

Nadler, Steven. *Spinoza: A Life* (Cambridge: Cambridge University Press, 1999).

Nadler, Steven. *Spinoza's 'Ethics': An Introduction* (Cambridge University Press: Cambridge, 2006).

Negri, Antonio. 'Democracy and Eternity in Spinoza'. In *Subversive Spinoza: (Un)contemporary Variations*, edited by Timothy S. Murphy (Manchester: Manchester University Press, 2004), 101–112.

Negri, Antonio. 'Prefazione all'edizione italiana'. In Crawford B. MacPherson, *Libertà e proprietà alle origini del pensiero borghese: La teoria dell'individualismo possessivo da Hobbes a Locke* (Milan: Istituto Editoriale Internazionale Milano, 1961), 13–22.

Negri, Antonio. 'The *Political Treatise*, or, the Foundation of Modern Democracy'. In *Subversive Spinoza: (Un)contemporary Variations*, edited Timothy S. Murphy (Manchester: Manchester University Press, 2004), 9–27.

Negri, Antonio. '*Reliqua Desiderantur*: A Conjecture for a Definition of the Concept of Democracy in the Final Spinoza'. In *The New Spinoza*, edited by Warren Montag and Ted Stolze (Minneapolis: University of Minnesota Press, 1998), 219–247.

Negri, Antonio. *The Savage Anomaly: The Power of Spinoza's Metaphysics and Politics*, translated by Michael Hardt (Minneapolis: University of Minnesota Press, 1991).

Nesbitt, Nick. *Universal Emancipation: The Haitian Revolution and the Radical Enlightenment* (Charlottesville: University of Virginia Press, 2008).

Oakeshott, Michael. 'Introduction to *Leviathan*'. In *Rationalism in Politics and Other Essays* (Indianapolis: Liberty Press, 1991), 221–294.

Paganini, Gianni. 'Hobbes's Critique of the Doctrine of Essences and Its Sources'. In *The Cambridge Companion to Hobbes's 'Leviathan'*, edited by Patricia Springborg (Cambridge: Cambridge University Press, 2007), 337–357.

Paul, Joanne. 'Counsel, Command and Crisis'. *Hobbes Studies 28* (2015): 103–131.

Pettit, Philip. *Made with Words: Hobbes on Language, Mind, and Politics* (Princeton, NJ: Princeton University Press, 2008).

Price, J. L. *The Dutch Republic in the Seventeenth Century* (New York: St. Martin's Press, 1998).

Prins, J. 'Hobbes and the School of Padua: Two Incompatible Approaches of Science'. *Archiv für Geschichte der Philosophie 72*, no. 1 (1990): 26–47.

Prokhovnik, Raia. *Spinoza and Republicanism* (Houndmills: Palgrave Macmillan, 2004).

Qudrat, Maryam. 'Confronting Jihad: A Defect in the Hobbesian Educational Strategy'. In *Hobbes Today: Insights for the 21st Century*, edited by S. A. Lloyd (New York: Cambridge University Press, 2013), 229–240.

Rawls, John. *Political Liberalism, with a New Introduction and the 'Reply to Habermas'* (New York: Columbia University Press, 1996).
Rawls, John. *A Theory of Justice*, rev. ed. (Cambridge, MA: Belknap, 1999).
Read, James H. 'Thomas Hobbes: Power in the State of Nature, Power in Civil Society'. *Polity 23*, no. 4 (1991): 505–525.
Rosenthal, Michael A. 'The Siren Song of Revolution: Spinoza on the Art of Political Change'. *Graduate Faculty Philosophy Journal 34*, no. 1 (2013): 111–132.
Rosenthal, Michael A. 'Spinoza's Political Philosophy'. In *The Oxford Handbook of Spinoza*, edited by Michael Della Rocca (New York: Oxford University Press, 2018).
Rosenthal, Michael A. 'Spinoza's Republican Argument for Toleration'. *Journal of Political Philosophy 11*, no. 3 (2003): 320–337.
Rosenthal, Michael A. 'What Is Real about "Ideal Constitutions"? Spinoza on Political Explanation'. In *Spinoza's 'Political Treatise': A Critical Guide*, edited by Yitzhak Melamed and Hasana Sharp (Cambridge: Cambridge University Press, 2018), 12–28.
Rosenthal, Michael A. 'Why Spinoza Chose the Hebrews: The Exemplary Function of Prophecy in the *Theological-Political Treatise*'. *History of Political Thought 18*, no. 2 (1997): 207–241.
Rousseau, Jean-Jacques. *On the Social Contract*, translated by Donald A. Cress (Indianapolis: Hackett, 1987).
Rudolph, Ross. 'Conflict, Egoism and Power in Hobbes'. *History of Political Thought 7*, no. 1 (1986): 73–88.
Rudolph, Ross. 'The Microfoundations of Hobbes's Political Theory', *Hobbes Studies 4*, no. 1 (1991): 34–52.
Saar, Martin. 'The Immanence of Power: From Spinoza to "Radical Democracy"'. *Mededelingen Vanwege Het Spinozahuis 106* (Uitgeverij Spinozahuis, 2014).
Sanders, Lynn M. 'Against Deliberation'. *Political Theory 25*, no. 3 (1997): 347–376.
Schoneveld, Cornelis W. *Intertraffic of the Mind: Studies in Seventeenth-Century Anglo-Dutch Translation* (Leiden: Brill, 1983).
Schumpeter, Joseph A. *Capitalism, Socialism and Democracy*, 3rd ed. (New York: Harper Perennial, 2008).
Shapin, Steven and Schaffer, Simon. *Leviathan and the Air-Pump: Hobbes, Boyle, and the Experimental Life* (Princeton, NJ: Princeton University Press, 2011).
Sharp, Hasana. 'Eve's Perfection: Spinoza on Sexual (In)equality'. *Journal of the History of Philosophy 50*, no. 4 (2012): 559–580.
Sharp, Hasana. 'Family Quarrels and Mental Harmony: Spinoza's *Oikos-Polis* Analogy'. In *Spinoza's 'Political Treatise': A Critical Guide*, edited by Yitzhak Melamed and Hasana Sharp (Cambridge: Cambridge University Press, 2018), 93–110.
Sharp, Hasana. *Spinoza and the Politics of Renaturalization* (Chicago: University of Chicago Press, 2011).
Sharp, Hasana. 'Spinoza's Commonwealth and the Anthropomorphic Illusion', *Philosophy Today 61*, no. 4 (2017): 833–846.
Sharp, Hasana. 'Violenta Imperia Nemo Continuit Diu: Spinoza and the Revolutionary Laws of Human Nature', *Graduate Faculty Philosophy Journal 34*, no. 1 (2013): 133–148.
Sharp, Hasana. 'Why Spinoza Today? or, "A Strategy of Anti-fear"', *Rethinking Marxism 17*, no. 4 (2005): 591–608.
Sieyès, Emmanuel Joseph. 'What Is the Third Estate?'. In *Emmanuel Joseph Sieyès: The Essential Political Writings*, edited by Oliver W. Lembcke and Florian Weber (Leiden: Brill, 2014), 43–117.

Silverthorne, Michael. 'Political Terms in the Latin of Thomas Hobbes'. *International Journal of the Classical Tradition 2*, no. 4 (1996): 499–509.

Skinner, Quentin. 'Hobbes on Persons, Authors and Representatives'. In *The Cambridge Companion to Hobbes's 'Leviathan'*, edited by Patricia Springborg (New York: Cambridge University Press, 2007), 157–180.

Skinner, Quentin. *Reason and Rhetoric in the Philosophy of Hobbes* (Cambridge: Cambridge University Press, 1996).

Slomp, Gabriella. 'The Inconvenience of the Legislator's Two Persons and the Role of Good Counsellors'. *Critical Review of International Social and Political Philosophy 19*, no. 1 (2016): 68–85.

Smith, Steven B. 'What Kind of Democrat Was Spinoza?', *Political Theory 33*, no. 1 (2005): 6–27.

Sommerville, Johann P. *Thomas Hobbes: Political Ideas in Historical Context* (Houndmills: Macmillan, 1992).

Sorell, Tom. *Hobbes* (London: Routledge & Kegan Paul, 1986).

Sorell, Tom. 'Law and Equity in Hobbes', *Critical Review of International Social and Political Philosophy 19*, no. 1 (2016): 29–46.

Spragens, Thomas A. *The Politics of Motion; The World of Thomas Hobbes* (Lexington: University Press of Kentucky, 1973).

Springborg, Patricia. *Western Republicanism and the Oriental Prince* (Austin: University of Texas Press, 1992).

Sreedhar, Susanne. *Hobbes on Self-Defence: Defying the Leviathan* (Cambridge: Cambridge University Press, 2010).

Steinberg, Justin D. 'Benedict Spinoza: Epistemic Democrat'. *History of Philosophy Quarterly 27*, no. 2 (2010): 145–164.

Steinberg, Justin D. 'Spinoza on Being *Sui Juris* and the Republican Conception of Liberty'. *History of European Ideas 34* (2008): 239–249.

Steinberg, Justin D. 'Spinoza on Civil Liberation'. *Journal of the History of Philosophy 47*, no. 1 (2009): 35–58.

Steinberg, Justin D. 'Spinoza's Political Philosophy'. *The Stanford Encyclopedia of Philosophy*, Winter 2013 ed., edited by Edward N. Zalta, http://plato.stanford.edu/archives/win2013/entries/spinoza-political/.

Steinberg, Justin D. *Spinoza's Political Psychology* (Cambridge: Cambridge University Press, 2018).

Strauss, Leo. *The Political Philosophy of Hobbes: Its Basis and Its Genesis*, translated by Elsa M. Sinclair (Chicago: University of Chicago Press, 1963).

Tarlton, Charles D. 'The Creation and Maintenance of Government: A Neglected Dimension of Hobbes's *Leviathan*'. *Political Studies 26*, no. 3 (1978): 307–327.

Thum Ping Tjin. 'Living in a Time of Deception', *The History of Singapore*, Podcast Episode 23 (2016), http://thehistoryofsingapore.com, accessed 19 November 2018.

Tronti, Mario. 'The Strategy of Refusal'. *Autonomia: Post-political Politics 3*, no. 3 (1980): 28–35.

Tuck, Richard. *Hobbes* (Oxford: Oxford University Press, 1989).

Tuck, Richard. 'Hobbes and Democracy'. In *Rethinking the Foundations of Modern Political Thought*, edited by Annabel Brett, James Tully, and Holly Hamilton-Bleakley (Cambridge: Cambridge University Press, 2006), 171–190.

Tuck, Richard. 'Introduction'. In *On the Citizen*, edited by Richard Tuck and Michael Silverthorne (Cambridge: Cambridge University Press, 2006), viii–lii.

Tuck, Richard. *The Sleeping Sovereign: The Invention of Modern Democracy* (Cambridge: Cambridge University Press, 2015).

Tucker, Ericka. 'The Multitude'. In *Spinoza: Key Concepts*, edited by André Santos Campos (Exeter: Imprint Academic, 2015), 129–141.

Viljanen, Valtteri. 'Spinoza's Actualist Model of Power'. In *The World as Active Power: Studies in the History of European Reason*, edited by Juhani Pietarinen and Valtteri Viljanen (Leiden: Brill, 2009), 213–228.

Virno, Paolo. *A Grammar of the Multitude: For an Analysis of Contemporary Forms of Life*, translated by Isabella Bertoletti, James Cascaito, and Andrea Casson (Los Angeles; New York: Semiotext(e), 2004).

Walzer, Michael. *Spheres of Justice* (New York: Basic Books, 1983).

Warrender, Howard. *The Political Philosophy of Hobbes: His Theory of Obligation* (Oxford: Clarendon Press, 1957).

Watkins, John W. N. *Hobbes's System of Ideas: A Study in the Political Significance of Philosophical Theories* (London: Hutchinson, 1965).

Weeks, Kathi. *The Problem with Work: Feminism, Marxism, Antiwork Politics, and Postwork Imaginaries* (Durham, NC: Duke University Press, 2011).

Zagorin, Perez. *A History of Political Thought in the English Revolution* (London: Routledge & Kegan Paul, 1954).

Zagorin, Perez. *Rebels and Rulers, 1500–1660*, Vol. 2 (Cambridge: Cambridge University Press, 1982).

Zourabichvili, François. *Le conservatisme paradoxal de Spinoza: Enfance et royauté* (Paris: Presses universitaires de France, 2002).

Index

An 'n.' following a page number indicates a footnote

For the benefit of digital users, indexed terms that span two pages (e.g., 52–53) may, on occasion, appear on only one of those pages.